Donald J. Trump as U.S. President: "It's all about me!"

DONALD J. TRUMP AS U.S. PRESIDENT

"It's all about me!"

JOHN DIXON
with the assistance of
CHRISTINA DIXON

Westphalia Press
An Imprint of the Policy Studies Organization
Washington, DC
2018

Westphalia Press
An imprint of Policy Studies Organization
1527 New Hampshire Ave., NW
Washington, D.C. 20036
info@ipsonet.org

ISBN-10: 1-63391-666-9
ISBN-13: 978-1-63391-666-1

Cover and interior design by Jeffrey Barnes
jbarnesbook.design

Daniel Gutierrez-Sandoval, Executive Director
PSO and Westphalia Press

Updated material and comments on this edition
can be found at the Westphalia Press website:
www.westphaliapress.org

For Tina, Piers, Aliki, David, and Isabella

President Barack Obama to President Donald J. Trump

January 20, 2017

... we are just temporary occupants of this office. That makes us guardians of those democratic institutions and traditions—like rule of law, separation of powers, equal protection and civil liberties—that our forebears fought and bled for. Regardless of the push and pull of daily politics, it is up to us to leave those instruments of democracy at least as strong as we found them.

CONTENTS

PREFACE

This is a wide-ranging book. Its focus is on the man, Donald J. Trump, who was elected the 45th president of the United States (US) on November 8, 2016 and was inaugurated on January 20, 2017. Its premise is that Trump's rhetoric and actions as president become more understandable, perhaps even more predictable, in the light of his personality and his worldview and view-of-the-world. It, therefore, has two goals:

- To delineate his personality traits and his worldview, so as to surmise on how he thinks about himself, others, and the world-at- large, and how he perceives and takes meaning from reality he experiences.
- To elucidate his idiosyncratic views on governance, government, the presidency, public administration, and public policy.

To achieve these goals required drawing upon concepts, frameworks, paradigms, and theories from economics, management, organizational theory, philosophy, political science, psychiatry, psychology, public administration, social theory, and sociology to understand his personality and worldview, and his views of the world-at-large, governance, government, and public policy. This necessitated its distinctive style. First, it has very extensive footnotes, at the bottom of each page to make the text accessible. These serve five functions:

- to document the electronic sources used;
- to define all the technical definitions needed to make the text accessible;
- to elucidate the relevant American political institutions and processes needed to make the text accessible;
- to elaborate on relevant meaning nuances; and
- to contextualize by interrelating subject matters.

Second, it has a thematic index of both the text and footnotes, one that relates exclusively to Trump. Finally, it provides an extensive array or electronic and printed sources to enable the reader to further explore issues of interest.

I have deliberately targeted this book at those for whom the Trump phenomenon—as a presidential candidate and as president—is both fascinating and baffling, and who are not intimately familiar with Trump the man of some notoriety—a family business tycoon and a reality TV celebrity—or with American political institution, processes, and politics. It is important to appreciate that it is neither a chronology of events (up to early December 2017) nor encyclopedic in its scope.

All authors are inevitably debtors. My intellectual debt is to the hundreds of journalists and op-ed writers across the world whose reports and reflections I have cited. They have been my eyes and ears. Professionally, they reported, unpicked, dissected, triangulated, and judged Trump's utterance and actions. I must also thank, again, the editorial and production team at Westphalia Press. Their professionalism is evidenced by the end product. I owe a particular professional debt to Ken Saycell, who unearthed a number of very useful sources and shared them with me. To my wife, Christina, I owe a very significant professional and personal debt. Without her diligent and insightful culling of the electronic news sources this book would not have been completed as quickly as it has been. And she has, yet again, put up with me writing yet another book. Indeed the years of marriage she has endured is now less than the number of books and book-length manuscripts she has endured, which is evidence of something after 47 years.

1
DONALD J. TRUMP: HIS PUBLIC PERSONA AND WORLDVIEW

INTRODUCTION

Donald J. Trump was elected the 45th president of the United States on November 8, 2016 and inaugurated on January 20, 2017. Like any US president, he does not govern alone, for that necessarily involves Congress and the Federal Executive, not to mention the Federal Judiciary. He has, nevertheless, considerable authority to make decisions and take actions. So, how he thinks about himself, others, and how he perceives and takes meaning from reality as he sees it, are matters of importance. Trump's rhetoric and actions become more understandable, perhaps even more predictable, in the light of his personality and his worldview.

TRUMP'S PUBLIC PERSONALITY

A person's "[p]ersonality is that pattern of characteristic thoughts, feelings, and behaviours [personality traits] that distinguish one person from another and that persist over time and situations" (Phares and Chaplin 1997, 2). These personality traits influence a person's adaptive capacity in different situations (Allport 1937; Cattell 1965, 1980; Eysenck 1970). As Cattell (1965, 117–118) succinctly remarks, personality is "that which tells what [a person] will do when placed in a given situation." The major—Big 5—behavioral (observable) personality traits have been identified as (Tupes and Christal [1961] 1962; Digman 1990; Costa and McCrae 1992; Goldberg 1993):

- *openness*, the extent of openness to new ideas and experiences;
- *conscientiousness*, the extent of carefulness and vigilance;
- *extraversion*, the extent of having a directing interests beyond self;
- *agreeableness*, the extent of having behavioral characteristics that reflect kindness, sympathy, cooperativeness, and considerateness; and

- *neuroticism*, the extent to which feelings of anxiety, anger, envy, and guilt, and depressed moods are experienced.

The personality traits discernible from Trump's public behavior, reveal his public persona. However, one psychologist, Dr Karl Albrecht[1] has said of Trump:

> Pundits, politicians, people who despise him, and even people who worship him can't seem to grasp the simple truth of this man, which is: **He Is Actually As Simple as He Appears**. He isn't "hard to figure out"—what you see is what you'll get (Albrecht 2017, emphasis in original).

Yet, it may well be that his public persona is a personality he deliberately seeks to portray, rather than being his private persona. As Vladimir Putin, the Russian President, is reported to have said after meeting Trump: "TV Trump is different than the real Trump."[2] Klapp (1964, 36) offers an explanation; a "leader" has to "typify" the wants and desires of his targeted audience, which, thereby, become symbolically significant. These typifications become an essential part of his Jungian "mask"—his front or guise—presented as his public persona for external consumption (Stevens 1990). Jung ([1934] 1981) noted that people with big egos relate to the world at large through a flexible public persona, elements of which may eventually be absorbed into their personal persona. The result can be a state of mind that is "utterly unconscious of any distinction between themselves and the world in which they live. They have little or no concept of themselves as beings distinct from what society [their publics] expects of them" (Dawson 1977, 267). Trump has, arguably, publicly revealed the following personality traits.

The first personality trait is his low degree of *openness*, because he is reluctant to accept new ideas that are in conflict with, and so challenge, his own firmly held beliefs, for he does not permit himself any conscious self-doubt or any questioning that threatens his own understanding of world as he sees it. This includes his fantasies about his own brilliance.

[1]   See: https://www.psychologytoday.com/experts/karl-albrecht-phd.
[2]   Retrieved from: http://www.bb unpicked, dissected, and judged c.co.uk/news/av/world-40545067/putin-tv-trump-is-different-than-real-trump.

Indicative is his own assessment of his high IQ: "Sorry losers and haters, but my IQ is one of the highest—and you all know it! Please don't feel so stupid or insecure, it's not your fault" (Twitter, May 2013, cited in Piehler 2016, 11). Indeed:

> During the presidential campaign, Donald Trump liked to invoke his late uncle, MIT research scientist John Trump[3], as evidence of the family's exceptional gene pool, proof should voters need it that Donald Trump is smart, like really smart.
>
> "It's in my blood," he says.[4]

That is as may be,[5] but undoubtedly, "he is sorely lacking in sophistication, knowledge of the world, understanding of government and a rudimentary grasp of economics."[6]

The second personality trait is his low degree of *conscientiousness*, because he is inclined to act impulsively, seemingly unable to resist temptations, urge or impulses even if they may ultimately hurt him or others.

---

[3] See: https://www.aip.org/history-programs/niels-bohr-library/oral-histories/ 5062.

[4] Retrieved from: http://www.thedailbeastcom/the-good-trump-was-a-genius -and-a-gentleman.

[5] There are, however, said to be five laws of stupidity (Cipolla 1976, retrieved from: http://harmful.cat-v.org/people/basic-laws-of-human-stupidity/):

- "A stupid person is a person who causes losses to another person or to a group of persons while himself deriving no gain and even possibly incurring losses."
- "The probability that a certain person be stupid is independent of any other characteristic of that person."
- "A stupid person is the most dangerous type of person."
- "Always and inevitably everyone underestimates the number of stupid individuals in circulation."
- "Non-stupid people always underestimate the damaging power of stupid individuals. In particular non-stupid people constantly forget that at all times and places and under any circumstances to deal and/or associate with stupid people always turns out to be a costly mistake."

[6] Retrieved from: http://www.independent.co.uk/voices/donald-trump-dimmest- us-president-ever-personal-mobile-phone-number-security-concerns-a77 66271.html.

One of his biographers, Michael D'Antonio[7]—*Never Enough: Donald Trump and the Pursuit of Success*[8] (2015) and *The Truth about Donald Trump*[9] (2016)—has recently dubbed him the little boy president, because he "acts in a way that would be expected of a 6-year-old boy."[10] And as has been observed:

> When six-year old throws a tantrum because it does not get his own way, everyone except the child's parents may shrug and say thank god he's not my kid.

> When the President of the United States throws a tantrum, no one smiles. People tremble.[11]

And another media observation made after a presidential tantrum is even more colorful: "You feel like you've got to give the president of the United States a pacifier and a rattle and put him in the crib."[12] This is the president who told supporters in Youngstown, Ohio in late July

> Sometimes, they say, "He doesn't act presidential," Trump said of his critics. "And I say, 'Hey look—great schools, smart guy—it's so easy to act presidential. But that's not going to get it done. ... With the exception of the late, great Abraham Lincoln, I can be more presidential than any president that's ever held this office. That I can tell you. It's real easy."

Perhaps he is being "modern-day presidential".[13]

---

[7] See: http://www.huffingtonpost.com/author/michael-dantonio.

[8] See: https://www.barnesandnoblecom/w/never-enough-michael-dantonio/1121862017.

[9] See:https://us.macmillan.com/thetruthabouttrump/michaeldantonio/9781250105288/.

[10] Retrieved from: http://google.com/newsstand/s/CBIwkKjv8jQ.

[11] Retrieved from: https://newsstand.google.com/articles/CAIiEGtR133yHzr VaVkPOfeYteIqFQgEKg0IACoGCAowrqkBMKBFMKGBAg.

[12] Retrieved from: http://www.huffingtonpost.com/entry/trump-pacifier-rattle_us_591655f3e4b0031e737dc72e.

[13] Retrieved from: http://www.bbc.co.uknews/av/world-us-canada-40746735/do-trump-voters-think-he-s-presidential.

Trump gets bored easily, and so has very limited ability to subdue his impulsiveness in order to achieve longer-term goals.[14] Of Trump, Albreicht (2017) suggests:

- He has a very short attention span (attention deficit disorder[15]).

- He is given to acting on his first reaction (low impulse control[16]).

- He might even have a limited proficiency in reading,[17] spelling,[18] and writing[19] (dyslexia[20]).

---

[14] See: http://www.msnbc.com/morning-joe/watch/-no-impulse-control-trump-s-focus-on-the-short-game-891026499969.

[15] See: http://www.healthline.com/health/adhd/difference-between-add-and-adhd. See also: http://www.huffingtonpost.com/george-sachs-psyd/unfit-unfocused-or-is-tru_b_11568002.html;https://www.quora.com/Does-Donald-Trump-have-ADHD.

[16] See: https://www.mentalhelp.net/articles/defining-features-of-personality-disorders-impulse-control-problems/. See also: https://www.entrepreneur.com/article/283480; https://www.washingtonpost.com/business/donald-trumps-most-enduring--and-unbefitting--trait/2016/07/15/f5684848-488b-11e6-acbc-4d4870a079da_story.html?utm_term=.a37e9458a458; http://www.msnbc.com/morning-joe/watch/-no-impulse-control-trump-s-focus-on-the-short-game-891026499969; https://www.ft.com/content/1cf9a2fe-8738-11e6-a75a-0c4dce033ade?mhq5j=e3.

[17] It is known, however, that Trump is not much of a reader. In 2016 he claimed his favorite book was Earnest Hemingway's *All Quiet on the Western Front*, although in 2015 it was the *Bible*. When asked in an interview, prior to becoming president, the name of the last book he read his response was "I read passages, I read areas, chapters, I don't have the time." Retrieved from: https://newrepublic.com/minutes/133566/donald-trump-doesnt-read-books.

[18] Was "covfevfe"—probably "coverage"—in a Trump tweet in late May a typing error or a spelling error? See: http://www.independent.co.uk/news/world/americas/us-politics/trump-ce-tweet-sean-spicer-president-small-group-explanation-a7766141.html; see also: https://www.wired.com/2017/06/asked-lawyers-vet-trumps-controversial-tweets/; http://www.politico.com/story/2016/01/trump-liberty-university-bible-217938.

[19] "It appears that his only out-bound [written] communication channel is Twitter [limited to 140 characters]" (Albrecht 2017). As Trump asserts: "I'm the Ernest Hemingway of 140 characters [Tweets]" (*Washington Times*, November 2015, cited in Piehler 2016, 35).

[20] This a general term for disorders that involve difficulties in acquiring and processing language, which interferes with an individual's ability in read or interpret words, letters, and other symbols, but do not affect general intelligence.

Such deficiencies "would have a huge impact on the way he processes information—and the way others communicate with him. I don't believe he uses a computer or email, or reads very much (his ghost-writers [of his 15 authored books] report that he hasn't read the books they wrote for him)" (Albrecht 2017).

Trump evidences little concerned with any unintended or unexpected consequences of his decisions, as he is indifferent about how they affect others, or, indeed, even himself. He believes that the rules, laws, and norms that apply others do not apply to him. "From his ongoing refusal to release his tax returns to his stonewalling of requests to disclose visitor logs at the White House, he has indicated normal rules do not apply to him."[21] So, they are meaningless and do not deserve forethought. So, nothing stops him doing what he really wants to do. He lacks any sense of remorse, shame, or guilt.

The third personality trait is his low degree of *extraversion*, because his dominant ego has created a grandiose sense of self[22]: "The show is 'Trump'. And it is sold-out performances everywhere" (*Playboy*, March 1990, cited in Piehler 2016, 11). This is further evidenced by his proclivity for illeism. It is the judgment of Kim Schneiderman,[23] a psychotherapist[24] that "Trump talking about himself in the third person reflects his perception of himself as being a larger-than-life character in the world stage."[25] John Altman, a contemporary American thriller writer,[26] in the same vein, ... considers that Trump is stranger than any fictional character a writer would dare create:

See: http://dyslexia.yale.edu/Stu_whatisdyslexia.htm; https://dyslexiaida. org/definition-of-dyslexia/. See also: https://www.youtube.com/watch?v=Lz 4gpBH2n-E; https://www.youtube.com/watch?v=bd79UsXSLWg; https:// www.youtube.com/watch?v=KXGuJlTVXfw; https://www.youtube.com/ watch?v=NXUhcVWOyuI.

[21] Retrieved from: http://www.bbc.co.uk/news/world-us-canada-39724045.

[22] Rosenberg (1979) defined the self-concept as "the totality of the individual's thoughts and feelings having reference to himself [sic] as an object." Allport (1955, 40) refers to it as "proprium," which embraces "all aspects of personality that make for inward unity."

[23] See: http://stepoutofyourstory.com/.

[24] See: http://www.bbc.com/news/magazine-33943762.

[25] Retrieved from: http://www.bbc.com/news/magazine-33943762.

[26] See: http://www.johnaltman.net/author.html.

... the Age of Trump challenges writers of fiction, and particularly writers of political fiction, to produce work that meets this standard.

For starters: Any day's news supplies plots so fantastic that most make-believe story lines pale in comparison. Elections stolen in collusion with the Kremlin? A White House spokesperson endorsing the Orwellian concept of "alternative facts"[27]? Another denying that Hitler used chemical weapons against his own people? A president firing the Director of the FBI—even as the agency investigates charges of Russian interference in that president's election? ... And Trump's version of reality feels palpably far-fetched. Using a patio at a Florida golf club as a makeshift situation room during a North Korean missile test—as a guest posts pics to Facebook? Really? An author describing this scene risks taxing suspension of disbelief beyond repair. Real and plausible are not the same thing.[28]

Trump is ever likely to exaggerate his achievements and talents, as he is publicly preoccupied with his fantasies about his success, power, and brilliance, even his handsomeness and physical attributes.[29] His dominant requirement is for constant acclaim; his perpetual fear is the loss of self-esteem. But, as Ellis (2005, 3) notes, to

self-esteem one's self on a global measure of self-worth

---

[27]   This is a reference to Kellyanne Conway, Trump's White House Counselor, who used this phrase, which she considers "a mistake that she has not been allowed to 'brush off.'" Retrieved from: https://www.theguardian.com/us-news/2017/mar/03/kellyanneconway-alternative-facts-mistake-oscars. See also: http://www.dailymail.co.uk/news/article-4508310/Mika-Brzezinski-says-Kellyanne-Conway-hates-DonalFRepublicanPartyrump.html; https://www.nytimes.com/2017/05/15/business/media/mika-joe-kellyanne-conway.html.

[28]   Retrieved from: https://newsstand.google.com/articles/CAIiED4_9nKvcLElp6Rl-mPUtRgqFwgEKg4IACoGCAowjKxcMOvhCzC-kLcB, Definitely see also: https://www.theguardian.com/commentisfree/2017/may/25/is-this-real-life-or-is-this-a-cabaret-of-the-von-trump-family-on-tour.

[29]   Retrieved from: http://www.telegrapco.uk/news/2017/05/29/comedy-writer-blocked-trump-gives-hilarious-account-social-media/.

is unhealthy and dysfunctional. First, it is irrational because there are no objective bases for making global evaluations of one's self. Second, focusing on one's self-esteem will make a person vulnerable to life's little setbacks, rejections, or mistakes, so that even people with generally high self-esteem may be predisposed to blow these out of proportion with resultant negative consequences. Third, a concern about self-worth can lead to a preoccupation with comparing oneself with others at the expense of engaging in healthy and productive endeavors and pursuits.

Trump considers everything in life to be a game that he must win—even handshakes.[30] And most importantly, his perceived competitors must definitely loose. So, at the interpersonal level, competition inevitably overwhelms cooperation, particularly when he concludes that he must adopt a hyper-competitive stance towards others—involving incessant and indiscriminate competition—in order to attain personal superiority—power—over other them: "The psychic result ... is a diffuse hostile tension between individuals" (Horney 1937, 285–286). Such interpersonal hostility is multidimensional (Mathews 1997):

- At the *cognitive* level, it manifests as cynicism and mistrust.

- At the *affective* level, it gives rise to anger, ranging from irritation to rage.

- At the *behavioral* level, it produces actions intending to manipulate, exploit, or show aggression, derisiveness, and humiliation, in order to cause emotionally or even physically harm to the other person.

So, Trump's disposition toward interpersonally hostile hyper-competitiveness, justifies him cheating, lying, stealing, perhaps even using—or encouraging others to use—violence. Adler ([1933] 1973) saw this striving for personal superiority in every area of a person's life giving rise to a destructive lifestyle, one that provides fertile grounds for neurosis.

---

[30] French President Emmanuel Macron bested Trump in their first handshake in Brussels, which apparently irritated him. See: https://www.vice.com/en_us/article/j5xq3d/a-frenchmans-firm-handshake-may-have-doomed-the-paris-deal-vgtrn.

Trump is also unable to accept responsibility for his actions, so he seeks to shift blame to others for any adverse outcomes they may cause. He is a convincing—pathological—liar who finds it almost impossible to be consistently truthful.[31] As Professor Dan P. McAdam[32] (Psychology, Northwestern University) has observed: "One possible yield [from Trump's personality traits] is an energetic, activist president who has a less than cordial relationship with the truth."[33] This makes Trump unreliable and unpredictable, evidencing no commitment to fulfilling or honoring any obligations and assurances he makes, for if he later decides that there is no benefit to him in following through, he will not do so. He will, of course, never apologize; in his own words: "I think apologizing's a great thing, but you have to be wrong. I will absolutely apologize, sometime in the hopefully distant future, if I'm ever wrong" (*The Tonight Show*, September 2015, cited in Piehler 2016, 11).

The fourth personality trait is his low degree of *agreeableness*, because he considers himself to be superior, which makes him arrogant and conceited:

- "Some people cast shadows [as I do], and other people choose to live in those shadows" (*New York Times*, September 2005, cited in Piehler 2016, 20).
- "You have to treat [women] like shit" (*New York Magazine*, November 1992, cited in Piehler 2016, 117).
- "Cause [sic] I like kids. I mean, I won't do anything to take care of them. I'll supply funds and she [my wife] will take care of the kids. Its not like I'm gonna be walking the kids down Central Park" (Howard Stern Show, 2005, cited in Piehler 2016, 117).

He can be charming, but behind that facade he is covertly domineering and manipulative. He probably has few intimate relationships and trusts very few people (Albrecht 2017). He expects to be recognized as being

---

[31] See, for example: http://edition.cnn.com/2017/08/03/politics/donald-trump-mexico-boy-scouts-lies/index.html); http://www.politico.com/magazine/story/2017/01/donald-trump-lies-liar-effect-brain-214658.

[32] See: http://www.psychology.northwestern.edu/people/faculty/core/profiles/dan-mcadams.html.

[33] Retrieved from: http ://www.theatlantic.com/magazine/archive/2016/06/the-mind-of-donald-trump/480771/.

superior even without the achievements that warrant that presumption. He demands unquestioning—but unreciprocated—loyalty and full compliance with his wishes, for he does not recognizes others people's rights. It seems that he prefers to surround "himself with dim yes men who know little more than he and, in any event, tremble at the prospect of correcting their 'Dear Leader.'"[34]

He presumes that he has a right to manipulate others to get what he wants. He can be envious of important others, believing they are envious of him. He is unwilling—perhaps unable—to recognize the needs of others and to understand and share their feelings and emotions. This makes him callous and lacking in sympathy if not empathy[35].[36] He has a limited range or depth of feelings, in spite of displaying signals that suggest he is open and gregarious. This makes him emotionally shallow, for when showing what seem to be warmth, joy, love, and compassion it is feigned and serves only his ulterior motives. This enables him to see others as exploitable opportunities.

The fifth personality trait is his high degree of *neuroticism*. This is because he is paranoid[37]; he becomes upset or emotional when his all-too-fragile ego is threatened.[38] So, those who threatened his ego cannot be trusted.

---

[34] Retrieved from: http://www.independent.co.uk/voices/donald-trump-dimmest-us-president-ever-personal-mobile-phone-number-security-concerns-a7766271.html.

[35] See; https://www.psychologytoday.com/basics/empathy.

[36] For a discussion of the difference between sympathy and empathy, see https://www.youtube.com/watch?v=3GswbktiW7I.

[37] Those with a paranoid personality disorder "are preoccupied with unjustified doubts about the loyalty or trustworthiness of others", and they are "reluctant to confide in others and tend to blame them and hold grudges even when they themselves are at fault" (Davison and Neale [1976] 2001, 360). It "involves intense anxious or fearful feelings and thoughts often related to persecution, threat, or conspiracy. ... Paranoia can become delusions, when irrational thoughts and beliefs become so fixed that nothing (including contrary evidence) can convince a person that what they think or feel is not true." Retrieved from: http://www.mentalhealthamerica.net/conditions/paranoia-and-delusional-disorders.

[38] See: http://www.independent.co.uk/news/world-0/donald-trump-dangerous-mental-illness-yale-psychiatrist-conference-us-president-unfit-james-gartner-a7694316.html.

This paranoia was directed at James Comey[39], who he fired as the Director of the Federal Bureau of Investigation (FBI) in May for reasons that included his refusal to exculpate Trump publicly, and to give him his pledge personal loyalty[40].[41] *The Telegraph*, a London-based newspaper, reported an insightful incident on May 15:

> Taken aback by the fallout from his sudden dismissal of James Comey, the FBI director, and on the hunt for someone to blame, the president was said to be toying with firing senior allies, from Reince Priebus, his chief of staff [who has since resigned], to Sean Spicer, his combative press secretary [who has since resigned]."[42]

Indeed, over the reaction to his firing of Comey firing: "... He's frustrated, and angry at everyone" [said] one confidant."[43]

Trump's inner feelings seem to fluctuate uncontrollably, driven by his publicly well-suppressed self-doubts and his enviousness of significant others who threaten his vanity, both of which feed his hyper-competi-

---

[39] See: https://gizmodo.com/donald-trump-just-fired-fbi-director-james-comey-1795069390; https://www.theguardian.com/us-news/2017/sep/02/donald-trump-russia-investigation-obstruction-of-justice.

[40] Trump's response was to ask the question: "Who would ask a man to pledge allegiance?" Retrieved from: http://www.bbc.co.uk/news/av/world-us-canada-40229997/trump-who-would-ask-a-man-to-pledge-allegiance, but see. https://www.nytimes.com/2017/05/11/us/politics/trump-comey-firing.html?mcubz=3. See also: http://google.com/newsstand/s/CBIwjerI8jQ.

[41] See: http://www.bbc.com/news/av/world-us-canada-39866898/trumps-love-hate-relationship-with-comey; http://google.com/newsstand/s/CBIwg_yX8jQ; http://www.bbc.com/news/av/world-us-canada-39945092/a-wild-week-for-trump-in-washington; http://google.com/newsstand/s/CBIwvPyW0Dk; http://google.com/newsstand/s/CBIwiLLd8TQ; http://google.com/newsstand/s/CBIwnfDx8zQ. See also: http://google.com/newsstand/s/CBIwzbOY0Dk.

[42] See: http://www.independent.co.uk/news/world/americas/us-politics/donald-trump-white-house-infighting-tweet-us-news-media-fake-news-michael-flynn-reince-priebus-steve-a7616486.html#gallery.

[43] Retrieved from: http://www.telegraph.co.uk/news/2017/05/14/frustrated-fallout-sacking-fbi-director-trump-considerspurging/; https://newsstand.google.com/articles/CAIiEKuHw8VJzN5pATolmC3NbaYqFggEKg4IACoGCAowm6R6MMKqCTCfrxU.

tiveness. As von Goethe in remarked in his classic *The Sorrows of Young Werther* ([1749] 2011, 56–57): "ill-humour arises from an inward consciousness of our own want of merit, from a discontent which ever accompanies that envy which vanity engenders." Trump lives perpetually on the edge—tense, nervous, or irritable—so verbal outbursts and punishments are normal. He has poor behavioral control.

Trump is, then, self-centered, with a strong sense of his own importance, albeit with a fragile ego. This fragility demands that he receives constant expressions of recognition, praise, and appreciation, and unquestioning compliance with his wishes. Criticism—particularly when it is expressed as humor, irony, exaggeration, or ridicule[44]—must, at all costs, be stopped where possible,[45] otherwise deflected or denigrated. Inevitably, this involved him fighting back hard by means of notoriously childish twitter retorts that often involved schoolyard insults, that only revealed his immaturity not his strength. He has resorted to banning from his twitter account those he considered who "replied to his tweets with mocking or critical comments".[46] This includes a person who accused him "of having a 'small willy [penis]'".[47]

His mental health has been the subject of speculation[48] by numerous mental health professionals. Professor Dan P. McAdam, a psychiatrist, has observed: "Donald Trump's basic personality traits suggest a presidency that could be highly combustible .... Tough. Bellicose. Threatening. Explosive."[49] This is all very much in in evidence.[50] To some Trump

---

[44] See: http://edition.cnn.com/2017/04/30/opinions/trump-whcd-contrast-opinion-obeidallah/index.html; see, particularly: http://edition.cnn.com/2013/02/06/showbiz/trump-bill-maher-suit/.

[45] In Iran a cartoon contest has been held to mock Trump. See: http://www.independent.co.uk/arts-entertainment/art/news/iran-holds-donald-trump-cartoon-contest-a7822046.html.

[46] Retrieved from: http://www.bbc.co.uk/news/world-us-canada-40577858.

[47] Retrieved from: http://www.telegraphco.uk/news/2017/05/29/comedy-writer-blocked-trump-gives-hilarious-account-social-media/.

[48] For a discussion of the appropriateness of such presidential speculation see: https://newsstand.google.com/articles/CAIiEOiA5NGuxPeSyFSEWti hb7wqGQgEKhAIACoHCAowocv1CjCSptoCMKrUpgU.

[49] Retrieved from: http://www.theatlantic.com/magazine/archive/2016/06/the-mind-of-donald-trump/480771/.

[50] See, for example: http://www.mercurynews.com/2017/08/16/jackie-speier-

observers,[51] his public persona evidences personality traits that can be associated with those of a narcissist[52], a sociopath[53], and even a psychopath[54] (see Appendix). Hara Estroff Marano,[55] the Editor at Large of

calls-for-trumps-removal-from-office-under-25th-amendment/; http://money.cnn.com/2017/08/20/media/trump-carl-bernstein-reliable-sources/index.html.

[51] See, for example: https://www.theatlantic.com/magazine/archive/2016/06/the-mind-of-donald-trump/480771/; https://www.nytimes.com/2017/02/17/opinion/is-it-time-to-call-trump-mentally-ill.html; http://www.zerohedge.com/news/2017-04-22/yale-psychiatrists-just-warned-there-something-seriously-wrong-trump; http://www.theblaze.com/news/2017/04/24/psychiatry-experts-claim-that-trump-is-unfit-for-presidency-due-to-dangerous-mental-illness/. For international media speculation see: http://www.bbc.com/news/world-us-canada-38881469; http://www.bbc.com/news/world-us-can71; http://google.com/newsstand/s/CBIwjfyhqjQ; https://www.indy100.com/article/keith-olbermann-donald-trump-psychopath-test-results-gq-resistance-webseries-7657321?utmsource=indy&utm_medium=top5&utm_campaign=i100; http://www.nydailynews.com/opinion/ex-trump-executive-knew-ill-35-years-article-1.2959293; http://google.com/newsstand/s/CBIwzteIzDQ; http://www.salon.com/2017/05/25/psychiatrist-bandy-lee-we-have-an-obligation-to-speak-about-donald-trumps-mental-health-issues-our-survival-as-a-species-may-be-at-stake/.

[52] This is a person with a narcissistic personality disorder. See: https://www.psychologytoday.com/blog/communication-success/201409/10-signs-youre-in-relationship-narcissist; http://www.mayoclinic.org/diseases-conditions/narcissistic-personality-disorder/basics/symptoms/con-20025568; http://dsm.psychiatryonline.org/doi/book/10.1176/appi.books.9780890425596.

[53] This is a person with an antisocial personality disorder. See: https://www.psychologytoday.com/basics/psychopathy; https://www.psychologytoday.com/articles/201305/how-spot-sociopath; http://www.nhs.uk/Conditions/antisocial-personality-disorder/Pages/Introduction.aspx; http://www.healthyplace.com/personality-disorders/sociopath/signs-of-a-sociopath-are-big-time-scary/; http://www.mcafee.cc/Bin/sb.html; http://www.mayoclinic.org/diseases-conditions/antisocial-personality-disorder/home/ovc-20198975.

[54] This is a person with a psychopathic personality disorder. See: https://www.psychologytoday.com/blog/communication-success/201409/10-signs-youre-in-relationship-narcissist; http://www.mayoclinic.org/diseases-conditions/narcissistic-personality-disorder/basics/symptoms/con-20025568; http://dsm.psychiatryonline.org/doi/book/10.1176/appi.books.9780890425596;see: https://www.psychologytoday.com/basics/psychopathy. See also: https://www.psychologytoday.com/articles/201305/how-spot-sociopath; http://www.nhs.uk/Conditions/antisocial-personality-disorder/Pages/Introduction.aspx; http://www.healthyplace.com/personality-disorders/sociopath/signs-of-a-sociopath-are-big-time-scary/; http://www.mcafee.cc/Bin/sb.html; http://www.mayoclinic.org/diseases-conditions/antisocial-personality-disorder/home/ovc-20198975.

[55] See: https://www.bookbrowse.com/biographies/index.cfm/author_

Psychology Today, has concluded:

> Donald Trump may or may not be mentally ill. He may
> or may not have an organic brain disease. Despite those
> unknowns, a group of prominent mental health profes-
> sionals today [20 April] agreed that they have an ethical
> obligation to expose to the public every instance of re-
> ality distortion, impulsive decision-making, and viola-
> tion of presidential norms of behaviors that singularize
> the Trump presidency.[56]

Indeed, some 60,000 mental health professionals have publicly declared
that Trump has "serious mental illness".[57] Their petition, addressed to
US Senator Chuck Schumer[58] (Democrat-New York),[59] read:

> We, the undersigned mental health professionals
> (please state your degree), believe in our professional
> judgment that Donald Trump manifests a serious men-
> tal illness that renders him psychologically incapable of
> competent discharging the duties of President of the
> United States. And we respectfully request that you re-
> move the powers and duties of his office.[60]

A debatable issue is whether psychiatrists should speak out against
Trump, despite the Goldwater rule[61] in their professional code of con-

---

number/1554/hara-estroff-marano.

[56] Retrieved from: https://www.psychologytoday.com/blog/brainstorm/201704/
shrinks-define-dangers-trump-presidency. See also: https://thepsychologist.bps.
org.uk/volume-30/march-2017/psychologists-and-donald-trump.

[57] Retrieved from: https://xk.psychologytoday.com/blog/me-we/201708/60000-
psychologists-say-trump-has-serious-mental-illness.

[58] See: https://www.schumer.senate.gov/.

[59] See: https://www.forbes.com/sitesemilywillingham/2017/02/19/psychologist
-calls-on-colleagues-to-sign-petition-for-trumps-removal/#35cd8e9e64f3.

[60] Retrieved from: https://www.change.org/p/trump-is-mentally-ill-and-must-be-
removed.

[61] This ethical rule forbids members of the American Psychiatric Association
from publicly commenting on "the psyches of living public figures whom they
have not personally examined." See: http://www.newyorker.com/magazine/
2017/05/22/should-psychiatrists-speak-out-against-trump.

duct? Opinions differ. Dr John Zinner,[62] a practicing psychiatrist, has reportedly suggested:

> ... that, as doctors, who swear an oath to protect their patients, psychiatrists have an obligation to speak out about the menace posed by Trump's mental health. "It's my view that Trump has a narcissistic personality disorder," Zinner said later. "Trump is deluded and compulsive. He has no conscience." He said that psychiatrists have a constructive role to play in advising policymakers to add checks on the President's control over nuclear weapons. "That supersedes the Goldwater rule," he said. "It's an existential survival issue".[63]

Professor Emeritus, Allen Frances[64] (Psychiatry, Duke University School of Medicine), who wrote the defining clinical characteristics for narcissistic personality disorder, has said of Trump:

> He may be a world-class narcissist, but this does not make him mentally ill, because he does not suffer from the distress and impairment required to diagnose mental disorder. Mr. Trump causes severe distress rather than experiencing it and has been richly rewarded, rather than punished, for his grandiosity, self-absorption, and lack of sympathy if not empathy.[65]

And:

> You don't have to be a psychoanalyst to understand Trump. He's the most transparent human being who ever

---

[62] See: https://npidb.org/doctors/allopathic_osteopathic_physicians/psychiatry_2084p0800x/1710044342.aspx.

[63] Retrieved from: http://www.newyorker.com/magazine/2017/05/22/should-psychiatrists-speak-out-against-trump.

[64] See: http://www.psychiatrictimes.com/authors/allen-frances-md.

[65] Retrieved from: https://www.nytimes.com/2017/02/14/opinion/an-eminent-psychiatrist-demurs-on-trumps-mental-state.html?mcubz=3&mtrref=www.google.co.uk&gwh=3B404D86E45BF32481BF6863B0FA1708&gwt=pay&assetType=opinion.

lived. Giving it a name doesn't explain it or change it.[66]

Penultimately, in Trump own words: "Who knows what's in the deepest parts of my mind" (*Buzzfeed*, February 2014, cited in Piehler 2016, 37). And finally, his biographer, Michael D'Antonio, has recently remarked: "Donald Trump is stuck in his own skull ... It's a very cluttered place to be, a fine-tuned machine spewing a torrent of chaos, cruelty, confusion, farce and transfixing craziness."[67]

It is somewhat easier, of course, to observe, and draw implications from, Trump's observed body language[68]—his non-verbal communications through which he expresses his attitudes and feelings by conscious and unconscious movements and postures:

> People are constantly throwing off a storm of signals. These signals may be silent (non-verbal) messages communicated through the sender's body movements, facial expressions, voice tone, and loudness. Microexpressions, hand gestures, and posture register unfilled almost immediately, a silent orchestra that can have long-lasting repercussions.[69]

Experts have analyzed Trump's body language in a variety of presidential settings.[70] A lot about his state of mind can be deduced from his telltale bodily gestures and motions.

---

[66] Retrieved from: http://www.newyorker.com/news/daily-comment/donald-trumps-state-of-mind-and-ours.

[67] Retrieved from: https://www.nytimes.com/2017/02/18/opinion/sunday/trapped-in-trumps-brain.html.

[68] See: https://www.psychologytoday.com/basics/body-language; http://www.businessballs.com/body-language.htm

[69] Retrieved from: https://www.psychologytoday.com/basics/body-language.

[70] See, for example: https://www.linkedin.com/pulse/body-language-analysis-33 96-donald-trumps-first-interview-brown; http://www.bodylanguagesuccess. com/2017/05/body-language-analysis-no-3395-donald.html; http://www. bodylanguagesuccess.com/2017/02/nonverbal-communication-analysis-no_13.html; http://www.bbc.co.uk/news/av/election-us-2016-37088990/what-trump-s-hand-gestures-say-about-him; http://www.bbc.co.uk/news/av/world-40534986/analysing-trump-and-putin-s-body-lang//uage-at-g20-meeting.

Dominance is evidenced by Trump's default—signature—handshake. This involves:

- pulling the other person's hand very close to, and often touching, his lower or mid-chest level; while

- patting the other person's left upper arm or shoulder.

"This is handshake choreography cluster, when displayed frequently, as part of a long-term pattern, is highly indicative of Narcissistic Personality Disorder."[71]

The now famous test of the handshakes between Trump and the much younger, Canadian Prime Minister, Justin Trudeau[72] at the White House steps[73] is revealing:

> As the men shake hands, Justin Trudeau grips just below Donald Trump's right shoulder—while Trump grips the top of Trudeau's. Although both of these maneuvers are alpha components of their greeting, Trump's is more so. Yet this is not the whole story ....
>
> Notice Prime Minister Trudeau's jaw—it is jutting forward (more prominently above). This is a sign of momentary increased adrenaline—and that the Canadian is exerting considerable physical effort with his grip strength.
>
> A moment later, their torsos' separate and we see that it is PM Trudeau who is pulling Trump's arm toward his lower chest. What we are witnessing here, is a sort of arm-wrestling between World leaders.
>
> Also very notable is the morphology of their hand grip. Both hands are cupped—without (or with minimal) palm contact. This configuration is seen during

---

71 Retrieved from:http://www.bodylanguagesuccess.com/2017/05/body-language-analysis-no-3394-donald.html.

72 See: https://www.liberal.ca/rt-hon-justin-trudeau/.

73 See:https://www.theguardian.com/usnews/video/2017/feb/14/donald-trumps-strange-handshake-style-and-how-justin-trudeau-beat-it-video-explainer.

attempts of greater grip strength (which is of course transpiring)—but also when one or both people really are not very enthusiastic about touching the other (yet they have to).[74]

Also revealing was Trump's response when he was bested in a handshake contest the France's President Emmanuel Macron[75], who was, apparently, ready and up to the challenge—"My handshake was not innocent," calling it "a moment of truth"[76]—is insightful. On being told of Macron's comments, Trump, so it is reported, got all "grumbly and bothered."[77] Publicly he remarked: "He's a great guy—smart, strong, loves holding my hand."[78]

Deception is evidenced when Trump points with the index finger of his right hand during a speech:

> The finger-point hand-chop is highly correlative with deception (as well as deception combined with anger). This association is even greater when displayed during moments of defending against the accusation of a lie. It's one of many examples of hyper-alpha body language. This disproportional and additionally out-of-context nonverbal display, is emblematic of defensive overcompensation associated with lying.[79]

Anxiety is evidenced when Trump:

- does consecutive hard swallows ("to generate more saliva and

---

74 Retrieved from: http://www.bodylanguagesuccess.com/2017/02/nonverbal-communication-analysis-no_13.html.

75 See: https://www.facebook.com/EmmanuelMacron/.

76 Retrieved from: https://www.vice.com/en_us/article/j5xq3d/a-frenchmans-firm-handshake-may-have-doomed-the-paris-deal-vgtrn.

77 Retrieved from: https://www.vice.comen_us/article/j5xq3d/a-frenchmans-firm-handshake-may-have-doomed-the-paris-deal-vgtrn.

78 Retrieved from: https://www.nytimes.com/2017/07/19/us/politics/trump-macron-holding-hands.html?mtrref=undefined&gwh=DACCE2F5421FAC8B366292BFD6D7C6CA&gwt=pay.

79 Retrieved from: http://www.bodylanguagesuccesscom/2017/05/body-language-analysis-no-3394-donald.html.

move it down the throat when it becomes dry in moments of nervousness"[80];

- looks in his lower right quadrant ("It is in this lower right quadrant where people most frequently and briefly gaze during moments of high-anxiety (particularly right-hand dominant individuals such as Donald Trump)"[81]; and

- substantially increasing his blinking frequency ("Increased blink frequency (compared with the baseline rate) has a strong correlation with anxiety"[82]) and ("Trump's eyelids [being] closed for at least 1.25 seconds—which is extremely prolonged and very telling"[83]).

Sincerity, a measure of which is the sincerity of his smile, is evidenced when Trump's smile reveals he has:

- relaxed his forehead ("although he has had Botox treatments in this part of his face, so it's difficult to assess his forehead status objectively"[84]);

- drawn together with vertical creases the area between his brows ("however these are longstanding and the creases are passive [not contracted])—if we did not have this prior knowledge, this finding may lead us astray"[85];

- partially but mostly closed his eyes ("consistent with a sincere smile"[86]);

80 Retrieved from: https://www.linkedin.com/pulse/body-language-analysis-3396-donald-trumps-first-interview-brown.

81 Retrieved from: https://www.linkedin.com/pulse/body-language-analysis-3396-donald-trumps-first-interview-brown.

82 Retrieved from: https://www.linkedin.com/pulse/body-language-analysis-3396-donald-trumps-first-interview-brown.

83 Retrieved from: https://www.linkedin.com/pulse/body language-analysis-3396-donald-trumps-first-interview-brown.

84 Retrieved from: http://www.bodylanguagesuccesscom/2017/05/body-language-analysis-no-3395-donald.html.

85 Retrieved from: http://www.bodylanguagesuccesscom/2017/05/body-language-analysis-no-3395-donald.html.

86 Retrieved from: http://www.bodylanguagesuccesscom/2017/05/body-language-analysis-no-3395-donald.html.

- fleeting concaved-up furrows in each of his lower eyelids ("also consistent with a sincere smile"[87]); and

- displayed his upper teeth ("also indicative of sincerity"), the corners of his mouth are vectored above the lateral (indicating "full sincerity"[88]).

Trump's policy rhetoric and actions become even more understandable, perhaps even more predictable, in the light of his worldview.

TRUMP'S WORLDVIEW

A worldview provides the lens through which a person interrogates and judges social reality (Smith 1980; Dixon 2003; Dixon, Dogan, and Sanderson 2009). It provides insights into how a person prefers to think about the actuality of Marcel's (1952, 164) "world of persons"—social reality or the social world. It demarcates his preferred social-reality disposition, comprising a set of firmly held propositions about

- how best to describe, explain, and understand social reality (his epistemological disposition), and

- how best to explain and predict the social actions of others and self (his ontological disposition).

On the basis of these mental processes (process cognitions) used to gain knowledge and comprehension (understandings or product cognitions) (Lycan 1990; Brandimonte, Bruno, and Collina 2006)), particular attitudes are portrayed and particular actions are justified. As Camus ([1942] 2005, 5) remarked: "man is always prey to his truths", regardless of their propositional certainty (the truth beyond doubt). This demarcates his mentality—his prevailing thinking and behaviour patterns. These always sit in the context of the prevailing mentifacts—the ideas and ways of thinking, concepts, and interpretations—prevalent in a society's mental culture (Posner 2004, 70). Semiotically, these are the prevailing societal codes—texts (Siefkes 2010, 231–232)—and

---

[87] Retrieved from: http://www.bodylanguagesuccesscom/2017/05/body-language-analysis-no-3395-donald.html.

[88] Retrieved from: http://www.bodylanguagesuccesscom/2017/05/body-language-analysis-no-3395-donald.html.

conventional signs—such as languages and dialects, scientific theories, and moral values).

Insights into the cognitive processes involved can be gained from Lewin's (1948, 1952, 1972) concept of life space. This has four dimensions (de Board 1978): cognitive (existential or perceptual), affective (evaluation), relational (cathartic), and directive (intentional). These intermingle to provide the interface that enables a person to construct meaning about anticipated events (his personal construct system (Kelly 1955). This include important firmly held beliefs that are central to self-identity (core constructs), relatively unimportant and changeable beliefs (peripheral constructs), poorly defined and unstable beliefs that lead to erratic and perhaps invalid predictions (loose constructs), and unarticulated assumptions (nonverbal constructs). These are the idiosyncratic means by which a person seeks to understand and explain the world he experiences, and so guide his practical action and social roles in concrete situations and relationships. Indeed, the mind can frame questions and answers, accusations, and defenses all at the same time.

Kelly postulated that "a person's [thought] processes are psychologically channelized by the ways by which he [sic] anticipates events" (1955, 1, 46); that "a person anticipates events by construing their replications" (p. 51); and that "each person characteristically evolves, for his [sic] convenience in anticipating events, a construction system embracing ordinal relationships between constructs" (p. 59). To the extent that a person can understand another person's internal constructions of reality, he can predict what that person will do (Kelly 1955).

Constructed is a person's holistic mental environment. This comprises a set of conscious experiences that make up a system of dynamic relationships (Koffka 1935; Wertheimer 1945)—his dynamic Gestalt psychological environment. This enables the construction the world "as the individual sees it"—his assumptive world—consisting of "his conscious and unconscious goals, dreams, hopes and fears, his past experiences and future expectations" (de Board 1978, 51)—giving rise to a hierarchically arranged sets of truths; truth propositions; explanations of what it is to be a human being; human nature suppositions; ways of acquiring genuine knowledge (truths); and ethical principles that determine what is moral conduct). These become part of his immutable core values (enduring beliefs); adaptive attitudes (learned dispositions); or changeable opinions (unsubstantiated beliefs) (Parsons 1995, 375).

This set of assumptions permits the assembling of the explanatory filter that guides that person's attitudes and social actions, thereby enabling him to engage appropriately in the "selecting, organizing, interpreting, and making sense of complex social reality to provide guideposts for knowing, analyzing, judging, persuading, and acting" (D'Andrade 1984, 109). Such framing[89] gives rise to "a stable mental state derived from a sense of continuity and order in events" (Bilton et al. 1996, 665) (ontological security) by providing a "perspective from which an amorphous, ill-defined, problematic situation can be made sense of and acted on" (Rein and Schön 1993, 146).

A person's assumptive world is assembled as a result of his interaction with other individuals. As social relationships are constitutive of who a person is, how he thinks, what he does, and who he is becoming, a particular meaning system builds up over time. This constitutes "whatever one has to know or believe in order to operate in a manner acceptable to members [of his reference group in a particular situation]" (D'Andrade 1984, 89). It permits him to take meaning from any situation he confronts (D'Andrade 1984, 96–101). That meaning can be

- *representational*: knowledge and beliefs about the world expressed as true or false propositions;
- *constructive*: understandings about what people agree counts as what;
- *directive*: the needs or obligation that require something to be done; or
- *evocative*: the distinct and well shared emotional states or feelings that are aroused.

This enables him to make sense of his interactions with others in particular situations. These guide attitude formation and motivate social actions. Indeed, Cutting and Kouzmin (1997, 86) argue: "it can be seen that the individual's sense of identity and values and beliefs run deep

---

[89]   Goffman (1974, 15) defines a frame as "definitions of a situation [that] are built

and are likely to be very stable held together by strong interconnect-ing patterns of neuronal processes." Beliefs and values can, thus be the prime determinants of individual motivation. This enables him to en-gage in reality as he imagines it to be (Geertz 1983). These understand-ings may well be held without awareness of their hypothetical nature and on the presumption that that social reality is the way his internalized images depict it. Indeed, Bacon ([1623] 1997) considered that a person is inevitably imprisoned in his own theoretical frameworks, which cause him to be misled because of the way he view the world, akin to the plight of Plato's ([c360 BC] 1955) imprisoned cave-dweller shackled by his illusions of the outside world.

Distilled from a person's assumptive world are his mindsets. These are the states of mind he brings to—and thus precedes his thinking about—tasks to be performed or actions to be taken (Duncker [1935] 1945). Each mindset is the set of assumptions, beliefs, and values (cognitive dispositions) that are held such that it creates an incentive to adopt pri-or behaviours, choices, or methods of analysis. This set of "preparatory cognitions" (Erel and Meiran 2011, 150) formulates the appropriate in-tentional mental states[90] (Farthing 1992; Flanagan 1992), so reflecting the interplay between cognitive and motivational processes, and em-body a set of "cognitive procedures" that promote successful navigation through the respective action phases (Fujita, Gollwitzer, and Oettingen 2007, 48). This involve the adoption of a configuration of cognitive in-formation processing resources (Erel and Meiran 2011, 150) that short-ened ways of thinking (Marbe 1901[91] cited in Gollwitzer and Bayer 1999, 11)—"mental shortcuts" (Eagly et al. 1999).

Five relevant categories of mindsets can be identified, each of which can be a pervasive feature of a person's mental life (Roese 1994; Gollwitzer and Bayer 1999; Ramnarayan 2003; Galinsky and Kray 2004; Fujita, Gollwitzer, and Oettingen 2007):

---

up in accordance with the principal of organization which governs events—or at least social ones—and our subjective involvement in them."

[90]   This is a relational mental state that connects a person to a proposition in a way that involves holding particular attitudes (expectancies and values) towards and/or intentions (hopes, aspirations, and goals) about that proposition (Cresswell 1985; Lycan 1990; Rey 1997).

[91]   See: http://www.psychologie.uni-wuerzburg.de/w_schule/WSCHOOL2a.pdf.

- A *counterfactual* mindset, which reflections on what can be learnt from past errors. It respects what could, would, or might have happened in the past—for better or for worse. This fosters the creation of alternative pasts, which permits history to be reconstructed, thereby raising awareness of alternative future realities. Thinking about what might have been also helps identifying the necessary conditions for avoiding previous errors, and so can influence the course of future actions and so future events.

- A *deliberative* mindset, which reflects on what are the desirable and feasible goals to be sought. It respects the careful appraisal of potentially competing goals, the weighing of likely pros and cons with respect to each potential goal, and consideration of the feasibility of these goals (expectancy-value considerations). This mindset foster relatively even-handed and accurate appraisal of evidence, which prolongs the consideration of pros and cons, thereby delaying decision-making and action-taking.

- An *implementation* mindset, which reflects on what are the appropriate actions to be taken in order to achieve the chosen goals. It respects the concentrated of post-decisional thoughts on goal achievement—the essential elements of planning—by focusing attention on the when, where, and how of goal implementation, and so on information that is relevant to the achievement of the desired goals.

- A *spectator* mindset, which reflects on what ideas for improvement. It respects not only the picking up of signals from the environment or getting an idea for improvement, but also the ignoring of the inability to act on that learning or insight, so making more ritualistic the performance of activities.

- An *actor* mindset, which reflects on what are the right actions to be taken on the basis of learning acquired. It respects acting on the basis of learning gained that leads to the right action being taken.

The assumptive world in which these states of mind are embedded is grounded in default standpoints on:

- What can be known about social reality and how can it best be known (a default epistemological disposition).

- What exists in social reality that has causal capacity—the power to engender social actions (a default ontological disposition).

- How should the morality of the social actions of self and others in that reality be judged (a default ethical disposition).

- What constraints are tolerated on individual autonomy when establishing relationships in that reality (a default social control disposition).

Trump's Epistemology

Epistemology

This is concerned with the nature, extent, sources, and legitimacy—truthfulness—of knowledge (Devitt 1984; Kirkham 1992). Truth (Baggini 2017) can be understood individualistically (so justified by reference to reason, individual experience, intuition or common sense, or revealed wisdom) or socially (so justified by reference to testimony, consensus, or received wisdom (tradition) (Aquinas [1259–1964] 1905; Grave 1960; Natanson 1963; Hollis 1994). Truth can, then, be characterized as objective—"If I know that twice two is four ... I need not struggle to make it my own; it is a reliable piece of lumber in my mental attic" (Barrett 1958, 152), or subjective—"a truth that must penetrate my own personal existence, or it is nothing; and I must struggle to renew it in my life each day ... it is not a truth that I have, it is a truth that I am" (Barrett 1958, 153).

So, different truth-standards can be applied to enable judgments to be made about what constitutes sufficient justification—sufficient evidence—to warrant the status of truth being assigned to a belief—whether that evidence is objective (naturalist epistemology) or subjective (hermeneutic epistemology) (Hollis 1994). A true belief, then, can be justified in many ways:

- On the evidence of sensory experiences, so becoming *a posteriori* knowledge (Kant [1781–87] 1956).

- If it is logically deduced from a set of premises, so becoming *a priori* knowledge (Kant [1781–87] 1956).

- If it is logically consistent with, and mutually supported by, other knowledge claims that, together, offers the simplest explanation of a phenomenon (Rescher 1973).

- If there are sufficiently good justifications grounded in cognitive processes of direct apprehension—sensory perception and memory—or reasoning that has produced a high proportion of true beliefs (Alston 1989).

- If its *prima facie* justification cannot be made defective, as a source of genuine knowledge, by being overridden or defeated by additional and previously unknown evidence (Shope 1983).

- If it is beyond doubt, as a result of a combination of experience and reason and does not need any further justification (Moser 1989; DePaul 2000).

- if experts who have sufficient relevant knowledge or experience to judge it truthfulness agree that it is true (Scheffler 1974; Murphy 1990; Mounce 1997);

- If it is substantiated by discourse (Berger and Luckmann 1966).

- If the degree of certainty—the probability—with which a belief is held to be true as measured by the believer's willingness to accord the status of truth to a belief on the basis of the axioms of probability theory (Rosenkrantz 1977).

- If it is useful to believe it to be true, as James remarks: "our obligation to seek truth is part of our obligation to do what pays" (James [1897] 1979) quoted in Russell 1946, 844).

Clearly, a *true* proposition cannot be genuine knowledge if it is *false*. Does this mean that the evidence proffered as proof must be objective and so secure as to be beyond all doubt, thereby giving rise to propositional certainty? Under the Platonic conception of knowledge, for a truth proposition to be genuine knowledge requires the evidence to give rise to propositional certainty that can never become false. Descartes ([1641] 1975), in this tradition, held that nothing should be believed unless it is absolutely certain that it is true—*de omnibus dubitandum* [every thing is to be doubted] (Cartesian doubt). However, to James (1896, Sect. IV): "Objective evidence and certitude are doubtless very fine ideals to play with, but where on this moonlit and dream-visited planet are they found?"

Trump's Existential Epistemological Disposition

Trump's epistemological disposition is clearly grounded in subjectivity (hermeneutic epistemology) based on self-knowledge (existential epistemology). To Sartre ([1946] 1973, 23, 26, 44), this truth is grounded "upon pure subjectivity—upon the Cartesian 'I think.'" and so "we must begin from the subjective."

Trump individually constructs the meaning and significance of social reality on the basis of pure existential subjectivity. So, in the Nietzschean nihilist tradition,[92] he holds that is there no "objectively true" social reality. Social knowledge—facts about the world of persons—are entirely subjective, and so are relative to the vagaries of a person's thoughts and experiences (Nietzsche [1886] 1998).[93] This is a foundational presumption of existential epistemology (Kierkegaard [1846] 1941; Nietzsche [1886] 1998; Schopenhauer [1818/1844] 1969). Kierkegaard's related propositions were that "in regard to every other reality external to the individual it can only be known through 'thinking it'" (Stack 1977, 197, n. 19), and that "existence, in its true or authentic form, is a subjective teleological activity for man, an activity characterized by dialectical tension and an intensification of subjectivity" (Stack 1977, 199, n. 40). Thus, the foundation of social knowledge is the individual's self-knowledge (Kierkegaard [1846] 1941; Schopenhauer [1818/1844] 1969). The world is, then, a manifestation of will—"the world is my idea" (Schopenhauer [1818/1844] 1969, 1) thus "no will: no idea, no world" (Schopenhauer [1851] 1970, 56). This doctrine of the primacy of will means that what a person believes to be real is the basis for reasoning. The real social world is, therefore, the self who has an idea. All social knowledge is based on immediate personal experience: "Our existence has no foundation on which to rest except the transient present" (Schopenhauer [1851] 1970, 52). To Sartre ([1946] 1973, 26) "we must begin from the subjective [because it] is the absolute truth of consciousness as it attains to itself" (Sartre [1946] 1973, 26).

---

92   Nietzsche, according to (Stack 1977, 17), saw nihilism's central concept being that "existence must not be interpreted in terms of 'purpose', 'unity', 'Being', or 'truth.'" For the Nietzschean nihilist there is no 'true' world at all.

93   This can be extended to the radical form of solipsism, which that holds that nothing at all exists apart from one's own mind and mental states (Russell 1948,

Thus, the social reality contains a multitude of subjective truths grounded in first-person mental discernments—intuition,[94] common sense,[95] or revealed wisdom[96] (Warnock 1970, 8–9). Social knowledge is, then, ultimately unique to the individual, such self-knowledge requires the recognition of past determinants, the acknowledgement of present concerns, and alertness to future possibilities (Heidegger [1927] 1967).

Trump is epistemologically elastic. He happily blurs, when personally convenient, the boundaries between:

- *Truths*: propositions that are objectively true—*a posteriori* or *a priori* knowledge (Kant [1781–87] 1956).

- *Beliefs*: propositions firmly held on grounds short of proof (Mill [1843] 1988).

- *Humbug*: propositions that are deceptive misrepresentations—unavoidable whenever a person is require to talk without knowledge—but just short of deliberate lying, achieved by the use of pretentious words or deeds to express thoughts, feelings, or attitudes (Black 1983).

- *Bullshit*: propositions that are intended to deliberately deceive—in order to misrepresent reality—by conveying false impressions, so as to divert attention away from the alternative accounts of that reality, including the correct one (Frankfurt 2005), the truth-value of which can be grounded in the charisma of the speaker (Baggini 2017, 22).

- *Lies*: propositions that are known to be not matters of fact. Yet, as Baggini (2017, 102) notes, "falsehood masquerades as truth by retreating into incomplete networks of beliefs where convenient

Part III, Ch. 2).

[94] Bergson saw intuition as an "instinct that has become disinterested, self-, and capable of reflecting upon its object and of enlarging it indefinitely" (quoted in Russell 1946, 821).

[95] These are beliefs that come naturally to mind to all people, as responsible agents, based on memory, reason, moral sense and taste—carry their own authority, despite accepted perceptual fallibilities, because people, proceeding cautiously, are capable of knowing the world (Moore 1959; Grave 1960).

[96] This is Aquinas' ([1259–64] 1905) truths of revelation: "Wisdom ... conferred by God as a particular endowment" (Rofe 2001).

facts are overstated and inconvenient ones ignore or just simply denied." And then there are lies made grand or noble by their civic purpose—the noble lie (Schofield 2007)—"[a] falsehood propagated to serve a higher goal. Sometimes, however, the purpose of such lies is self-interest" (Baggini 2017, 35).

On this, Bacon ([1597–1625] 1972, 7) wryly observed:

> Doth any man doubt, that if there were taken out of men's minds vain opinions, flattering hopes, false valuations, imaginations as one would, and the like, but it would leave the minds of a number of men poor shrunken things, full of melancholy and indisposition, and unpleasing to themselves.

Trump is an intuitive, right-brained thinker.[97] He has the capacity to deny the factuality of information that threaten his fantasies:

> Among his recent fantasies, he asserted that the investigation into possible Russian interference in the 2016 election, headed by the special counsel Robert Mueller,[98] was "not an investigation"; he ventured that Medicaid funding "actually goes up" under a Senate bill that would have cut it sharply; and he said that he had signed more bills "than any President, ever," ignoring Bill Clinton, Jimmy Carter, Harry Truman, and F.D.R., all of whom, the Times noted, had signed more at this point in their terms. And finally, this week, Trump seemed to mistake a visit to a crowd of children and teen-agers for a political rally, reminiscing with an audience of Boy Scouts about an election-night event that probably happened past their bedtime: "Do you remember that incredible night with the maps, and the Republicans are red and the Democrats are blue, and that map was so red, it was unbelievable, and they didn't know what to say?"[99]

---

[97] See: http://brainmadesimple.com/left-and-right-hemispheres.html

[98] See: http://www.newyorker.com/news/news-desk/robert-mueller-to-head-russia-trump-probe-first-thoughts.

[99] Retrieved from: http://www.newyorker.com/news/daily-comment/donald-

Further evidenced is his insistence, without providing any confirming evidence, that that he won the presidential popular vote (because, he alleged, there was widespread voter fraud orchestrated by the Democrats) and that the former President Barak Obama used the FBI, or even a British intelligence agency[100]—the Government Communications Headquarters (GCHQ)[101]—to tap his Trump Tower communications system. In his own words: "Terrible! Just found out that Obama had my 'wires tapped' in Trump Tower just before the victory. Nothing found. This is McCarthyism!"[102] (Tweet, March 4, 2017).[103] Of course, as Congressman Ted Lieu (Democrat-California) tweeted: "If wiretap was on Trump Tower, that means fed [federal] judge found probable cause phone lines used by agents of foreign power."[104]

Trump is, thus, forever caught between delusion and denial.[105] As Kierkegaard ([1847] 1962, quoted in Marino 2001, 12) remarked: "Indeed, one can be deceived in many ways; one can be deceived in believing what is untrue, but on the other hand, one is also deceived in not believing what is true." This is because "Where ignorance is bliss, 'tis folly to be wise" (Thomas Gray,[106] *Ode to a Distant Prospect of Eton College* (1742)[107]). This means, despite

> [s]itting atop arguably the great resource on the planet—the body of knowledge retained by American

---

trumps-state-of-mind-and-ours.

[100] http://google.com/newsstand/s/CBIw6cLfzDQ; but see http://google.com/newsstand/s/CBIwkv7ezTQ.

[101] See: https://www.gchq.gov.uk/features/welcome-to-gchq.

[102] See: https://www.britannica.com/topic/McCarthyism.

[103] Retrieved from: https://www.theguardian.com/us-news/2017/mar/17/whitehouse-will-not-be-repeat-claims-gchq-spied-trump-. But see: https://www.indy100.com/article/donald-trump-accuses-barack-obama-wiretapping-twitter-waking-up-breitbart-7611011.

[104] Retrieved from: https://twitter.com/tedlieu/status/838046638065123328.

[105] But his fans do not seem to care if he lies. See: https://www.debatepolitics.com/general-political-discussion/245159-do-trump-supporters-care-if-he-lies-them-29.html.

[106] See: https://www.poetryfoundation.org/poets/thomas-gray.

[107] Retrieved from: https://www.poetryfoundation.org/poems-and-poets/poems/detail/44301.

government experts on everything from economics to medicine to military history—he remains blissfully ignorant on a range of subjects [worryingly, including American history[108]].[109]

And, of course, there is "the convenient willed ignorance: "I've got my mind made up, so don't confuse me with the facts."[110]

Trump's flexibility with the truth suggests he is intellectually shallow. Intelligent he may well be, but he evidences little interest in theories, doctrines, policies, and plans. He disinclination to be truthful certainly makes him unpredictable, even unprincipled. The risk he takes is that people will eventually stop believing what he says. Indeed, some have said his credibility crisis had arrived less than 3 months after taking office,[111] with a majority of Americans even then thinking that Trump does not keeps his promises[112].

A Relevant Platonic Insight

In one of Plato's[113] early Socratic dialogues[114]—the *Euthyphro*[115]—Socrates[116] travels to the Athenian court to defend himself against trumped-

---

[108] See:http://edition.cnn.com/2017/08/19/politics/trump-history-facts-historians/index.html; https://www.justplainpolitics.com/showthread.php?83637-Trump-s-muddled-view-on-American-history; https://congressionalblackcaucus.com/trumps-muddled-view-of-american-history/; http://www.dispatch.com/news/20170611/is-president-trumps-foreign-policy-strategic-or-simply-muddled.

[109] Retrieved from: http://www.independent.co.uk/voices/donald-trump-dimmest-us-president-ever-personal-mobile-phone-number-security-concerns-a7766271.html.

[110] See: http://www.iep.utm.edu/fallacy/#Willed%20ignorance

[111] See: https://www.theatlantic.com/politicsarchive/2017/03/trumps-credibility-crisis-arrives/520347/?utm_source=feed.

[112] See: http://www.gallup.com/poll/208640/majority-no-longer-thinks-trump-keepspromises.aspx?g_source=position1&g_medium=related&g_campaign=tiles.

[113] See: http://www.iep.utm.edu/plato/.

[114] See: https://www.circeinstitute.org/2011/03/what-is-socratic-dialogue.

[115] See: http://www.indiana.edu/~p374/Euthyphro.pdf.

[116] See: http://www.iep.utm.edu/socrates/.

up charges. As he approaches the court, he runs into his friend Euthyphro, a young man who is on his way to the same place to prosecute his own father for the killing of another man. Euthyphro insists that he is doing what piety demands. Yet after critical questioning by Socrates, it became clear that Euthyphro did not understand piety. So, his ignorance of his ignorance about piety meant that he cannot really know whether prosecuting his father is, in fact, the right thing to do. The central lesson to be drawn from is that a person who is ignorant of his ignorance not only cannot understand the subject up which he is ignorant but also places no importance on correcting that ignorance.

The Public Trump: Does Ignorance Prevail?

Trump's ignorance of his own ignorance, and his willingness to blur the truth, permits him to assert confidently "alternative facts"[117] (see Baggini 2017, 75–76) or "post truths"[118] that are intended to delude or deceive people into accepting his representation of reality[119,120]. This reflects the intensity of his desire to have others believe to be true what he wants them to believe. He achieves this by lying[121] to evoke their emotions—perhaps supported by conspiracy theories—in a way that overwhelms any contrary evidence—the emotional resonance of a lie[122]—as the basis for verifying truthfulness. It also enables him to at least delay, if not avoid, changing his mind on matters of importance to him, particularly if any such changes of mind challenge his fantasies about his own success, power, and brilliance. The conclusion to be drawn is that he is caught between delusion and denial.

---

[117] See, for example: http://www.nydailynews.com/news/national/trump-hates-fake-news-spreads-unsubstantiated-claims-article-1.2988895; https://www.wired.com/story/president-trumps-lies-and-untruths/.

[118] See: https://en.oxforddictionaries.com/definition/post-truth.

[119] For a list all Trump's deceptions see: http://flackcheck.org/globalsearch/?mssearch=Trump&msp=1&mswhere=all.

[120] For an exploration of the many ways that the truth is manipulated by government and corporations in the US see Lewis 2014.

[121] See: https://www.theguardian.com/books/2017/may/12/post-truth-worst-of-best-donald-trump-sean-spicer-kellyanne-conway.

[122] See: http://www.thedailybeast.com/the-emotional-resonance-of-liesand-what-we-can-do-to-defeat-them.

Trump has, some have argued, begun to understand what he does not know. According to his apologists, he is growing into the job by showing a capacity to learn, and, as a result, a willingness to adapt to presidential realities (by "flip-flopping", as necessary, on campaign promise).[123] This suggests that his campaign rhetoric was based in his instincts—alternative facts—what he had a will to say—some of which he has firmly believed for years (such as China's currency manipulation practices[124]). Such core ideas are typically enduring—difficult to change—thereby becoming immutable core values. These are central to his personal construct of reality—reality as he imagines it to be—or, perhaps more importantly, to his self-identity, particularly if such change, in any way, is likely to diminish the acclamation his adoring and protective fans give him.[125] When policies grounded in such enduring beliefs shift so dramatically, with little or no explanation, they can obviously shift (back?) again. The important question is: Has Trump begun to understand that, because the presidential world of public policy, politico-administration, and diplomacy is far more complicated than he had ever thought would be, he must be willing to change his firmly held beliefs when they conflict with established facts.

Insightfully, in a recent interview with *The Wall Street Journal* Trump is reported to have said:

> "After listening for 10 minutes, I realized it's not so easy," the president said after a discussion with Chinese President Xi Jinping that included his hopes that China's pressure could steer North Korea away from its nuclear efforts. "I felt pretty strongly that they had a tremendous power" over North Korea. "But it's not what you would think."[126]

---

[123] See also: https://www.washingtonpost.com/news/fact-checker/wp/2017/03/13/president-trump-the-king-of-flip-flops/; http://www.bbc.com/news/world-us-canada-39591032.

[124] See: https://www.axios.com/trumps-tweets-for-the-past-6-years-tell-a-different-story-2357875234.html.

[125] See: https://www.aol.com/articlenews/2017/04/30/trump-rally-goer-roughed-up-after-being-wrongly-ided-as-a-protester/22061975/.

[126] Retrieved from: http://www.mediaite.com/tv/anderson-cooper-stunned-by-

Such self-assuredness suggests that Trump is not accustomed to being forced to considering the veracity of that which he finds convenient to deny. As President, he has evidenced little that would suggest that he engages in any kind of introspective reflection that would reveal the importance to him of filling his governance, government, and policy knowledge gaps. So far, policies espoused and actions taken by Trump are against a backdrop of deep ignorance. Only time will tell if he is flexible enough to accept, on a regular basis, evidence-based policy advice that seriously questions his firmly held beliefs.

Trump's Ontology

Social Ontology

This seeks to provide a consistent account of the nature and coherence of what exists in the world of persons and what phenomena possess causal efficacy—the capacity to give rise to social actions. The causal phenomenon can be within the individual (agential-causation or free will)—agency ontology—or it can be external to the individual (structural-causation or societal determinism)—structuralist ontology (Archer 2000; Dixon, Dogan, and Sanderson 2009). Free will holds that a person is free to determine and control his own actions, because he has the capacity to perform actions consciously (knowingly and responsibly) and voluntarily (unconstrained by the freedom-limiting punitive, oppressive, coercive, compulsive, manipulative or social conditioning factors over which he or she has no control) that are chosen from an array of alternative courses of action (Kane 2002). Social determinism explains social actions in terms of societal determining conditions over which the action-taker has little or no control (Butterfield 1998). Such determining conditions economic processes and relations (economic determinism), the group beliefs, tendencies and practices that an action-taker adopts to become integrated into that group (social determinism), culturally specific cognitive structures expressed cultural acts and artifacts (cultural determinism), and thought- and behaviors-shaping language the language used to shape the way an action-taker creates meaning about, and behaves in, the world (linguistic determinism) As

trumps-i-realized-its-not-so-easy-comments-on-china-north-korea/.

Schopenhauer ([1839] 1999) epigrammed: "A man can surely do what he wills to do, but he cannot determine what he wills."

Trump's Existential Individualism Disposition

Trump's ontological disposition is clearly grounded in agency ontology, in recognition that individuals are self-determining agents who are ultimately accountable for their own destiny and character. They are free to determine and control their own actions and so "could have chosen or acted otherwise" (Kane 2002, 5). His intuitive proclivity is towards existential individualism. This is the proposition that a person is free to exercise his will to determine his own destiny and character. So, he has the existential freedom to be who he wants to be, and so to be able to engage with social reality—as he imagines it to be—in any way he chooses. Trump, by his drive and determination to pursue whatever goals he sets himself, is exercising Nietzsche's instinct for freedom ([1887] 2006)—his incarnate will-to-power ([1895] 1967)—thereby making possible the Sartrian proposition of seeing "a possibility as my possibility" (Sartre [1943] 1957, 34). So, he is seeking to live in the way he find most valid and fulfilling.

Insightfully, Frankl ([1948/75] 2000, 138), an existential psychologist, argued that to be able exercise the will-to-power requires a person to overcome "a certain inner condition, namely, the feeling of inferiority ... by developing the striving for superiority." A sense of who a person is—and can become—is grounded in the existential notion that an individual simply exist—"existence comes before essence" (Sartre [1946] 1973, 44):

> Man simply is. Not that he is simply what he conceives himself to be, but he is what he wills, and as he conceives himself after already existing—as he wills to be after that leap toward existence. Man is nothing else but that which he makes of himself (Sartre [1946] 1973, 28).

To May (1967, 8), "the human dilemma is that which arises out of man's capacity to experience himself as both subject and object at the same time", a product of simultaneously living in a world of biological needs and drives, a world of interrelationships, and a world of self-awareness and self-relatedness. It is, then, up to him to decide his own fate, and so determine his own destiny—his purpose for being. A person searching for his own authentic self-identity is required have what Camus ([1942] 2005, 55, emphasis in original) called "the freedom to *be*." To accomplish this search, according to Sartre ([1943] 1957), requires him to achieve a synthetic unity between his capacity to transcend his knowledge of self in the contemporaneous now—who self is now—so be able to project himself into future unrealized possibilities—who self might become—and his knowledge of what it is about him that can be changed as necessary in order to exploit those future possibilities. Exercising the necessary free will to achieve this authenticity involves him engaging in an internal struggle with his subjective interpretations of others' discernments of him, particularly that of significant others. These discernments can ameliorate his capacity to recognize his own unique consciousness, thereby inclining him to self-impose constraints on his exercising of free will, unless he wills otherwise. As Greek tragedy suggests, a person who has the will-to-power to create his world as he believes it should be can face self-destructive (see, for example, Owen 2007). This can occur if the pride and arrogance that follows his success become addictive, and gives rise to feelings of invincibility, causing him to construct individually the meaning of reality as he prefers it to be, thereby sowing the seeds of his subsequent ruination—the "Hubris Syndrome."[127] As Sophocles had his blind prophet, Teiressias, in *Antigone*[128] (scene 5) remark: "Think: all men make mistakes, but a good man yields when he knows his course is wrong, and repairs the evil. The only crime is pride."[129]

---

[127] This a syndrome that affects people who have exercised substantial power over a length of time. Its major manifestations are (Owen and Davidson 2009):
- using power for self-glorification;
- focusing excessively on personal image;
- being excessively self-confident, with a contempt for advice or criticism of others;
- loosing contact with reality;
- speaking as a messiah;
- being reckless and taking impulsive actions; and
- having supreme overconfidence that leads to inattention to details.

[128] See: http://classics.mit.edu/Sophocles/antigone.html.

[129] Retrieved from: https://genius.com/2255983.

Trump is a man who never has enough success (D'Antonio 2015), however measured. The yardsticks by which he has measured his currency of selfhood—the success he has achieved—are:

- *Wealth accumulation*: "The beauty of me is that I am very rich" (*Time*, April 2011, cited in Piehler 2016, 18).

- *TV ratings*: "If you get good ratings, they'll cover you even if you have nothing to say" (Dallas Texas, September 2015, cited in Piehler 2016, 75).

- *Popular acclaim*: "People love me. And you know what, I have been very successful. Everyone loves me" (CNN, July 2015, cited in Piehler 2016, 40).

How he measures his success as President is difficult to judge, but his default measure is most likely to be the acclaim of his supporters.

Trump, despite his past success, evidences a fragility of self-identity—ego. He deals with this existential insecurity by creating a false self. This embodies a set of psychological defense mechanisms ("the ego's struggle against painful or unendurable ideas or effects" (Freud [1936] 1948, 45)). There are a wide variety of Freudian and neo-Freudian defense mechanisms (Freud [1936] 1948; Horney 1945; Cramer 1991; Planet-Psych 1999–2006) available to a person seeking to protect his fragile ego:

- *arbitrary rightness*: asserting the rightness of preferred understandings despite the contrary factual evidence;

- *denial*: refusing to recognize anxiety-provoking contrary factual evidence;

- *repression*: blotting out anxiety-provoking contrary factual evidence by not thinking about it;

- *rationalization*: using plausible but erroneous arguments to reconcile contrary factual evidence with preferred understandings;

- *compartmentalization*: placing anxiety-provoking contrary factual evidence into categories that conceal their factual inconsistencies or contradictions;

- *fantasy*: channeling anxiety-provoking understandings into imaginative unacceptable or unattainable desires;

- *displacement*: redirecting thoughts and feelings away from anxiety-inducing understandings to safer and more acceptable ones;

- *reaction formation*: adopting opposite understandings to the anxiety-provoking understandings, so as to make the emotions experienced acceptable;

- *regression*: reverting to an earlier stage of development to avoid facing unsustainable anxiety-provoking understandings;

- *compensation*: emphasizing strengths to counterbalancing perceived weaknesses caused by sustaining unsustainable anxiety-provoking understandings;

- *projection*: attributing to others the undesirable behaviors or thoughts attributable to sustaining unsustainable anxiety-provoking understandings;

- *intellectualization*: rationalizing in a way that dissociates anxiety-provoking understandings from feelings; and

- *sublimation*: channeling anxiety-provoking understandings toward activities that are more acceptable.

Trump draws upon this set of defense mechanisms to protect his fragile ego.

The fragility of his ego continually drives Trump to strive for—and very frequently assert—his superiority over others. This he achieves by the cultivation of fear,[130] and by never admitting he has been wrong and certainly never apologizing if he is wrong: "I think apologizing's a great thing, but you have to be wrong. I will absolutely apologize, sometime in the hopefully distant future, if I'm ever wrong" (*The Tonight Show*, September 2015, cited in Piehler 2016, 11). This all means that he is able to make decisions on the basis of, in the words of Pascal ([1670] 1966, 34), "pure will free of the perplexities of intellect."

A Relevant Nietzscheian Insight

Nietzsche's novel *Thus Spoke Zarathustra* ([1883] 1967) has Zarathus-

---

[130]   Retrieved from: http://www.politico.com/story/2017/03/trump-white-house-paranoia-236069; See also: https://www.theguardian.com/us-news/2017/aug/13/donald-trump-white-house-steve-bannon-rich-higgins.

tra, his main character, describing his heroic character—an *ubermensch* (a super-man or over-man). This is a man who has is able to establish his own idiosyncratic values and thus able to exercise—constructively or destructively—the will-to-power in order to create *his* world—perhaps even *the* world—as he believes it should be. To achieve this he not only has freed himself from all external influences, and, thereby, able to rise above social conventions, but also has dominated the thoughts and values of others—using the power of his will—and thereby, curb or, preferably remove, any of their desires that are in conflict to his vision of the world as it should be. Sometimes this can result in violent behavior, which, Nietzsche considered, is intrinsic to the nature of men.

Being a Nietzscheian *ubermensch*, however, is also about being self-overcoming—repressing any immediate instincts for power by means of cruelty and aggression—so as to achieve a more refined expression of power. This permits the "creator within" to prevail over the "animal within", achieved by self-examination and inner struggle, a process that makes him a deeper and stronger person, one with an independence of mind, able to address his self-constraints. To achieve this he has to foster an attitude toward life that accepts that there are no absolute truths, merely different perspectives that can be believed at will. Thus, rather than embarking upon a search for the objective and rational "truth" before taking action, he must be pragmatic and flexible enough to be able to draw upon as many different perspectives as possible. Such a manner of thinking recognizes the importance of not inhibiting and thwarting the passions and emotions that give rise to actions by demanding rational analysis before taking action. This pragmatic approach to truth permits the Dionysian[131] dimensions life—its irrationalities—to be taken just as they are experienced, without the close examination needed to establish their true nature or causation. On life's irrationalities, G.K. Chesterton ([1908] 2007, 97) offers the following insight: "Life is not an illogicality; yet it is a trap for logicians. It looks just a little more mathematical and regular than it is; its exactitude is obvious, but its inexactitude is hidden; its wildness lies in wait." Thus, the will-to-believe (James 1896) becomes a necessary antidote to the will-to-truth (Nietzsche [1886]

---

[131] Dionysus in ancient Greek mythology is the god of irrationality and chaos, who appeals to emotions and instincts (Nietzsche [1871] 1993).

1998), for James was contemptuous of the proposition that knowing the truth produces better life outcomes, thereby acknowledging that there can be dangerous knowledge that can make life unbearable.

Trump as President: An Ubermensch?

Undoubtedly, Trump's presidential behaviors would suggest he sees himself as a heroic character intent on changing the presidential politico-administrative landscape. At a speech given in January 2016 at Liberty University (Lynchburg, Virginia), he remarked:

> And you'll say if I am president ... "Please, Mr. President, we're winning too much. We can't stand it anymore. Can't we have a loss?" and I'll say no, we are going to keep winning, winning, winning, ... because we're going to make America great again. And you'll say, "Okay, Mr. President, Okay" (cited in Piehler 2016, 45).

He certainly sees himself as having led a momentous, perhaps even meaningful, life, evidenced by his self-proclaimed mega-success in a family business and as a reality TV star. He considers that this prepared him for his heroic role on the presidential campaign stage. He considers that he has risen above political conventions to establish his idiosyncratic ways of becoming president. He believes that he has the independence of mind of a deep and strong person. He imagines that he has the strength of will to create his worlds—his presidential world, his family business world, and perhaps, even *the* world—as he believes they should be, by dominating the thoughts and values of others, so molding them to his will and his world vision. He considers that he has a manner of thinking that does not inhibit and thwart the passions and emotions that give rise to his actions (evidenced by his hasty decision to launch the Syrian airbase missile attack), because he does not demand rational (duty-of-care facts-based) analysis before he acts[132] (evidenced by his criticism of, and unwillingness to engage with, the Washington intelligence community,[133] and by his dismissal of the Congressional Budget

---

[132]   See: https://www.wasingtonpost.com/blogs/plum-line/wp/2017/03/30/trump-has-nothing-but-contempt-for-facts-and-reality-based-policy-now-its-backfiring/?utm_term=.323755276e4a.

[133]   See: http://www.huffingtonpost.comentry/donald-trump-intelligence-agencies

Office's critical analysis of the proposed Obamacare[134] repeal and replacement legislation[135]).

The Heroic Trump he may be to his faithful followers—some of whom even consider that he has been "anointed by God"[136]—who expect him to keep his promises.[137] In any event, Trump has failed to achieve Nietzsche's demanding heroic standards in relation to self-overcoming. There is no evidence that he has ever embarked on a cathartic self-examination or inner struggle that have made him a deeper and stronger person, able to repress his dominant instinct for power by means of aggression.

TRUMP'S WORLDVIEW

Man not only strives to perceive his environment as a meaningful totality, but he strives to find an interpretation which will reveal him as an individual with a purpose to fulfill ... pointing up man's distinctive ability to find meaning not merely in what is, but in what can be (Crumbaugh 1973, 29).

_us_58a52530e4b045cd34be99aa?. See also, particularly: http://edition.cnn.com/2017/01/05/politics/russian-hacking-hearing-senate-republicans/?sr=.

134 Formally, the Patient Protection and Affordable Care Act, 2010. See: https://www.hhs.gov/sites/default/files/ppacacon.pdf; see also: https://www.whitehouse.gov/repeal-and-replace-obamacare.

135 See: https://www.cbo.gov/publication/52486; https://www.cbo.gov/publication/52939; https://www.google.com.tr/search?q=obamacare+repeal+congressional+budget+office&oq=Obamacare&aqs=chrome.2.69i57j69i60j69i59l2j69i60j0.5468j0j1&sourceid=chrome&ie=UTF-8#q=obamacare+repeal+congressional+budget+office&start=10.

136 See: www.churchmilitant.com/video/episode/vortex-donald-constantine-trump. But see also Spadaro and Figueroa (2017) available at: http://www.laciviltacattolica.it/articolo/evangelical-fundamentalism-and-catholic-integralism-in-the-usa-a-surprising-ecumenism/.

137 See: https://www.usatoday.com/story/opinion/2017/08/24/evangelicals-squander-their-moral-authority-sticking-trump/589241001/; https://www.theatlantic.com/magazine/archive/2017/05/a-match-made-in-heaven/521409/. See also: https://assets.donaldjtrump.com/_landings/contract/O-TRU-102316-Contractv02.pdf. But see also: https://qz.com/971930/trumps-100-days-a-scorecard-trump-made-28-promises-in-a-contract-with-the-american-people/?utm_source=.

The Contending Worldviews

Social reality can be viewed through one of fours contending lens—grounded on the epistemological dichotomy (naturalism and hermeneutics) and ontological dichotomy (agency and structuralism)—through which a cognitively consistent person can choose to frame the world of persons, each of which demarcates a Model of Man—a metaphysical views of what it means to be a human being (Dixon 2003, 2016; Dixon, Dogan, and Sanderson 2009):

Hermeneutic Agency

This lens—Trump's lens—is grounded on the proposition that social realty is as it is subjectively experienced by those who engage in it, the meaning and significance of which is individually constructed on the basis of self-knowledge, and it exists as a collection of mutually unknowable individuals. This means that that the social actions of those present can never fully predict, so inclining each of them toward self-referentiality in his social relationships, which means acting and interacting in ways each one believes to be necessary. This worldview denotes Existential Man.

Naturalist Structuralism

This lens is grounded on the proposition that social realty is entirely material in form with objectively factual qualities, and it exists as perceptible, structurally functional, and stable patterns of interpersonal relationships, which give rise to social institutions that reflect interdependence and can sustain social order. This means that the social actions are most appropriately explained by analyzing the economic, social, cultural, and linguistic influences that shape the perceived patterns of social interactions, and so mold the social roles and social practices that influence, if not determine, the intentional mental state that give rise to social actions. This worldview denotes Hierarchical Man.

Naturalist Agency

This lens is grounded on the proposition that social realty is entirely material in form with objectively factual qualities, and its existence is contingent on the known patterns of voluntary and self-determined social relationships. This means that that the social actions are most appropriately explained by the reference to the revealed wishes and desires of people in pursuit of as much material happiness (pleasure) as possible. This worldview denotes Economic Man.

Hermeneutic Structuralism

This lens is grounded on the proposition that social realty is as it is subjectively experienced by those who engage in it, the meaningfulness and significance of which is socially constructed by a process of reflexive discourse. It exists as a site in which various sociocultural constructs and discursive formations are created and sustained, giving rise to sets of common beliefs, worked-out norms, and agreed social roles and practices. This means that social actions are most appropriately understood by reflecting on sociological, psychological and linguistic factors that influence, if not determine, the cognitive structures that give rise to social actions. This worldview denotes Social Man.

Trump's Hermeneutic Agency Worldview

Trump's intuitive predilection is for the hermeneutic-agency worldview—social reality is an idea in his mind and his relationships with other people are self-determined in whatever way he considers is necessary to meet his life's challenges. This offers him a distinctive and coherent philosophy of life, one that informs and justifies his way he conducts his life. It is the lens through which he interrogates—describes, explains, understand, and predicts—the world of persons as he assumes it to be—his assumptive world. This gives him a stable orientation for decisions and actions, because it justifies his distinctive ways of thinking (acquiring, validating, and using information), feeling (emotional arousals and responses), and acting (personal and social behaviors).

However, this lens gives Trump his blind spots—those elements of social reality that are obscured or denied because of the limitations of his default cognitive dispositions. The first is a knowledge blind spot, caused by his denial that social knowledge can be acquired either by objectively investigation or from discourse. This means that the only social knowledge he accepts as valid is that grounded in his own opinions—

propositions that he finds palatable, and thus, trustworthy. This makes problematic any predictions he may make about the future course of events. The second is a behavioral-response blind spot, caused by his willingness to accept that people's real intentions are unknowable to him, and, thus, cannot be reliably presumed or predicted. So, at the interpersonal level, this means that most people cannot be trusted. This restricts his capacity to anticipate the courses of action followed by others in general. These blind are the product because of his:

- *ignorance* (his lack of knowledge);
- *delusion* (his willingness to believe what is not genuine knowledge); or
- *denial* (his willingness to ignore genuine knowledge).

These implications of these blind spots will become very apparent in the next chapter.

CONCLUSION

This chapter has explored and explicated the public persona of Donald J. Trump, and elucidated how he takes meaning from the world of persons as he sees it. He is self-centered, with a strong sense of his own importance, albeit with a fragile ego. He is disdainfully flexible with the truth. He is ever eager to divert attention away from unpalatable truths about, or related to, himself—what he says and does—making him willing to deceive others by conveying false impressions, perhaps with a hint of a supportive conspiracy theory. He presumes that he has the freedom to be who he wants to be, and so to be able to engage with reality—as he imagines it to be—in any way he chooses.

He sees life as a game he must win and every other player must lose. So, to this end, any means necessary are justified. This extends to

- making outlandish and unsubstantiated allegations and insinuations about his competitors—political opponents, even their families (notably, Obama,[138] the Clintons,[139] and even his fellow

---

[138] See: http://edition.cnn.com/2017/06/28/politics/trump-obama-relationship/index.html.

[139] See: https://www.theguardian.com/us-news/2017/sep/08/hillary-clinton-

Republican Party members, some of whom were also presidential candidates[140]); and

- making unrealistic, even misleading, promises to win over supporters—promises that raised their expectations beyond those that he could possibly deliver with any certainly (for example, restoring the American manufacturing to its former glory or having the Mexican's finance his cherished Mexican wall).

APPENDIX: ON NARCISSISTS, SOCIOPATHS, AND PSYCHOPATHS

The Archetypal Narcissist

Narcissists (Lasch 1979) are people with a narcissistic personality disorder (Baumeister 1993; Bushman and Baumeister 1998). This is a mental health condition that affects how they relate to others. They have pervasive, narrow-minded, and overly indulgent obsession with self: "Infatuated with his own reflection in a pool, Narcissus pined away and died of self-love."[141] It is promoted by their emphasis on developing and expressing characteristic attributes and potentials in a way that enables the attainment of achievements they judge to be good, thereby comprehensively disclosing their real nature. They are often successful in the outside world, because they have confidence and do not fear failure. They also respond well in a crisis, because it gives them a chance to bring glory upon themselves. They are forever seeking adoration. They need parasitic relationships to reinforce their self-love, which means they want to be associated with people who reinforce their fragile self-image. They have a low tolerance of frustration, inadequacy, and strong emotional feelings, due to the lack of ego development. They are inclined to violence in the face of perceived insulting provocations. They want to punish those who threaten their favorable views of themselves. They, thus, feel an inner emptiness, fluctuating as they do between self-love

---

memoir-what-happened-election-trump-sanders.

[140] See: http://www.nationalreview.comarticle/449521/donald-trump-republicans
-congress-has-failed-adap.

[141] Retrieved from: https://www.theguardian.com/books/2017/jun/12/selfie-will-
storr-review-me-myself-trump-age-ego.

and self-hatred. They have desire to formulate relationships only with those willing to give them confirming and admiring feedback. They are hyper-sensitive to slights, criticism, and rejection. They have a proclivity to overreact to perceived failures, threatening situations, or perceived insulting provocations. They have a low tolerance of boredom and frustration. They are incapable of strong emotional feelings, due to a lack of ego development; and they feel a sense of inner emptiness, fluctuating between the mental states of self-love and self-hatred.

The profile of a narcissist is a person who exhibits an array of the following personality traits:[142]

- He expects to be recognized as superior even without achievements that warrant it.

- He exaggerates his achievements and talents.

- He is preoccupied with fantasies about his success, power, brilliance, beauty or being the perfect mate.

- He believes that he is superior and can only be understood by or associate who are equally special people.

- He requires constant admiration.

- He expects special favors and unquestioning compliance with his wishes.

- He takes advantage of others to get what he wants.

- He has an inability or unwillingness to recognize the needs and feelings of others.

- He is envious of others and believes they are envious him.

- He behaves in an arrogant or haughty manner.

The Archetypal High Functioning Sociopath

Sociopaths (Partridge 1930) are people with an antisocial personality disorder, which is a mental health condition that affects how they think, perceive, feel, and relate to others. It is characterized by behaviors that

---

[142] See http://www.mayoclinic.org/diseases-conditions/narcissistic-personality-disorder/basics/symptoms/con-20025568; http://dsm.psychiatryonline.org/doi/book/10.1176/appi.books.9780890425596.

are impulsive and irresponsible and that are made without concern for other people's feelings.[143] By all appearances, they are conventional and normal, but perhaps a little too good to be true. They exude charisma, radiate charm, and have excellent verbal and nonverbal communication skills—capable of intense, captivating, unwavering eye contact—making them alluring, fascinating, and captivating, capable of completely overshadowing anyone in *any* room. Everyone loves a sociopath.

Having complete control over the drives that govern their lives means that they can choose to act on them, or not as the case may be, depending on circumstances, even whim. Their morality is governed by an internal code of behaviors. They are, by temperament, authoritarian,[144] paranoid, and secretive. They deny having a mental health condition. They are contemptuous of those who seek to understand them in these terms.

The profile of a sociopath is a person who exhibits an array of the following personality traits:[145]

- He considers everything in life to be a game he must win, so justifying cheating, lying, stealing, and even violence.
- He is always charming, but covertly domineering and manipulative, as he never recognizes others people's rights, but willingly accepts, as permissible, their self-serving behaviors, and sees them merely as instruments to be used, dominated, and humiliated as necessary.

---

[143] See: https://www.psychologytoday.com/blog/communication-success/201409/10-signs-youre-in-relationship-narcissist; http://www.mayoclinic.org/diseases-conditions/narcissistic-personality-disorder/basics/symptoms/con-20025568; http://dsm.psychiatryonline.org/doi/book/10.1176/appi.books.9780890425596.

[144] Adorno et al.'s (1950) enunciation of the authoritarian personality is insightful. Authoritarians are characterized by, among other things, their arrogance toward those they consider inferior; their capacity for prejudice; their unwillingness to tolerate ambiguity; and their readiness to punish those who challenge their authority (but see Madge 1962).

[145] See: http://www.nhs.uk/Conditions/antisocial-personality-disorder/Pages/Introduction.aspx; http://www.healthyplace.com/personality-disorders/sociopath/signs-of-a-sociopath-are-big-time-scary/; http://www.mcafee.cc/Bin/sb.html; http://www.mayoclinic.org/diseases-conditions/antisocial-personality-disorder/home/ovc-20198975.

- He is a convincing liar who finds it almost impossible to be consistently truthful, so he is able to construct complex belief about his own powers and abilities.

- He has a deep-seated and so repressed rage. This enables him to see others only as exploitable opportunities, and so is indifferent to the consequences of his decisions or actions for others—or, indeed, for himself—thus, nothing stops him from doing what he wants to do, as he lacks any sense of remorse, shame, or guilt.

- He is emotionally shallow, for when showing what seem to be warmth, joy, love, and compassion it is feigned and serves only his ulterior motive.

- He is living on perpetually on the edge—tense, nervous, or irritable—so verbal outbursts and physical punishments are normal, and promiscuity is common.

- He believes that the rules, laws, and norms that exist for others do not apply to him, so they are meaningless.

- He has a grandiose sense of self, so he feels entitled to certain things as a matter of right.

- He acts quickly and without deliberation, for he neither has the time nor inclination to assess hazards or to judge risks, so he is a risk-taker, one who lives in the present purely to gain pleasure, excitement, and instant gratification, without concern for the consequences of his actions on self or others.

- He is unreliable, for if after making a commitment he later decides that there is no benefit to him in following through, he will not honor that commitment—but he will not apologize—so he is unpredictable.

- He is a thrill-seeker whose life must always be extraordinary, always needing excitement when boredom looms, and so has a need for change.

The Archetypal Psychopath

Psychopaths are people with an a psychopathic personality disorder, where the psychopathic traits are innate, ascribed to "a chaotic or violent upbringing"[146] that tips the scales for those who are predisposed to psychopathic behaviors that are unstable, aggressive, and can even be violent.

The profile of a psychopath is a person who exhibits an array of the following personality traits:[147]

- He has a glib and superficial charm.
- He has a grandiose sense of self.
- He has low self-discipline because boredom comes easily.
- He is a pathological liar.
- He uses deceit and deception for personal gain.
- He lacks any feelings of remorse or guilt.
- He has a limited range or depth of feelings, in spite of signs suggesting openness and gregariousness.
- He is callousness reflecting a lack of empathy.
- He is manipulative, selfish, and exploitative of others.
- He is unable to begin or complete responsibilities.
- He has poor behavioral control.
- He is promiscuous sexual behaviors.
- He is unable to develop, or persist with, realistic, long-term goals;
- He is impulsive.
- He repeatedly failure to fulfill or honor obligations and commitments.
- He is unable to accept responsibility for his own actions.
- He is inconsistent, undependable, and unreliable about meeting any life commitments he has made.

---

[146] https://www.psychologytoday.com/basics/psychopathy.

[147] https://www.sociopathicstyle.com/psychopathic-traits/; http://www.minddisorders.com/Flu-Inv/Hare-Psychopathy-Checklist.html; https://www.healthyplace.com/personality-disorders/psychopath/psychopathic-traits-and-characteristics-of-a-psychopath; https://www.thoughtco.com/characteristics-of-the-psychopathic-personality-973128.

2
DONALD J. TRUMP: THE INTUITIVE EXISTENTIALIST

INTRODUCTION

Donald J. Trump is, intuitively, an existentialist in his thoughts and actions. He lives only in the present; as Schopenhauer ([1813/1877] 2017, s. 51) remarked: "The present is always passing through to a dead past; the future is quite uncertain and always short." In Trump's view, the present "That's where the fun is" (Twitter, July 2014, cited in Piehler 2016, 148). He individually constructs the meaning and significance of social reality on the basis of his existential subjectivity—"upon pure subjectivity" (Sartre [1946] 1973, 26). This makes the trustworthiness of knowledge about the world of persons contingent upon the vagaries of his thoughts and experiences. He presumes that he has the existential freedom to be who he wants to be—able to make the necessary leap in the dark in expectation of success—by exercising Nietzsche's incarnate will-to-power ([1895] 1967). He believes he is able to engage with social reality as he imagines it to be in any way he chooses. So, he has the drive for worldly success and power over others, which makes possible "a possibility as my possibility" (Sartre [1943] 1957, 34). Yet, his life experience seems to have taught him that to be successful he must, in the process of exercising his existential freedom, preserver with competitive aggression, in order to take up and defeat life's endless cycle of trials and tribulations—Nietzsche's ([1883] 1967) law of eternal recurrence. This epitomizes the existential belief that events in life can never be entirely under anyone's control—luck, fate, and unpredictable external forces are always lurking—with mal-intent—in a social world that is objectively unknowable and so is unpredictable.

THE EXISTENTIAL TRUMP

Trump sees social reality as an idea in his mind. He makes sense of any situation—and his position in it—only on the basis of his own inimitable first-person mental discernments—essentially intuition drawn from insights gained from such previous or similar situations. Other people are a challenge to him. Their traits and attributes he would consider understandable and acceptable only after he has judged the meaning of his first-hand experience with them, based upon his pure subjectivity. He would search for the relevant heuristic clues in their behavior, upon which he would draw conclusions—particularly about their trustworthiness and loyalty—that, with the first-person authority of self-knowledge, he would privilege with the presumption of truth.

In his assumptive world, his social engagement style—the way he construes his place in his world—is predicated on him being an active (or influencing) agent, which "implies an engagement with an environment by 'doing' or acting in it" (McKinney 1981, 359). His role relationship with others is self-determined, in accord with whatever he considers necessary to meet the challenges he faces. He sees his social context as always one where everyone has a place, relative to him, but no one belongs and, ultimately, he does not care about anyone.

His interpersonal relationships are governed by his behavioral norms—essentially, distrust, hostility, and hyper-competitiveness—that constitute the ingrained rules by which he conduct himself and his affairs. This is not too surprising considering the two dominant influences in his life were both strong willed people. One was his father, Frederick Trump,[148] who was noted for his "alleged racial discrimination against potential tenants",[149] and who has been described as "strict and demanding, he was family. He loved his son and bailed him out of financial scrapes, not to mention providing him with an ample inheritance upon his death."[150] In Trump on words: "My legacy has its roots in my father's legacy."[151]

---

[148] See: http://metro.co.uk/2016/10/20donald-trumps-fortune-is-built-on-money-from-prostitutes-and-brothels-6203104/.

[149] Retrieved from: http://heavy.com/news/2016/01/donald-trump-father-fred-trump-woody-guthrie-photos-real-estate-developer-wife-mary-family-kkk-arrest-death-net-worth-children-born/.

[150] Retrieved from: https://newsstand.google.com/articles/CAIiEGtR133yHzrVa VkPOfeYteIqFQgEKg0IACoGCAowrqkBMKBFMKGBAg.

[151] Retrieved from: https://www.washingtonpost.com/news/wonk/wp/2015/08/10/the-middle-class-housing-empire-donald-trump-abandoned-for-luxury-building/?utm_term=.5decca021e30.

Trump's other mentor was Roy Cohen[152], "the infamous chief aide to Senator Joseph McCarthy[153] during the Red Scare[154] of the early 1950s. Cohn then went on to make his career as a no-holds-barred attorney who would stop at nothing—including the law—to win for his client. [Cohn was ultimately disbarred prior to his death in 1986.]"[155] As Peter Fraser, "who as Mr. Cohn's lover for the last two years of his life spent a great deal of time with Mr. Trump,"[156] is reported to have said:

> I hear Roy in the things he [Donald Trump] says quite clearly, ... That bravado, and if you say it aggressively and loudly enough, it's the truth—that's the way Roy used to operate to a degree, and Donald was certainly his apprentice.[157]

Trump is perpetually struggling with his interpretation of other people's discernments of him. This feeds his proclivity to distrust everyone until his trust has been earned; but distrust is always only just around the corner. So, he uses a set of Jungian masks to portray the social impressions that enables him to play whatever roles are necessary in order to manipulate them to achieve what he wants without disclosing his true feelings about them. These masks constitute "a compromise ... between the demands of the environment and the necessities of the individual's inner constituents" (Jacobi 1962, 19). Haselbach (1994, 45–46) elaborates:

> Where life situations of individuals are segmented, where individuals fulfill different roles, where individuals have experienced, learned, and actually use different

---

152 See: https://www.nytimes.com/2016/06/21/us/politics/donald-trump-roy-cohn.html.

153 See: https://www.britannica.com/biography/Joseph-McCarthy.

154 See: http://www.history.com/topics/cold-war/red-scare.

155 Retrieved from: https://www.forbes.com/forbes/welcome/?toURL=https://www.forbes.com/sites/johnbaldoni/2017/05/12/president-trump-knows-no-composure/&refURL=https://www.google.com.tr/&referrer=https://www.google.com.tr/.

156 Retrieved from: https://www.nytimes.com/2016/06/21/us/politics/donald-trump-roy-cohn.html.

157 Retrieved from: https://www.nytimes.com/2016/06/21/us/politics/donald-trump-roy-cohn.html.

registers of behaviors, we find plural identities .... If ... we link "identity" with development (of the personality), change (over time), interaction (with others), responsiveness and adaptation (to a variety of dissimilar situations encountered and to evaluations of these situations and of our responses by others, i.e. to the never-ending processes of calibration), we end up with plural identities of the individual and with a notion of identity, of those plural identities, that have a process character, something which one cannot possess but

In terms of Riesman's (1950) inner-other directedness dichotomy, Trump has an inner-directedness orientation—preferring to act independently and in accordance with his personal code of conduct. Thus, he continually strives to deal with the real by discerning reality as it becomes or manifests; draw upon his experience to shapes his individuality: "Man has no nature; what he has is history," so "I am myself and my circumstances" (Ortega y Gasset [1929–31] 2002, 53) and "in what we do we recognize what we are" (Schopenhauer [1839] 1999, 109).

On the Levenson's locus-of-control spectrum (1981, 49–52), Trump is among the externalists who see external factors—essentially other people—conspiring against him, and so he holds them responsible—blameworthy and punishable—for whatever adversely happens to him. This may, of course, be a convenient belief that enables negative consequences to be attributed to others.

TRUMP'S EXISTENTIAL DISPOSITIONS

Trump's existentialist disposition inclines him to a set of propositions (Dixon, Dogan, and Sanderson 2009), with a twist, of course, given his personality traits.

On the Poorly Educated Common and Mediocre Masses

Trump's ontological disposition inclines him to share Sartre's ([1943] 1957) proposition that in the process of individual interaction individuals have to struggle to absorb each other's freedom. As Trump is only concerned about how others perceive him, especially his poorly educated[158] core supporters—Nietzsche's ([1886] 1998) herd—to curry favor he ingratiated himself by publicly declaring his love for them.[159] Yet, it has been mooted, probably correctly, that "Trump doesn't understand ordinary people. This is because he was born with a silver spoon in his mouth and has led a charmed life only the progeny of the rich lead."[160] He tells them that they are the smartest and most loyal people,[161] but, according to Trump's son-in-law, Jared Kushner, he lies to them "because he thinks they're stupid."[162] They may well be easily misguided, god-fearing, sometimes fatalistic,[163] always skeptical of the establishment and its

---

158 See: https://www.youtube.com/watch?v=Vpdt7omPoa0; https://www. usatoday.com/story/news/politics/onpolitics/2016/02/24/donald-trump-nevada-poorly-educated/80860078/; http://www.rollingstone.com/politics/news/watch-trump-brag-about-uneducated-voters-the-hispanics-20160224; http://www.huffingtonpost.com/entry/donald-trump-poorly-educated-voters_us_56cf9ee1e4b0bf0dab3191f7; https://sputniknews.com/us/201602241035297279-trump-loves-uneducated-voters/. But see: http://elitedaily.com/humor/donald-trump-loves-poorly-educated/1396865/; https://qz.com/623640/i-love-the-poorly-educated-read-donald-trumps-full-nevada-victory-speech/.

159 See: https://www.youtube.com/watch?v=Vpdt7omPoa0; https://www. usatoday.com/story/news/politics/onpolitics/2016/02/24/donald-trump-nevada-poorly-educated/80860078/; http://www.rollingstone.com/politics/news/watch-trump-brag-about-uneducated-voters-the-hispanics-20160224; http://www.huffingtonpost.com/entry/donald-trump-poorly-educated-voters_us_56cf9ee1e4b0bf0dab3191f7; https://sputniknews.com/us/2016022 41035297279-trump-loves-uneducated-voters/. But see: http://elitedaily.com/humor/donald-trump-loves-poorly-educated/1396865/; https://qz.com/62 3640/i-love-the-poorly-educated-read-donald-trumps-full-nevada-victory-speech/.

160 Retrieved from: http://www.independent.co.uk/voices/bannon-fired-trump-breitbart-work-already-done-embrace-white-nationalists-a7901416.html.

161 Retrieved from: https://www.youtube.com/watch?v=ydF_gniBkx0.

162 Retrieved from: http://www.independent.co.uk/News/world/americas/jared-kushner-donald-trump-lied-base-stupid-voters-supporters-president-son-in-law-white-house-a7764791.html.

163 Fatalists blame fate on the premise that no one can be held responsible, morally or otherwise, for their actions, as no one can be a completely free agent (Strawson 1986; Cicero [44 BC] 1991). They "expect conspiracy, but it does not shock or surprise them" (Douglas 1994, 110). They are prone to put a brave face on hopelessness, allowing them to embrace a genial fatalism (Douglas and Ney

rational experts, and, perhaps, even alienated.[164] They, adoringly, want to hear, ferociously devour, and take to heart, his populist, anti-intellectual,[165] and authoritarian rhetoric. They believe that only he—and he alone—can give them back what they have lost: their jobs, their communities, their hopes and aspirations, and their self-respect—"I am with you, I am your voice."[166] This brings to the mind the process understood by Trotsky—his concept of substitutionism[167]—whereby the Communist Party "substitute itself for the working classes" (Cliff 1960). So, the Party—Trump—acts as proxy in their name and on their behalf, regardless of what they think or want.

Trump instinctively—perhaps even cynically—understands what other have found by research: "that people who have lower levels of education and fewer qualifications tend to subscribe to more socially conservative and more authoritarian positions."[168] They also make very clear link between values and culture. This may explain why Trump, seeing the need, in late August, to shore-up his core support, advanced a no-holds-barred law and order agenda—police militarization[169] and tough policing[170]—to consolidate his image as a relentless and uncompromising enforcer of law and order.[171] Indeed, he pardoned former Arizona Sheriff, Joe Arpaio—"a major Trump supporter during last year's cam-

---

1998, 114; see also Douglas 1996).

[164] This is a state-of-mind being experienced as a sense of estrangement as a first-person mental state (BonJour 2002, see also Hegel [1807] 1977, Marx [1844] 1963, Maslow [1962] 1968, Rogers 1961).

[165] See: https://www.theguardian.com/us-news/2016/oct/16/white-college-graduates-donald-trump-support-falling.

[166] Retrieved from https://www.youtube.com/watch?v=zbAqJf-OuDI.

[167] See: http://www.gutenberg.us/articles/substitutionism.

[168] Retrievedfrom:http://www.newsweek.com/donald-trump-brexit-austria-french-presidential-election-national-front-525281.

[169] See: http://edition.cnn.com/2017/08/28/politics/police-military-gear-ban-lifted/index.html; http://edition.cnn.com/2017/08/28/politics/police-military-gear-ban-lifted/index.html?sr=.

[170] See: http://edition.cnn.com/2017/08/28/politics/police-military-gear-ban-lifted/index.html?sr=.

[171] See: http://edition.cnn.com/2017/08/28/politics/police-military-gear-ban-lifted/index.html?sr=.

paign"[172]—who was awaiting sentencing after being found guilty[173] in July of "criminal contempt for ignoring a federal judge's order to stop detaining people because he merely suspected them of being undocumented immigrants."[174] Trump obviously considered that he was "convicted for doing his job"[175]—ruthless law enforcement.[176]

His poorly educated core support base willingly became Trump's loyal and obedient foot soldiers on his crusade to win the presidency. To them, he promised to give power back to the people.[177] He has not; quite the contrary.[178] But still they must continue to pay him their dues. They must be willing to give him, on demand at any time, an injection of unfettered acclaim, nay, devotion, to restore his faith in himself. Yet there

---

[172] Retrieved from: https://www.washingtonpost.com/politics/trump-holds-campaign-style-rally-amid-large-protests-in-arizona/2017/08/22/dd7c83c0-8796-11e7-961d-2f373b3977ee_story.html?utm_term=.fcb46cb15733.

[173] See: http://edition.cnn.com/2017/08/24/politics/why-joe-arpaio-was-found-guilty/index.html.

[174] Retrieved from: https://www.washingtonpost.com/politics/trump-holds-campaign-style-rally-amid-large-protests-in-arizona/2017/08/22/dd7c83c0-8796-11e7-961d-2f373b3977ee_story.html?utm_term=.fcb46cb15733.

[175] Retrieved from: https://www.washingtonpost.com/politics/trump-holds-campaign-style-rally-amid-large-protests-in-arizona/2017/08/22/dd7c83c0-8796-11e7-961d-2f373b3977ee_story.html?utm_term=.fcb46cb15733.

[176] Retrieved from: https://www.washingtonpost.com/politics/trump-holds-campaign-style-rally-amid-large-protests-in-arizona/2017/08/22/dd7c83c0-8796-11e7-961d-2f373b3977ee_story.html?utm_term=.fcb46cb15733. See: http://edition.cnn.com/2017/08/28/politics/donald-trump-joe-arpaio-pardon/index.html. Trump has now set "a legal precedent of effectively pardoning someone for abusing the constitutional rights of an ethnic minority. Done in a manner that employs the pardon power as a reward for political loyalty. Resulting from a process that evidently did not involve the normal review and recommendation of the Justice Department's pardon attorney." Retrieved from: https://www.washingtonpost.com/politics/trump-holds-campaign-style-rally-amid-large-protests-in-arizona/2017/08/22/dd7c83c0-8796-11e7-961d-.

[177] See: http://thehill.com/homenews/administration/315275-trump-were-giving-power-back-to-the-people; https://www.aol.com/article/news/2017/01/20/trump-vows-to-give-power-back-to-you-the-people-as-he-becomes-45th-president/21659429/.

[178] See: http://www.latimes.com/projects/la-ed-trumps-authoritarian-vision/; amp-politics/la-times-scorches-authoritarian-trump-its-most-blistering-editorial-date.

is a catch—their loyalty is never reciprocated. Beneath the thin veneer of love—and he loved a lot of things during his campaign[179]—he seems to "despises the very voters who elected him."[180] This is evidenced by his intention to introduce policy and budgetary measures detrimental to their best interests—most notably his fiscal austerity measures that cut welfare programs.[181] This is not surprising, for his poorly educated core support base represents what he clearly despises, weak-willed people unable to take the bull—life—by the horns and win, despite whatever fate decrees, just as he believes he has done all his life. Indeed, to Trump, life is all about the exercising the will to power—taking control of life at any cost to anyone, including strangers, acquaintances, friends, and, if really necessary, even family.

Trump would, no doubt, generally endorse the existentialist explanation for their plight:

- They are prisoners of their own learnt or inherited mental constructs—Sartre's ([1960] 2004) concept of practico-inert.[182]

- They lack an "appetite for life" (Wilson [1956/1967] 2001, 118).

- They fear success—Maslow's Jonah complex.[183]

- They have a sense of fatalism—manifesting as feelings of anomie (Durkheim [1897] 1952) and distrust (Sztompka 1996)—

---

[179] See: https://www.youtube.com/watch?v=rXj_yrEkFJI.

[180] Retrieved from: http://www.salon.com/2017/05/27/paul-krugman-trump-clearly-despises-the-very-voters-who-elected-him_partner/.

[181] See: https://www.nytimes.com/2017/05/22/us/politics/trump-budget-cuts.html.

[182] This means the practical activities and social structures inherited from previous generations limit or nullify true freedom of action. See:

https://plato.stanford.edu/entries/sartre/; http://oxfordindex.oup.com/view/10.1093/oi/authority.20110803100034159; https://is.muni.cz/el/1423/jaro2015/SOC757/um/3b_Reckwitz.pdf.

[183] This is the fear of success that a person has when he fears that the use of his talents and creativeness could bring new responsibilities and duties, which could threaten his of sense of safety, security, and belongingness (Maslow [1962] 1968, 59), thereby threatening to initiate a total personal transformation. It is named after the Biblical Old Testament Jonah, who was a timid merchant whose fear and pride cause him to run from God (Book of Jonah).

that they cannot shake off, leading them to blame bad luck, fate, the mystical forces of God's will,[184] or the other powers that be, for what they are now—the forgotten forsaken—the socially marginalized, even the socially alienated.[185] They are frustrated by their powerlessness in the face of economic and political oppression. They hate "the system" that has taken way who their jobs,[186] their hopes, and their self-respect. This gives rise to feelings of hatred and a desire for revenge—Nietzsche ([1887] 2006) concept of *ressentiment.*

- They stand in isolation, unsure about whom they are (Ortega y Gasset [1935] 2001), which generates a detachment: "a sense of strangeness, of unreality" (Wilson ([1956] 1957, 15) and a disconnection with life—"life is a dream, it is not real" (Wilson ([1956] 1957, 18). This focuses awareness on the human soul in its direst straits—confronting all life's paradoxes, ambiguities, and absurdities.

On the Individual Other

Trump's ontological disposition necessitates him constantly reflecting on how others falsify him. This feeds his paranoia, which inclines him to categorize others into two categories: his trusted disciples (loyal family

---

184 Devine determinism posits that a person's actions are determined by divine agency, a manifestation the divine nature of all-powerful God. Occasionalists believe that God is the only true causal agent, one who is able to cause both bodily and mental states by exercising, on occasions, his necessary efficacious power (Malebranche [1774–75] 1980, Nadler 1993, but see also Teresa and Kolodieichuk 2007).

185 Social alienation is "a condition in social relationships reflected by a low degree of integration or common values and a high degree of distance or isolation between individuals, or between an individual and a group of people in a community or work environment" (Ankony 1999, 120).

186 Marx argued that individuals are alienated because they are unable to attain the full self-realization that comes with the process of transforming the world in their own image through labor: "he [the worker] does not fulfill himself in his work but denies himself, he has a feeling of misery rather than well-being, does not develop freely his mental and physical energies but is physically exhausted and mentally debased. The worker, therefore, feels himself at home only during leisure time, whereas at work he feels homeless" (Marx [1844] 1963, 124–125).

members, servants, and retainers), and the rest (all of whom are his enemies until proven otherwise). According to his whim, trusted disciples who show any disloyalty can be quickly demoted to the status of enemy; and enemies who show their personal loyalty can be promoted to trusted-disciple status.

His narcissistic traits inclined him to view his dealings with others through a win–lose lens, ever seeking to attain an advantage—dominance—over them. This would incline him to prefer what Buber ([1923] 1958) described as I-It interpersonal relationships, whereby the other person is perceived as an object—having specific, isolated qualities—but the relationship is one of separateness and detachment, degrees of which is directly correlated with relative importance of the other person.

So, from those with whom he must engage to advance his cause, he demands continual evidence of their personal loyalty and their uncritical compliance with his wishes. Such loyalty, of course, goes unreciprocated. He presumes the right to manipulate them to get what he wants, as his rights trump their rights. This enables him to see others only as exploitable opportunities. He judges that he has no need to value those he considers play only a passing, trivial, and trifling role in the creation of his desired self-identity. Include in this category are:

- Those who were willingly taken in by his political rhetoric—particularly the uneducated common and mediocre masses—to whom he lies because he considers them to be stupid[187] and who he can be abandoned at will.

- Those whose political or administrative nous is only of instrument value to him, who have outlived their usefulness and so can be publicly demoted, humiliated, or even discharged at will.

- Those who never evidence any personal loyalty to him, whose interests can be totally ignored at will. These include:
  - Those who do not willingly share his beliefs and values: particularly the *Democrats*. They should have supported his

---

[187]   Retrieved from: http://www.independent.co.uk/News/world/americas/jared-kushner-donald-trump-lied-base-stupid-voters-supporters-president-son-in-law-white-house-a7764791.html.

first excellent Obamacare repeal and replacement initiative: "We had no votes from the Democrats, ... They weren't going to give us a single vote so it's a very difficult thing to do [to appeal an Act when the majority-holding Republican Party is divided]."[188]

- Those who are not suitably impressed by his rhetoric, particularly cynical *journalists*, who Trump believes the FBI should consider throwing into jail.[189]

- Those who threaten his finely crafted fantasies about his success, power, and brilliance, particularly educated and long-standing *heads of state*, especially if they are *female* (Dr Angela Merkel,[190] the German Chancellor[191]), and *forthright heads of state* (such as,[192] the Australian Prime Minister[193]). Malcolm Turnbull

Trump never, of course, underestimates the value of those—living or dead—he considers play and on-going, vital, and central—thus important—role in the creation of his desired self-identity. These include:

- *Andrew* Jackson,[194] the seventh US president (1828–1836), with whom he would like to be associated in the popular mind,

---

188 Retrieved from: http://www.vox.com/obamacare/2017/3/24/15055232/donald-trump-ahca-statement).

189 See: http://edition.cnn.com/2017/05/22/politics/trump-comey-jail-journalists/index.html.

190 See: https://www.biography.com/people/angela-merkel-9406424.

191 See: http://www.independent.co.uk/voices/donald-trump-angela-merkel-megyn-kelly-hillary-clinton-a76of 38176.html; http://www.independent.co.uk/voices/donald-trump-angela-merkel-megyn-kelly-hillary-clinton-a7638176.html; http://www.marketwatch.com/story/merkel-slams-trumps-decision-to-quit-paris-climate-accord-2017-06-02.

192 See: https://www.pm.gov.au/.

193 See: http://www.bbc.com/news/world-australia-38837263; http://www.bbc.com/news/world-us-canada-38849257; http://www.telegraph.co.uk/news/2017/02/02/worst-call-far-donald-trump-told-malcolm-turnbull-attacking/.

194 See: https://www.whitehouse.gov/1600/presidents/andrewjackson; https://www.biography.com/people/andrew-jackson-9350991; http://www.smithsonianmag.com/history/andrew-jackson-americas-original-anti-establishment-candidate-180958621/.

so as to enhance, by reflection, his own self-glory. This is because Jackson was the original anti-establishment president—a populist outsiders. Trump considers him to be a great president with "a big heart".[195] Unlike Trump, however, he was a seasoned politician comfortable in high office before becoming president, given his background as lawyer, a military man of some repute—"The Old Hero"—as well as having been both a Congressman and a Senator. He also, notoriously, led a military campaign against Native Americans to relocate or exterminate them. Trump's choice of a presidential role model is insightful.

- Those who evidence the necessary personal loyalty and willingness to comply with his wishes, particularly, his daughter *Ivanka Kushner* nee *Trump*[196] and son-in law *Jared Kushner*.[197]

- Those who can stroke his fragile ego, perhaps by mere association, or, possibly, by their flattery or even their indulgence—the all-important *business CEOs*[198] and *billionaires*, particularly those willing to serve loyally in his administration. As has been observed:

---

195 See: m/us-news/2017/may/01/donald-trump-civil-war-cause-andrewjackson).

196 See: http://www.businessinsider.com/jared-kushner-russia-back-channel-testimony-2017-7; http://www.motherjones.com/politics/2017/07/the-trump-russia-conspiracy-is-now-very-simple/. See also http://www.thedailybeast.com/trump-russia-scandal-now-threatens-to-ensnare-ivanka.

197 See: https://www.vanityfair.com/news/2017/07/jared-kushner-trump-campaign-russia-investigation; http://www.independent.co.uk/news/world/americas/us-politics/jared-kushner-lying-contacts-russia-watergate-prosecutor-jill-wine-banks-msnbc-a7862106.html; http://nymag.com/daily/intelligencer/2017/07/jared-kushner-keeps-making-the-russia-scandal-so-much-worse.html; http://www.businessinsider.com/jared-kushner-russia-back-channel-testimony-2017-7.

198 So he would probably be astonished that at "[from a] gathering of 125 leaders at a Yale School of Management CEO Summit ... [50% graded ... his first 130 days in office as] ... A big fat F [fail .... [He] garnered merely a D from 21% of the respondents and only 18% gave him a C [10% gave him a B and only 1% gave him an A grade]." Retrieved from: https://www.forbes.com/sites/laurensonnenberg/2017/06/16/ceos-gather-at-summit-to-give-president-trump-a-failing-grade/; see also: http://www.independent.co.uk/news/world/americas/us-politics/trump-ceos-job-performance-rating-grading-yale-summit-favourability-a7792376.html.

Trump seems to enjoy trouping CEOs of major companies into the White House while he holds court. He likes to consider himself among his own kind, fellow business leaders. There is one major difference. Most if not all of those CEOs are heads of public companies; Trump ran his family's business. Those CEOs report to boards and shareholders. Trump reported to himself.[199]

- Those who, somewhat enviously, considers to be almost role models, because that have exhibited at least some of necessary political acumen needed to be strong head of state, including *Vladimir Putin*,[200] *Kim Jong-Un*,[201] *Saddam Hussein*,[202] and *Recep Tayyip Erdoğan*[203].

On Reasoning and Rationality

Trump's epistemological disposition inclines him toward both the trial and error learning style (Schwarz and Thompson 1990, 66) and non-rationality (Portes 1972; Elster 1985), "where the canons of rationality, validity, truth, and efficiency are simply beside the point—irrelevant!" (Shweder 1984, 38). So, according to Heidegger "thinking only begins at the point where we have come to know that Reason, glorified for

---

[199] Retrieved from: https://newsstand.google.com/articles/CAIiEGtR133yHz rVaVkPOfeYteIqFQgEKg0IACoGCAowrqkBMKBFMKGBAg.

[200] Retrieved from: http://beforeitsnews.com/alternative/2016/06/putin-repeats-praise-of-trump-hes-a-bright-person-3371208.html; see particularly: http://edition.cnn.com/interactive/2017/03/politics/trump-putin-russia-timeline/; but see also: https://www.usnews.com/news/world/articles/2016-12-23/the-5-best-quotes-from-vladimir-putins-press-conference.

[201] Retrieved from: https://www.theguardian.com/us-news/2017/may/01/donald-trump-kim-jong-un-meeting-north-korea; https://www.theguardian.com/us-news/2017/may/01/donald-trump-kim-jong-un-meeting-north-korea; http://abcnews.go.com/Politics/trump-north-korean-leader-kim-jong-gotta-give/story?id=36198345.

[202] Retrieved from: https://www.nytimes.com/2016/07/06/us/politics/donald-trump-saddam-hussein.html.

[203] Retrieved from: http://www.hurriyetdailynews.com/i-give-erdogan-great-credit-for-turning-the-coup-around-trump-.aspx?pageID=238&nID=101949&NewsCatID=358.

centuries, is the most obstinate adversary of thinking" (cited in Barrett 1958, 184). Hence, statements about an objectively unknowable world cannot be confirmed or disproved, as no evidence or experience can possibly be considered as proof. Thus what he believes to be real is the basis for reasoning. This begs the question: How does Trump think?

> Some would say he is incapable of it. Ignorant and incurious, given to impromptu rants, jerked to and fro by a cabal of conspiracy theorists, shock jocks and doom-mongers, he is the very epitome of thoughtlessness. Beneath that curvaceous quiff, behind that perma-tanned pout, his mind is a broiling elemental chaos.

> There is no telling what Trump thinks because he takes opposite views of all subjects, sometimes simultaneously.[204]

This means outcomes are to be enjoyed or endured, never sought. Hoppe (2000) describes this as inspirational-strategic rationality, which gives no credence to any information purporting to consist of "objective truths" derived by "experts." As Weick (1979, 56) observed: "how do I know what I think until ... I see how I act." So, making sense of any situation involves rolling or serial hindsight, driven by plausibility—plausible bullshit—rather than truthfulness (Weick 1995).

Trump has revealed his preferred way of thinking, which is quintessentially existential: "I don't look forward or not look forward" (*Washington Post*, July 2015 cited in Piehler 2016, 11). "I try to learn from the past, but I plan for the future by focusing exclusively on the present. That's where the fun is" (Twitter, July 2014, cited in Piehler 2016, 148). A counterfactual mindset he might have—although it is not apparent that as President he learns from his errors; a spectator mindset he probably has; but a deliberative mindset he certainly does not have. He feels comfortable with his way of thinking about family business by utilizing his spectator mindset. This way of thinking about politics, policy and administration is problematic, because it reveals his lack of a delibera-

---

[204] Retrieved from: https://newsstand.google.com/articles/CAIiEI2rgLZ4ROQJN wYjGHJtEY4qFggEKg4IACoGCAowl6p7MN-zCTCOvRU.

tive, an implementation, or an agent mindset. So, he would, no doubt willingly accept the validity of Schopenhauer's [1851] 1970, 56) doctrine of the primacy of will—the real world is the self who has an idea. Trump's knowledge of that world is based on what he intuitively finds useful to say. This is the basis of his reasoning.

On Risk-taking

Trump is an instinctive risk-taker. His epistemological disposition means, however, that risks cannot be objectively measured or evaluated by anyone, as the future is unknowable in a world that is random and disordered, and so constituted as a zero-sum game (Thompson and Taylor 1986, 22). This means that all that can be done, particularly if avoid hazards—in the hope of minimizing the possibility of future failure—is unacceptable—is to shrug them off (Douglas and Ney 1998, 137), after, of course, deflecting responsibility.

Trump accepts risk-taking because he has no inclination to assess fully the possible consequences of his decisions or actions. Indeed, whether or not he should impose risks on others is beside the point, for he—as one of the powers that be—decides what should be done, and then exercises the necessary coercive power at his disposal to do it. He always ensures, however, that in the event of failure he can readily and speedily deflect responsibility—blame—for any detrimental outcomes to others. As the causation of any failure cannot be objectively determined, fate (Strawson 1986; Cicero [44 BCE] 1971) decides to whom it is convenient to assign blame. Trump's usual list of suspects are the traitors within the White Houses[205]—those individuals or factions disloyal to him—or the enemies beyond—disloyal factions within the congressional Republican Party,[206] the Democratic Party,[207] treacherous

---

[205] See: http://www.nydailynews.com/news/national/trump-hates-fake-news-spreads-unsubstantiated-claims-article-1.2988895; http://www.independent.co.uk/voices/donald-trump-white-house-fake-news-source-washington-dc-government-politics-russia-hillary-clinton-a7763136.html.

[206] Retrieved from: http://www.vox.com/obamacare/2017/3/24/15055232/donald-trump-ahca-statement).

[207] Retrieved from: http://www.vox.com/obamacare/2017/3/24/15055232/donald-trump-ahca-statement.

federal judges,[208] Barack Obama and his undercover operatives in the bureaucracy—the "deep state"[209]; and, of course, "the enemy of the people"[210]—the fake media and its journalists[211].

On Problem-solving

Trump is not inclined to do a careful study of a policy or administrative problem, or even to reflect on, and apply to, any problem a well thought through set of problem-solving notions. His epistemological disposition leads him to see problems as occurring in unstable and unknowable environments. This makes it wise to presume no certainties, so avoiding contestable problem knowledge, and to articulate no expected ends or means, on the ground that they are knowable only with experience. So, problems should have neither a structure imposed upon them nor their causation presumed. All possible solutions should be kept open, so as to maximize opportunities for escaping the clutches of fate.

Trump's preference is to make his own judgment on how best to address a problem, after he seeks out opinions on possible solutions, from which he would choose the one that is most advantageous to the advancing his own agenda.

On Decision-Making

Trump adopts a distinctive approach to decision-making. His epistemological disposition means that decision analysis can only involve random search behaviors and inspiration, on the presumption that there are no certainties. Thus, surprise dominates. Intelligence cannot improve ig-

---

208 See: https://www.theguardian.com/us-news/live/2017/mar/16/trump-travel-ban-blocked-nationwide-hawaii-court-live; see particularly: http://www.telegraph.co.uk/news/2017/02/04/donald-trump-slams-so-called-judge-blocked-ban-vows-overturn/.

209 Retrieved from: http://www.telegraph.co.uk/news/2017/03/11/deep-state-shadowy-network-obama-holdovers-undermining-donald/; see also http://google.com/newsstand/s/CBIwj628vDk.

210 See: http://www.independent.co.uk/news/world/americas/donald-trump-us-news-media-enemy-of-the-people-coverage-fixation-tv-west-wing-white-house-president-a7622216.html.

211 See: http://www.politico.com/magazinestory/2017/04/23/trump-loves-media-reporters-white-house-215043.

norance. Goals and values are luxuries. Any judgments that need to be made are limited, wherever possible, to Vickers' ([1983] 1995) action judgments: What action should be taken? Decision-making is, thus, inspirational (Thompson 1967), on the premise that disagreement follows uncertainties about outcome preferences and cause-and-effect relations, both of which are inevitable. So, it can only involve a garbage-can decision-making process (March and Olsen 1976), characterized as "a collection of choices looking for problems, issues, and feelings looking for decision situations in which they may be aired, solutions looking for issues to which they may be answers, and decision makers looking for work" (Cohen, March, and Olsen 1972, 2), or perhaps even as a lottery (Hood 1998). The decision-making outcome sought is to produce a workable intervention that builds, intuitively, on a sense-making interpretation of reality (Weick 1995). Pugh and Hickson (1996, 124–125) describe this as a:

> continual weaving of sense from beliefs, from the implicit assumptions, from tales from the past, and from ideas about what will happen as a result of what can be done. The whole sense-making process gives ostensible orderliness to what has gone on, and, indeed, is going on.

Trump, however, can be, according to psychologist Dan P. McAdam, "a daring and ruthlessly aggressive decision maker who desperately desires to create the strongest, tallest, shiniest, and most awesome result—and who never thinks twice about the collateral damage he will leave behind."[212] He can even be an audacious decision maker, when he feels the need to make a decision that gives him instant gratification—his core supporters' adulation (an example being his first Travel Ban Executive Order), and when the needed information at his disposal he judges to be palatable, and so trustworthy. Yet, if he chooses he can be apathetic in his decision-making—doing nothing unless, and until, absolutely necessary—when he needs to make anxiety-creating decisions and the needed information at his disposal is unpalatable, and thus, untrustworthy (for example, when needing to replace Obama appointees who remain in place in the Federal Executive at his pleasure, with people how

---

[212] Retrieved from: http ://www.theatlantic.com/magazine/archive/2016/06/the-mind-of-donald-trump/480771/.

should, first and foremost, be loyal to him).

Trump's approach to decision-making reflects the trust he has in his instincts:

> But as Trump passed the six-month mark in office, facing historic unpopularity and a raft of investigations involving his campaign and his family, his comments and his political behaviours have become only more bizarre, as if driven by the centrifugal force of his instincts.[213]

So, he is intuitive, impulsive, informal, and inevitably seeking to make extraordinary—even outrageous—decisions that advance his fantasies about his own success, power, and brilliance. His disposition is to avoid immoderation in anything he does—"A little more moderation would be good. Of course, my life hasn't exactly been one of moderation" (Twitter, June 2014, cited in Piehler 2016, 19). So, he is disposed, where he can, to quick decision-making, without apparent concern for the consequences of his decisions for others or, perhaps, even for himself. However, if after making a decision he later decides that there is no benefit to him in following through, he will not honor any commitments made, evidenced by his flip-flopping on inconvenient campaign promises.

Indeed, his decisions are driven by random stimuli—what he is told by whoever his trusted confidents are at the time a decision has to be made or by his trusted family members—or by shifts in mood—induced by what he sees on his favorite cable telephone news network—*Fox News*[214]. This is evidenced by his symbolic military response in Syrian to what he saw on the cable news—Syrian children being injured and dying from gas poisoning.[215] Making decisions prior to any duty-of-care pre-decision analysis is his decision-making predisposition, on the presumption that success will be forthcoming because he has decreed it to be so, with

---

[213] See: http://www.newyorker.com/news/daily-comment/donald-trumps-state-of-mind-and-ours.

[214] See: http://www.huffingtonpost.com/entry/trump-pacifier-rattle_us_591655 f3e4b0031e737dc72e.

[215] See: http://www.foxnews.com/world/2017/04/05/syria-chemical-attack-doctors-civilians-recall-children-suffocating-dying-on-streets-sarin-gas-suspected.html.

the caveat, of course, that responsibility for any failure—blame—can be externalized to the traitors within or the enemies beyond.

Trump's salient decision-making risks are threefold. First, a situation that demarcates the decision-making context may not be fully understandable solely by reference to his epistemologically subjective, intuitive self-knowledge that he finds useful to say. This makes his knowledge subject to severe relativism and open to constant revision, thereby making prediction problematic. Second, the roles that he has self-assigned himself, on the basis of what he considers necessary to meet the challenges he faces, may not be appropriate. Third, the behavioral responses he anticipates soliciting from others may not be forthcoming from the engagement approach he has decided to adopt.

On Power and Compliance

Trump's ontological dispositions means he has no reservations about using the power of threats (Boulder 1990) and coercion (French and Raven 1959) to make people do what they would not otherwise want to do. The use of such powers is likely to solicit coercive compliance, so giving rise to alienative compliance (Etzioni 1961). This sense of alienation may be relieved only by the unilateral actions people are willing to take in defiance of Trump's power-exercising authority, such as minor, irregular or occasional disobediences, including the leaking of confidential documents or embarrassing anecdotes to the media.

On Ethics and Moral Conduct

Trump's epistemological disposition guides him to judge the morality of his and others conduct by own personal code of ethics, as moral beliefs are not absolute. They can only be opinions that reveal moral sentiments (Hume [1777] 1902, 285–s94): "a virtue has to be our invention, our more personal defense and necessity ... each one of us should devise his own virtue, his own categorical imperatives" (Nietzsche [1888] 1969, 121). Moral beliefs, moreover, do not need further justification: "that there are no moral truths, that there is no moral knowledge, that in morals and politics all that we can ultimately do is to commit ourselves" (Bambrough 1979, 14). Holding such a moral position reflects discomfiture with any universal moral code, perhaps because "it is in the everyday world of space and time that moral decisions are made and moral struggles take place" (Walsh 1972, 29). So, what constitutes moral conduct is fluid, flexible, sometimes ambiguous, always situational, and only held after self-justification. The resultant personal ethical code is one that requires a person to act in a manner that is compatible with his underlying moral predispositions. This makes morality the product of circumstances, particularly, as Nietzsche ([1881] 1997) argued, in relation to, for example, the desire for power. Thus, how a person should conduct himself is contingent upon his emotions and desires, which are, typically, pluralistic and conflicting, which means that morality can never be immune to luck (Williams [1976] 1993, 1981; Nagel [1976] 1993). Others can hold no one morally responsible for their conduct, as it is self-referential (Cicero [44 BC] 1971).

TRUMP'S WORLDVIEW: ITS TENSIONS WITH ITS CONTENDERS

Trump's disposition to view social reality through the hermeneutic-agency social-reality lens—worldview—would inexorably antagonize those with different perspectives on social reality because they prefer to view it through different social-reality lens (Dixon, Dogan, and Sanderson 2009).

Contending Truth Perspectives

Trump's preferred truth criterion is what he intuitively finds useful to say and so believe. He would, then, deny the veracity of:

- *empirical* knowledge (social facts), thereby denying the Hierarchical Man worldview;

- *logical* knowledge (logical facts), thereby denying the Economic Man worldview; or

- *socially constructed* knowledge (social understandings), thereby denying the Social Man worldview.

This would make him unable to agree with adherent to other worldviews on what is knowable and true about the social world, which makes any communications between them problematic.

Contending Perspectives on Being Human

Trump prefers to see people as essentially unique and free human beings able—if they have the will—to determine their own fate. He would, then, deny the human nature propositions that consider people are

- *inherently errant human beings,* indolent and always seeking to avoid responsibility, thereby denying the Hierarchical Man worldview;
- *free human beings,* intent of pursuing their own material self-interests, thereby denying the Economic Man worldview; or
- *inherently good human beings,* with a capacity for real moral progress, thereby denying the validity of the Social Man worldview.

This makes him unable to agree with adherent to other worldviews on what it means to be human, which makes problematic the possibility of judging and addressing any human dilemmas, predicaments, and quandaries in a way that is acceptable to everyone.

Contending Social Action Perspectives

Trump prefers to consider individuals as self-determining agents who "could have chosen or acted otherwise" (Kane 2002, 5) and so are able to determine their own destiny and character. He would, then, deny that social actions are the product of a person's desire:

- to *conform* with the norms, roles, and practices that constitute the rules or code of conduct in any societal, institutional, or social group—whether they be:
  - pre-existent, thereby denying the validity of the Hierarchical Man worldview, or
  - group negotiated, thereby denying the validity of the Social Man; or
- to *maximize* their material wellbeing, thereby denying the validity of the Economic Man worldview.

This makes him unable to agree with adherent to other worldviews on how best to explain and predict a person's social actions, which makes problematic how best to achieve any desired behavior change.

Contending Moral Conduct Perspectives

Trump prefers to judge the morality of his own and others conduct on the basis of his personal ethical code. He would, then, deny that anyone can properly judge morality by reference to:

- its *moral rightness*: conduct that is in accord with moral principles, embedded in a set of moral rules or laws, that express what conduct is permitted or acceptable, and what is forbidden or unacceptable (deontological ethics) (Blackburn 2001), thereby denying the validity of the Hierarchical Man worldview;

- its *moral virtue*: conduct that is virtuousness because the action-taker has virtuous character traits, which makes virtue of a disposition that precedes the choice of a right conduct (virtue ethics) (Aristotle [350 BC] 2004), thereby denying the validity of the Social Man worldview; or

- its *consequences*: conduct that produces, or is likely to produce, good consequences (consequential ethics) (Gouinlock 1972)—the greatest happiness (pleasure) for the greatest number of people (Mill [1861] 1968; Bentham [1789] 1970; Austin [1832] 1995), thereby denying the validity of the Economic Man worldview.

This makes him unable to agree with adherent to other worldviews on how the morality a person's conduct should be judged, which makes problematic the articulating of generally acceptable ethical foundations for determining right actions.

Contending Trust Perspectives

Trump would believe that extending trust can only be justified on the basis of trust-inducing past personal experience. He would, then, deny that trust should be extended on the basis of:

- having *a common set of innate moral values* (moralistic *trust*) (Uslaner 2002), thereby denying the validity of the Hierarchical Man worldview;

- building up *mutual expectations of reciprocity*—sufficient goodwill—through discourse (goodwill trust) (Ring and van de Ven

1994), thereby denying the validity of the Social Man world-view; or

- having *knowledge of the probable risk* of extending trust (Gam-betta 1988)—the net beneficial consequences—of so doing (*knowledge-based trust*) (Yamigishi and Yamigishi 1994), there-by denying the validity of the Economic Man worldview.

This makes him unable to agree with adherent to other worldviews on how best to decide on the trustworthiness of others, which makes trust-ing problematic. Rothstein (2005) describes such a situation as a social trap, where individuals are unable to cooperate because of mutual dis-trust and the lack of social capital, even if such cooperation is, in fact, mutually beneficial.

Contending Decision-Making Perspectives

Trump would hold that decision-making should involve using his intui-tive knowledge to make plausible sense of reality. He would, then, deny the merit of gathering:

- *objective information* required to facilitate:
  - *satisficing decisions* (Simon [1947] 1960, 1956; Schwartz 2004) that everyone ought to agree with, premised on the accepted need for reason to be constrained by hierarchically determined values and beliefs, thereby denying the validity of the Hierarchical Man worldview; or
  - *optimizing decisions* (Schwartz 2004), premised on self-evi-dent need for successful risk-taking that creates opportuni-ties for personal material reward, thereby denying the valid-ity of the Economic Man worldview; or
- *subjective (socially constructed) information* required to facilitate *compromising decisions* (Foucault 1978; de Haven-Smith 1988; Gergen and Thatchenkey 1998) that have the direct consent of all those involved, premised on the agreed need to achieve the sensible and practicable good, thereby denying the validity of the Social Man worldview.

This makes him unable to agree with adherent to other worldviews on what basis decisions should be made, which makes decision-making problematic.

TRUMP'S WORLDVIEW: WILL IT EVER CHANGE?

Not unreasonably, Trump wants his worldview to dominate Washington. However, he faces competitors in the form of contending worldviews, the adherents to which are aggressively asserting that their worldview is the "right" one. One voice—Trump's—is seeking to drown out all the others because they have the "wrong" view of the world of persons. The end result is a dialogue of the deaf (Hirschman 1991): all the voices talking but none listening. The issue is under what circumstances, if any, would anyone abandon his worldview (Dixon 2003; Dixon, Dogan, and Sanderson 2009).

The paradigmatic jousting among the contending worldviews can open the door to change. This can occur when a worldview is no longer capable of delivering on its expectations. Whether this realization leads a person to choose a different worldview, however, requires him to first reconsider, fundamentally, the set of expectations he has about his social status and roles. This is because choosing to follow a different worldview would necessitate him adopting a new way of describing, explaining, understanding, and judging social reality, and a new way of forming social relationships. The process by which a person adopts a new lens through which to interrogate social reality is, thus, linked to a that person's referred way of arranging his social relationships and, therefore, linked to his social-control preference weightings (his preferred degree of individual autonomy). This determines the boundaries of his other-control comfort zone—akin to Barnard's (1938) "zone of indifference"—defined by his tolerance of the limitations being imposed by others on his decision-choices, and his social actions, interactions and relationships.

Trump's Other-Control Comfort Zone

Trump seems intent, for the moment, on remaining in his very restricted—intolerant—other-control comfort zone, grounded in his unwillingness to compromise—in his own words: "I'm not big on compromise. I understand compromise. Sometimes compromise is the right answer, but oftentimes compromise is the equivalent of defeat, and I don't like being defeated" (*Life*, January 1989, cited in Piehler 2016, 69). His disposition, in terms of Olli's (1995, 60) plausible models of the individual, is to be "consistent, solid and single-minded" about his autonomy, making him one of Olli's "coherent individual". This is a person who, by nature, is not reflexive and, thus, does not care to question the premises of his circumscribed worldview. The attitudes and opinions he holds are central to his self-identity and held with a firmness grounded in the certitude of his core values. They are "very close to becoming a permanent trait of the individual, almost like a personality" (Olli 1995, 60). Sagan (1996, 23) captures the essence:

> All of us cherish our beliefs. They are, to a degree, self-defining. When someone comes along who challenges our belief system as insufficiently well-based or who, like Socrates, merely asks embarrassing questions that we haven't thought of or demonstrates that we've swept key underlying assumptions under the rug it becomes much more than a search for knowledge. It feels like a personal assault.[216]

Trump would, seemingly, tolerate little variation in either his preferred degrees of individual choice sovereignty or his self-determination of his social actions, interactions, and relationships, as he, no doubt, consider the status and role relationships he has with others to be sacrosanct. To sustain the *status quo*, he would seem willing to do everything necessary to ensure that does no need to move out of his restricted other-control comfort zone. What, then, might motivate him to do so to the point where choosing to a different worldview becomes desirable? The theory of surprise[217] provides such a motivation.

The Theory of Surprise

Surprise occurs when the unexpected outcomes of a person's decision or action cause his beliefs—the expected outcomes—and certainties—the actual outcomes—to move out of alignment. In other words, the

---

[216] Socrates' method—*elenchus* in classical Greek, which has with connotations of belittlement—involved him asking questions that forced those with whom he verbally engaged in the public domain to examine their own assumptions and logic, ultimately obliging them to admit their ignorance (a process known in classical Greek as *diatribai*, literally whiling away time) (Navia 2007; Wilson 2007).

[217] This theory has its origins in the ecology literature (see Holling 1986).

lens through which social reality is read is causing double vision—contradictory understandings: "What disturbs men's minds is not events but their judgments on events" (Epictetus[218] cited in Matheson 1916). While the occurrence of unexpected outcomes of events may be surprising, if the supporting evidence is contrary to a person's thoughts, beliefs, expectancies, attitudes or perceptions, then, as Festinger (1957) established, it may be rejected initially, and it may even, counter intuitively, reinforce that person's faith in those understandings, making him prone to Hirschman's (1991, 168) "rhetoric of intransigence." There is, however, a point reached where the cumulative effect of belief-disconfirming evidence serves to threaten seriously those product cognitions, so initiating the agonizing motivational state of cognitive dissonance: when "two opinions, or beliefs, or items of knowledge are dissonant with each other if they do not fit together; that is, if they are inconsistent, or if, considering only the particular two items, one does not follow from the other" (Festinger 1957, 25). The magnitude of the dissonance experienced depends on the relative importance to a person's self-identity of the contradictory product cognitions involved.

Ultimately, everyone is capable of being surprised by the unexpected outcomes of events, but it would take very much longer for a person who is well practiced in the denial of the truth and utterly self-delusional. To such a person, as one of Olli's (1995) coherent individual, if confronted with an unexpected outcomes of events that threatened to give rise to a mental state of cognitive dissonance, may well, choose not to notice those outcomes, or if they are noticed, his defense mechanisms would come into play—such as arbitrary rightness, denial, repression, and regression. This would motivate him, for example, to assert—by means perhaps of distorting bullshit, reinforced by conspiracy theories that cannot be negated, the rightness of his understandings, thereby reinforcing the certitude with which the core values that are central to his self-identity are held, and the firmness with which he holds derivative attitudes and opinions. This would reinforce his faith in the aptness of his worldview, so making him even more intransigent. In any case, there would be no incentive for him to change what he considers to be the

---

[218] "Epictetus ... was an exponent of Stoicism [as "a type of eudaimonic virtue ethics"] who flourished in the early second century C.E." Retrieved from: http://www.iep.utm.edu/epictetu/.

tolerable degree of constraints that others can put on his individual de-cision sovereignty or the self-determination of his social actions, inter-actions, and relationships. This means he would be unwilling to change his other-control comfort-zone boundaries, preferring to maintain his existing pattern of social relationships.

If, however, the cumulative effect of a long sequence of surprises moves him toward his disillusionment threshold, then he confronts two choic-es. The first is that he can change important, firmly held beliefs that are central to his self-identity, thereby enabling him to inculcate new atti-tudes, at least to the extent required to dissipate the effects of the cogni-tive dissonance he is experiencing. This would be problematic for one of Olli's (1995) coherent individuals. Thorngate (2001, 95–105) explains the challenges to be confronted in the process of attitudinal change. A person needs to be convinced that the attitudinal change is desirable largely on the basis of:

- *direct experience* or hands-on learning;
- *functional experience* in the form of social pressures for confor-mity, whether the product of experiencing either:
- *normative influences,* as a person seeking to avoid embarrass-ment, censure, or ostracism; or
- *informational influences,* as a person observing the responses of others to his actions or his opinion.

But, actually changing attitudes requires the satisfaction of one or more of five discrete but interrelated personality-function imperatives (Shavitt 1989; Smith, Bruner, and White 1956; Katz 1960):

- He must receive information that initiates deep reflection be-fore he begins to question his cognitive dispositions (the *knowl-edge* function requirement).
- His disillusionment must increase the distance from his old atti-tude (the *ego-defensive* or *externalization* function requirement).
- He must want to achieve consistency within his cognitive awareness, by realigning his core values (the value-expressive function requirement).
- He must be willing and able to engage fully with the new group

of other people who are aligned with the attitude to be acquired (the *social adjustment* function requirement).

- He must believe that tangible benefits will follow attitudinal change (the *adjustive-utilitarian* function requirement).

For Trump, as one of Olli's coherent individual, he would be initially averse to making such cognitive changes. Indeed, such is his capacity for self-delusion and to applying his impressive array defense mechanisms to deny any contradictions in his product cognitions, as he has made himself almost immune to the consequences of cognitive dissonance. Over time, however, cognitive changes may—just may—occur, but only with considerable reluctance, for such changes would require Trump to consider affecting a personality change in order to express his newly acquired beliefs and attitudes. Eventually, he may well appreciate that he is approaching his disillusionment threshold—his capacity for delusion and denial may—just may—have its limits—to which his face-saving response may well be to disengage from the disillusioning situation.

CONCLUSION

Trump, intuitively, is an existentialist in his thoughts and actions. He sees social reality as an idea in his mind, so he believes he is able to engage with it as he imagines it to be in any way he chooses. He presumes he has the freedom to be who he wants to be, so he believes he is able to make any necessary leaps in the dark in expectation of success. He has a strong sense of his self-importance, Yet, he is confronting Nietzsche's ([1883] 1967) law of eternal recurrence, a challenge that nobody—not even he—can entirely meet, as fate cannot always be forced to bend to anyone's will.

His disposition toward the hermeneutic-agency worldview has, not unexpectedly, inexorably antagonized those in Washington and elsewhere with different worldviews. Not unreasonably, but certainly naively, he wants his worldview to dominate. The end result has been a dialogue of the deaf (Hirschman 1991): all the voices talking but none listening.

He has brought to the US presidential politics and administration very different cognitive and behavioral perspectives, grounded in a very idiosyncratic set of social reality assumptions, one that he would probably not be willing or is unable to change. He has made himself almost immune to the consequences of cognitive dissonance. His capacity for delusion and denial may, of course, have its limits, to which his face-saving response may well be to disengage rather than change.

3
DONALD J. TRUMP:
ON GOVERNING AND HIS GOVERNMENT

INTRODUCTION

Trump's political philosophy is, by his words and actions, that of a reluctant etatist.[219] He certainly not a statist in the Hegalian tradition (Hegel [1806] 1998, [1807] 1977), one who believes that "the state is a spiritual entity" (Dixon 2015, 37); nor is he one in the Rand tradition, who believes that "man's life and work belong to the state ... and that the state may dispose of him in any way it pleases for the sake of whatever it deems to be its own tribal, collective good" (Rand 1967, 47). As a reluctant collectivist, he accepts the collective values of social intervention and cooperation—state has an obligation, in the Millsian social liberalism tradition, to intervene in the marketplace when private actions do harm to others, so as to correct any resultant adverse consequences that could give rise to social costs that, ultimately, could undermine economic and social stability (Mill [1859] 1963, [1863] 1968; see also Green [1895] 2006; Keynes [1936] 2007, 1972). This requires balancing, by the use of the power of the state, "enablement" (advancing positive freedom—freedom from—by constraining negative freedom—freedom to) over "liberty" (advancing negative freedom by constraining positive freedom).[220] Such a balancing clearly differentiates social liberalism from classical liberalism (Ashford 2016), neoliberalism (Dixon 2016), and libertarianism (Vallentyne and van der Vossen 2014).

Trump's right-wing critics have certainly asserted his statist inclinations, which they consider to be contrary to the spirit of conservatism.[221] As the Conservatives and Libertarians Against Donald have pointed out:

---

[219] Derived from the French *étatisme* meaning government control (Mises 1944).

[220] According to Berlin (1969), negative freedom is the right of self-determination, which is identified with the Hobbesian idea of the absence of constraint on, or obstacles to, individual freedom; and positive freedom is the right to be able to take control of one's life, which is identified with Rousseau's ([1762] 1973) notion of moral self-government.

[221] See, for example: https://www.facebook.com/againsttrump/posts/200973979 987848; http://ariarmstrong.com/2016/07/the-statist-convergence-of-trump-and-clinton/.

> He's donated thousands of dollars to anti-freedom, gun-grabbing, socialist Democrats like Hillary Clinton, Ted Kennedy, John Kerry, Harry Reid, Joe Lieberman, and others. He has also called for "universal health-care." Please do not be deceived.[222]

But they were.

Trump chooses to present himself as a populist. His ensemble of rhet-oric was attractive because he used the populist imagery meaningful to those with a "deep cynicism and resentment of existing authorities, whether big business, big banks, multinational corporations, media pun-dits, elected politicians and government officials, intellectual elites and scientific experts, and the arrogant and privileged rich" (Inglehart and Norris 2016, 6). His personal mission was, first and foremost, to win the presidency, by whatever means necessary, so as to ensure that Hillary Clinton did not become president. He did nothing to prepare himself to be president, perhaps because he did expect—did not want[223]—to be president.[224] He had not, for example, seriously consider how, if he won the presidency, he might need to re-arrange his family business affairs so as to avoid any conflicts of interest.[225] (He, finally, decided he needed to

[222] See, for example: https://www.facebook.com/againsttrump/posts/200973979 987848; http://ariarmstrong.com/2016/07/the-statist-convergence-of-trump-and-clinton/.

[223] See: http://www.politico.com/magazine/story/2017/06/22/trump-doesnt-want-to-be-president-215292; http://www.foxnews.com/opinion/2017/05/17/does-donald-trump-still-want-to-be-president.html; https://www.theguardian.com/film/2016/aug/17/michael-moore-donald-trump-does-not-want-to-be-president; http://www.esquire.com/news-politics/news/a53040/does-trump-want-to-be-president/; https://bullshit.ist/the-signs-are-clear-donald-trump-really-doesnt-want-to-be-president-4787ff8ea159; http://www.huffingtonpost.com/peter-dreier/donald-trump-want-to-be-president_b_8176016.html; http://www.politicalstorm.com/letterman-trump-didnt-really-want-president-now-hes-stuck/.

[224] For media speculation see: http://www.reuters.com/article/us-trump-leaks-commentary-idUSKCN18D013; http://www.newsmax.com/Politics/weekly-standard-calls-trump-leaker-in-chief/2017/07/26/id/803929/; http://www.newsmax.com/Politics/weekly-standard-calls-trump-leaker-in-chief/2017/07/26/id/803929/.

[225] See: http://www.bbc.com/news/world-us-canada-38069298; https://www.

build a wall of paperwork around his family business interests, transferring full responsibility to his children, which he claimed would protect his presidency from allegations of conflicts of interest,[226] a debatable proposition[227].)

Trump clearly had the skill-set needed to win the presidency; being a successful president, however, requires a different skill-set, one that Trump clearly does not have. This inclines him to blur the distinction between presidential campaigning and governing (Doherty 2012). Indeed, he has remained in "spectacle mode," and has never really entered "governing mode." Joshua Green, author of *Devil's Bargain*[228] (2017)—about the Trump-Bannon[229] relationship during the presidential campaign—captures the essence when he remarked during a media interview:

> The kind of tragic, Shakespearean irony of the Donald Trump-Steve Bannon relationship is that Bannon finally did find the vessel for his ideas who could get elected president ... [but who] now doesn't have the focus, the wherewithal, the self-control to even do the basic things that a president needs to do.[230]

Indeed, "the evidence is becoming overwhelming that Trump lacks the temperament, basic knowledge or intelligence to be a minimally competent president."[231] Yet, according to Michael D'Antonio, his biographer:

---

theatlantic.com/business/archive/2017/08/donald-trump-conflicts-of-interests/508382/.

[226] See: http://www.wsj.com/graphics/donald-trump-potential-conflicts-of-interest/.

[227] See: https://www.theguardian.com/us-news/2017/jan/11/donald-trump-conflicts-of-interest.

[228] See: http://www.penguinrandomhouse.com/books/557633/devils-bargain-by-joshua-green/9780735225022/.

[229] See: https://www.nytimes.com/2016/11/27/us/politics/steve-bannon-white-house.html.

[230] Retrieved from: http://www.npr.org/templates/transcript/transcript.php?storyId=537885042

[231] Retrieved from: https://www.theguardian.com/commentisfree/2017/jun/01/donald-trump-incompetence-white-house-staff-intervention.

Despite claiming to be above politics, Donald Trump wants so much to be re-elected that he formed a 2020 campaign committee weeks after moving into the White House. With the power of the incumbency and a head start on his opponents, the President has everything going for him—except his own big mouth.

In the annals of American politics, no president has done so much to undermine himself as Trump. ...

Trump has frequently acted as a child, impulsively blurting out claims and condemnations that call into question his fitness to serve. It is these statements that imperil both his presidency and his hopes for re-election.[232]

ON BECOMING PRESIDENT: TRUMP THE POPULIST CANDIDATE

Shortly after 11 a.m. on June 16, 2015 "Donald Trump entered the presidential race with a bang,"[233] as a contender for nomination as the Republican presidential candidate. His presidential campaigning saw him doing what comes naturally—selling rhetoric to those who want to hear it and destroying the opposition by whatever means necessary—lies, fake news, and character assassination by smears and innuendo (but see Coulter 2016; Lake 2016; Schlafly, Martin, and Decker 2016; see also Lewis 2014). He brought to his campaign a strong distaste for the Washington politico-administrative system, which he saw as being indifferent to the people's needs—a "swamp"[234] full of crocodiles. His *bête*

---

[232] Retrieved from: http://edition.cnncom/2017/06/05/opinions/trump-threatens-presidency-opinion-dantonio/index.html. There is some evidence that Trump's impulsive blurting out of false claims and condemnations is wearing thin, even on his supporters. See: https://www.washingtonpost.com/news/post-politics/wp/2017/08/23/as-trump-ranted-and-rambled-in-phoenix-his-crowd-slowly-thinned/?utm_term=.c1f29fcb210d. See also: https://newsstand.google.com/articles/CAIiEPhjrfrHNqpMCJGKU5Oak_oqGQgEKhAIACoHCAowocv1CjCSptoCMPrTpgU.

[233] Retrieved from: http://money.cnn.com/2016/06/16/media/trump-announcement-one-year-later/index.html.

[234] See: https://www.donaldjtrump.com/press-releases/trump-pledges-to-drain-the-swamp.

noire were self-serving bureaucrats;[235] their clients and their lobbyists; politicians who listen to all of them rather than to the people; and, of course, the news media, most of which he perpetually moaned about, as is his want, because, he alleges,[236] it produced "fake news"—news that he does not like[237]—even if it is true[238]—because it is very often personally embarrassing.[239]

Trump's economic nationalism, in the words paraphrasing his campaign policy guru Steve Bannon, who became his White House Chief Strategist, is "the antithesis of 'globalism', which he characterizes as a governing creed which has put the economic interests of multinational firms and a wealthy international elite above those of ordinary working class."[240] This meant *trade protectionism,* which resonated with his main core support base, principally those located in the Mid-West Rust Belt,[241] which, many decades ago, were the powerhouse of American mining and manufacturing industries. They now denote the broken relationship that

---

235   See: http://www.govexec.com/federal-news/fedblog/2016/08/donald-trump-has-great-faith-federal-bureaucrats/130578/; https://www.washingtonpost.com/news/powerpost/wp/2016/11/21/trump-republicans-plan-to-target-government-workers-benefits-and-job-security/?utm_term=.6719e0061817.

236   See: http://www.washingtonexaminer.com/trump-claims-anonymous-sources-made-up-by-fake-news-writers/article/2624356http://ew.com/tv/2017/06/27/donald-trump-fake-news-twitter/; http://www.teenvogue.com/story/donald-trump-shared-actual-fake-news-facebook-page.

237   See: https://newsstand.google.com/articles/CAIiEIernu4S0xWt9oToIMv_xK4qGQgEKhAIACoHCAowocv1CjCSptoCMI29pgU.

238   See, for example: https://www.washingtonpost.com/graphics/2017/politics/australia-mexico-transcripts/?utm_term=.047641142a56.

239   See: http://www.chicagotribune.com/news/opinion/huppke/ct-trump-fake-news-cnn-huppke-20170628-story.html.

240   Retrieved from: http://www.independent.co.uk/news/business/news/steve-bannon-economic-nationalism-what-is-it-explained-donald-trump-cpac-2017-a7598181.html.

241   "The Rustbelt covers a section of the northeast US, running from the east of the state of New York, through Pennsylvania, Ohio and Michigan, then ending in north Indiana and east Illinois and Wisconsin. ... It now includes three swing states key to the 2016 US election: Pennsylvania, Ohio and Michigan." Retrieved from: http://www.independent.co.uk/news/world/americas/us-elections/rust-belt-what-is-it-us-ohio-michigan-pennsylvania-election-2016-donald-trump-hillary-clinton-a7405141.html.

exists between elite whites and working-class whites (Williams 2017). They are his beloved loyal uneducated,[242] to whom he is willing to lie because, according to his son-in-law, Jared Kushner, he believes they are stupid.[243] They were looking for a savior to believe in—a Nietzscheian *ubermensch*—someone who can give them hope that they have a realistic opportunity to win back their self-respect by being able to take back personal responsibility for their own fate. And Trump was their man. As the French Philosopher, Bernard-Henri Lévy,[244], has remarked:

> The people listen less and less to policy and they even seem less concerned about whether the candidates are telling the truth or not. ...

> They are more interested in the performance, in the theatrical quality of what is said than whether it is true.[245]

Trump presented to his audiences a world that is simple to understand—a post-complexity world—"a powerful message in a disconcertingly uncertain world" (Baggini 2017, 8). In effect, he became the chief of the tribe[246]—

---

[242] See: https://www.usatoday.com/story/news/politics/onpolitics/2016/02/24/donald-trump-nevada-poorly-educated/80860078/; http://www.rollingstone.com/politics/news/watch-trump-brag-about-uneducated-voters-the-hispanics-20160224; http://www.huffingtonpost.com/entry/donald-trump-poorly-educated-voters_us_56cf9ee1e4b0bf0dab3191f7; https://sputniknews.com/us/201602241035297279-trump-loves-uneducated-voters/. But see: http://elitedaily.com/humor/donald-trump-loves-poorly-educated/1396865/.

[243] Retrieved from: http://www.independent.co.uk/News/world/americas/jared-kushner-donald-trump-lied-base-stupid-voters-supporters-president-son-in-law-white-house-a7764791.html.

[244] See: http://www.bernard-henri-levy.com/en/.

[245] Retrieved from: p://www.telegraph.co.uk/news/2016/11/20/leading-french-philosopher-marine-le-pen-may-win-election-as-peo/.

[246] Tribalism denotes a group of people who have a strong sense of cultural identity, which separates and distinguishes them from other groups (James 2006). They possess strong feelings about, and exhibit particular behaviour and attitudes that stem from, their strong sense of tribal loyalty. They have strong negative feelings for people who are not members of their tribe. Tribalism can be all pervasive and is readily able to override reason (Rozenblit 2008). See also: https://www.theatlantic.com/health/archive/2016/11/stoking-stribal-bia/508175/; http://www.salon.com/2014/03/25/robert_reich_tribalism_is_tearing_america_apart_partner. See also: https://www.psychologytoday.com/blog/how-risky-

the Trump Tribe,[247] which, needless to say, even has its own Trump line of artifacts.[248]

Trump's ethnic nationalism—tinged with bigotry—manifested as a blaming of Mexicans, Muslims, and African-Americans for America's problems,[249] and as a flirtation with anti-Semitic metaphors.[250] This meant blocking, then restricting, the entry into the US of Muslims and Latinos and deporting illegal Latino immigrants. This resonated with his other significant support base, he has long courted[251] followers of "alt-right"[252] and allied movements. The alt-right movement has as its dual focuses the promotion of *white identity* and the preservation of *western civilization*. It can be distinguished from, although its rhetoric overlaps with, allied movements, including:

- *White Nationalism*: "... this movement seeks to expand its influence mainly through argument and persuasion directed at its target audience of white Americans aggrieved over racial double standards, race-based affirmative action policies, high black-

---

is-it-really/201205/how-tribalism-makes-risky-word-even-more-dangerous; http://www.bbc.com/future/story/20160823-how-modern-life-is-destroying-democracy.

[247] See http://www.trumptribemovie.com/. The video can be retrieved from: https://vimeo.com/ondemand/trumptribe. See also: https://www.facebook.com/pg/TrumpTribeMovie/photos/?ref=page_internal.

[248] See: https://shop.donaldjtrump.com/.

[249] See: https://www.nytimes.com/2017/04/25/opinion/le-pen-trump-ethnic-nationalism.html.

[250] See: https://www.washingtonpost.com/posteverything/wp/2017/02/17/president-trump-thinks-asking-him-to-condemn-anti-semitism-is-insulting-why/?utm_term=.d836523fa414.

[251] See: http://www.aljazeera.com/indepth/opinion/2017/05/trump-canwill-break-trump-170518085955594.html; http://www.slate.com/blogs/the_slatest/2017/08/14/donald_trump_s_ties_to_alt_right_white_supremacists_are_extensive.html; http://www.slate.com/blogs/the_slatest/2016/07/28/how_donald_trump_s_reddit_ama_rewarded_hateful_trolls.html.

[252] This advances itself as the right-wing alternative to the Republican Party. It regards "mainstream or traditional conservatives as weak and impotent, largely because they do not sufficiently support racism and anti-Semitism." Retrieved from: https://www.adl.org/education/resources/backgrounders/alt-right-a-primer-about-the-new-white-supremacy.

on-white crime rates, and liberal immigration policies" (Swain [2002] 2004: front matter).

- *White Supremacy*: This is a populist movement that propagates "the belief that white people are superior to people of color"[253] and asserts that the New World Order is conspiring to "end the purity of the white race."[254]

- *Ku Klux Klan*: "The Ku Klux Klan [KKK], with its long history of violence [sine 1865], is the most infamous—and oldest—of American hate groups. Although black Americans have typically been the Klan's primary target, it also has attacked Jews, immigrants, gays and lesbians and, until recently, Catholics."[255]

- *Neo-Nazism*: "Neo-Nazi groups share a hatred for Jews and a love for Adolf Hitler and Nazi Germany. While they also hate other minorities, gays and lesbians and even sometimes Christians, they perceive 'the Jew' as their cardinal enemy, and trace social problems to a Jewish conspiracy that supposedly controls governments, financial institutions and the media."[256]

- *Right-wing militia groups*: such as the *American Guard*,[257] which advocates "the preservation of western culture;" the *Proud Boys*, [258] a group of "Western chauvinists;" and the *Three Percenters*,[259] which advocates armed resistance to any government overreach that it believes infringes the US Constitution.[260]

---

[253] Retrieved from: https://www.thoughtco.com/white-supremacy-definition-302 6742.

[254] Retrieved from: http://www.salon.com/2017/04/23/what-is-white-supremacy-a-brief-history-of-a-term-and-a-movement-that-continues-to-haunt-america/.

[255] See: https://www.splcenter.org/fighting-hate/extremist-files/ideology/ku-klux-klan.

[256] Retrieved from: https://www.splcenter.org/fighting-hate/extremist-files/ideology/neo-nazi.

[257] See: https://en-gb.facebook.com/theamericanguard/.

[258] See: https://en-gb.facebook.com/proudboysunite/.

[259] See: https://en-gb.facebook.com/ThreePercenters/.

[260] Retrieved from: http://www.independent.co.uk/news/world/americas/us-politics/trump-rally-washington-crowd-size-juggalos-insane-clown-posse-national-park-service-a7951046.html.

According to Professor Douglas G. Brinkley[261] (History, Rice University), "10–15%" of Trump's voter base are followers of the Ku Klux Klan[262], white nationalists, and "alt-right" movement."[263]

Trump's future core supporter base has long expected the powers that be to exercise the necessary power to govern as they see fit—at best they were the subjects of compassion without respect (Williams 2017). They had little or no expectations of government. Sometimes they may have considered government to be benign in intent, the consequences of which were unknowable in advance, but it was inevitably malevolent in action, the consequences of which they experienced. So, they expect to be coercively alienated from those who govern them from Washington. They were Wildavsky's politically mute (1984), and so "cut off from political maneuvering and influence" (Douglas and Ney 1998, 123). They had long experienced Sztompka's (1996, 38) "syndrome of distrust," whereby their social relations were dominated by insulation. As Banfield (1958, 162) explained: "trust and cooperation within the family coexisted with complete distrust and morally unrestrained cheating among individuals not belonging to the same family." So, most people cannot be trusted. As Machiavelli ([1513] 1961) remarked: "men are wretched creatures who would not keep their word to you" (p. 100), and they will "always do badly by you unless they are forced to be virtuous" (p. 127). At the extreme, their individual autonomy is minimal. This made some of them unwilling to engage in any way with governmental processes. They had lost any trusted they may had in government. Trump's political metanarrative captured their imagination because it was what they wanted to hear—it vilified the incompetent Washington elite. They were willing to place presidential power in Trump's hands—as an uncontaminated outsider—willing to be embodiment of their will, not to mention God's will.

Some of his core supporters certainly believed that Trump has been anointed by God—perhaps with "the nostalgic dream of a theocratic

---

[261]   See: http://www.history.rice.edu/faculty/douglas-g-brinkley.

[262]   See: https://www.splcenter.org/fighting-hate/extremist-files/ideology/ku-klux-klan.

[263]   Retrieved from: http://www.dailywire.com/news/19663/cnns-brinkley-10-15-percent-trumps-supporters-are-robert-kraychik.

type of state."[264] He has, indeed, been the subject of divine prophesies for 10 years or more.[265]

God has, allegedly, spoken about Trump as a future president to three people. The first was Kim Clement,[266] a South African "singing prophet," through whom He predicted in 2007 that Trump would, at some—unspecified—time in the future, win the presidency as God's choice and that he will become known as a "prayerful president." Clements sang:

> Trump shall become a trumpet. I will raise up the Trump to become a trumpet and Bill Gates to open up the gate of a financial realm for the church, says the Lord.
>
> It shall come to pass that the man I place in the highest office shall go in whispering my name. But God said, when he enters into office, he will be shouting out by the power of the spirit. For I shall fill him with my spirit when he goes into office and there will be a praying man in the highest seat in your land.
>
> There will be a praying president, not a religious one, for I will fool the people, says the Lord. I will fool the people, yes I will, God says, the one that is chosen shall go in and they shall say, "He has hot blood." For the spirit of God says, yes, he may have hot blood, but he will bring the walls of protection on this country in a greater

---

[264] Retrieved from: http://www.laciviltacattolica.it/articolo/evangelical-fundamentalism-and-catholic-integralism-in-the-usa-a-surprising-ecumenism/.

[265] See:http://gods-kingdom-ministries.net/daily-weblogs/2016/11-2016/kim-clements-prophecies-regarding-donald-trump-and-hillary-clinton-with-my-comments/; https://www.youtube.com/watch?v=zt7_KaPoybIhttp://gods-kingdom-ministries.net/daily-weblogs/2016/11-2016/kim-clements-prophecies-regarding-donald-trump-and-hillary-clinton-with-my-comments/; https://www.reddit.com/r/The_Donald/comments/5e39bu/trump_shall_become_my_trumpet_to_the_american/; http://www.silverdoctors.com/headlines/world-news/the-donald-trump-prophesy-a-president-raised-up-by-god-himself/; https://hellochristian.com/5411-incredible-2007-prophecy-on-election-trump-shall-become-a-trumpet.

[266] See: https://www.kimclement.com/update-on-kim.php.

way and the economy of this country shall change rapidly, says the Lord of hosts.

Listen to the word of the Lord, God says, "I will put at your helm for two terms a president that will pray, but he will not be a praying president when he starts," Clement continued. "I will put him in office and then I will baptize him with the Holy Spirit and my power," says the Lord of hosts.[267]

The second was Jeremiah Johnson,[268] a protestant minister, through whom He said in 2015:

Trump shall become My trumpet to the American people, for he possesses qualities that are even hard to find in My people these days. Trump does not fear man nor will he allow deception and lies to go unnoticed. I am going to use him to expose darkness and perversion in America like never before, but you must understand that he is like a bull in a china closet.[269]

The third was Lance Wallnau,[270] a business consultant, who has a divinity doctorate, through whom He said in 2016:

"Donald Trump is a wrecking ball to the spirit of political correctness" fighting a global "demonic agenda", and is "raising the warning cry about the destruction of America." And so he is doing His work. This prophecy has been dubbed the Cyrus Prophecy, after Cyrus the Great,[271] the powerful, rich and pagan Persian king who conquered Babylon in 539 BC and freed the Jews (Isaiah 45).[272]

---

267 Retrieved from: http://beholdthemanministries.com/prophesy-donald-trump-shall-become-the-trumpet/.

268 See: http://beholdthemanministries.com/author/jeremiahjohnson/.

269 Retrieved from: http://beholdthemanministries.com/prophesy-donald-trump-shall-become-the-trumpet/. See also: http://www.stevebremner.com/2015/07/judging-prophetic-words-with-discernment/.

270 See: https://lancewallnau.com/.

271 See: http://www.iranchamber.com/history/cyrus/cyrus.php.

272 See: https://www.theguardian.com/commentisfree/2017/mar/23/cyrus-

Trump, in his presidential Nowruz[273] Statement on March 22, issued as a White House Press Release,[274] quoted Cyrus the Great—the fictional one—as if he was the historical one—in Larry Hedrick's historical novel, *Xenophon's Cyrus the Great: The Art of Leadership and War*[275] ([1906] 2006):

> freedom, dignity, and wealth together constitute the greatest happiness of humanity. If you bequeath all three to your people, their love for you will never die.[276]

So, Trump's campaign rhetoric, with or without God's assistance, coincided with the prejudices of his core supporters. It was readily accepted as reality. When Trump said that he is the only one who *can* "Make American Great Again", it was taken to means that he *could, would,* and *will* do so. This suggests that this supporters were happiest under the influence of what might have seems to them to be an innocent delusion, one that was always entertaining and may even, perhaps, be beneficial to them, if it came to fruition. His populist political metanarrative reinforced their preoccupation with the condition of their life; with their skepticism about experts and their facts and their rational reasoning that has never helped them; with their belief that Washington is distant, capricious, and unresponsive to their needs; and with the irreducibility of their experience.

During his presidential campaign,[277] Trump presented himself as a will-

---

prophecy-evangelical-support-donald-trump. See also: https://www1.cbn.com/content/lance-wallnau-donald-trump-wrecking-ball-spirit-political-correctness.

[273]   See: http://www.refinery29.uk/2017/03/146082/persian-new-year-nowruz-tradition-meaning.

[274]   Retrieved from: https://www.whitehouse.gov/the-press-office/2017/03/22/statement-president-donald-j-trump-nowruz.

[275]   See: https://us.macmillan.com/xenophonscyrusthegreat/larryhedrick/9780312364694/.

[276]   See: https://us.macmillan.com/author/larryhedrick/; see also: particularly: http://www.cogwriter.com/news/prophecy/donald-trump-of-god-cyrus-or-apocalyptic/; https://mic.com/articles/171903/trump-used-a-fake-cyrus-the-great-quote-to-wish-iranians-happy-new-year#.cZprlgLeU.

[277]   For an interesting insight in the Trump campaign from the perspective a sympathizer see Gingrich 2017.

ing fighter for the forsaken—those left behind in the rush towards globalization and the neoliberal nirvana (Dixon 2016)—which meant free trade, small government with little interest in the poor and uneducated, lower taxes for rich, and more individual responsibility. Through his rhetoric Trump sought to create a cult of personality around himself. In the words of the iconic, overtly political, signature song of the 1980s hard rock band, *Living Colour*[278]—"The Cult of Personality"[279] (1988):

> Look in my eyes, what do you see?
> The cult of personality
> I know your anger, I know your dreams
> I've been everything you want to be
> I'm the cult of personality.
>
> Like Mussolini and Kennedy
> I'm the cult of personality
> ...
>
> Neon lights, a Nobel Prize
> Then a mirror speaks, the reflection lies
> You don't have to follow me
> Only you can set me free
> I sell the things you need to be
> I'm the smiling face on your T.V.
> I'm the cult of personality
> I exploit you still you love me.
>
> I tell you one and one makes three
> I'm the cult of personality
> Like Joseph Stalin and Gandhi
> I'm the cult of personality
> ...
>
> Neon lights, a Nobel Prize
> A leader speaks, that leader dies
> You don't have to follow me
> Only you can set you free

---

[278] See: http://www.livingcolour.com/.

[279] See: https://www.youtube.com/watch?v=7xxgRUyzgs0.

You gave me fortune
You gave me fame.

You gave me power in your own god's name
I'm every person you need to be
Oh, I'm the cult of personality
....[280]

During his campaign, Trump resorted, very effectively, to controversial line of rhetoric bullshit that was disdainful of both political correctness, personal sensitivities, and the etiquette of international diplomacy. The values at the forefront of his bombastic rhetoric were greed and selfishness—"The point is, you can never be too greedy" (Twitter, March 2016, cited in Piehler 2016, 69)—and hate and prejudice. These underpinned his twin signature presidential campaign mantras: "America First" and "Make America Great Again," the latter echoing the American fascists in the 1930s.[281] His campaign promises—which became his presidential policy agenda—can be encapsulated by his often repeated but vacuous political slogans, "Buy American, Hire American" and "Making America Safe Again." The good society he envisioned was one in which the best interest of his adoring supporters would be advanced by him becoming a president because he would promote both ethnic nationalism (restricting the entry into the US of Latinos and Muslims, and deporting illegal immigrants, including Syrian refugees), and economic nationalism (imposing trade barriers that would create jobs in their communities for them and their children) and so the give them back their self-respect.

Trump, no doubt, found that selling his visionary rhetoric was a great deal of fun—eliciting much adulation. Not surprisingly, in the setting of large, adoring, and cheering campaign audiences, he perpetually

---

[280] Retrieved from: https://www.google.com.tr/search?q=cult+of+personality&oq=cult+of+personality&aqs=chrome..69i57j0l5.11119j0j1&sourceid=chrome&ie=UTF-8

[281] See: https://www.jacobinmag.com/2015/12/trump-coughlin-nazis-christian-front-kristallnacht-antisemitism-kasich-fascism/. Spy novelist, John le Carré, has drawn comparisons between the Trump era and the rise of 1930s fascism in Spain, Germany, and Japan. See: https://www.theguardian.com/books/2017/sep/07/john-le-carre-on-trump-something-truly-seriously-bad-is-happening?CMP=Share_AndroidApp_Gmail.

pumped-up the rhetorical hyperbole—what Trump calls "truthful hyperbole"—"an innocent form of exaggeration" and "a very effective form of promotion" the purpose of which is to "play to people's fantasies" (cited in Baggini 2017, 65–66). After all, as Goethe ([1749] 2011, 51) observed, "man is but man; and whatever be the extent of his reasoning powers, they are of little avail when passion rages within." But, as Goethe soberingly reminds those with innocent delusions: "All men are disappointed in their hopes, and deceived in their expectations" (Goethe [1749] 2011, 77). More soberingly for Trump supporters, Diodorus, an Athenian, during the Mytilenian Debate of 427 BC, observed that the impulses of men will lead them to act dangerously for as long as their ambitions are fed by pride and insolence, their poverty and greed requires them to act boldly, and their life is dominated by endless passion, for the forces of law cannot restrain human nature from pursuing its course: "Cities and individuals alike, all are by nature disposed to do wrong, and there is no law that will prevent it" (cited in Thucydides [401 BC] 1972, 3.45).

ON GOVERNING

Governance—from the Latin *gubernare,* meaning to rule or to steer (Eilon 1974)—has been defined as "a mode of social co-ordination or order" (Mayntz 1993, 11) or as the "social institutions or sets of rules guiding the behavior of those engaged in identifiable social practices" (Young 1994, ix).[282] It needs to be distinguished from *government*—"organizations or entities established to administer provisions of governance systems" (Young 1994, ix). The two poles of governance—the governed's response to the processes of those who seek to govern them—are the constituents of Foucault's (1991) concept of *governmentality*. Whether the governed's response is one of compliance or antagonism depends upon how they justify, to themselves and to others, the limitations that they tolerate their governors imposing upon them (Dixon 2003). At is-

---

[282] Developing this definition, Garland (1997, 174) considers that it constitutes, "the forms of rule by which various authorities govern populations, and the technologies of self through which individuals work on themselves to shape their own subjectivity." Kooiman (1999, 70) defines it as: "all those interactive arrangements in which public as well as private actors participate aimed at solving societal problems, or creating societal opportunities, and attending to the institutions within

sue is, in the words of Juvenal (Decimus Junius Juvenalis) the first century AD Roman satirist: "*Sed quis custodiet ipsos custodes*", freely trans-
lated as "but who will govern the governors?" It is all about who should
exercise power of the state (Morris 1987) and by what means.[283]

The Washington politico-administrative environment that awaited
Trump's inauguration reflected the increasing diversity, dynamics, and
complexity of America's socioeconomic, political, cultural, and natural
environments in recent decades. Like other advanced liberal democ-
racies, America has experienced the impact of dynamic processes of
economic and social differentiation, which have made it "institutional-
ly rich" (Streeck 1991, 27). This has changed the role of government,
particularly as it seeks to address the perceived incapacity of hierarchical governing structures, processes, and instruments to respond to the
governance challenges of a new globalizing world (Dixon 2003). These
challenges have been identified by Moran (2000, 11) as "distrust, fear of
risks, consumerism, legalism and democracy."

The response has been a gradual transition away from hierarchical governance modes[284] toward new patterns of state–society interactions, or
forms of sociopolitical governance (Dixon 2003). Two such societal
governance modes are: market self-regulation governance[285] and net-

---

which these governing activities take place."

[283] French and Raven (1959) offer a power taxonomy from a "power-over"
perspective: position or legitimate power (individuals conform because they
believe that those exercising power have the right to have power over them), expert
power (individuals conform because they believe that those exercising power
have superior knowledge and skills), personal or referent power (individuals
conform because they are attracted by, and identify with the person exercising
power), resource or reward power (individuals conform to receive benefits
from the person exercising power) and physical or coercive power (individuals
conform to avoid punishment) (see also Boulder 1990; Hales 2001).

[284] Hierarchical governance is where individuals or groups of individuals
(organizations) are subject to a set of enforceable rights and obligations designed
and implemented by politico-administrative institutions with a territorial
mandate.

[285] Market self-regulation is the self-regulating market form of society in which
buyers and sellers negotiate enforceable contracts, with a zero noncompliance
tolerance and full restitution as the ultimate sanction. They conduct their affairs
in accordance with their contractual obligations within the rules of the law of

work (interactive) governance[286] (Kooiman 1993, 1999), which, as Hay (1998, 39) sensibly argues, do not exist independently of each other. This has led to much debate about the purpose and accountability of government for its actions and performance.

It has been argued that one consequence of this new sociopolitical environment has been the creation of a state too big for small problems, yet too small for big problems. Given the increased plurality of agents— contending policy advocates (special interests) participating in the policy process—and the growing complexity of the policy issues to be decided upon, it is perhaps not surprising that some people—most notably Foucault (1991)—have questioned whether modern societies are, in fact, governable. This legitimation crisis reflects the "exhaustion of the traditional forms of state intervention" (Merrien 1998, 57). Others have contemplated on the desirable alternatives governing models—characterized as the minimal state (Nozick 1974), the enabling state (Gilbert and Gilbert 1989), the active society (Etzioni 1968), or the network society (Messner 1997).

In any event, a consensus has begun to emerge that democratic societies can no longer be readily directed or controlled by the use of direct command or coercive power by a governing elite—those engaged in directing (the political elite) or administering (the administrative elite) a polity. This brings into question the merit of Plato's guardian-style polity, which he described in *The Republic*[287] as the entrusting of rulership to that minority of people who, by reason of their superior insight and virtue, are particularly qualified to govern (Hendriks and Zouridis 1999, 125). It also brings to mind Hennis' pleading for a state with the "power to create unity," and able to act as "protector, guardian, promoter of morality ... guarantor of moral standards" (cited in Messner 1997, 80). This style of governances requires government to be elitist,

---

property, tort and contract (Dixon 2003).

[286] Network, interactive or co-governance is a situation in which individuals or groups of individuals voluntarily cede some autonomy to a voluntary network to which they belong, in return for agreed common rights and acceptable common obligations. By so belonging, they share, with other network members, its commitment to a common set of governance values and a presumption that network interactions are on the basis of loyalty and reciprocity.

[287] Retrieved from: http://www.idph.net/conteudos/ebooks/republic.pdf.

stable, and strong. It demand and expects loyalty and compliance. The role of the state has, however, been increasingly constrained by the ineffectiveness of command-type public policy instruments in the context of constitutional constraints, fiscal constraints, and the constraints engendered by globalization forces in the form of ecological, economic, financial, and technological interdependencies.

It is into this complex governance environment that an ill-equipped and ill-prepared Donald J. Trump stepped on Friday January 20, 2017 to begin his reign as president and so take up the reins of government.

ON GOVERNING AMERICA

Trump is unwilling to master the art and science of governing a complex and diverse society with a rich set of institutions. His presidential mindset seems to be in line with that of a medieval monarch, one who demands of his inner circle the swearing of an oath of fealty:

> I promise on my faith that I will in the future be faithful to the lord, never cause him harm and will observe my homage to him completely against all persons in good faith and without deceit.[288]

Upon making this oath they become his vassals, who must unquestionably accept their subservient or subordinate positions. The Medieval pageantry involved in this oath taking is something Trump would undoubtedly enjoy:

> The vassal would appear before the lord bareheaded and without weapons. The vassal would then kneel before the lord, clasping his hands as in prayer, which he would stretch outward toward his lord. This position signified total submission. The vassal then swore the Oath of Fealty. The lord would then take the hands of the vassal and announce his acceptance.[289]

In any event, Trump became president with a very naïve view of gov-

---

[288]   Retrieved from: http://www.lordsandladies.org/oath-of-fealty.htm.

[289]   Retrieved from: http://www.lordsandladies.org/oath-of-fealty.htm.

ernment and without any governance philosophy. To him, governing America was straight forwardly simple;[290] just like governing his family business—The Trump Organization[291]. Since becoming president, he has, however, changed his mind: "I thought it would be easier."[292] So easy, perhaps, that early in his presidency, he drafted himself as his own best messenger: "To control and edit the messages radiating out of the White House is media hound Trump's keenest ambition."[293] It might well be that he also aspires to be the White House "bullshitter-in-chief"[294] or "liar-in-chief"[295] Perhaps also the associated position of "leaker-in-chief",[296] suggestive of which is his sharing of highly classified information with Sergey Lavrov, the Russian Foreign Minister in mid-May[297]. [298]

[290] Retrieved from: https://www.vox.com/policy-and-politics/2017/5/30/156317 10/trump-bullshit.

[291] See: http://www.trump.com/; http://www.businessinsider.com/what-is-the-trump-organization-2016-12/#-3; http://www.investopedia.com/updates/donald-trump-companies/.

[292] Retrieved from: http://www.reuters.com/article/us-usa-trump-100days-idUSK BN17U0CA?feedType=RSS&feedName=politicsNews.

[293] Retrieved from: http://www.politico.com/magazine/story/2017/06/22/trump-doesnt-want-to-be-president-215292.

[294] Retrieved from: https://www.vox.com/policy-and-politics/2017/5/30/156317 10/trump-bullshit.

[295] Retrieved from: http://www.rollingstone.com/politics/features/donald-trump-liar-in-chief-w475917.

[296] Retrieved from: http://www.reuters.com/article/us-trump-leaks-commentary-idUSKCN18D013.

[297] See: https://www.washingtonpost.com/blgs/right-turn/wp/2017/05/15/bombshell-trump-tells-secrets-to-russia/?utm_term=.f1974e2ea9e5; http://www.aljazeera.com/news/2017/05/trump-disclosed-secrets-russia-washington-post-170515222926350.html, but see: https://www.washingtonpost.com/politics/white-house-offers-shifting-explanations-of-trumps-disclosures-to-russians/2017/05/16/23c6c456-3a4b-11e7-8854-21f359183c8c_story.html?utm_term=.9f54f2db3d23.

[298] For media speculation see: http://www.reuters.com/article/us-trump-leaks-commentary-idUSKCN18D013; https://www.dailykos.com/stories/2017/8/7/1687708/-Leaker-in-Chief-Could-Trump-Be-Prosecuted-Under-the-New-Department-of-Justice-Directive; http://www.newsmax.com/Politics/weekly-standard-calls-trump-leaker-in-chief/2017/07/26/id/803929/; http://www.weeklystandard.com/the-leaker-in-chief/article/2008995; https://www.belfercenter.org/publication/americas-leaker-chief-trump-and-

Having been elevated to the highest political office in Washington, he expected to have the right to reign as he sees fit, simply because he is the embodiment of the will of the people. In practice, this meant, essentially, one-man rule. Insightfully, at his inaugural ball, for his first presidential dance he choose Frank Sinatra's signatures song *My Way*[299]:

> Yes, there were times, I'm sure you knew
> When I bit off more than I could chew.
> But through it all, when there was doubt,
> I ate it up and spit it out.
> I faced it all and I stood tall;
> And did it my way.[300]

By so doing, some would say he was giving a musical clue as to how he intends to govern: "Trump would be Trump. The anti-politician had morphed into the anti-president."[301]

The Guardian, a London-based newspaper, considers his presidency to be illegitimate, as he is without a true mandate from the American people:

> Trump walks and talks instead like an authoritarian, and
> seems to believe he is above the people and the law, and
> need not answer to either. He wants to be untouchable.
> He behaves with impunity and acts as if legal standards
> like obstruction of justice don't apply to him.[302]

His authoritarian inclinations became very clear when he publicly

---

russia; https://newsstand.google.com/articles/CAIiELv6lm83ValJl-SbyQpo QTcqGAgEKg8IACoHCAowi4-MATDXsRUwhP2ZAg; http://www.independent.co.uk/news/world/americas/us-politics/then-trump-new-york-times-fake-tips-maggie-haberman-news-lies-a7749821.html.

[299] Retrievable from: https://play.google.com/music/preview/Traxlz23in2hs7abcy i3mueqq2q?lyrics=1&utm_source=google&utm_medium=search&utm_campaign=lyrics&pcampaignid=kp-lyrics.

[300] Retrieved from: http://www.lyricsfreak.com/f/frank+sinatra/my+way_20056 378.html.

[301] Retrieved from: http://www.bbc.co.uk/news/world-us-canada-39724045.

[302] Retrieved from: https://www.theguardian.com/commentisfree/2017/may/11/ donald-trump-illegitimate-president-james-comey.

praised—identified with—a variety of authoritarian heads of state, namely:

- Russia's *Vladimir Putin*, who he sees as a strong leader—"He's done an amazing job—he's put himself really at the forefront of the world as a leader in a short period of time"[303]—a man, about whom he wondered if "he will become my new best friend."[304] "I think that I would probably get along with him very well."[305] Putin reciprocated, calling Trump a "talented person" and "the absolute leader of the Presidential race," to which Trump responded:

  > It is always a great honor to be so nicely complimented by a man so highly respected within his own country and beyond ... I have always felt that Russia and the United States should be able to work well with each other towards defeating terrorism and restoring world peace, not to mention trade and all of the other benefits derived from mutual respect.[306]

- North Korea's *Kim Jong-Un*, who he considers to be a "pretty smart guy"[307] who he would be "honored" to meet under the "right circumstances"[308], although he is a "maniac"—not to mention paranoid about America having a plot to kill him[309]—

---

[303] Retrieved from: https://www.theguardian.com/us-news/2017/sep/18/trump-in-moscow-what-happened-at-miss-universe-in-2013.

[304] Retrieved from: http://beforeitsnews.com/alternative/2016/06/putin-repeats-praise-of-trump-hes-a-bright-person-3371208.html; see particularly: http://edition.cnn.com/interactive/2017/03/politics/trump-putin-russia-timeline/; but see also: https://www.usnews.com/news/world/articles/2016-12-23/the-5-best-quotes-from-vladimir-putins-press-conference.

[305] Retrieved from: https://www.newyorker.com/news/ryan-lizza/trumps-real-estate-ambitions-in-moscow.

[306] Retrieved from: https://www.newyorker.com/news/ryan-lizza/trumps-real-estate-ambitions-in-moscow.

[307] Retrieved from: https://www.theguardian.com/us-news/2017/may/01/doSwampnald-trump-kim-jong-un-meeting-north-korea.

[308] Retrieved from: https://www.theguardian.com/us-news/2017/may/01/donald-trump-kim-jong-un-meeting-north-korea.

[309] See: http://google.com/newsstand/s/CBIw74Tv7zQ.

but "you gotta give him credit" for the "incredible" way he removed his political opponent.[310]

- *China's ruling elite,* whose actions in the 1989 Tiananmen Square "riot" he considers "horrible" and "vicious" but it just "shows you the power of strength."[311]

- Iraq's *Saddam Hussesin,* who he judges to be "a really bad guy" but "you know what he did well? He killed terrorists. He did that so good. They didn't read them the rights. They didn't talk. They were terrorists. It was over."[312]

- Turkey's *Recep Tayyip Erdoğan,* whom he praised following the failed 2016 *coup d'état* attempt: "I give great credit to him for being able to turn that around."[313] Indeed, the similarities between Trump and Erdoğan have been noted:

The presidents of the US and Turkey are both nationalists who have promised to make their countries great again. Both have turned governing into a family business and rely heavily on their respective sons-in-law, Jared Kushner and Berat Albayrak. Both are despised by metropolitan elites but often adored outside big cities. Both have accused their countries' permanent bureaucracy of plotting against them.[314]

Trump's self-image demanded that he portrays himself as a strong—authoritarian—leader who should be able to exercise what he believes to be his presidential power without regard to existing politico-judicial institutions or to any bodies of law, including the constitution.[315]

---

[310] Retrieved from: http://abcnews.go.com/Politics/trump-north-korean-leader-kim-jong-gotta-give/story?id=36198345.

[311] Retrieved from: https://www.washingtonpost.com/news/worldviews/wp/2016/03/11/trump-just-called-tiananmen-square-a-riot-the-communist-party-will-be-pleased/?utm_term=.13846d116fea.

[312] Retrieved from: https://www.nytimes.com/2016/07/06/us/politics/donald-trump-saddam-hussein.html.

[313] Retrieved from: http://www.hurriyetdailynews.com/i-give-erdogan-great-credit-for-turning-the-coup-around-trump-.aspx?pageID=238&nID=101949&NewsCatID=358.

[314] Retrieved from: https://www.ft.com/content/3156a004-3713-11e7-bce4-9023f8c0fd2e

[315] See: http://www.bbc.com/news/uk-politics-39289427.

Trump has repeatedly expressed his desire to reform the quagmire of Washington politics[316]—by "draining the swamp"[317] so as to eliminate what he saw as corruption in national politics—thereby curbing the influence of Washington's lobbyists[318] and special interests[319]:

> Every effort must be made to reduce the influence of special interests have on our federal government. Along with seeking a Constitutional amendment to limit the terms of members of Congress, we should seek a Constitutional amendment to balance the budget. Tax reform would be the third reform necessary to greatly diminish the corrupting influences of special interests on our government.[320]

Yet, he has recruited an unknown number of lobbyists as White House staff: "Trump's budget director, Mick Mulvaney, asked the Office of Government Ethics director, Walter Shaub, in May to halt his inquiry into lobbyists-turned-Trump administration employees."[321]

Trump may, of course, seek to be even more heroic by doing more than tinkering with Washington's political institutions and processes.[322] His

---

[316] For his politic-administrative reform agenda see his "Contract with the American Voter" see: https://assets.donaldjtrump.com/_landings/contract/O-TRU-1023 16-Contractv02.pdf. But see also: https://qz.com/971930/trumps-100-days-a-scorecard-trump-made-28-promises-in-a-contract-with-the-american-people/?utm_source=.

[317] Retrieved from: https://www.donaldjtrump.com/press-releases/trump-pledges-to-drain-the-swamp.

[318] Retrieved from: https://www.theguardian.com/us-news/2017/may/23/trump-government-ethics-office-lobbyists-mick-mulvaney. See also: https://www.theguardian.com/us-news/2017/may/23/trump-government-ethics-office-lobbyists-mick-mulvaney.

[319] http://www.businessinsider.com/trump-first-100-days-promises-2pop017-4?utm_source=googleplaynewsstand&utm_medium=referral.

[320] Retrieved from: https://www.teapartypatriotscitizensfund.com/official-tppcf-primary-registration/donald-trump/?roi=echo7-22089092107-45865753-4d6e 12f3e1e31f39739a7595888b38e1&mid=9180712.

[321] Retrieved from: https://www.theguardian.com/us-news/2017/may/23/trump-government-ethics-office-lobbyists-mick-mulvaney.

[322] See: https://www.youtube.com/watch?v=n82bEVTp1uI.

authoritarian predisposition and his utter lack of knowledge and experience in politics and government, means he has little appreciation of—and perhaps has only contempt for[323]—the constitutional intentions of the Founding Fathers of Federation to restrict one-man rule with the power of an absolute monarch. So, perhaps he might be inclined to try and re-define—perhaps even replace[324]—America's constitutional democracy.[325] However, the *British Broadcasting Corporation (BBC)*[326] has speculated that "Trump isn't anti-establishment; He's pro-establishment so long as he's the establishment."[327] Indeed, he is not a fully paid-up Republican. He is not committed to small government—just a government that does what he believes needs to be done in the Keynesian pump-priming[328] tradition. He is not committed to free trade—just to fair and reciprocal trade[329] that permits the rebuilding the American manufacturing sector, even if it means tit-for-tat trade wars and the inevitable inflationary pressures.

Trump, no doubt to his chagrin, has found that putting his campaign promises into effect is not as simple as issuing instructions—Executive Orders[330] and Presidential Memorandums[331]. Indeed, his only accom-

---

[323] https://www.theguardian.com/us-news/2017/apr/29/trump-blames-constitution-for-first-100-days-chaos-presidency.

[324] See: http://www.salon.com/2017/05/01/historian-timothy-snyder-its-pretty-much-inevitable-that-trump-will-try-to-stage-a-coup-and-overthrow-democracy/.

[325] See: https://www.theguardian.com/us-news/2017/apr/29/trump-blames-constitution-for-first-100-days-chaos-presidency.

[326] See: http://www.bbc.co.uk/corporate2/insidethebbc/managementstructure/bbcstructure

[327] Retrieved from: http://www.bbc.com/news/world-us-canada-39483715.

[328] Trump claims he invented this term. See https://newsstand.google.com/articles/CAIiENo9uUDIEV7dNAuqjfcqCLgqFggEKg0IACoGCAowm_EEMKAiMMq9zA), which was probably coined by US President Herbert Hoover.

[329] See: https://www.economist.com/news/briefing/21721935-idea-reciprocity-animates-white-houses-view-trade-what-donald-trump-means-fair; https://www.cnbc.com/video/2016/03/10/donald-trump-free-trade-has-to-be-fair-trade.html; https://www.usatoday.com/story/money/2017/03/06/trump-advisor-free-fair-and-reciprocal-trade-deals-priority/98801640/.

[330] See: http://www.presidency.ucsb.edu/data/orders.php; https://www.whitehouse.gov/briefing-room/presidential-actions/executive-orders.

[331] See: https://www.quora.com/Whats-the-difference-between-a-presidential-

plishments achieved by this means are a product of his passionate dedication to destroying the presidential legacy of Barack Obama.[332] Trump seems to hold the expectation that everyone involved with the Washingtonian politico-administrative and judicial processes were obliged to respect the "will of the people." This is not surprising since, as a populist, he considers that he, and only he, represents, the people. As Trump explained in his presidential inaugural speech, because he now controls the executive, the people now control the government.[333] And so, by implication, all opposition is illegitimate—opposing Trump means opposing the people.

So, all federal political, administrative, and judicial institutions were expected to facilitate—certainly not block—any presidential administrative instruction that he considers met his campaign promises, not withstanding any constitution and budgetary constraints. He soon learnt—from bitter trial-and-error experience—implementing his campaign promises—even if they were long-standing Republican Party policies, such as, repealing and replacing Obamacare[334]—is a matter of public administration, congressional politics, and, undoubtedly, constitutional law, of which his sadly lacking both knowledge and experience. More importantly, perhaps, his senior advisors have been similarly ignorant and inexperienced in the use of the levers of government.

THE CONSTITUTIONAL SEPARATION OF POWERS

The American constitution embodies the political doctrine under which the three branches of government—the executive, the legislative,

---

memorandum-executive-memo-and-an-executive-ordergb; https://www. whitehouse.gov/briefing-room/presidential-actions/presidential-memoranda.

[332] See: http://www.latimes.com/politics/la-na-pol-trump-obama-legacy-201707 18-story.html; https://www.usatoday.com/story/news/politics/2017/08/15/ trump-reverses-obama-legacy-court-battles-justice/565525001/; http://www. latimes.com/politics/la-na-pol-trump-obama-legacy-20170718-story.html.

[333] See: https://www.theguardian.com/world/2017/jan/20/donald-trump-inauguration-speech-full-text; but see: https://www.theguardian.com/world/20 17/jan/20/donald-trump-inauguration-speech-analysis.

[334] See: http://www.vox.com/carecare/2017/3/24/15055232/donald-trump-ahca -statement

and the judicial—are kept separate to prevent the abuse of power. Each branch has been given powers to be able to impose checks and balances the other branches. Trumps has made it clear that he considers this to be an obsolete doctrine, perhaps, as has been suggest, because "it will not allow him to govern like a 'Third World' leader."[335] Indeed, in an interview with *Fox News* on April 29, Trump said of the system of constitutional checks and balances: "It's a very rough system ... It's an archaic system ... It's really a bad thing for the country."[336] His has been, insightfully, satirized on this subject by *The New Yorker* (Friday, February 10):

> WASHINGTON (The Borowitz Report)—Hinting darkly that "there's something going on," Donald J. Trump complained on Friday that he has been treated "very unfairly" by the people who wrote the United States Constitution.
>
> "If the Constitution prevented me from doing one or two things, I'd chalk that up to bad luck," he said. "But when literally everything I want to do is magically a violation of the Constitution, that's very unfair and bad treatment."
>
> Lashing out at the document's authors, Trump said that "America is a great country, but we have maybe the worst constitution writers in the world."
>
> "Russia has much better constitution writers than we do," he said. "I talked to Putin, and he said their constitution never gives him problems."
>
> "The situation is very unfair!" he added.
>
> In an ominous warning, Trump said that, as of Friday [today], he was putting the writers of the US Constitution "on notice."

---

[335] Retrieved from: http://www.aljazeera.com/indepth/opinion/2017/05/trump-canwill-break-trump-170518085955594.html.

[336] Retrieved from: https://www.theguardian.com/us-news/2017/apr/29/trump-blames-constitution-for-first-100-days-chaos-presidency. But see: https://newsstand.google.com/articles/CAIiEOqgliWP4BRNDdOQ3d-Yqgoq FwgEKg4IACoGCAowis8wMLmCBjD_oNQD.

"I don't have their names yet, but that's something I'm looking into," he said. "These jokers are not going to get away with this."[337]

THE US JUDICIARY

Created by the American Constitution, the federal court system administers justice with respect to the Constitution, all federal legislation, and all presidential administrative instructions (Executive Orders and Presidential Memorandums).[338] It comprises the Supreme Court, America's highest court, below which are 94 district level trial courts and 13 courts of appeals. They have the power of judicial review, under which a court can judge the constitutionality of the actions taken by the other two branches government. This includes judging whether presidential administrative instructions are unconstitutional, which can only happen when constitutionality is brought up in a case that has been presented to a court. Ultimately, the Supreme Court is the final adjudicator.

Trump's preference, no doubt, would be for the federal court system to:

- *Uphold law and order and the protection of property rights* in accordance with his conception of the public interest.

- *Restrict freedom of access to any public information* because, in his view, it must remain secret in the national interest.

- *Refrain from engaging in judicial policymaking.*

- *Refrain from exercising its power of judicial review over presidential executive actions.*

Trump considers that the power of judicial review being exercised by federal judges to constrain his administrative orders—by blocking or unilaterally changing his Presidential Executive Orders[339]—is contrary

---

[337] Retrieved from: http://www.newyorker.com/humor/borowitz-report/trump-says-he-has-been-treated-very-unfairly-by-people-who-wrote-constitution.

[338] See: http://www.uscourts.gov/; https://www.fjc.gov/history/judges.html.

[339] See: https://www.forbes.com/forbes/welcome/?toURL=https://www.forbes.com/sites/andyjsemotiuk/2017/05/26/trumps-immigration-promises-stymied-by-courts/&refURL=https://www.google.co.uk/&referrer; https://www.google.co.uk/; https://www.washingtonpost.com/news/volokh-

to the "will of the people." After all, he is only doing what the people elected him to do.[340]

THE US CONGRESS

Congress is the bicameral federal legislature, comprising the Senate[341] (100 Senators) and the House of Representatives[342] (435 voting Representatives[343]). Its powers under the American Constitution are as follows:

- *Express powers*—these are embedded in the Constitution and include, among other things, the power to impose taxes, borrow money, regulate commerce and currency, organize all US courts below the Supreme Court, and, above all, the power [under Article 1, Section 2, Clause 18]:

  > To make all Laws which shall be necessary and proper for carrying into Execution the foregoing Powers, and all other Powers vested by this Constitution in the Government of the United States, or in any Department or Officer thereof.[344]

- *Implied powers*—these are granted by the Supreme Court to extend its powers "assumed to exist due to their being necessary to implement the expressed powers [under Article 1, Section

conspiracy/wp/2017/04/25/federal-court-rules-against-trumps-executive-order-targeting-sanctuary-cities/?utm_term=.4b77da98ab4c; http://www.msnbc.com/rachel-maddow-show/trumps-latest-defeat-court-smacks-down-another-executive-order.

340   See: http://www.independent.co.uk/news/world/americas/seattle-federal-judge-restraining-order-donald-trump-immigration-ban-a7562406.html.

341   See: https://www.senate.gov/.

342   See: https://www.house.gov/.

343   "The number of voting representatives [also called Congressman and women] in the House is fixed by law at no more than 435, proportionally representing the population of the 50 states. Currently, there are five delegates representing the District of Columbia, the Virgin Islands, Guam, American Samoa, and the Commonwealth of the Northern Mariana Islands. A resident commissioner represents Puerto Rico." Retrieved from: https://www.house.gov/.

344   Article I, Section 8. Retrieved from: https://www.whitehouse.gov/1600/constitution. See also: http://press-pubs.uchicago.edu/founders/tocs/a1_8_18.htm/.

2, Clause 18] that *are* named in Article I."[345] This has given it, for example, powers to impose environmental and labor regulations, and legislate on educational and health matters.[346]

- *Inherent powers*—these are granted by the Supreme Court, under Article 1, Section 2, Clause 18, to extended its powers

> over and beyond those explicitly spelled out in the Constitution or which can reasonably be implied from express grants [of congressional power] ... The US Supreme Court has discovered federal inherent powers to take land through eminent domain proceedings, to acquire land by discovery and occupation, to exclude or admit aliens, and to sell munitions to belligerent nations.[347]

- *Non-legislative powers*—these are embedded in the Constitution and including the power to impeach a president (remove him from office), to confirm or deny all major appointments made by a president (US judges, cabinet officers, and major officials of executive agencies), and to confirm or deny an international treaty (requiring a two-thirds vote of the Senate for any treaty to acquire the force of law).[348]

Trump's evidences little or no understanding of the constitutional nuances and complexities of Congress's governance role and legislative procedures. This is hardly surprising.

On the Republicans in Congress

Trump's relationship with the ideologically divided[349] Republican Party,[350]

---

[345] Retrieved from: http://www.shmoop.com/legislative-branch/implied-powers-of-congress.htm.

[346] See: http://www.shmoop.com/legislative-branch/implied-powers-of-congress.html.

[347] Retrieved from: https://definitions.uslegal.com/i/inherent-powers-constitution/.

[348] See: Article I, Section 8 Retrieved from: https://www.whitehouse.gov/1600/constitution.

[349] See: http://www.mcall.com/opinion/letters/mc-sb2-fisher-20170913-story.html; https://www.usnews.com/news/politics/articles/2017-04-17/gop-seen-as-divided-party-poll.

[350] See: https://www.gop.com/; https://www.gop.com/histor; https://www.gop.

which controls both chambers of Congress, is ambiguous. He owes its leadership nothing. He was elected president despite, not because of, them:

> Congressional leadership thinks if they and Trump disagree, clearly Trump should give way and follow their lead. But why? He beat them, and they couldn't beat him. The party didn't go for any of the other candidates because they wanted him. Yet since his inauguration congressional Republicans have acted like they have an equal seat at the table. They don't have that, and they don't deserve it. And Trump should stop pretending they do.

He is, effectively, an independent president, perhaps one interested in establishing his own party to contest the 2020 presidential election. He is not swayed by conservative ideological pressures, whatever their hue. Yet, in practice, he needs the support of the Republicans in Congress to get his requested budget[351] approved and to enact his legislative agenda. They need him, as he is the elected Republican president, at least until his presidential approval rating collapses to the point that the Republicans control of the Senate, and even the House of Representatives, is under very serious threat.

Indeed, the Republicans in Congress begun to pull away from Trump in mid-May, worried about his volatility.[352] This is further evidenced in early October by an ill-tempered Trump twitter row—dual[353]—with

---

com/platform/.

[351] See: https://www.theguardian.com/us-news/2017/may/23/republicans-opposition-trump-budget-medicaid-spending; https://www.forbes.com/sites/stancollender/2017/05/21/due-tuesday-2018-budget-could-be-trumps-biggest-failure-yet/#372bd35557e9; https://www.usatoday.com/story/opinion/2017/05/24/donald-trump-2018-budget-turn-off-voters-column-stan-collender/102074618/http://equitablegrowth.org/equitablog/should-read-stan-collender-this-weeks-rollout-of-trump-2018-budget-could-be-his-biggest-failure-yet/.

[352] See: https://www.nytimes.com/2017/05/14/us/politics/trump-republican-senators.

[353] See: http://www.bbc.com/news/world-us-canada-41419190.

Senator Bob Corker[354] (Republican, Tennessee), the Chair of the Senate Foreign Relations Committee, during which Corker "hit back that the White House had become an 'adult day care centre'".[355] Then, Trump begun to ditch the Republican Party in early September, intent on governing around them. He is frustrated with the incapacity of the Republican leadership—Mitch McConnell[356] (Senate Majority Leader) and Paul Ryan[357] (Speaker of the House of Representatives)—to bring together the ideologically split Republican factions, because he is worried about whether there is sufficient congressional support to raise the federal public debt ceiling—to enable the financing of his proposed 2018 budget, with its substantial public expenditure increases and its ambitious tax reductions—given the resistance within the Republican ranks to so doing.[358]

Trump, when faced with unreceptive Republican majorities in Congress, chose to embrace bipartisanship. This shift toward the center ground of American politics would make him the highest ranking RINO—Republican in Name Only.[359] Ben Domenech, the publisher of the right-

---

[354] See: https://www.corker.senate.gov/public/; but see also: https://www.theatlantic.com/international/archive/2017/10/corker-north-korea-trump/542514/; http://time.com/4977185/bob-corker-donald-trump-feud-reality-show/.

[355] Retrieved from: http://www.bbc.com/news/world-us-canada-41546140; see also: https://www.reuters.com/article/us-usa-trump-corker/senator-corker-says-trump-risks-putting-u-s-on-path-to-world-war-three-idUSKBN1CD0OP; https://www.cnbc.com/2017/10/08/president-donald-trump-is-blasting-senator-bob-corker-on-twitter.html; https://www.vox.com/policy-and-politics/2017/10/8/16443694/trump-bob-corker-twitter-tax-reform-iran-world-war-iii-reelection.

[356] See: https://www.mcconnell.senate.gov/public/.

[357] See: https://www.speaker.gov/about.

[358] See: https://www.nytimes.com/2017/05/23/us/politics/congress-budget-republicans.html?mcubz=3; http://thehill.com/policy/finance/335346-five-tax-reform-issues-dividing-republicans; https://www.washingtonpost.com/powerpost/trumps-push-for-tax-cuts-is-coming-up-against-a-familiar-challenge-divided-gop/2017/09/11/bd7a875c-9763-11e7-82e4-f1076f6d6152_story.html?utm_term=.7baaac975d24.

[359] This is a Republican who is willing to abandon conservative principles when it is in his interests to do so. In particular he does not adhere to Republican values of limited-government, free-market, pro-family. See: http://www.conservapedia.

wing online magazine *The Federalist*,[360] has expressed his prognosis:

> The [Republican Party] voters don't want Ryanism or ...
> McConnellism. They want Trumpism—or at least what
> they think that is. GOP [the "Grand Old Party", which
> is the colloquial name of the Republican Party] voters
> want leaders who mesh with Trump and his agenda be-
> cause that reflects the mandate he won. They can't stand
> the fact that their Congressional leaders are crosswise
> with the president. So it's a dysfunctional relationship,
> because McConnell and Ryan are operating from a false
> perception that they are in charge. They're not. Trump
> hasn't yet cemented that fact in his own mind, but when
> he does, things will change—and this could be the first
> indication that they are changing.[361]

On the Democrats in Congress

In September, Trump reach across party lines to do a deal with the Democrats[362],[363] when he began negotiations with the Democrat congressional leaders, Charles (Chuck) Schumer[364] (Leader of the Democratic
Caucus in the Senate) and Nancy Pelosi[365] (Democratic Leader of the
House of Representatives).[366] His starting point was to do a deal that

---

com/RINO; but see also: federalist.com/2016/01/15/rino-doesnt-mean-anything-any-more/.

[360] See: https://mediabiasfactcheck.com/the-federalist/

[361] Retrieved from: http://thefederalist.com/2017/09/07/trumps-potential-triangulation/.

[362] See: https://www.democrats.org/; but see also: http://time.com/4951191/divided-democratic-party-debates-its-future/.

[363] See: https://www.nytimes.com/2017/09/14/us/trump-schumer-pelosi-daca.html?mcubz=3; http://edition.cnn.com/2017/09/14/politics/chuck-schumer-senate-donald-trump/index.html.

[364] See: https://www.schumer.senate.gov/.

[365] See: https://pelosi.house.gov/.

[366] See: https://www.newyorker.com/humor/borowitz-report/in-stunning-new-deal-with-democrats-trump-agrees-to-be-impeached; https://www.nbcnews.com/politics/congress/trump-talking-daca-democrats-has-republicans-edge-again-n801291; https://www.thetimes.co.uk/article/trump-backers-in-despair-

would raise the federal public debt ceiling:

> The debt ceiling deal itself was pretty simple: Donald Trump ditched, with zero ceremony, his own Republican team[367] and joined with the slightly bemused Democrats to raise the amount of debt the US is legally allowed to possess.
>
> Actually, it was not a deal: he just accepted the Democrats' position. It was the first time in his presidency that he reached across to Democrats to solve a major political issue. It will not be the last.[368]

Indeed, the current deal could, much to the chagrin of his core supporters:

- Give "legal status to about 700,000 young undocumented immigrants—known as 'dreamers'—who were brought into the US as children,"[369] and who were protected under Barack Obama's Deferred Action for Childhood Arrivals (DACA) program.[370]

- Defer the construction of the Mexican wall: "We're working on a plan, subject to getting massive border controls," Mr Trump said [on September 14]. "The wall will come latter."[371] True to form, Trump soon modified his position: "If there is not a wall,

---

at-democrat-talks-ck283xk7f; http://forum.woodenboat.com/showthread.php?228660-Donald-Trump-backers-in-despair-at-talks-with-Democrats.

[367] See: http://www.powerlineblog.com/archives/2015/07/trump-no-longer-even-pretends-to-be-a-republican.php.

[368] Retrieved from: https://www.thetimes.co.uk/article/trump-no-longer-even-pretends-hes-republican-tn6gchbxz; see also: https://www.theatlantic.com/politics/archive/2017/09/trump-democrats-debt-ceiling/539148/; http://edition.cnn.com/2017/09/06/politics/trump-deal-democrats-republicans/index.html.

[369] Retrieved from: https://www.thetimes.co.uk/article/trump-backers-in-despair-at-democrat-talks-ck283xk7f.

[370] See: https://undocu.berkeley.edu/legal-support-overview/what-is-daca/; see also: http://www.independent.co.uk/topic/daca.

[371] Retrieved from: https://www.thetimes.co.uk/article/trump-backers-in-despair-at-democrat-talks-ck283xk7f.

we're doing nothing." Democrats must agree "not to obstruct the wall."[372]

- Raise taxes on the wealthy: Trump reportedly said "he would not cut taxes on the wealthy and may raise them."[373] Trump and the Democrats are, however, at loggerheads over inheritance tax, which Trump has promised to abolish.[374]

- Reverse his decision to withdraw the US from the Paris Climate Accord.[375]

Clearly, in the longer term, Trump will have to set his policy agenda in accord with the policies that are most popular to both Democrats and Republicans. His premise may well be that neither party would want to be seen to responsible for the failure of a popular bipartisan approach to politics and public policy merely to placate the prejudices of their core bases at either end of the political spectrum.

The full political ramifications for Trump are unclear.[376] Will he be able to step to the right or left at a whim, and still keep his core right-wing base on side with tough rhetoric? This will be a testing challenge, given in recent months he has infuriated both the end of the political spectrum, and he has always been disdainful of the middle ground—

[372] See: https://www.washingtonpost.com/video/politics/trump-if-we-dont-have-the-wall-were-doing-nothing/2017/09/14/21015e06-9965-11e7-af6a-6555caaeb8dc_video.html?utm_term=.f3557391a8ec.

[373] Retrieved from: https://www.thetimes.co.uk/article/trump-backers-in-despair-at-democrat-talks-ck283xk7f. See also: https://newsstand.google.com/articles/CAIiEG3YAi3hai4WjpLor5mDLqQqGAgEKg8IACoHCAowjtSUCjC30X-Qwzqe5AQ; https://www.washingtonpost.com/news/wonk/wp/2017/09/13/trump-says-his-plan-could-hike-taxes-on-the-wealthy-contradicting-experts-and-his-own-treasury-secretary/?utm_term=.6288c4c3cf02; https://www.washingtonpost.com/news/wonk/wp/2017/09/13/trump-says-his-plan-could-hike-taxes-on-the-wealthy-contradicting-experts-and-his-own-treasury-secretary/?utm_term=.921e6f0302bc; http://www.reuters.com/article/us-usa-tax/trump-says-rich-might-pay-more-in-taxes-talks-with-demo-crats-idUSKCN1BO1HM.

[374] Retrieved from: https://www.thetimes.co.uk/article/taxes-will-test-the-bipartisan-spirit-d7zz8dq0w.

[375] See: http://www.bbc.co.uk/news/world-us-canada-41300036.

[376] See: http://www.bbc.co.uk/news/world-us-canada-41275221.

inevitably the zone of compromise. To some of his supporters, it is already clear that Trump has lost it all.[377] He has, thereby, committing political suicide. One Republican Congressman, Steve King[378]—well known for his animosity to amnesty: "I adamantly oppose amnesty, regardless of the guise under which it is presented. Amnesty pardons immigration lawbreakers and rewards them with the objective of their crime—citizenship"[379]—believes that the "Trump base is blown up, destroyed, irreparable and disillusioned beyond repair. No promise is credible."[380] Only time will tell whether his flirtation with the Democrats becomes a dalliance—at a price—and, ultimately, an affair to remember.[381]

On Working with Congress

Regardless of outcome of his overtures with the Democrats and his deteriorating relationship with the Republicans, Trump needs to get his budgetary and legislative agendas enacted, which some have argues is already dead in 2017.[382] To this end, he would need to become a president who is willing and able to solicit the support of specific members of Congress—perhaps from both parties—to sponsor his bills and to lobby other members—perhaps from both parties—to facilitate their passage into law. His staff, particularly the Vice President and his Chief of Staff, would also need to be willing and able lobby Congress in support of these agendas. Trump and his senior staff have still to learn how to navigate proposed legislation through Congress. So far, the Trump administration has evidenced little enthusiasm for—or capacity to—engage with the Republican's in Congress—let alone the Democrats—as evidenced by its handling of the Obamacare repeal and replacement legislation—

---

[377] See: http://rendevouswithdestiny.blogspot.co.uk/2017/09/gop-congressman-if-daca-deal-is-true.html.

[378] See: https://steveking.house.gov/.

[379] See: https://steveking.house.gov/.

[380] Retrieved from: https://www.thetimes.co.uk/article/trump-backers-in-despair-at-democrat-talks-ck283xk7f.

[381] See: http://edition.cnn.com/2017/09/15/politics/donald-trump-base-support/index.html.

[382] See: https://www.forbes.com/sites/stancollender/2017/05/14/the-comey-fallout-trump-legislative-agenda-is-dead-in-2017/#ef379652c84e.

essentially, too little, too late.[383] Perhaps it will have more success with the Democrats, but to be successful Trump will still need the support of some—moderate?—Republicans. A measure of his mishandling of Congress, it has, in a rare bipartisan initiative, told him that it does not trust him on matters Russian.[384] The *Countering America's Adversaries Through Sanctions Bill*[385]—the Russian sanctions bill that enacted Obama's 2016 sanctions against Russia, and imposed new sanctions on Iran and North Korea—passed through both chambers of Congress with an almost unanimous—veto-proof[386]—bipartisan support, expressly placing constraints on Trump's authority to remove sanctions on any of these countries without congressional approval.[387] Trump reluctantly signed the bill into law, albeit angrily.[388] The press coverage on this is insightful:

> It shows the degree that the president has fallen out with the people in Congress he most needs to succeed as president. Congressional Republicans, for their part, are increasingly willing to ignore Trump or shoot back at him.[389]

---

[383] See: https://www.vox.com/policy-and-politics/2017/7/19/16000408/voxcare-trump-hates-obamacare; http://thehill.com/homenews/administration/342 809-trump-plays-hardball-on-obamacare-repeal; https://www.reuters.com/ article/us-usa-healthcare-idUSKBN1A40UX; http://www.bbc.co.uk/news/ world-us-canada-40754257.

[384] See: https://www.theguardian.com/us-news/2017/jun/13/us-senators-reach-deal-to-stop-w-easing-russia-sanctions-without-approval; http://time.com/48 77685/trump-russia-sanctions-bill-capitol-hill/.

[385] See: https://www.whitehouse.gov/legislation/hr-3364-countering-americas-adversaries-through-sanctions-act.

[386] Congress can override a presidential veto by passing the act by a two-thirds vote in both the House and the Senate. See https://www.archives.gov/files/legislative/ resources/education/veto/background.pdf.

[387] See: https://www.vox.com/policy-and-politics/2017/7/28/16055630/ congress-trump-russia-sanctions-veto; https://www.nytimes.com/2017/07 /22/us/politics/congress-sanctions-russia.html.

[388] See: http://time.com/4884001/donald-trump-signs-russia-sanctions-bill/; https://www.vox.com/world/2017/8/4/16090812/trump-russia-sanctions-congress-putin; https://www.vanityfair.com/news/2017/08/donald-trump-russian-sanctions-bill-congress. But see: http://www.telegraph.co.uk/news/20 17/08/02/donald-trump-signs-russia-sanctions-bill-calls-significantly/.

[389] Retrieved from: https://www.vox.com/world/2017/8/4/16090812/trump-

> This is a president who clearly doesn't understand the current political environment. He remains bereft of any major wins and is facing an investigation that's threatening his presidency. His desperation and frustration appear to be leading him to attack his own party more and more openly.[390]

And:

> Russia's Prime Minister Dmitry Medvedev reacted strongly to the bill's signing, saying ... that "the Trump administration demonstrated complete impotence, in the most humiliating manner, transferring executive powers to Congress."[391]

This all means that Trump is struggling to be the consummate political dealmaker in Washington—the fierce fighter and inevitable winner—he portrayed himself to be during his presidential campaign and still does.[392] Instead, he is willing the blame others—even the Democrats—for the consequences of his and his senior staff's political ineptitude. So he blames the minority Democratic Party for its obstructionist stance in Congress—Trump curiously holds the view that "If they [the Democrats] weren't obstructionists, I would normally get Democratic support."[393] The veracity of this intriguing proposition is being tested by his September public debt ceiling overtures to the Democrats. Trump is, quite clearly, the ultimate political pragmatist, loyal to no one but himself. At one point, he was even prepared to bring about a "good shutdown" of government when this current round of appropriations

---

russia-sanctions-congress-putin.

[390] Retrieved from: https://www.vox.com/world/2017/8/4/16090812/trump-russia-sanctions-congress-putin.

[391] Retrieved from: http://edition.cnn.com/2017/08/02/politics/donald-trump-russia-sanctions-bill/index.html.

[392] See: http://www.salon.com/2017/06/29/donald-trumps-myth-is-coming-unglued-how-did-the-supposed-master-dealmaker-become-a-spectacularly-incompetent-president/; http://www.washingtontimes.com/news/2017/jun/27/donald-trump-winning-as-president-not-as-deal-make/.

[393] Retrieved from: https://www.vanityfair.com/news/2017/07/trump-claims-he-has-a-secret-plan-to-tax-the-rich-but-democrats-wont-let-him.

expires in September[394] to "fix the mess" in the Republican-controlled Congress, in order to get his beloved Mexican wall funded by Congress.[395] That issue, however, seems to be off the negotiating table[396] at least in the short-term. Trump seems to believe that it is the Democrats who hold the key to the funding of his tax reforms and infrastructure development aspirations by more public borrowing.

THE EXECUTIVE BRANCH

Trump's want is to create a public sector that is, first and foremost, loyal to him and compliant with his wishes as the duly elected president, one who sees himself as the embodiment of the will of the people. Then, it has to be lean and financially disciplined—like a well-run business—allowing government to achieve and sustain a balanced budget. During his presidential campaign, Trump told the Tea Party Patriots Citizens Fund[397]:

> I will ... propose strict budget discipline. I will propose budgets that freeze overall spending levels until such time as the budget comes into balance. This approach eliminates the existing resources to reshape spending priorities. Congress, knowing that I will not sign a budget that increases spending until the budget is balance, will work with the Executive branch and the American people to do what is best for the country.[398]

---

[394]   See: https://www.vox.com/policy-and-politics/2017/5/2/15514594/trump-shutdown-tweets; http://www.news.com.au/world/north-america/donald-trump-wants-government-shutdown-in-september-to-fix-mess-in-senate/news-story/8a172afc1c44c1fa3cac131cf2498672; https://www.theatlantic.com/politics/archive/2017/05/president-trump-wants-a-government-shutdown/525051/. See also: https://twitter.com/realDonaldTrump.

[395]   See, for example: http://thehill.com/policy/finance/347680-ryan-shutdown-over-border-wall-not-necessary; http://edition.cnn.com/2017/08/23/politics/paul-ryan-border-security-funding/index.html; http://talkingpointsmemo.com/livewire/paul-ryan-govdernment-shutdown-not-necessary-trump-threat.

[396]   See: https://www.thetimes.co.uk/article/trump-backers-in-despair-at-democrat-talks-ck283xk7f.

[397]   See: https://www.teapartypatriotscitizensfund.com/.

[398]   Retrieved from: https://www.teapartypatriotscitizensfund.com/official-tppcf-

Finally, he wants the public sector to be accountable and working effectively and efficiently to deliver those programs that he considers to be necessary for the betterment for the American people. This would seem to prioritize defense of his realm, homeland security, border protection, and immigration control, which leaves no space in his priorities for environmental, education, and anti-poverty programs.

On Administrative Reorganization

Trump is instinctively distrusting of the departments and agencies in his Executive Branch, which he considers to be bloated and inefficient. His thinking has been dominated by three considerations.

Creating A Lean and Mean Bureaucracy with a Heart

His first concern reflects his campaign promise that "government will become lean and mean, except—except it will have a big, fat, beautiful heart. We will have an effective and responsible and honest government for a change."[399] In the words of his initial Chief Strategist, Steve Bannon, "the deconstruction of the administrative state," is a top priority for the Trump administration.[400]

Trump's starting points are three-fold. First, he wants to reduce or abolish "unnecessary" or "undesirable" public—mainly social—program, thereby reducing public expenditures (by $478 billion). This sits within the context of Trump's first budget outline presented in mid-March—*America First: Budget Blueprint to Make America Great Again*.[401] This set out the programs that the Trump administration considered are unnecessary, out-dated, or simply not working: Medicaid and the Children's Health Insurance Program (saving $616 billion), welfare programs (saving $272 billion), repeal and replacement of Obamacare (saving $250

---

primary-registration/donald-trump/?roi=echo7-22089092107-45865753-4d6e 12f3e1e31f39739a7595888b38e1&mid=9180712.

[399] Retrieved from: http://www.govexec.com/management/2016/08/trump-government-lean-and-mean-big-fat-beautiful-heart/131182/.

[400] Retrieved from: http://www.reuters.com/article/us-usa-trump-regulations-idU SKBN1631NV.

[401] Retrieved from: https://www.whitehouse.gov/sites/whitehouse.gov/files/omb/budget/fy2018/2018_blueprint.pdf

billion), student loans (saving $143 billion), unspecified government payments to individuals (saving $142 billion), disability programs (saving $72 billion), and retirement benefits for federal employees (saving $63 billion).[402] He needs a to reduce federal expenditure in this way in order to offset some of the budgetary costs of his ambitious tax reform plan, which is officially uncosted. The Committee for a Responsible Budget has estimated, however, that

> the plan could cost $3 to $7 trillion over a decade—our base-case estimate is $5.5 trillion in revenue loss over a decade. Without adequate [expenditure or revenue growth offsets, tax reform could drive up the federal debt, harming economic growth instead of boosting it.[403]

Added to this are his ambitious proposals to increase defense expenditure (by $469 billion),[404] to provide an infrastructure investment (by $200 billion),[405] and, at the time, to finance the building of his ambitious Mexican wall (officially uncosted, but it could be as much as $21.6 billion)[406].

Second, he wants to move forward on deregulation. His campaign promise was to ask Congress to support legislation requiring the nullification of two regulations for every new regulation imposed by a federal agency.[407] To that end he appointed fellow billionaire, Carl Ichan,[408] as his unofficial advisor on regulatory overhaul.[409] Trump's *Presidential*

[402] See: https://www.nytimes.com/2017/05/22/us/politics/trump-budget-winners-losers.html.

[403] Retrieved from: http://www.crfb.org/blogs/how-much-will-trumps-tax-plan-cost.

[404] See: https://www.nytimes.com/2017/05/22/us/politics/trump-budget-winners-losers.html.

[405] See: https://www.nytimes.com/2017/05/22/us/politics/trump-budget-winners-losers.html.

[406] See: http://www.reuters.com/article/us-usa-trump-immigration-wall-exclusive-idUSK.BN15O2ZN.

[407] See: https://www.c-span.org/video/?417256-1/donald-trump-campaigns-johnstown-pennsylvania.

[408] See: https://www.forbes.com/profile/carl-icahn/.

[409] See: https://www.forbes.com/sites/nathanvardi/2016/12/21/billionaire-carl-

Executive Order on Enforcing the Regulatory Reform Agenda[410] issued on February 24 requires every federal department and agency:

- to designate regulatory reform officers, who will "oversee the implementation of regulatory reform initiatives and policies" (Section 2);

- to establish a Regulatory Reform Task Force, which will review all regulations and make recommendations on which ones are economically burdensome and so should be repealed, replaced, or modified (Section 3); and

- to measure and report on (with 90 days) on its regulatory reform progress (Section 4) with respect to "improving implementation of regulatory reform initiatives and policies "and identifying regulations for repeal, replacement, or modification" (Section 3).

So, deregulation became an administrative strategy that would "Roll Back Burdensome Regulations"[411]:

> We must eliminate every outdated, unnecessary, or ineffective federal regulation, and move aggressively to build regulatory frameworks that stimulate—rather than stagnate—job creation. Even for those regulations we must leave in place, we must strike every provision that is counterproductive, ineffective, or outdated.[412]

In response, Ichan decided to resign in mid-August because, as he states:

---

icahn-to-be-trumps-adviser-on-regulatory-overhaul/#3be3c0c17264.

[410] See: https://www.whitehouse.gov/the-press-office/2017/02/24/presidential-executive-order-enforcing-regulatory-reform-agenda.

[411] See: https://books.google.co.uk/books?id=yfwxDwAAQBAJ&pg=PT36&lpg=PT36&dq=%E2%80%9CRoll+Back+Burdensome+Regulations%E2%80%9D&source=bl&ots=DsmqYLd9I1&sig=mvcDmxCf5YPwSz8AqWNgCvu4iXo&hl=en&sa=X&ved=0ahUKEwiT-KaFhvrVAhVKIsAKHee8DUsQ6AEINTAD#v=onepage&q=%E2%80%9CRoll%20Back%20Burdensome%20Regulations%E2%80%9D&f=false.

[412] Retrieved from: https://www.forbes.com/sites/waynecrews/2017/05/24/in-todays-world-trumps-balanced-budget-will-require-regulatory-reform/#453bdb2f695f. See also: http://www.nationalreview.com/article/447074/trump-hundred-days-regulation-rollback-has-begun.

I did not want partisan bickering about my role to in any way cloud your administration or Ms. [Neomi] Rao's important work. (Rao[413] was confirmed as administrator of the Office of Information and Regulatory Affairs by the Senate in July).[414]

Third, Trump wants to reorganize the Executive Branch. To this end, he issued an Executive Order—*Comprehensive Plan for Reorganizing the Executive Branch*[415] on March 13. This is

> intended to improve the efficiency, effectiveness, and accountability of the executive branch by directing the Director of the Office of Management and Budget [OMB[416]] to propose a plan to reorganize governmental functions and eliminate unnecessary agencies, components of agencies, and agency programs.

In April, the OMB issued on March 13 very detailed, follow-up instructions to all executive departments and agencies on the implementation of the proposed reorganization—*Comprehensive Plan for Reforming the Federal Government and Reducing the Federal Civilian Workforce.*[417] Its opening gambit is neoliberal in tone:

> Despite growing citizen dissatisfaction with the cost and performance of the federal government, Washington often crafts costly solutions in search of a problem. Too often the focus has been on creating new programs instead of eliminating or reforming programs which are no longer operating effectively. The result has been too many

---

[413]   See: http://timesofindia.indiatimes.com/nri/us-canada-news/indian-american-to-head-white-house-regulatory-affairs-office/articleshow/59551003.cms.

[414]   Retrieved from: https://www.forbes.com/sites/maggiemcgrath/2017/08/18/carl-icahn-steps-down-from-role-as-unofficial-trump-adviser/#159b5b481727.

[415]   Executive Order 13781, retrieved from: https://www.whitehouse.gov/the-press-office/2017/03/13/presidential-executive-order-comprehensive-plan-reorganizing-executive.

[416]   See: https://www.whitehouse.gov/omb.

[417]   Retrieved from: https://www.whitehouse.gov/sites/whitehouse.gov/files/omb/memoranda/2017/M-17-22.pdf.

overlapping and outdated programs, rules, and process-es, and too many federal employees stuck in a system that is not working for the American people. Through the actions described below, President Trump aims to make government lean, accountable, and more efficient.

To begin addressing this challenge, on January 23, 2017, the President issued a Memorandum imposing a Federal "Hiring Freeze." This ensured immediate action was taken to halt the growth of the federal workforce until a "long-term plan to reduce the size of the federal government's workforce" is put in place. On March 16, 2017, the President submitted his Budget Blueprint to Congress proposing to eliminate funding for programs that are unnecessary, outdated, or not working. Addi-tionally, on March 13, 2017, the President issued an Executive Order (Reorganization EO) directing the Office of Management and Budget (OMB) to submit a comprehensive plan to reorganize Executive Branch departments and agencies.

According to the OMB, the reorganization objectives are two-fold:

- to create a lean, accountable, more efficient government that works better for the American people; and
- to focus the federal government on effectively and efficiently delivering those programs that are the highest needs to citizens, but only where there is a unique role to be played by the federal government.

This, however, raises a complicating tension between the elitist—pres-idential and congressional—perceptions that federal departments and agencies should offer only "services" that they consider the people—as service recipients—need, and the populist perception that federal de-partments and agencies should offer services that the people want. To diminish this tension requires a full examination of the role of the federal government, which might be too daunting—even too threatening—for the Keynesian-inclined president who is flirting with—playing off—all sides of American politics.

Creating a Loyal Bureaucracy

Trump's second concern is the Executive Branch's political allegiance to him. Every new president has the opportunity to appoint his own senior government officials. Indeed, he has the option to make 4,000 political appointments across a bureaucracy of some 2 million workers. There are four categories of such appointments:[418]

- *Presidential Appointments with Senate Confirmation*: There are 1,212 senior leaders to be appointed, including the Cabinet secretaries and their deputies, the heads of most independent agencies and ambassadors, who must be confirmed by the Senate. These positions first require a Senate hearing in addition to background checks and other vetting.

- *Presidential Appointments without Senate Confirmation*: There are 353 such positions to be filled, which make up much of the White House staff, although they are also scattered throughout many of the smaller federal agencies.

- *Non-career Senior Executive Service*: These members of the Senior Executive Service (SES)[419] work in key positions just below the top presidential appointees, bridge the gap between the political leaders and the civil service throughout the federal government. While most SES members are career officials, up to 10% of the SES can be political appointees. There are up to 680 non-career members of the SES to be appointed.

- *Schedule C Appointments*: There are 1,403 such appointments to be made. They serve in a confidential or policy role, ranging from schedulers and confidential assistants to policy experts.

Trump's concern about these appointments reflects his belief that he is expected to nominating officials for top management positions, including ambassadors, without knowing what precisely they do—"I look at some of the jobs, and it's people over people over people ... I say, 'What

---

[418] Retrieved from: http://presidentialtransition.org/blog/posts/160316_help-wanted-4000-appointees.php. See also: https://www.gpo.gov/fdsys/pkg/GPO-PLUMBOOK-2012/pdf/GPO-PLUMBOOK-2012.pdf; https://www.fas.org/sgp/crs/misc/R42720.pdf; https://fas.org/sgp/crs/misc/RL30365.pdf.

[419] See: https://www.opm.gov/policy-data-oversight/senior-executive-service/

do all these people do?'"[420]—and, above all, whether they are loyal to him and the Trump Cause. They must be utterly trustworthy—that is, dependably compliant of his wishes when need be.[421] Insightfully, a White House source has reported:

> When Secretary of State Rex Tillerson wanted to appoint Elliott Abrams, a veteran of the Ronald Reagan and George W. Bush White Houses, as his No. 2, someone in the president's orbit made sure Trump was freshly aware of Abrams' anti-Trump comments from 2016, such as a Weekly Standard op-ed in which Abrams wrote, "The party has nominated someone who cannot win and should not be president."

> Trump personally intervened to block Abrams' appointment.[422]

In a similar vein, another White House source has reported that when Ryan Zinke, Trump's Secretary of the Interior, complained to Trump about unfilled key position in his organization, he was told that he would get his people. But, only "as long as they're our people."[423] This means that they are not liberals, not Hillary Clinton donors, or not publicly associated with the Obama administration, even as career civil servants.[424] As was explained by a White House source briefed on this incident:

> If you [a Cabinet Secretary] want somebody [to fill a key position vacancy], that's fine, but they have to be vetted because, one, you know, Zinke is not the president. This is Presidential Personnel, and … they [senior

---

[420] Retrieved from: https://www.usatoday.com/story/opinion/2017/05/09/president-trump-help-wanted-editorials-debates/101019046/.

[421] See: http://www.businessinsider.com/whos-running-the-government-trump-unfilled-executive-branch-positions-2017-4.

[422] Retrieved from: http://www.politico.com/story/2017/02/elliott-abrams-no-deputy-secretary-of-state-234908.

[423] See: https://www.axios.com/white-house-at-war-over-personnel-2306708580.html.

[424] See: https://www.axios.com/white-house-at-war-over-personnel-2306708580.html.

White House staff] keep having this conversation with these department secretaries and administrators, and it's just not clicking.[425]

As another White House sources has been reported as saying:

These Secretaries have these egos that this is their little kingdom now, and it's their way or the highway. So it's been creating a logjam ... No way will the White House rubber stamp Hillary people; never Trumpers and flat-out liberals.[426]

Trump has not managed, after 6 months in office, to make most of the important political appointments, particularly deputy secretaries and ambassadors. Indeed, it was reported that, as of July 28, of the 575 key positions requiring Senate confirmation, the nomination status was:[427]

- confirmed: 50
- formally nominated: 165
- awaiting nomination: 3
- no nominee: 357

Having so many unfilled key positions, particularly in senior positions at or just below the top presidential appointees—the political appointees to the Senior Executive Service—is a problem,[428] but not a catastrophic one. For as the Master of Deceit and Intrigue observed:

The choice of servants [secretaries of the princes] is of no little importance to a prince. ... And the first opinion which forms of the prince, and of his understanding, is by observing the men he has around him; and when they are considered capable and faithful he may always

[425] Retrieved from: https://www.axios.com/white-house-at-war-over-personnel-2306708580.html.

[426] Retrieved from: https://www.axios.com/white-house-at-war-over-personnel-2306708580.html.

[427] Retrieved from: https://ourpublicservice.org/issues/presidential-transition/political-appointee-tracker.php.

[428] See, for example, http://www.bbc.co.uk/news/world-us-canada-40534572.

be considered wise, because he has known how to recognize the capable and to keep the faithful (Machiavelli [1513] 2011, 101).

Once nominations requiring Senate confirmation have been made, the Trump administration has the power to make acting appointments while the Senate is vetting them. These are usually career civil servants who are chosen by the president from a narrowly defined pool of candidates. Their interim status, however, diminishes their effectiveness and, as career civil servants, they are likely to be less inclined to make hard decisions with any political ramifications. However, when a department or agency has many unfilled key roles the political risks for Trump become all too evident,[429] because he does not have enough advocate to impress upon the bureaucratic mind his determination to make his "Make America Great Again" vision a reality. This can inhibit the design, enactment, and implementation planning of his long-term policies.

Disengaging the Deep State

Trump's third Executive Branch concern reflects his belief that there is "shadowy network of Obama holdovers that constitute the 'deep state'"[430] intent on sabotaging his presidency. Sean Spicer, when he was White House Press Secretary, argued these undercover saboteurs are:

> affiliated with, joined [to] and continue to espouse the agenda of the previous administration. ... I don't think it should come as any surprise that there are people burrowed into government during eight years of the last administration and may have believed in that agenda and want to continue to seek it. I don't think that should come as a surprise to anyone.[431]

---

[429] For department and agency details see: https://ourpublicservice.org/issues/presidential-transition/political-appointee-tracker.php.

[430] Retrieved from: http://www.telegraph.co.uk/news/2017/03/11/deep-state-shadowy-network-obama-holdovers-undermining-donald/; see also http://google.com/newsstand/s/CBIwj628vDk.

[431] Retrieved from: http://www.telegraph.co.uk/news/2017/03/11/deep-state-shadowy-network-obama-holdovers-undermining-donald/; see also http://

The Obama holdovers are, of course, *in situ* at Trump's pleasure. He can replace them whenever he has the will to do so. It may well be that he is unknowingly following the advice of the Master of Deceit and Intrigue: "a wise prince, when he has the opportunity ought with craft to foster some animosity against himself, so that, having crushed it, his renown may rise higher" (Machiavelli [1513] 2011, 94). Who better to blame when things are not going to plan than Obama's secrete army of officials, the disloyalty of members of which Trump can expose to the acclaim of his core support base (as happened in the case of Sally Yates, his short-lived Acting Attorney General[432]).

It may well be, of course, that the absence a concerted—loud—Trump organizational voice has permitted some departments and agencies to actively undermine his downsizing agenda.[433] This may be motivated by a desire to protect the interests of their existing stakeholders or to maintain their structural integrity. Indeed, a former Labor Secretary, Robert Reich,[434] has suggested that there is a "vast upsurge of resistance [to Trump's policy and administrative agendas] inside government".[435] He concludes: "You see, most government workers want to do their jobs, and they believe in democracy. In the months and years ahead, they'll also be an important source of whistle-blowing."[436]

CONCLUSION

As has been insightfully observed, "[b]ullshitting is easy, but governing

---

google.com/newsstand/s/CBIwj628vDk.

[432] Retrieved from: http://www.bbc.co.uk/news/world-us-canada-39826934

[433] See: https://www.washingtonpost.com/politics/resistance-from-within-federal-workers-push-back-against-trump/2017/01/31/c65b110e-e7cb-11e6-b82f-687d6e6a3e7c_story.html?utm_term=.2143541c8d7a.

[434] See: https://gspp.berkeley.edu/directories/faculty/robert-reich.

[435] Retrieved from: https://www.facebook.com/RBReich/posts/1457837370895521. See also: https://www.washingtonpost.com/politics/resistance-from-within-federal-workers-push-back-against-trump/2017/01/31/c65b110e-e7cb-11e6-b82f-687d6e6a3e7c_story.html?utm_term=.35c217361285; see also: http://www.washingtonexaminer.com/exclusive-far-left-green-groups-invited-to-advise-epa-on-scientific-integrity/article/2623512.

[436] Retrieved from: https://www.facebook.com/RBReich/posts/1457837370895521.

is hard."[437] The idea that government should be run like a business is a popular one (Dixon 2016), being run by inexperienced business magnates at the organizational levels is a novel one, but the West Wing of White House being run as a family business is, at best, a worrying one. Little wonder Trump finds governing to be messy and complicated.[438] He is accustomed to telling people what to do and then fire them if they do not do it. But government does not work that way, which, by now, he should have discovered.[439] Being president, he now realizes involves more work than running a global family business.[440] He has also come to two important—but very basic—realizations;

- *The enormity of the federal government*:

  > It's massive. And every agency is, like, bigger than any company. So you know, I really just see the bigness of it all, but also the responsibility.[441]

- *The importance of the human factor in the world of politics*:

  > And the human responsibility. You know, the human life that' is involved in some of the decisions.[442] Well in business, you don't necessarily need heart, whereas here, almost everything affects people. So if you're talking about health care—you have health care in business but you're trying to just negotiate a good price on health care, et cetera, et cetera. You're providing health. This is (unintelligible). Here, everything, pretty much everything you do in government, involves heart, whereas in business, most things don't involve heart.[443]

But does he fully understand that a President needs the bureaucracy to

---

[437] Retrieved from: https://www.facebook.com/Vox/posts/671821166338822.

[438] See: http://news.nationalpost.com/full-comment/kelly-mcparland-trump-runs-into-the-problem-with-government-its-messy-and-complicated.

[439] See: https://www.indy100.com/article/t-anecdote-donald-trump-7612076.

[440] See: http://www.reuters.com/article/us-usa-trump-100days-idUSKBN17U0CA?feedType=RSS&feedName=politicsNews.

[441] Retrieved from: https://apnews.com/c810d7de280a47e88848b0ac74690c83.

[442] Retrieved from: https://apnews.com/c810d7de280a47e88848b0ac74690c83.

[443] Retrieved from: https://apnews.com/c810d7de280a47e88848b0ac74690c83.

come up with, and implement, policy? He must, by now, have realized that his presidential power is limited not only by the size, but also by the controllability of the Republican Congressional majorities, and by the legislative rules and the courts. Finally, he must have come to realize that he should not expect support from the Democrats merely at his whim. Trump is certainly on a presidential learning curve: "He's still learning how to be president" according former House Speaker John Boehner, a Republican, who considers " President Donald Trump's time in office has been a "complete disaster" aside from foreign affairs".[444]

Every president faces a steep learning curve when he enters the White House; Trump is not an exception. He seems, however, to be genuinely surprised by the scope of his duties, by the contending interests he must balance, by the methods he has at his disposal to get things done.[445] His surprise should not be surprising, as he became president as a person with little interest in how the government worked or how policy is made, enacted, or implemented. This suggests that he did little to prepare himself for the presidency, perhaps because he did not expect to become president. Indeed, his naivety is in his thought that being president would be easy.[446]

And, if he believes his own rhetoric, he has a lot more to learn about navigating congressional politics, policymaking, and processes. In late April he asserted:

> I have great relationships with Congress. I think we're
> doing very well and I think we have a great foundation

---

[444] Retrieved from: http://www.reuters.com/article/us-usa-trump-boehner-idUS KBN18M2AO.

[445] See: https://www.nytimes.com/2017/04/13/us/politics/donald-trump-policy-reversals.html; http://www.bbc.com/news/world-us-canada-39587855; https://www.csmonitor.com/USA/Politics/2017/0427/Trump-s-steep-learning-curve; https://www.csmonitor.com/USA/Politics/2017/0427/Trump-s-steep-learning-curve; https://www.csmonitor.com/USA/Politics/2017/0427/Trump-s-steep-learning-curve; http://daily-iowan.com/2017/06/12/trumps-learning-curve/.

[446] See: http://www.reuters.com/article/us-usa-trump-100days-idUSKBN17 U0CA; https://www.theguardian.com/us-news/2017/apr/28/i-thought-being-president-would-be-easier-trumps-reuters-interview-highlights.

for future things. We're going to be applying, I shouldn't tell you this, but we're going to be announcing, probably on Wednesday [May 24], tax reform. And it's— we've worked on it long and hard. And you've got to understand, I've only been here now 93 days, 92 days. President Obama took 17 months to do Obamacare. I've been here 92 days but I've only been working on the health care, you know I had to get like a little bit of grounding right? Health care started after 30 day(s), so I've been working on health care for 60 days. ...You know, we're very close. And it's a great plan, you know, we have to get it approved.[447]

And:

So the Republican Party has various groups, all great people. They're great people. But some are moderate, some are very conservative. The Democrats don't seem to have that nearly as much. You know the Democrats have, they don't have that. The Republicans do have that. And I think it's fine. But you know there's a pretty vast area in there. And I have a great relationship with all of them. Now, we have government not closing. I think we'll be in great shape on that. It's going very well. Obviously, that takes precedent.[448]

---

[447] Retrieved from: https://apnews.com/c810d7de280a47e88848b0ac74690c83.

[448] Retrieved from: https://apnews.com/c810d7de280a47e88848b0ac74690c83.

4

DONALD J. TRUMP:
ON THE PRESIDENCY AND HIS WHITE HOUSE

Trump is isolated in the White House, out of his milieu, unable to shape the story, forced to interact with people he doesn't own. Even the staffers folding his clothes aren't on his payroll. [449]

Maureen Dowd, *The New York Times*, February 7, 2017

INTRODUCTION

Trump brought to the White House the leadership nous and management skills acquired over decades as the CEO of a global family business. He lacks the capacity—the temperament, knowledge, and skills—to manage a large, complex and accountable system of public organizations. Robert Reich, the renowned Berkeley public policy academic,[450] captured the reality of Trump's governance capacity:

> America is in a crisis of governance. There is no adult in charge ... Instead, we have as president an unhinged narcissistic child who tweets absurd lies and holds rallies to prop up his fragile ego ... He's advised by his [unpaid[451]] daughter, his [unpaid[452]] son-in-law, and an oddball who once ran a white supremacist fake-news outlet [Steve Bannon] ... His cabinet is an assortment of billionaires, CEOs, veterans of Wall Street, and ideologues, none of whom has any idea about how to govern and most of whom don't believe in the laws their departments are in charge of implementing anyway ... He has downgraded or eviscerated groups responsible for giving presidents professional advice on foreign

---

[449] https://www.tlc.com/tv-shows/my-600-lb-life/full-episodes/dianas-story

[450] See: https://gspp.berkeley.edu/directories/faculty/robert-reich.

[451] See: http://www.independent.co.uk/news/world/americas/us-politics/donald-trump-ivanka-unpaid-federal-employee-job-father-advisor-a7657141.html.

[452] See: https://www.bloomberg.com/news/articles/2017-01-09/trump-s-son-in-law-kushner-said-to-take-unpaid-white-house-role.

policy, foreign intelligence, economics, science, and domestic policy. He gets most of what he learns from television.[453]

Trump clearly prefers not to rule America as his predecessors had done. About them, he has disdainfully remarked in 2016: "We are led by very, very stupid people" (cited in Piehler 2016, 87). Traditionally, a president before making decisions would:

- *engage with experts*—Trump rejects this because they are untrustworthy;
- *read reports*—Trump has difficulty doing this; and
- *seek differing opinions*—Trump considers this to be irrelevant.

Rather, he sees ruling as being seen to be unusually, if not uniquely, active, by addressing a wide range of issues and problems on a daily basis, especially those that relate to criticism and slurs about him. He readily claimed records for his diligence in office, when compared with other presidents, because he has issued many Executive Orders (49 up to September 29)[454] and Presidential Memorandums (68 up to September 14),[455] and signed many bills (57 up to August 18)[456].[457] But:

> More than 6 months into his presidency, the number of bills Trump has signed stands at 53 … In all, two of the laws have created a new policy, 15 have rolled back rules and regulations issued under Obama's administration, 10 had to do with designating something or working to create a new initiative, 11 changed or expanded existing legislation, and 15 were related to government funding or operations.[458]

---

[453] Retrieved from: http://www.salon.com/2017/03/22/robert-reich-donald-trum ps-government-faces-a-crisis-because-theres-no-adult-in-charge/.

[454] See: https://www.whitehouse.gov/briefing-room/presidential-actions/execut ive-orders?term_node_tid_depth=51.

[455] See: https://www.whitehouse.gov/briefing-room/presidential-actions/preside ntial-memoranda.

[456] See: https://www.whitehouse.gov/briefing-room/signed-legislation.

[457] See, for example: http://www.politifact.com/truth-o-meter/statements/ 2017/ apr/27/sean-spicer/trump-has-signed-more-bills-100-days-any-president/; http://www.npr.org/2017/04/26/525764669/as-president-trump-nears-100th-day-white-house-touts historic-accomplishments.

[458] Retrieved from: http://edition.cnn.com/2017/06/29/politics/president-trump -legislation/index.html.

Trump's propensity to overstate his achievements and to mislead knows no limits.[459]

TRUMP'S SURREAL WHITE HOUSE

Trump's presidency has been characterized as a "reality show" presidency[460]—undoubtedly one "on steroids"?[461]—with a president who thinks like a reality TV performer[462]:

> It has become a global ritual: you wake up each morning and grab your phone to catch up on the latest episode of *The Trump Show*, the addictive reality TV series... [that] perches between fiction and non-fiction, which is the spot where Trump feels happiest.[463]

> The cast consists of Trump—the star of the show, his relatives—who cannot be removed from the *Trump Show*, and his aids—who are all dispensable and so can be removed.[464] He is, as would be expected of the reality star, an uninhibited narcissist ever willing to plumb and reveals the deepest parts of his mind. Certainly, his presidency is "not the usual presidency. This is something strange... Adjectives such as 'unconventional' lack sufficient verve. 'Surreal' comes closer."[465] From leaked sources, the following incident, if true, is indicative.

> White House chief of staff Reince Priebus issued a stern

[459] See: https://www.nytimes.com/2017/04/29/us/politics/fact-checking-president-trump-through-his-first-100-days.html.

[460] Retrieved from: https://www.forbes.com/sites/markjoyella/2017/07/29/donald-trumps-reality-show-presidency-has-killed-off-the-network-evening-news/#13dd28ff33aa.

[461] Retrieved from: http://www.bbc.co.uk/news/world-us-canada-40954179.

[462] See: http://www.newyorker.com/magazine/2017/07/31/the-tv-that-created-donald-trump.

[463] Retrieved from: https://www.ft.comcontent/a41f0638-7c89-11e7-ab01-a13271d1ee9c.

[464] For a visual image see: https://www.vox.com/policy-and-politics/2017/8/18/16170400/bannon-fired-trump-administration.

[465] Retrieved from: https://www.washingtonpost.com/politics/the-epic-and-bizarre-first-110-days-of-the-trump-presidency/2017/05/10/4d0b85ca-3593-11e7-b373-418f6849a004_story.html?utm_term=.9a4f49c37b8a.

warning at a recent senior staff meeting [in mid-May]: Quit trying to secretly slip stuff to President Donald Trump.

Just days earlier, K.T. McFarland, the deputy national security adviser, had given Trump a printout of two Time magazine covers. One, supposedly from the 1970s, warned of a coming ice age; the other, from 2008, about surviving global warming, according to four White House officials familiar with the matter.

Trump quickly got lathered up about the media's hypocrisy. But there was a problem. The 1970s cover was fake, part of an internet hoax that's circulated for years.[466] Staff chased down the truth and intervened before Trump tweeted or talked publicly about it.

The episode illustrates the impossible mission of managing a White House led by an impetuous president who has resisted structure and strictures his entire adult life.[467]

Moreover:

While the information stream to past commanders in chief has been tightly monitored, Trump prefers an open Oval Office with a free flow of ideas and inputs from both official and unofficial channels. And he often does not differentiate between the two. Aides sometimes slip him stories to press their advantage on policy; other times they do so to gain an edge in the seemingly endless *Game of Thrones*[468] inside the West Wing.

The consequences can be tremendous, according to a half-dozen White House officials and others with direct

---

[466] See: http://science.time.com/2013/06/06/sorry-a-time-magazine-cover-did-not-predict-a-coming-ice-age/.

[467] Retrieved from: http://www.politico.com/story/2017/05/15/donald-trump-fake-news-238379.I

[468] See: http://www.imdb.com/title/tt0944947/.

interactions with the president. A news story tucked into Trump's hands at the right moment can torpedo an appointment or redirect the president's entire agenda.

Current and former Trump officials say Trump can react volcanically to negative press clips, especially those with damaging leaks, becoming engrossed in finding out where they originated.[469]

Rumors abound:

Priebus [as White House Chief of Staff] and White House staff secretary Rob Porter have tried to implement a system to manage and document the paperwork Trump receives. While some see the new structure as a power play by a weakened chief of staff—"He'd like to get a phone log too," cracked one senior White House adviser—others are more concerned about the unfettered ability of Trump's family-member advisers, Jared Kushner[470] and daughter Ivanka[471], to ply the president with whatever paperwork they want in the residence sight unseen.

"They have this system in place to get things on his desk now," the same White House official said. "I'm not sure anyone follows it."

Priebus has implored staff to do so in order to abide by presidential record-keeping laws, which require cataloguing what the president sees for the archives.[472]

This brings to mind, life in the courts of Renaissance princes (Machiavelli [1513] 1961). The courtiers would each push their own secret agenda and would they each jockey for power and status, by presenting their

---

[469]   Retrieved from: http://www.politico.com/story/2017/05/15/donald-trump-fake-news-238379.

[470]   See: http://time.com/collection/2017-time-100/4742700/jared-kushner/. See also https://www.cnbc.com/jared-kushner/.

[471]   See: http://time.com/ivanka-trump-pictures-photographs/. See also: http://www.independent.co.uk/topic/ivanka-trump.

[472]   Retrieved from: http://www.politico.com/story/2017/05/15/donald-trump-fake-news-238379.

views and proposals in terms what is personally beneficial to their Prince. Palace intrigues become both the norm and an obsession.

Trump always adopts a hyper-competitive stance toward others in order to have power over them, thereby creating diffuse hostile interpersonal tensions. This has created White House that is in accord with Morgan's (1986) "psychic prisons"—one in which its staff are trapped in a particular cognitively and emotionally dominant organizational mindset of keeping the president happy at any cost. So, suppositions about the president's impetuous wishes fuel perceptions and perceptions fuel emotions in a way that does not allow them to see organizational reality clearly from any other perspective. Thus, it has become an organization that is in accord with Morgan's (1986) instruments of domination—one that glorifies Trump at the expense of festering hostility that feeds his need to sacrifice any staff member who evidences the slightest hint of disloyalty. The resultant organizational culture is one that tolerates, if not encourages, manipulation, exploitation, bullying, and public humiliation; and so encourages infighting between the warring factions—and there may well be as many as six of them[473]—and acts of disloyalty.

Of course, Trump is always seeking evidence of disloyalty. One tactic he uses is to give his trusted senior officials an opportunity to reconfirm their pledge of loyalty in the presence of their peers, as he did at his first full Cabinet meeting[474]: "They came to praise President Donald Trump, not focus on the controversies engulfing him."[475] He has also done this prior making a major announcement.[476] It matters not to his trusted senior officials that such behavior is reinforcing Trump's self-delusions. Another tactic is to demand that senior officials sign an *ex post facto* pre-drafted memo supportive of one of his decision:

---

[473] See: http://www.independent.co.uk/voices/bannon-fired-trump-breitbart-work-already-done-embrace-white-nationalists-a7901416.html.

[474] See: https://www.theguardian.com/us-news/2017/jun/12/donald-trump-first-cabinet-meting-praise. But see also: https://www.theguardian.com/us-news/video/2017/jun/13/trump-trolled-by-democrats-after-staff-take-turns-praising-the-president-video; http://www.reuters.com/article/us-usa-trump-cabinet-idUSKBN19400P.

[475] Retrieved from: http://www.reuters.com/article/us-usa-trump-cabinet-idUSK BN19400P.

[476] See: http://edition.cnn.com/2017/06/03/opinions/inexhaustible-egos-of-donald-trump-and-hillary-clinton-opinion-dantonio/index.html.

> A maddening type of official document has emerged
> as a tool of the Trump Administration. This document
> [drafted by the White House for subsequent signature
> by senior officials] is short and inadequate to its stated
> task: providing a rational basis for a highly suspect ex-
> ecutive decision. Often, the document contradicts the
> words or actions of the President himself.[477]

It matter not to his trusted senior officials that by putting their names
on such documents, they are "signing away one of the rule of law's last
defenses."[478]

Any hint of disloyalty feeds Trump's proclivity for presidential witch-
hunts. This, in turn, feeds his paranoia in a way that demands retribution. It diverts his and others energies, so making the White House
dysfunctional, thereby weakening his power.[479] The likely suspects
would, of course, be traitors within—disloyal White House staff—
and those in the "shadowy network of Obama holdovers that constitute the 'deep state.'"[480]

As Dan Rather, the iconic former CBS News anchor,[481] notes of the
Trump White House: "Even the most grounded of presidents must fight
to keep themselves moored to the real world. The Oval Office can be
a bubble. Power attracts sycophants and cynics. But I have never seen
anything like this."[482] The personal impact of Trump's paranoid style of

---

477 Retrieved from: http://www.newyorker.com/news/news-desk/the-bogus-
     memos-of-the-trump-administration.

478 Retrieved from: http://www.newyorker.com/news/news-desk/the-bogus-
     memos-of-the-trump-administration.

479 See: https://www.theguardian.com/commentisfree/2017/apr/06/donald-
     trump-weak-paranoid-president-government.

480 Retrieved from: http://www.telegraph.co.uk/news/2017/03/11/deep-state-
     shadowy-network-obama-holdovers-undermining-donald/; see also http://
     google.com/newsstand/s/CBIwj628vDk; see also: http://www.telegraph.
     co.uk/news/2017/03/11/deep-state-shadowy-network-obama-holdovers-
     undermining-donald/; see also http://google.com/newsstand/s/CBIwj628vDk.

481 See: http://www.politico.com/magazine/story/2017/04/26/dan-rather-
     comeback-facebook-donald-trump-215050.

482 Retrieved from: http://www.independent.co.uk/news/world/americas/us-
     politics/donald-trump-dan-rather-paranoia-untenable-cbs-anchor-working-
     republic-us-president-white-house-a7617316.html.

politics[483]—by no means a style that is new to America[484]—is becoming apparent. One of Trump's friends is reported to have said in early June "He now lives within himself, which is a dangerous place for Donald Trump to be. I see him emotionally withdrawing. He's gained weight. He doesn't have anybody whom he trusts."[485] This has been made worse by the resignation in late September of his "wing man"—his "emotional anchor" and "security blanket"—Keith Schiller, who had been his chief security officer for 18 years.[486] Indeed, in early October it was reported:

> A cadre of White House insiders and close associates of President Donald Trump have painted a grim picture of an increasingly volatile Trump, who in the past few weeks has found himself at the center of near-constant battles that have frequently spilled out into the public ... One person close to Trump likened the president to a "pressure cooker," according to The [Washington] Post.
>
> The ongoing tirades—covering his displeasure with people he considers disloyal, outrage over media coverage, and more—show no signs of ending. And that has prompted some of Trump's allies and detractors to question his capacity to fulfill his duties as president. "He concerns me," [Senator Bob] Corker said, according to the [New York] Times. "He would have to concern anyone who cares about our nation."[487]

The impact of Trump's paranoid style of politics on the White House depends crucially, on the responses of the mandarins—the public officials—and courtiers—the sycophants. Their willingness to cooperate rather than to compete and defend themselves has not been much in evidence. The *Washington Post* reported, within days of Trump's inauguration: "The turbulence and competing factions that were a hallmark of Trump's campaign have been transported to the White House."[488] As has been observed:

---

483 See: https://hanskundnani.com/2017/03/19/trump-and-the-paranoid-style/; https://twitter.com/nfergus.

484 See: https://harpers.org/archive/1964/11/the-paranoid-style-in-american-politics/.

485 Retrieved from: http://edition.cnn.com/2017/06/03/opinions/inexhaustible-egos-of-donald-trump-and-hillary-clinton-opinion-dantonio/index.html.

486 Retrieved from: https://www.thetimes.co.uk/article/donald-trump-left-isolated-as-his-security-blanket-quits-b6xbjkrl7.

487 Retrieved from: http://www.businessinsider.com/trump-behavior-in-white-house-bob-corker-tillerson-tweets-feuds-2017-10. See also: https://www.youtube.com/watch?v=zaZznShmxnc.

488 Retrieved from: http://www.independent.co.uk/news/world/americas/us-

Rivalries over ideas can be healthy. Dissent over issues provokes debate and ideally deliberation. Rivalries among people spark animus, and that can be destructive to individuals and ultimately the organization.[489]

The tone of the Trump administration had been set;[490] but it is one that would have worried the Master of Deceit and Intrigue:

> I do not believe that factions can ever be of use; rather it is certain that when the enemy comes upon you in divided cities you are quickly lost, because the weakest party will always assist the outside force and the others will not be able to resist (Machiavelli [1513] 2011, 94).

On Paranoia and Factionalism

Trump's paranoia is undoubtedly having its effect on his administration—distrust breeds distrust—making chaos the natural state of the White House. Rule by chaos prevails. It has been reported that

> in the White House, Trump has failed to unite his team ... around an organizing principle that is larger than defending the president's own reputation. Without a common purpose, factions feel the need to leak against one another.[491]

So, White House senior officials and staff are looking over their shoulders, to see if Trump is still happy with them, fearing that they may be the next to be blamed or punished for his faults or incompetence. Trump, of course, blames those around him when things are not going to plan. Reportedly, "Trump fumes at staff yesterday [March 4] [because they allowed the media to focus too much on Attorney General Jeff Sessions alleged meeting with Russian officials and so not enough on him].

politics/donald-trump-white-house-infighting-tweet-us-news-media-fake-news-michael-flynn-reince-priebus-steve-a7616486.html.

[489] Retrieved from: https://newsstand.google.com/articles/CAIiEGtR133yHzrVa VkPOfeYteIqFQgEKg0IACoGCAowrqkBMKBFMKGBAg.

[490] See: https://www.vox.com/policy-and-politics/2017/5/19/15662842/trump-leaks-stop.

[491] Retrieved from: http://www.politico.com/magazine/story/2017/07/27/anthony-scaramucci-leaks-215429.

When things aren't going well, Trump never shoulders blame."[492] The following reported incident, if true, is also insightful:

> When Trump bellows about this or that story, his aides often scramble in a game of cat and mouse to figure out who alerted the president to the piece in the first place given that he rarely browses the internet on his own. Some in the White House describe getting angry calls from the president and then hustling over to Trump's personal secretary, Madeleine Westerhout, to ferret who exactly had just paid a visit to the Oval Office and possibly set Trump off.[493]

Not surprising, then, that POLITICO Pro, a European-based policy news service,[494] concluded in early March that "[a] culture of paranoia is consuming the Trump administration, with staffers increasingly pre-occupied with perceived enemies—inside their own government ... It's an environment of fear that has hamstrung the routine functioning of the executive branch."[495] Suspicions are rife: "that rival factions in the administration are trying to embarrass them, that civil servants opposed to President Donald Trump are trying to undermine him, and even that a 'deep state' of career military and intelligence officials is out to destroy them."[496] A culture of fear is growing.[497]

One life-and-death political struggle within the White House has been between US National Security Advisor, Lieutenant General H.R McMaster[498]

---

[492]   Retrieved from: https://twitter.com/maggieNYT/status/838245079802331136; see also: https://www.indy100.com/article/twitter-anecdote-donald-trump-7612076.

[493]   Retrieved from: http://www.politico.com/story/2017/05/15/donald-trump-fake-news-238379.

[494]   See: http://www.politico.com/pro.

[495]   Retrieved from: http://www.politico.com/story/2017/03/trump-white-house-paranoia-236069; See also: https://www.theguardian.com/us-news/2017/aug/13/donald-trump-white-house-steve-bannon-rich-higgins.

[496]   Retrieved from: http://www.politico.com/story/2017/03/trump-white-house-paranoia-236069.

[497]   See: https://www.forbes.com/forbes/welcome/?toURL=https://www.forbes.com/sites/cartoonoftheday/2017/07/23/why-the-trump-administration-win-an-emmy-for-house-of-cards/

[498]   See: https://www.hoover.org/profiles/h-r-mcmaster.

and Steve Bannon.[499] At stake is the survival of Trump's Bannon-inspired ethnic and economic nationalism agenda. Bannon seemed willing to use organizational guerrilla warfare tactics (such as, fabricated leaks, rumors, and character assassination) to destroy McMaster,[500] who he considered to be a "globalist", one of those conspiring to subvert Trump's presidency:[501]

> This is not politics as usual but rather political warfare at an unprecedented level that is openly engaged in the direct targeting of a seated president through manipulation of the news cycle ... Recognizing in candidate Trump an existential threat to cultural Marxist memes that dominate the prevailing cultural narrative, those that benefit recognize the threat he poses and seek his destruction.[502]

This factional in-fighting solicited an inflammatory seven-page memo entitled *POTUS* [President of the United States] *& Political Warfare* drafted and circulated in May by Rich Higgins,[503] the now former director for strategic planning for the National Security Council.[504] Higgins, who was "widely regarded as a Flynn [Trump's initial US National Security Advisor] loyalist who dislikes McMaster and his team," warned, in conspiratorial, apocalyptic, and overtly political language, that "...many close to the president have pushed him off his [alt-right] message when he was candidate Trump thus alienating him from his base thereby iso-

---

499   See: http://theweek.com/speedreads/718185/white-house-struggle-between-stephen-bannon-hr-mcmaster-apparently-coming-head.

500   See: http://theweek.com/speedreads/718185/white-house-struggle-between-stephen-bannon-hr-mcmaster-apparently-coming-head; see also http://www.cbsnews.com/news/john-mccain-calls-alt-right-attacks-on-h-r-mcmaster-disgraceful/. See also: https://www.wsj.com/articles/steve-bannon-on-politics-as-war-1479513161.

501   Retrieved from: http://www.businessinsider.com/heres-the-memo-that-blew-up-the-national-security-council-2017-8.

502   Retrieved from: https://www.nytimes.com/2017/08/11/us/politics/rich-higgins-memo-national-security-council.html?rref=collection%2Ftimestopic%2FNational%20Security%20Council&action=click&contentCollection=timestopics&region=stream&module=stream_unit&version=latest&contentPlacement=1&pgtype=collection.

503   See: https://www.scribd.com/document/356073046/Political-Warfare-NSC-memo#from_embed; http://foreignpolicy.com/2017/08/10/heres-the-memo-that-blew-up-the-nsc/.

504   See: https://www.whitehouse.gov/nsc.

lating him in the process ... When President Trump is not candidate Trump, he becomes dangerously exposed."[505] There are, Higgins intuitively knew, dark forces conspiring to remove Trump from the presidency with a view to imposing on the America "cultural Marxism"—a neo-Marxist plot to destroy capitalism from within, by advocating socially unnecessary constraints on individual freedom and, ultimately, the domination of the individual by the social, which means that anyone with progressive tendencies is presumed to be secret Communist.[506] This conspiratorial cabal includes hard leftist—Democrats, "deep state" government workers, globalists, bankers, Islamist and establishment Republicans, and even the Muslim Brotherhood,[507] the Council on American-Islamic Relations,[508] the American Civil Liberties Union,[509] Black Lives Matter,[510] and the United Nations[511]. The dilemma for Trump in late July was that he probably had to choose between McMaster, who, he apparently thinks, talks too much,[512] or Bannon, who could save him with his alt-right support base, but at what cost;[513] he could not have both.[514] Bannon's resignation was accepted in August.

---

[505] Retrieved from: https://www.nytimes.com/2017/08/11/us/politics/rich-higgins-memo-national-security-council.html?rref=collection%2Ftimestopic%2FNational%20Security%20Council&action=click&content Collection=timestopics&region=stream&module=stream_unit&version=latest&contentPlacement=1&pgtype=collection.

[506] See: http://knowyourmeme.com/memes/cultural-marxism.

[507] See: http://www.ikhwanweb.com/. But see also: https://www.theguardian.com/world/2011/feb/08/egypt-muslim-brotherhood-uncovered; https://www.washingtonpost.com/news/monkey-cage/wp/2016/03/07/is-the-muslim-brotherhood-a-terrorist-organization-or-a-firewall-against-violent-extremism/?utm_term=.14a7d122030d.

[508] See: https://www.cair.com/. But see also: http://www.meforum.org/916/cair-islamists-fooling-the-establishment; http://www.nationalreview.com/article/393614/cair-terror-group-daniel-pipes.

[509] See: https://www.aclu.org/.

[510] See: http://blacklivesmatter.com/. But see also: https://www.newyorker.com/magazine/2016/03/14/where-is-black-lives-matter-headed.

[511] See: https://www.nytimes.com/2017/08/11/us/politics/rich-higgins-memo-national-security-council.html?mcubz=3.

[512] See: http://www.newsweek.com/trump-mcmaster-israel-russia-fired-national-security-adviser-jared-kushner-616735.

[513] See: https://www.vanityfair.com/news/2016/08/breitbart-stephen-bannon-donald-trump-master-plan.

[514] See: https://www.nytimes.com/2017/07/29/us/politics/trump-presidency-setbacks.html?mtrref=undefined&gwh=02CFD587545D8DEE00F43FD38D72F69D&gwt=pay.

The conclusion to be drawn is the obvious one. "It's an environment [in the White House] of fear that has hamstrung the routine functioning of the executive branch ... the degree of suspicion had created a toxicity that is unsustainable."[515] Trump, of course, has denied that there is any White House infighting—"Don't let the FAKE NEWS tell you that there is big infighting in the Trump Admin. We are getting along great, and getting major things done."[516] It may well be that an infighting culture[517] is to his liking, because, according to his biographer, Tim O'Brien (*TrumpNation: The Art of Being the Donald*)[518]: "He's the emperor of chaos."[519] Trump, in his co-authored—ghost-authored—best-selling book *Trump: The Art of the Deal*[520] (1987)—said "I play it very loose... I try not to schedule too many meetings. I leave my door open ... I prefer to come to work each day and just see what develops."[521]

Indeed, Trump has a history of overseeing pressure-cooker organizations rife with suspicion, setting up sophisticated surveillance[522] in part to monitor employees at his properties, including at his campaign headquarters, where some campaign aides suspected their offices were bugged[523].[524] So, he deliberately encouraged rivalries:

> He named Priebus [as White House Chief of Staff]
> and Steve Bannon [as White House Chief Strategist]

515 Retrieved from: http://www.politico.com/story/2017/03/trump-white-house-paranoia-236069.

516 Retrieved from: http://www.independent.co.uk/news/world/americas/us-politics/donald-trump-white-house-infighting-tweet-us-news-media-fake-news-michael-flynn-reince-priebus-steve-a7616486.

517 See: https://www.theguardian.com/us-news/2017/jul/29/winners-losers-white-house-warring-factions.

518 See: https://www.amazon.com/TrumpNation-Donald-Timothy-L-OBrien/dp/0446578541.

519 Retrieved from: https://www.nytimes.com/2017/02/18/opinion/sunday/trapped-in-trumps-brain.html.

520 See: https://www.amazon.co.uk/Trump-Art-Deal-Donald-J/dp/0399594493.

521 Retrieved from: http://edition.cnn.com/2017/07/31/opinions/white-house-shakeup-opinion-louis/index.html.

522 Retrieved from: http://www.politico.com/story/2017/03/trump-white-house-paranoia-236069.

523 Retrieved from: https://www.nytimes.com/2016/05/28/us/politics/donald-trump-campaign.html?_r=1.

524 Retrieved from: http://www.politico.com/story/2017/03/trump-white-house-paranoia-236069.

as co-equal advisors, neatly undercutting the authority of the role [of Chief of Staff]. The President also allows selected aides and cronies—including White House counselor Kellyanne Conway, former Apprentice contestant Omarosa Manigault, and communications aide Hope Hicks—to walk into the Oval Office whenever they choose.[525]

Yet it is evident that "Trump was mad—steaming, raging mad"[526] about the leaks, setbacks, and accusations he has experienced. As the *Washington Post* reported on August 19:[527]

Trump's young presidency has existed in a perpetual state of chaos ... At the center of the turmoil is an impatient president increasingly frustrated by his administration's inability to erase the impression that his campaign was engaged with Russia, to stem leaks about both national security matters and internal discord and to implement any signature achievements.

Of concern to Dan Rather, the former CBS News anchor, is:

The sheer level of paranoia that is radiating out of the White House is untenable to the workings of a republic...I have a real question if President Trump actually believes what he is saying. Even Richard Nixon, the most paranoid president to date, ruled for years with a relatively calm hand...This Administration has been an off kilter whirlwind since the inauguration, and news reports suggest that seething anger from Mr. Trump is only getting

---

[525] Retrieved from: http://edition.cnn.com/2017/07/31/opinions/white-house-shakeup-opinion-louis/index.html.

[526] Retrieved from: https://www.washingtonpost.com/politics/inside-trumps-fury-the-president-rages-at-leaks-setbacks-and-accusations/2017/03/05/40713af4-01df-11e7-ad5b-d22680e18d10_story.html?utm_term=.460250cd1735.

[527] "This account of the administration's tumultuous recent days is based on interviews with 17 top White House officials, members of Congress and friends of the president, many of whom requested anonymity to speak candidly." Retrieved from: https://www.washingtonpost.com/politics/inside-trumps-fury-the-president-rages-at-leaks-setbacks-and-accusations/2017/03/05/40713af4-01df-11e7-ad5b-d22680e18d10_story.html?utm_term=.460250cd1735.

worse ... There is a growing consensus that the President may be "unhinged." It's a serious allegation, but even if it is not the case, Mr. Trump only has himself to blame.[528]

General John Kelly,[529] Priebus's replacement as White House Chief of Staff, in late July, undoubtedly inherited a nightmare organization—"a [White House] West Wing that has set a new standard for chaos, back-stabbing, factionalism, and inefficacy"[530]—with a near impossible pres-idential-granted remit of reducing its disfunctionality. He has, however, managed to gain of control over all White House staff, including, Trump's daughter Ivanka—dubbed the "Princess Royal" by some White House aids[531]—and her husband, Jared Kushner. This was a decision by Trump that, according to his biographer, Michael D'Antonio, is suggestive: "for a man who prizes loyalty and surrounds himself with family instead of those with policy expertise ... [this] further speaks to a sense of inner panic."[532]

So, Kelly controls who enters the Oval Office and what documents Trump reads. He has also pushed "incendiary rightwingers such as Bannon and British-born Sabastian Gorka, a national security advisor, out of the White House."[533] This pleased Republicans.[534] Managing

---

[528] Retrieved from: http://www.independent.co.uk/news/world/americas/us-politics/donald-trump-dan-rather-paranoia-untenable-cbs-anchor-working-republic-us-president-white-house-a7617316.html.

[529] See: http://www.businessinsider.com/who-is-john-kelly-marine-general-homeland-security-white-house-chief-of-staff-2017-8; http://www.cosmopolitan.com/politics/a8475057/john-kelly-homeland-security/.

[530] Retrieved from: https://www.theatlantic.com/politics/archive/2017/07/prie bus-kelly/535338/.

[531] Retrieved from: http://www.newsweek.com/ivanka-trump-secretly-referred-princess-royal-white-house-aides-according-656339. See also: http://uk. businessinsider.com/white-house-aides-ivanka-trump-nickname-princess-royal-2017-8;http://www.independent.co.uk/news/world/americas/us-politics/ivanka-trump-nickname-princess-royale-white-house-aides-nepotism-a7919266.htmlhttp://www.telegraph.co.uk/news/2017/08/29/ivanka-trump-dubbed-princess-royal-washington-enemies/.

[532] Retrieved from: http://edition.cnn.com/2017/08/01/opinions/trump-military-men-kelly-opinion-dantoo/index.html.

[533] Retrieved from: https://www.thetimes.co.uk/article/donald-trump-left-isolated-as-his-security-blanket-quits-b6xbjkrl7.

[534] See: https://www.nytimes.com/2017/08/11/us/politics/rich-higgins-memo-national-security-council.html?mcubz=3; https://www.mediaite.com/tv/richard-painter-demands-trump-fire-seb-gorka-and-steve-bannon-over-charlottesville-violence/.

upward, however, is undoubtedly his biggest challenge.[535] At issue is whether he can ever deal with a president that never struggles to control his impulses. *Newsweek* reported on August 29 an interview with Gorka:

> "He's definitely asserted control as one would expect from a military professional," Gorka said of Kelly. "The key unknown is whether his style will comport with the president's expectations and own style." ...

> "The president currently feels, to a certain extent, isolated," Gorka said of Trump. "Individuals don't have access to him as they did in the past." ...

> "So we know General Kelly wanted to impose a certain regimen on the system. But there are aspects of the new regime that the president is not satisfied with, let me leave it at that."[536]

And *The Times*, quoting a Trump administration source, reported on September 10:

> General Kelly is doing a sterling job but he may end up being a victim of his own success. He is managing to tame President Trump in the short term but ultimately President Trump is not a man who will allow himself to be tamed.

A Republican close to the White House was reported by *CNN* [*Cable News Network*] 10 days later as saying: "He [Kelly] doesn't care how long he stays. That's what makes him effective—for now", which leaves open "whether—or how soon—Trump will chafe under Kelly's stern hand."[537]

The Economist has drawn the obvious conclusion that "Donald Trump has no grasp of what it means to be president—U-turns, self-regard and

---

535 See: https://www.forbes.com/sites/brookmanville/2017/08/06/management-and-leadership-in-trumps-presidency/#780e404e7ac1.

536 Retrieved from: http://www.newsweek.com/kelly-trump-isolated-gorka-white-house-656639.

537 Retrieved from: http://edition.cnn.com/2017/09/20/politics/john-kelly-donald-trump-oval-office-access/index.html

equivocation are not what it takes."[538]

On Tweets and Policy Scripts

Oborne and Roberts (2017, 2) observed that Twitter allowed Trump during his presidential campaign:

> to appeal at a personal level to anyone who is against anything and make him or her feel like part of a vast shared community without having to meet or even acknowledge any of its other members. ... [and he] viscerally understood the power of this new medium to simplify complex ideas, to remove nuance and subtext and, above all, to remove any boundary between assertion and fact.

For Trump, every day is a new day with new challenges to his fragile ego. So, it offers countless distractions and irresistible urges in his holy twitter fingers.[539] He justifies his tweeting on the grounds that he keeping in touch with his community of followers—his tribe. So, he inundates the world with the thoughts that pass through his mind from time-to-time, frequently as responses to perceived personal slights and affronts, as put-downs of those with whom he is a personal dispute, or as brags, inevitably overstating his achievements, possessions, or abilities. He cares not that airing such undisciplined presidential thoughts not only reveal his quick temper—and his willingness to use his status to bully even the powerless—but also can be unsettling to both friend and foe alike.

Trump's communications preoccupation is with creating an illusory world, one that accords with his will to power, is impervious to reality, and is understandable to those who share his commitment to keeping complexity short and simple. However, it is a virtual world about which he makes outlandish statements that he would like to be able to dismiss

---

[538] Retrieved from: https://www.economist.com/news/leaders/21726696-u-turns-self-regard-and-equivocation-are-not-what-it-takes-donald-trump-has-no-grasp-what-it?frsc=dg%7Ce

[539] See: https://twitter.com/realDonaldTrump?ref_src=twsrc%5Egoogle%7Ctwc amp%5Eserp%7Ctwgr%5Eauthor. But see also: http://www.trumptwitterarchive .com/; https://www.wired.com/2017/06/asked-lawyers-vet-trumps-controversial-tweets/.

subsequently as irrelevant simply because they were tweeted: "In other words, the president's Twitter voice is an unreliable narrator[540]."[541] Phelan (2005, 34–37) identifies six types of unreliable narratives, which fall into two categories:

- *statements that are wrong*—misreporting, misinterpreting, and misevaluating; and
- *statements that are insufficient or incomplete*—underreporting, underinterpreting, and underregarding (disregarding).

Trump continues to tweet, despite the negative popular reaction his tweeting has induced—a *FoxNews* poll in late June suggests that 77% of voters believe his tweets are hurting his agenda[542]—and despite criticism from some in his own party. For example, Senator Ben Sasse (Republican–Nebraska): "Please just stop. This isn't normal and it's beneath the dignity of your office." Indeed, his irresistible urge to tweet belies any sense of presidential composure. As John Baldoni,[543] a writer on leadership and an executive coach, has observed:

> Composure—an ability to maintain a sense of calm and equanimity—is integral to leadership. An executive who cannot control his temper is someone to avoid. They create chaos and confusion and soon enough lose the respect of their peers as well as their direct reports.[544]

Keeping Trump focused on message, and so prioritizing the implementing of his campaign promises, has proved to be an enormous challenge for both Trump and his administration. It is one made more difficult because his campaign promises remain vacuous—and his rhetorical flourishes have become tired and repetitive—because they have not yet been converted into policy scripts—concrete goals, desired outcomes, plausible benefits, possible strategies, and realistic enactment and im-

---

[540] Booth (1961) first coined this term.

[541] Retrieved from: http://www.thedailybeast.com/trumps-twitter-problemand-ours.

[542] See: http://www.foxnews.com/politics/2017/06/29/fox-news-poll-voters-say-trumps-tweets-hurting-agenda.html.

[543] See: http://www.johnbaldoni.com/blog/; http://thinkers50.com/john-baldoni-video-blog/.

[544] Retrieved from: https://www.forbes.com/sites/johnbaldoni/2017/05/12/president-trump-knows-no-composure/#75148d66f014.

plementation timelines—for transmission to his germane political supporters and to the relevant stakeholders in policy communities and networks,[545] whose support he needs for their successful execution.

On Leaks and Whistle-blowing

Leaks—the intentional public disclosure of information deemed to be secret or confidential[546]— or, more fittingly, whistle-blowing—the intentional public disclosure of information or activity occurring in an organization that has been kept secret because it is deemed to be illegal, unethical, or simply not true[547]—generally fall into five categories: personal, political, bureaucratic, policy, and authorized. And, of course, as Weber (1946, 233) observed:

> Every bureaucracy strives to increase the superiority of its position by keeping its knowledge and intentions secret. Bureaucratic administration always seeks to evade the light of the public as best it can, because in so doing it shields its knowledge and conduct from criticism ...

Leaks are, quite clearly, a preoccupation with the secretive Trump,[548] particularly as they tend to be mostly personal, political, or bureaucratic in nature, and so, in his mind, reflect poorly on him.

On February 16, during a lengthy press conference at the White House, Trump said about the recent flood of White House media leaks:

> The leaks are real. You're the one who wrote about them and reported them. The leaks are real.

---

[545] The term "policy community" refers to the set of public and private actors who coalesce around a policy issue area and who share a common interest in shaping its development. This can be bifurcated into the attentive public, with its active watching brief on developments, and the sub-government, those actors actively engaged in policy design or implementation. The term policy network depicts the structural or power relationship between the actors in the sub-government sector of a policy community (Pross 1986; Coleman and Skogstad 1990).

[546] See: https://en.oxforddictionaries.com/definition/leak.

[547] See: https://www.transparency.org/topic/detail/whistleblowing//.

[548] He posted 86 "fake news" tweets between January 10 and July 24, See: http://www.trumptwitterarchive.com/.

The leaks are absolutely real. The news is fake because so much of the news is fake.[549]

But on May 28 he tweeted:

It is my opinion that many of the leaks coming out of the White House are fabricated lies made up by the #Fake-News media ... Whenever you see the words "sources say" in the fake news media, and they don't mention names ... it is very possible that those sources don't exist but are made up by fake news writers. #FakeNews is the enemy![550]

The anonymous leaking of information critical of Trump, or an opposing faction within his White House, to the "fake news" media is taken to be a manifestation of disloyalty. But, as has been observed:

Trump's White House is not leaky because of a few bad apples. The No. 1 reason why it leaks is because his team lacks unity ... The leaks are also the result of deep disloyalty, for which the president has only himself to blame ... If Trump wants loyalty from his Cabinet and staff, he must recognize that loyalty is a two-way street and show them more respect than he has to date ... Finally, even if the team is loyal and united, a political organization that does not promote self-discipline will always suffer from leaks ... the president's tweets and interviews show a lack of discipline ... In this environment, it's not realistic to expect discipline from staff when the boss sets a poor example.[551]

Trump's frustration is, of course, understandable.[552] He seemed, by late

---

[549] Retrieved from: http://thehill.com/homenews/administration/319939-trump-the-leaks-are-real-the-news-is-fake; http://www.independent.co.uk/news/world/americas/us-politics/donald-trump-russia-leaks-fake-news-claims-quote-a7584516.html.

[550] Retrieved from: http://thehill.com/homenews/administration/335453-trump-many-leaks-are-fabricated-lies-made-up-by-fake-news-media.

[551] Retrieved from: http://www.politico.com/magazine/story/2017/07/27/anthony-scaramucci-leaks-215429.

[552] Retrieved from: http://www.politico.com/magazine/story/2017/07/27/ant

July, to be in panic mode over leaks.[553] This is why he recruited Anthony Scaramucci[554]—"the Mooch"[555]—as Mike Dubke's[556] replacement
as Director of Communications. Scaramucci was seen as Trump's
"tough-talking alter ego who would ferociously fight for him the way
others had not."[557] His job was to stem the flow of leaks.[558] Scaramucci saw off Sean Spicer (White House Press Secretary), who Trump
has, since his inauguration, constantly second-guessed, routinely
contradicted him, and regularly expressed unhappiness with his performance.[559] He also saw off Reince Priebus (White House Chief of
Staff),[560] who was "a technocrat and consummate [Republican] party
man"[561] and who "[t]ried to present a united front with Bannon but ...
he is losing a power struggle".[562] Scaramucci was, however, soon seen
off by Priebus's replacement, General John Kelly. Within days, Scaramucci went too far in an epic media rant[563] using foal language and

hony-scaramucci-leaks-215429.

553 See: http://edition.cnn.com/2017/08/01/opinions/trump-military-men-kelly-
opinion-dantonio/index.html.

554 See: https://www.facebook.com/ascaramucci/. See also: http://fortune.com
/2017/09/28/anthony-scaramucci-news-site/; https://www.theguardian.com/
us-news/2017/oct/03/anthony-scaramucci-post-media-company.

555 Retrieved from: https://www.vanityfair.com/style/2017/09/anthony-scaramucci-
spreading-white-house-rumors-on-tmz-live.

556 See: https://finance.yahoo.com/news/white-house-communications-director-
resigns-amid-tensions-131134100--politics.html; https://www.theguardian.com/us-
news/2017/jul/31/trump-administration-firings-resignations-anthony-scaramucci.

557 See: https://www.nytimes.com/2017/07/31/us/politics/trump-white-house-
obamacare-health.html.

558 See: https://www.vox.com/vox-sentences/2017/8/4/16100150/vox-sentences-
sessions-trump-leaks.

559 See: https://www.bostonglobe.com/metro/2017/06/20/replacing-spicer-
wouldn-just-job-change-but-cultural-moment/iH8TF1nJN3A2I7snIInLsJ/story.
html;http://fortune.com/2017/05/18/trump-spicer-press/; http://fortune.
com/2017/05/18/trump-spicer-press/;http://fortune.com/2017/05/18/trump-
spicer-press/;https://www.theguardian.com/us-news/2017/mar/08/trump-
wiretapping-obama-russia-sean-spicer-response.

560 See: http://www.telegraph.co.uk/news/2017/07/21/anthony-scaramucci-new-
white-house-communications-director-edged/.

561 Retrieved from: https://www.theguardian.com/us-news/2016/nov/19/stephen-
bannon-jared-kushner-reince-priebus-trump-administration.

562 Retrieved from: https://www.theguardian.com/us-news/2017/mar/10/donal
d-trump-first-50-days-white-house-administration; See also: https://www.
theguardian.com/us-news/2016/nov/19/stephen-bannon-jared-kushner-
reince-priebus-trump-administration.

563 See: https://www.thesun.co.uk/news/4117622/donald-trumps-new-pr-

criticizing senior White House staff.[564] He was fired 10 days after his appointment.[565]

It would seem that the entire White House staff are preoccupied with leaks.[566] It has been reported that there is one widespread concern in the Trump White House: that "career intelligence operatives are working to undermine the new president through a series of leaks of classified information."[567] Another concern was expressed by a White House aid: "I do think there's a concerted effort to disrupt us," the aide said. "We're professional, we're courteous. But it's a one-way street. They [anti-Trump staffers] are out to hurt the administration, and you have to handle yourself accordingly."[568] So:

> Aides are going to great lengths to protect themselves. They're turning off work-issued smartphones and putting them in drawers when they arrive home from work out of fear that they could be used to eavesdrop. They're staying mum in meetings [not telling anyone anything] out of concern that their comments could be leaked to the press by foes. ... Some rank-and-file White House aides, meanwhile, have become convinced that intelligence agents may be monitoring their phone calls, emails, and text messages.[569]

The perception among some White House staff is that monitoring is so widespread that it has engendered even greater suspicion and anxiety. "We've got strict instructions not to talk to talk to the press," said one

---

chief-anthony-the-mooch-scaramucci-launches-into-epic-rant-saying-he-wants-to-kill-paranoid-schizophrenic-white-hous/; https://www.nytimes.com/2017/07/31/us/politics/trump-white-house-obamacare-health.html; but definitely see: leaks.html?mtrref=www.nytimes.com&gwh=0DF426302D25E69B37D63266DE25262A&gwt=pay.

564 See: https://www.nytimes.com/2017/07/27/us/politics/scaramucci-priebus-.

565 But see: https://www.theguardian.com/us-news/2017/oct/03/anthony-scaramucci-post-media-company#img-1.

566 See: https://en.oxforddictionaries.com/definition/leak.

567 Retrieved from: http://www.politico.com/story/2017/03/trump-white-house-paranoia-236069.

568 Retrieved from: http://www.politico.com/story/2017/03/trump-white-house-paranoia-236069.

569 Retrieved from: http://www.politico.com/story/2017/03/trump-white-house-paranoia-236069.

White House aide. "I assume I would get fired immediately."[570] Or worse.

The Attorney General, Jeff Sessions, who Trump has criticized as being "very weak" on leaks,[571] announced on August 4 that four people have been charges with "divulging classified material or concealed contacts with foreign intelligence officers."[572] He said the Trump administration has tripled the number of active leak probes since January.[573]

On Fake News

According to Albrecht (2017), Trump is "deeply suspicious of intellectuals and 'wordsmiths'—those who craft complex messages and confront him with his contradictions ... He tends to see journalists as dangerous, and almost universally to be despised or distrusted." His public distain of the media is intense and long standing.[574] But, privately, the media is central to his sense of self-identity. As Jack Shafer, POLITICO's senior media writer, has observed: "He's always loved to lie (*I mean, talk*) to reporters because he lives for having an attentive audience, and now that he's president reporters would line up to transcribe his words even if he started reciting a Maytag washer repair manual backward."[575]

To Trump, "fake news"[576] is any news using quotations from unnamed sources—making it anonymous testimony—with which he disagrees because it embarrasses or challenges his authority or credibility. He asserted that such quotations are fabricated by journalist[577] because they are liberals who support the Democrats. After all, he told a rally of supporters—incorrectly—that, according to the Center of Public Integri-

---

[570] Retrieved from: http://www.politico.com/story/2017/03/trump-white-house-paranoia-236069.

[571] See: https://www.theguardian.com/us-news/2017/aug/04/jeff-sessions-trump-leaks-doj-intelligence.

[572] Retrieved from: http://www.bbc.co.uk/news/world-us-canada-40829559.

[573] See: http://www.bbc.co.uk/news/world-us-canada-40829559.

[574] See: http://www.trumptwitterarchive.com/.

[575] Retrieved from: http://www.politico.eu/blogs/on-media/2017/06/donald-trump-doesnt-want-to-be-president-communications-director/.

[576] For a discussion of this concept see: http://edition.cnn.com/videos/tv/2017/02/26/how-trump-turned-fake-news-into-a-slur.cnn.

[577] See: http://www.politico.com/magazine/story/2017/04/23/trump-loves-media-reporters-white-house-215043.

ty,[578] "96 percent of journalists who made donations in the last election gave them to our opponent."[579] In fact, "Nearly all of that money—more than 96 percent—has benefited Clinton."[580] His presumption is that, like him, journalists naturally lie—"make up stories and make up sources."[581] His position is clear: "I'm against the people [journalists] that make up stories and make up sources. They shouldn't be allowed to use sources unless they use somebody's name. Let their name be[582] out there ... Let there be no more sources."[583] Of course:

> It's reasonable to question the reliability of anonymous sources. Putting your name on what you tell the press is one way to help readers assess your credibility. When you refuse to be named, you shield yourself from direct accountability. If you tell one story anonymously, and a named source tells a different story, thereby putting his skin in the game, that person seems more credible.[584]

But, when there is dispute over what happened at a White House meeting, it is not just a matter of the relative credibility of anonymous sources and named public officials. It is whether the specific claims made by anonymous sources—falsifiable factual allegations—are trumped by evasive non-denials made by named public officials, regardless of their status and standing.

So, Trump would have the "fake news" media required to disclose the names of their sources, presumably so as to make it easier for them to

---

[578] See: https://www.publicintegrity.org/about.

[579] Retrieved from: http://heavy.com/news/2017/04/donald-trump-harrisburg-pennsylvania-pa-rally-photos-pictures-crowd-size-pics-farm-expo-center-supporters-how-many/7/.

[580] Retrieved from: https://www.publicintegrity.org/2016/10/17/20330/journalists-shower-hillary-clinton-campaign-cash.

[581] Retrieved from: http://fortune.com/2017/02/25/trump-anonymous-media-sources/

[582] For a discussion of this concept see: http://edition.cnn.com/videos/tv/2017/02/26/how-trump-turned-fake-news-into-a-slur.cnn.

[583] Retrieved from: http://fortune.com/2017/02/24/donald-trump-cpac-fake-news-attack/. See also: http://www.washingtonexaminer.com/trump-claims-anonymous-sources-made-up-by-fake-news-writers/article/2624356http://ew.com/tv/2017/06/27/donald-trump-fake-news-twitter/.

[584] Retrieved from: http://www.slate.com/articles/news_and_politics/politics/2017/05/why_we_should_believe_anonymous_sources_over_h_r_mcmaster.html.

be prosecuted before being subjected to harsh punishment when they are found guilty. These anonymous sources who leak negative information to the "fake news" media about, or in relation to, a properly elected President need to be punished. They have been disloyal to him—the properly elected American president who embodies the will of the people—and so they are unpatriotic—perhaps even traitors.[585] An alternative, obvious, explanation for such whistle-blowing has been offered. White House aids, when dealing with the reality of civil war between White House factions,[586] "in the manner of children themselves, are calling attention to issues they hope Trump will notice when publicized."[587]

Curiously, and certainly cynically, Trump's "no more sources" diktat does not apply to his White House. It has resorted to quoting anonymous White House spokespersons that when Trump needed support he cannot otherwise get.[588] It did so when attacking the proposition that he has leaked "classified information,"[589] and when justifying his failure to condemn explicitly white supremacists[590] for the violence that turned deadly at a white supremacist demonstration in Charlottesville (Virginia) in mid-August.[591]

Asserting any news he does not like to be "fake news" is an important communication strategy used by Trump, particularly if he knows the

---

585   Retrieved from: http://www.telegraph.co.uk/news/2017/03/11/deep-state-shadowy-network-obama-holdovers-undermining-donald/; see also http://google.com/newsstand/s/CBIwj628vDk.

586   See: https://www.vanityfair.com/news/2017/04/jared-kushner-steve-bannon-white-house-civil-war.

587   Retrieved from: https://newsstand.google.com/articles/CAIiEGtR133yHzrVa VkPOfeYteIqFQgEKg0IACoGCAowrqkBMKBFMKGBAg.

588   See: https://www.theguardian.com/us-news/2017/aug/08/donald-trump-news-tweet-north-korea-fox-and-friends; http://elitedaily.com/news/politics/trump-sharing-story-anonymous-sources-hypocritical-gets/2039303/.

589   Retrieved from: http://www.rawstory.com/2017/05/white-house-uses-anony mous-spokesperson-to-contradict-brennan-testimony-and-decry-anonymous-leaks/.

590   An interesting error appeared in one White House statement: "neo-Nazi" became "nephew-Nazi"; a typing error or a Freudian slip? See: https://twitter.com/Porter_Anderson/status/896764950319960064.

591   Retrieved from: http://www.marketwatch.com/story/a-day-later-white-house-says-trump-meant-to-condemn-white-supremacists-2017-08-13; http://www.businessinsider.my/white-house-reponse-trump-charlottesvillewhite-supremacists-timeline-2017-8/.

leaked information is accurate. This is evidenced by his cries of "fake news" that have, in time, proven to be accurate.[592]

> "Almost every single time he's used that term, the news has been accurate," [Jake Tapper] said Monday [August 7] on CNN. "It's just been news he doesn't like."
>
> Tapper then ticked off examples, such as Trump's claim earlier this year that he had a "very civil conversation" on the phone with Australian Prime Minister Malcolm Turnbull, but the "FAKE NEWS media lied" with reports of tensions during the call.[593]

Transcripts leaked in early August[594] confirmed the media reports at the time were accurate and that Turnbull got he wanted and, in the process, bested Trump[595].[596]

To Trump, then, "fake news" is phony news intended to deliberately deceive by conveying false impressions about him, his policies, and his administration, in order to misrepresent reality as he prefers to see it. It, thus, diverts attention away from his "correct" understanding of that reality. Such news, he considers, is based on specious information, and is fabricated in order to cater to those who want to hear anything that diminishes his successfulness, powerfulness, and brilliance. He has dubbed the "fake news" media "the enemy of the people"[597] because they publish bullshit about his administration in order to destroy him—the embodiment of the will of the people—by whatever means necessary.

---

592 See, for example: https://www.usatoday.com/story/news/politics/onpolitics/2017/06/07/onpolitics-today-james-comey-says-fake-news-trump-true/102608082/.

593 Retrieved from: https://www.washingtonpost.com/world/national-security/no-gday-mate-on-call-with-australian-pm-trump-badgers-and-brags/2017/02/01/88a3bfb0-e8bf-11e6-80c2-30e57e57e05d_story.html?tid=sm_tw&utm_term=.2239be047450.

594 See: https://www.washingtonpost.com/graphics/2017/politics/australia-mexico-transcripts/?utm_term=.d36e66d060a1; see also http://www.huffingtonpost.com/entry/trump-world-leaders-phone-calls_us_59833035e4b06d4888748afa.

595 See: http://edition.cnn.com/2017/08/03/opinions/donald-trump-diplomacy-opinion-miller-sokolsky/index.html.

596 See: http://www.huffingtonpost.com/entry/jake-tapper-fake-news_us_5989286fe4b0d7937389b2c1.

597 See: http://www.independent.co.uk/news/world/americas/donald-trssump-us-news-media-enemy-of-the-people-coverage-fixation-tv-west-wing-white-house-president-a7622216.html.

What differentiates journalists' so-called phoney "fake news"—a report quoting anonymous sources—from Trump's genuine "fake news"—a crafted statement intended to create significant public confusion about current events—is that the latter, of course, deserves to be believed.

Trump has also signaled that there is a need to consult with the likes of Bill Gates, about "closing up the internet in some way. Somebody will say 'Oh, freedom of speech, freedom of speech.' these are foolish people. We have a lot of foolish people" (Address at Mount Pleasant, South Carolina, December 2015, cited in Piehler 2016, 72).

Trump's aggressive public attitude to the media, brings to mind a recent, disquieting, observation made by Ron Rosenbaum, the author of *Explaining Hitler The Search for the Origins of His Evil*[598] (1999):

> What I want to suggest is an actual comparison [of Trump] with Hitler that deserves thought. It's what you might call the secret technique, a kind of rhetorical control that both Hitler and Trump used on their opponents, especially the media. And they're not joking ... The playbook is *Mein Kamph*.[599]

Essentially, in Hitler's words:

> "If you tell a big enough lie and tell it frequently enough, it will be believed."[600]

> "Make the lie big, make it simple, keep saying it, and eventually they will believe it."[601]

---

[598] See: http://www.goodreads.com/book/show/54277.Explaining_Hitler.

[599] Retrieved from: https://lareviewofbooks.org/article/normalization-lesson-munich-post/; see also: http://www.vanityfair.com/style/2017/04/louis-ck-doesnt-take-back-trump-insult; http://www.bu http://www.vanityfair.com/news/2015/08/donald-trump-marie-brenner-ivana-divorce ssinsider.com/yale-professor-shouldnt-afraid-compare-trump-hitler-on-tyranny-comparison-politics-2017-4; http://www.dailymail.co.uk/news/article-4640492/Alastair-Campbell-compares-Donald-Trump-HITLER.html; https://www.thenation.com/article/trump-echoed-hitler-speech-withdrawing-paris-climate-accord/; http://www.dailymail.co.uk/news/article-4642104/N-Korea-likens-Trump-Hitler.html.

[600] Retrieved from: https://www.goodreads.com/author/quotes/30691.Adolf_Hitler.

[601] Retrieved from: https://www.brainyquote.com/quotes/quotes/a/adolfhitle385028.html.

That Trump has a copy of Mein Kampf, was acknowledged in 1990, when he responded to a Vanity Fair interviewer's question: "Actually, it was my friend Marty Davis from Paramount who gave me a copy of Mein Kampf, and he's a Jew."[602]

Unknowingly, Trump has, once more, followed the advice of the Master of Deceit and Intrigue's (Machiavelli [1513] 2011, 94) and crafted media animosities against himself, but whether he can crushed the media to his advantage is, to say the least, problematic.

TRUMP'S INCUBUS: THE SAGA OF RUSSIA'S MEDDLING IN THE 2016 PRESIDENTIAL ELECTION

Publicly, it all began back in July 2016 when Trump invited Russia to hack Hillary Clinton's emails:

> "I will tell you this, Russia: If you're listening, I hope you're able to find the 30,000 emails that are missing," the Republican nominee said at a news conference in Florida. "I think you will probably be rewarded mightily by our press."[603]

Over the ensuing months, it has been concluded that Russian hackers have been active in the 2016 presidential election:

> Russian hackers targeted 21 US state election systems in the 2016 presidential race and a small number were breached but there was no evidence any votes were manipulated, a Homeland Security Department official [Jeanette Manfra, the acting deputy undersecretary of cyber security] told Congress [the Senate Intelligence Committee] on Wednesday [21 June] ...
>
> US intelligence agencies have concluded the Kremlin orchestrated a wide-ranging influence operation that

---

[602] Retrieved from: http://www.vanityfair.com/news/2015/08/donald-trump-marie-brenner-divorce.

[603] Retrieved from: https://www.nytimes.com/2016/07/28/us/politics/donald-trump-russia-clinton-emails.html.

included email hacking and online propaganda to dis-
credit Democratic presidential candidate Hillary Clinton and help Donald Trump, a Republican, win the
White House in November.[604]

As to whether this involved collusion with the Trump Campaign, there
is a great deal of inconclusive circumstantial evidence, including many
odd events and interactions between Trump's campaign advisers and
Russians[605]:

> Michael Flynn[606] and other advisers to Donald Trump's
> campaign were in contact with Russian officials and
> others with Kremlin ties in at least 18 calls and emails
> during the last seven months of the 2016 presidential
> race, current and former US officials familiar with the
> exchanges told Reuters.[607]

As yet, there is limited tangible evidence supporting any specific collusion between the Trump Campaign and the Russian government to
relation to any Russian meddling in the 2016 presidential election. But,
"[i]t's getting harder to say Russian meddling didn't actually help lead to
Trump's victory and Clinton's loss".[608] There has been ceaseless flow of
rumors,[609] disclosures from James Comey (both when he was Director
of the FBI and after he was fired)[610] and Jared Kushner (Trump's son-
in-law),[611] and allegations of collusion[612] coming from the on-going—

---

[604] Retrieved from: http://www.reuters.com/article/us-usa-cyber-congress-idUSK
BN19C1Y3.

[605] See: http://edition.cnn.com/2017/07/22/politics/the-many-unearthed-interac
tions-between-trump-world-and-russia-documented/index.html.

[606] See: http://www.bbc.co.uk/news/av/world-us-canada-40137571/michael-flyn
n-the-man-at-the-centre-of-trump-s-russia-crisis.

[607] Retrieved from: http://www.reuters.com/article/us-usa-trump-russia-contacts-
idUSKCN18E106.

[608] Retrieved from: http://edition.cnn.com/2017/05/27/politics/russian-memo-
2016-election-schultz-comey-clinton/index.html.

[609] See: https://qz.com/989368/richard-clarke-why-the-journalists-spies-and-
politicians-warned-about-trumps-russia-ties-couldnt-believe-their-eyes/.

[610] See: https://www.nytimes.com/2017/06/08/us/politics/senate-hearing-
transcript.html.

[611] See: http://www.businessinsider.com/trump-senior-adviser-jared-kushner-full-
statement-russia-senate-intelligence-committee-2017-7; https://www.youtube.
com/watch?v=ekk_wA36XTc.

[612] See: http://www.dailymail.co.uk/news/article-4547694/NSA-boss-says-s-

sometimes very public—multiple investigations being conducted:[613] by the Senate Select Committee on Intelligence,[614] the House of Representatives Permanent Select Committee on Intelligence,[615] and the FBI.[616]

The FBI's long-standing, and more secretive investigations on Russian election meddling were taken over by a Special Counsel,[617] a former FBI

---

damning-evidence-Russia-collusion.htm; https://newsstand.google.com/articles/CAIiEOlMl7HTsYXtOj0cYTup90cqEwgEKgsIACoFCAowgGAwAD-CCrRE.

[613] See: http://www.npr.org/2017/06/08/531940912/there-are-many-russia-investigations-what-are-they-all-doing.

[614] "The Senate Select Committee on Intelligence is conducting a broad inquiry looking at what, exactly, Russia did to influence the 2016 elections and how that fits into broader 'cyberactivity and active measures' the country has used to target the United States. Part of that includes examining whether there is any evidence that members of President Trump's campaign collaborated with Russian operatives." Retrieved from: http://www.npr.org/2017/06/08/531940912/there-are-many-russia-investigations-what-are-they-all-doing. See also: https://www.buzzfeed.com/emmaloop/the-senate-intelligence-committees-russia-investigation-is?utm_term=.nuZO6GaMq#.tf3bWLzG6.

[615] "... the House Permanent Select Committee on Intelligence wants to write a report answering four questions:

What did Russia do to interfere in the 2016 election?

Were there any links between Russian operatives "and individuals associated with political campaigns"?

How did the federal government respond to these efforts?

How and why was classified information leaked during this process?

Retrieved from: http://www.npr.org/2017/06/08/531940912/there-are-many russia-investigations-what-are-they-all-doing.

[616] See: http://edition.cnn.com/2017/05/26/politics/russia-investigation-what-to-know/index.html; http://www.bbc.co.uk/news/av/world-us-canada-40268708/jeff-sessions-russia-collusion-claim-a-detestable-lie.

[617] "This person is appointed directly by the attorney general—and—this is the important part—is thus directly answerable to the attorney general. This person can pursue criminal indictments in grand jury investigations, but the attorney general can fire them at any time [but only for 'misconduct, dereliction of duty, incapacity, conflict of interest, or for other good cause, including violation of Departmental policies'] and overrule any decisions they make when it comes to investigating or prosecuting the case. However, "[i]n this case, [the Attorney General, Jeff] Sessions has already formally recused himself from participating in any Trump-Russia investigations, so the next person in line, Deputy Attorney General Rod Rosenstein, would be the one with the authority to appoint a special counsel." Retrieved from: https://www.vox.com/policy-and-politics/2017/5/10/15609794/independent-russia-trump-investigation-special-prosecutor (emphasis in original). See: https://www.justice.gov/opa/pr/attorney-general-sessions-statement-recusal. See also: https://www.cnbc.com/2017/05/18/what-the-special-counsel-can-and-cant-do-with-his-investigation;https://www.theatlantic.com/politics/archive/2017/05/a-special-prosecutor-is-not-the-answer/526662/.

Director Robert S. Mueller III,[618] who was appointed on May 17:

> Deputy Attorney General Rod J. Rosenstein[619] today announced the appointment of former Department of Justice official and FBI Director Robert S. Mueller III to serve as Special Counsel to oversee the previously-confirmed FBI investigation of Russian government efforts to influence the 2016 presidential election and related matters.[620]

On Mueller's appointment, Rosenstein is reported to have written: "What I have determined is that based upon the unique circumstances the public interest requires me to place this investigation under the authority of a person who exercises a degree of independence from the normal chain of command."[621] Mueller's remit is to investigate "any links and/or coordination between the Russian government and individuals associated with the Campaign of President Donald Trump; and any matters that arose or may arise directly from the investigation."[622] This includes investigating Trump for obstruction of justice,[623] because

---

[618]   See: http://www.newyorker.com/news/news-desk/robert-mueller-to-head-russia-trump-probe-first-thoughts.

[619]   It has been suggested that if there is an obstruction case against the President, one of the chief claims would be that Rosenstein's memo [that justified FBI Director Comey's firing] was a ruse orchestrated to shift attention away from the real reason for the Comey firing: the president's opposition to the FBI's investigation of whether Trump campaign aides colluded with the Russians to influence the presidential election campaign. Rosenstein will have to recuse himself from any supervisory role in the Mueller investigation due to this possible conflict of interest.

Retrieved from: http://edition.cnn.com/2017/06/16/opinions/rosenstein-conflict-of-interest-r ecuse-opinion-callan/index.html. See also: http://www.newyorker.com/news/ryan-lizza/why-trump-attacked-his-own-deputy-attorney-general.

[620]   Retrieved from: https://www.justice.gov/opa/pr/appointment-special-counsel.

[621]   Retrieved from: http://www.newyorker.com/news/ryan-lizza/why-trump-attacked-his-own-deputy-attorney-general.

[622]   Retrieved from: http://www.npr.org/2017/06/08/531940912/there-are-many-russia-investigations-what-are-they-all-doing. See also: https://newsstand.google.com/articles/CAIiEJl8a6KZleZ-TIgFJhnePHUqFggEKg0IACoGCAowt6AMMLAmMMT5lwM.

[623]   "In this case, if Trump intended to interfere with the investigation into the Russian collusion, even if ultimately the special counselor concludes no Russian collusion occurred, Trump could still be found guilty of attempted interference of an ongoing investigation" Retrieved from: https://thinkprogress.org/someone-

he fired FBI Director James Comey,[624] and probing Trump's finances[625];[626] as well as taking over "an ongoing investigation into Trump's former campaign manager's [Paul Manafort's] financial dealings in Ukraine[627]."[628] Mueller took a major step by empanelling a grand jury[629]

needs-to-explain-obstruction-of-justice-to-donald-trump-ff78862b7f3/. But see also: http://www.bbc.co.uk/news/world-us-canada-40283036; https://www.facebook.com/Newsweek/posts/10155255471781101; http://www.bbc.co.uk/news/world-us-canada-40283036.

[624] See: https://www.theatlantic.com/politics/archive/2017/06/donald-trump-is-under-investigation-for-obstruction-of-justice/530412/; https://www.washingtonpost.com/world/national-security/special-counsel-is-investigating-trump-for-possible-obstruction-of-justice/2017/06/14/9ce02506-5131-11e7-b064-828ba60fbb98_story.html?utm_term=.e3f680ce117a; http://www.slate.com/articles/news_and_politics/jurisprudence/2017/07/the_obstruction_of_justice_case_against_trump_is_already_a_slam_dunk.html; http://www.foxnews.com/politics/2017/08/10/muellers-russia-investigation-what-to-know.html; see also: https://www.forbes.com/forbes/welcome/?toURL=https://www.forbes.com/sites/jacobfrenkel/2017/06/29/why-president-trump-is-unlikely-to-face-obstruction-of-justice-charges/&refURL=https://www.google.com.tr/&referrer=https://www.google.com.tr/; https://www.cnbc.com/2017/06/07/it-would-be-difficult-to-bring-an-obstruction-charge-against-trump.html. But particularly see: http://edition.cnn.com/2017/05/19/opinions/obstruction-justice-case-against-trump-callan/index.html; and https://www.theguardian.com/us-news/2017/sep/02/donald-trump-russia-investigation-obstruction-of-justice.

[625] In a survey conducted by CNN in early August, respondents were "[a]sked if 'Mueller should be able to investigate whether Donald Trump had any financial dealings with Russia,' 70 percent of Americans said he should be able to, while only 25 percent agreed with Trump that his finances should be out of bounds." Retrieved from: https://www.commondreams.org/news/2017/08/10/70-percent-americans-think-mueller-should-be-free-go-after-trumps-finances; see also: http://edition.cnn.com/2017/08/10/politics/cnn-poll-russia-investigation-trump-finances/index.html.

[626] See: http://uk.businessinsider.com/russian-officials-reportedly-discussed-having-derogatory-information-about-trump-2017-5; http://www.salon.com/2017/05/30/russian-officials-discussed-having-derogatory-intel-on-trump-top-aides-report/; https://www.voanews.com/a/us-special-counsel-mueller-probes-trump-finances/3980602.html; http://edition.cnn.com/2017/08/03/politics/mueller-investigation-russia-trump-one-year-financial-ties/index.html; but see also: http://www.dailymail.co.uk/news/article-4773538/Trump-sent-private-messages-appreciation-Mueller;.html; http://edition.cnn.com/2017/08/06/opinions/rosenstein-should-curb-mueller-whittaker-opinion/index.html.

[627] See: https://www.bloomberg.com/news/features/2017-05-22/paul-manafort-s-lucrative-ukraine-years-are-central-to-the-russia-probe; http://edition.cnn.com/2017/04/14/politics/manafort-finances-ukraine-connection/index.html; https://www.vanityfair.com/news/2017/07/paul-manafort-reportedly-owed-millions-to-russian-oligarch-before-joining-trump-campaign.

[628] Retrieved from: http://www.foxnews.com/politics/2017/08/10/muellers-russia-investigation-what-to-know.html.

[629] "Typically made up of between 16 and 23 laypeople, grand juries are selected in a

"to look into the now infamous meeting in June 2016 between Russians and the President's son, Donald Trump Jr, along with other members of the President's inner circle."[630] This is a very significant development, as a grand jury has "the force of the law behind it to demand documents, put witnesses on oath and seek indictments if there's a suspicion of a crime having been committed."[631]

The Muller's wide-ranging investigations quite dramatically entered a new phase[632] in late October.[633]

> In [grand jury] court records unsealed on Monday [October 30], the FBI said George Papadopoulos "falsely described his interactions with a certain foreign contact who discussed 'dirt' related to emails" concering Democratic presidential candidate Hillary Clinton. Records also describe an email between Trump campaign officials suggesting they were considering acting on Russian invitations to go to Russia.

manner similar to a criminal trial in England or Wales.

They are given an outline of the case by the prosecutor, who will show them evidence or call witnesses to testify under oath ...

The proceedings are not public and only the people in the room have knowledge of what has been discussed, while there is no cross-examination of the defendant's case.

Unlike a traditional trial, jurors may ask questions themselves and witnesses are not allowed to have lawyers present.

After listening to the evidence and any witnesses, the grand jury retires and votes in secret on whether or not to formally accuse the defendant and compel them to stand trial." Retrieved from: http://news.sky.com/story/president-trump-russia-collusion-probe-what-is-a-grand-jury-10973229.

630 Retrieved from: http://news.sky.com/story/bad-means-fake-in-the-parallel-reality-of-president-trumps-movement-10973206; see also: https://www.bloomberg.com/news/articles/2017-08-06/rosenstein-says-special-counsel-not-on-trump-fishing-expedition.

631 Retrieved from: http://news.sky.com/story/bad-means-fake-in-the-parallel-reality-of-president-trumps-movement-10973206.

632 See: https://www.vox.com/world/2017/10/30/16570518/robert-mueller-paul-manafort-george-papadopoulos-strategy; http://nationalinterest.org/feature/manafort-mueller-the-plot-thickens-22966.

633 See: htttps://www.forbes.com/forbes/welcome/?toURL=https://www.forbes.com/sites/peterjreilly/2017/10/30/manafort-and-gates-thats-how-they-got-al-capone/&refURL=https://www.google.com.tr/&referrer=https://www.google.com.tr/; https://www.vox.com/world/2017/10/30/16570518/robert-mueller-paul-manafort-george-papadopoulos-strategy.

In addition, former Trump campaign chairman Paul
Manafort and former Trump campaign official Rick
Gates surrendered Monday to Justice Department spe-
cial counsel Robert Mueller.

The charges against top officials from Trump's campaign
signals a dramatic new phase of Mueller's wide-ranging investigation into possible collusion between the
Russian government and members of Trump's team
as well as potential obstruction of justice and financial
crimes.[634]

Paul Manafort,[635] Rick Gates,[636] and George Papadopoulos[637] are the
first members of Trump Campaign team to be charged in connection
with the investigations of the Special Counsel.[638] Manafort and Gates
each pleaded not guilty to

12 counts which include conspiracy against the US,
conspiracy to launder money, being an unregistered
agent of a foreign principal—in this case Ukraine, and
seven counts of failure to report foreign bank accounts
and transactions. [639]

Papadopoulos pleaded guilty to lying to—misleading—FBI investigators about his contacts with a [English] professor who he believed had

---

[634]   Retrieved from: http://edition.cnn.com/2017/10/30/politics/paul-manafort-
russia-investigation-surrender/index.html.

[635]   See: http://www.bbc.com/news/av/world-us-canada-41811939/manafort-s-
indictment-where-did-all-the-money-go.

[636]   See: https://www.theguardian.com/us-news/2017/oct/30/rick-gates-paul-manafort-
donald-trump. See also: http://www.bbc.com/news/world-us-canada-41808227;
https://www.nbcnews.com/news/us-news/trump-campaign-adviser-george-
papadopoulos-pleads-guilty-lying-n815596.

[637]   See: https://www.nbcnews.com/news/us-news/who-george-papadopoulos-
en ergy-expert-junior-trump-staffer-sought-be-n815826.

[638]   See: http://edition.cnn.com/2017/10/29/politics/nidictments-mueller-trump/
index.htm;http://edition.cnn.com/2017/10/30/politics/manafort-gates-indictment-
explained/index.html;   but   see: http://edition.cnn.com/2017/10/30/politics/
manafort-trumop-analysis/index.html.

[639]   Retrieved from: http://www.independent.co.uk/news/world/americas/paul-
manafort-charged-arrested-trump-russia-fbi-latest-news-conspiracy-us-mueller-
surrender-a8027301.html.

deep ties to Russia because he didn't want to contradict Trump's public denials of collusion with the Kremlin, a source told ABC News.

Papadopoulos was arrested in July and accepted a plea deal, admitting that he lied about interactions he had with a professor in England who offered "dirt" on Democratic presidential nominee Hillary Clinton.

The aide's faithfulness to his candidate was not returned by the President, who sought to diminish Papadopoulos' role in the campaign. "Few people knew the young, low level volunteer named George, who has already proven to be a liar," Trump tweeted after court documents detailing the case were unsealed.[640]

The White House response was, predictably; the denial of the relevance of the indictments, the denial of any Russian collusion, and another call for an investigation of whether Hillary Clinton and the Democrats colluded with the Russians during the 2016 presidential election campaign.[641] The question awaiting an answer is: who will be next?[642] Michael Flynn or even Jared Kushner? The answer came a month or so later:

> Ex-national security adviser Michael Flynn has pleaded guilty to making false statements to the FBI about meetings with Russia's ambassador weeks before Donald Trump became president.
>
> The charges were brought by Special Counsel Robert Mueller, as part of his inquiry into alleged Russian meddling in the 2016 US election.
>
> Mr Flynn is the most senior member of the administration to be indicted.

---

[640] Retrieved from: http://www.nydailynews.com/news/politics/ex-trump-adviser-papadopoulos licd-fbi-loyalty-report-article-1.3623515.

[641] See: http://www.bbc.com/news/world-us-canada-41808227; http://www.bbc.co m/news/world-us-canada-41796255; But see: http://www.bbc.com/news/world-us-canada-38966846; https://www.bloomberg.com/news/articles/2017-10-30/manafort-gates-ties-to-trump-campaign-run-deep-despite-denials.

[642] See: https://www.washingtonpost.com/opinions/manafort-gates-papadopolous-whos-next/2017/10/31/4502962e-be83-11e7-97d9-bdab5a0ab381_story.html?utm_term=.9addd158591c.

He also revealed he was co-operating with Mr Mueller's inquiry.[643]

Trump, undoubtedly, to his chagrin, has found that extricating himself and his family from the pesky and unacceptably intrusive FBI investigators who he considers are on a fishing expedition[644] is difficult. At a rally in Huntington, West Virginia, on August 3, Trump explained his position: The investigations are based on "the totally made up Russia story"[645] and "[t]hey're trying to cheat you out of the leadership that you won with a fake story that is demeaning to all of us."[646] Rob Rosenstein, the Deputy Attorney General with 25 years of experience working in the Department of Justice—through both Republican and Democratic administrations—made his department's position very clear "... we don't engage in fishing expeditions."[647]

Trump instinctively understanding the threat posed by Mueller, felt compelled go after him.[648] His attack began only hours after his appointment was announced:

> President Trump's silence lasted just over 12 hours. Then, he let it all out ... The appointment of a special counsel to investigate possible collusion between his campaign and Russia was the "single greatest witch hunt in American history," he tweeted.
>
> Hours later, during a news conference with Colombian President Juan Manuel Santos, Trump revisited the topic.

---

[643] Retrieved from: http://www.bbc.com/news/world-us-canada-42192080.

[644] See: http://www.politico.com/magazine/story/2017/08/05/swamp-diary-trump-mueller-grand-jury-215463.

[645] Retrieved from: http://www.smh.com.au/world/trump-campaign-russia-probe-not-a-fishing-expedition-rod-rosenstein-20170806-gxqjes.html. But see: http://www.salon.com/2017/05/23/no-the-russia-scandal-isnt-fake-news-or-conspiracy-theory-its-a-national-crisis-we-dont-fully-understand/.

[646] Retrieved from: https://www.theguardian.com/us-news/2017/aug/03/donald-trump-west-virginia-rally-russia-grand-jury.

[647] Retrieved from: https://www.bloomberg.com/news/articles/2017-08-06/rosenstein-says-special-counsel-not-on-trump-fishing-expedition.

[648] See: http://www.businessinsider.com/trump-tweets-leaks-mueller-investigation-russia-washington-post-2017-7.

"I think it's totally ridiculous. Everybody thinks so," Trump said when asked about the appointment. "Everybody, even my enemies, have said there is no collusion."[649]

Trump's thinly veiled threatening response to Mueller was clear, when he suggested that his

> investigation was a tool of the establishment that is still smarting from Hillary Clinton's election loss ... Trump, admittedly before a receptive audience [at a campaign rally in Huntington, West Virginia in early August], implied that any outcome of the probe that did not favor him or his associates would in itself represent a flouting of democratic norms.[650]

Trump drew a red line and warned Mueller that he would cross it if he began investigation of his personal finances apart from Russia. The question is:

> If that is where the investigation leads, would Trump fire Mueller? That seemed to be the implication, although he did not say so directly. (This comes in the context of a [New York] Times report that Deutsche Bank will co-operate with Mueller's requests for information on Trump's finances; the bank reportedly has lent Trump and his family millions over the years.) Again, Trump openly plays the intimidation game, unaware or untroubled by the potential that this will be seen as part of a scheme of obstruction and interference in an ongoing investigation.[651]

---

[649] Retrieved from: https://www.washingtonpost.com/politics/trump-cant-stop-talking-about-the-russia-investigation--even-if-it-might-hurt-him/2017/05/18/0964ce2e-3be9-11e7-9e48-c4f199710b69_story.html?utm_term=.3d19ce4b2bde.

[650] Retrieved from: http://edition.cnn.com/2017/08/04/politics/trump-mueller-political-argument/index.html; see also https://www.theguardian.com/us-news/2017/aug/03/donald-trump-west-virginia-rally-russia-grand-jury.

[651] Retrieved from: https://www.dailymaverick.co.za/article/2017-07-21-when-the-leadership-skills-are-missing-in-action-exhibit-trump/#.WXYAFyN95cw.

Undoubtedly, Trump wants Mueller fired,[652] but, according to White House Counselor, Kellyanne Conway in early August, the president "has not even discussed" nor is "discussing" firing Mueller.[653] Developments in late October have enraged Trump,[654] but he is resting any suggestion that he should fire Mueller.[655]

To be able to get Mueller fire, Trump must find a legitimate reason to do so. These are limited "misconduct, dereliction of duty, incapacity, conflict of interest, or for other good cause, including violation of Departmental policies[656]".[657] And some members of Congress have given notice that they are watching Trump very closely:

> Earlier on Thursday [August 3], Sens. Chris Coons (D-DE) and Thom Tillis (R-NC) introduced a bill [Special Counsel Integrity Act] that would give special counsel Robert Mueller the right to a court review in the event that Trump fired him. Right now Trump can basically fire Mueller, who's leading the escalating Russia collusion probe, at will [but only with good cause]; if Tillis-Coons [Bill] passes, then Trump would need to prove he has some kind of good reason to fire Mueller or else the court might overrule him and keep the for-

---

[652] See: https://www.vox.com/world/2017/7/24/16008272/robert-mueller-fbi-trump-russia-explained.

[653] Retrieved from: http://www.foxnews.com/politics/2017/08/10/muellers-russia-investigation-what-to-know.html.

[654] See: http://edition.cnn.com/2017/10/30/politics/donald-trump-mueller-reaction/index.html; http://www.abc.net.au/news/2017-10-30/trump-tweets-after-charges-reported-russia-inquiry/9098148

[655] See: http://edition.cnn.com/2017/10/30/politics/president-donald-trump-robert-mueller/index.html;http://thehill.com/homenews/administration/357943-trump-exasperated-disgusted-over-indictments-report. https://www.washingtonpost.com/politics/trump-resists-mounting-pressure-from-bannon-and-others-to-fight-mueller/2017/10/31/22b02ce0-be4b-11e7-97d9-bdab5a0ab381_story.html?utm_term=.14d4ca711ce0. See particularly: http://edition.cnn.com/2017/10/31/politics/president-donald-trump-robert-mueller-investigation/index.html.

[656] Retrieved from: https://www.cnbc.com/2017/05/18/what-the-special-counsel-can-and-cant-do-with-his-investigation.

[657] See: https://www.cbsnews.com/news/trump-lawyer-says-theres-no-basis-to-fire-robert-mueller/;https://www.vox.com/policy-and-politics/2017/7/28/16050148/trump-fire-sessions-recess-appointment.

mer FBI chief in his job.[658]

Whether the Tillis-Coons Bill can get an overwhelming—presidential veto-proof[659]—bipartisan support will depend on the continuance of Congress's extraordinary confrontational mood,[660] perhaps reflected in the thoughts of Senator Tom Cotton (Republican-Arkansas): "for decades, Congress has ceded too much authority to the executive branch. And we should exercise our constitutional responsibilities seriously and with vigor".[661] Whether such legislation is, however, constitutional is disputable matter.[662]

Trump's other response to the Mueller probe was more pragmatic:

> Trump has asked his advisers about his power to pardon[663] aides, family members and even himself in connection with the Justice Department's probe into Russia's efforts to influence last year's election, which is being led by special counsel Robert Mueller.

The result is that he considers that he "has the complete power to pardon:"[664]

> In practice a president could offer clemency or a commutation, i.e. reducing a prison sentence. A president

---

[658] Retrieved from: https://www.vox.com/world/2017/8/4/16090812/trump-russia-sanctions-congress-putin.

[659] "To pass a bill over the president's objections requires a two-thirds vote in each Chamber." Retrieved from: https://www.senate.gov/reference/glossary_term/override_of_a_veto.htm.

[660] See: https://www.vox.com/world/2017/8/4/16090812/trump-russia-sanctions-congress-putin; https://www.theguardian.com/us-news/2017/aug/03/trump-robert-mueller-senate-russia-firing

[661] Retrieved from: https://www.bloomberg.com/news/articles/2017-08-06/rosenstein-says-special-counsel-not-on-trump-fishing-expedition.

[662] For a discussion see: https://www.salon.com/2017/10/02/can-congress-stop-trump-from-firing-mueller_partner/; https://www.alternet.org/comments/can-congress-stop-trump-firing-special-prosecutor-robert-mueller; http://www.newsweek.com/can-congress-pass-law-protect-mueller-being-fired-trump-647806.

[663] Under the Constitution, The President "shall have power to grant reprieves and pardons for offenses against the United States, except in cases of impeachment." Retrieved from: https://www.law.cornell.edu/constitution/articleii.

[664] Retrieved from: https://twitter.com/realDonaldTrump/status/888724194820857857; see also http://www.bbc.co.uk/news/world-us-canada-40692709. But see: http://www.bbc.co.uk/news/world-us-canada-40699441.

can also offer a full pardon, in essence an official state-ment of forgiveness for a crime.

An individual does not have to be charged or convicted to receive a pardon, and a president cannot pardon peo-ple over state-level crimes.

In the context of the Russia investigation, Mr Trump could grant immunity to aides or family members, lim-iting Mr Mueller's scope.[665]

As to whether he could pardon himself:

The short answer is we do not know, given the short wording but broad application of the constitution, and the fact there is no precedent for a US leader issuing such a pardon.[666]

And Mark Tushnet,[667] a law professor at Harvard University, argues:

A self-pardon might well be outrageously improper ... but the response the Constitution creates for such mis-conduct is impeachment, a political rather than crimi-nal remedy.

A vivid speculation on what Trump's reactions might be to any adverse findings by Mueller on the "Russian thing" comes from Michael To-masky,[668] a Special Correspondent for *The Daily Beast* and the Editor of *Democracy: A Journal of Ideas*[669]:

The president is a caged and cornered animal ...

Trump will not just take this. He'll do ... something ... Here are four scenarios.

1. He tries to start a war ... North Korea is the first choice of a target, maybe ISIS [in Afghanistan?].

665   Retrieved from: http://www.bbc.co.uk/news/world-us-canada-40693249.
666   Retrieved from: http://www.bbc.co.uk/news/world-us-canada-40693249,
667   See: http://hls.harvard.edu/faculty/directory/10906/Tushnet.
668   See: https://www.facebook.com/mtomasky.
669   See: https://democracyjournal.org/author/mtomasky/

2. He tries to destroy everyone around him ... No one in his orbit is safe from this. Ivanka, I suppose. But not Jared, and not anyone else. [Indeed, Trump began in late May to distance himself from his son-in-law, when he "accused the media of exaggerating his relationship with Jared Kushner, asserting that "I don't know him very well ... He's someone I would see around the office and who, I guess, was working for me ... Beyond that, I couldn't tell you much about him ... I couldn't tell you if that's the kind of thing he'd do [have an improper contact with Russian spies during the transition]. You really should ask someone who knows him."[670]

3. He incites street violence[671] [perhaps mobilizing the neo-Nazis and White supremacists[672]] ... he'll hit the road and have more campaign-style rallies ... And he'll work his people into a rage ... And something will circulate online about taking up arms, and Trump brigades will form, and he'll finally have his very own private thug army. [Yale Historian, Timothy Snyder[673] considers that "it's pretty much inevitable" that Trump will try to stage a coup and overthrow democracy[674]].

4. He quits. I could see this, too. I can hear it:

---

670   Retrieved from: http://www.newyorker.com/humor/borowitz-report/trump-says-he-does-not-know-jared-kushner-very-well. But see also: http://www.telegraph.co.uk/news/2017/05/29/donald-trump-defends-jared-kushner-white-house-insists-not-taking/.

It has been suggested that Kushner is the domino that Trump can least afford to fall, as he has "improbably, emerged as a major policymaking force inside his father-in-law's ersatz administration."

Retrieved from: https://www.vox.com/policy-and-politics/2017/6/2/157147 08/jared-kushner-russia-domino.

671   For an interesting historical perspective see: https://www.theguardian.com/us-news/2017/aug/20/civil-war-american-history-trump.

672   See: http://www.huffingtonpost.co.uk/entry/alt-right-leaders-praising-donald-trump-response-charlottesville_uk_5993fe93e4b0e789a947f8a6; https://twitter.com/DrDavidDuke/status/897559892164304896.

673   See: http://history.yale.edu/people/timothy-snyder

674   Retrieved from: http://www.salon.com/2017/05/01/historian-timothy-snyder-its-pretty-much-inevitable-that-trump-will-try-to-stage-a-coup-and-overthrow-democracy/.

"Look. I did my job. I kept Crooked Hillary out of the White House. Gorsuch. I did Gorsuch. Quality guy ... I did a lot of things, beautiful things. But the press is so unfair. So unfair. And a lot of the people, frankly, I must tell you: mediocre ... And disloyalty. People are so disloyal. So look, I had a great life. I go back to my life."[675]

On Trump the caged and cornered animal, Putin's reportedly commented to a Russian Senator, in the context of Russian-American diplomacy: "Trump is like a prisoner ... And how can you talk to a prisoner?" This tells it all.

As Trump likes to win not loose, he likes to whine until he wins:

"Look at the way I've been treated lately, especially by the media [negatively[676] but not necessarily negatively bias[677]]" Trump said on Wednesday [17 May] during a speech to the Coast Guard Academy in Connecticut. "No politician in history, and I say this with great surety, has been treated worse or more unfairly."

He told the coast guard graduates: "You can't let them get you down." Responding to their cheers, he commented: "I guess that's why we won."[678]

Jennifer Rubin[679] put it this way in her *Washington Post* "Right Turn" column on 20 July:

"Trump is flailing, throwing mud in every direction in the vain hope that his words will disable his critics.

---

[675] Retrieved from: http://www.thedailybeast.com/donald-trumps-paths-all-lead-down. See also: http://www.nybooks.com/articles/2016/04/21/can-donald-trump-be-stopped/; http://www.nybooks.com/articles/2016/10/13/can-the-unthinkable-happen/

[676] See: http://www.zerohedge.com/news/2017-05-19/harvard-study-reveals-huge-extent-anti-trump-media-bias.

[677] See: https://www.forbes.com/sites/markjoyella/2017/05/19/trumps-getting-killed-in-the-media-but-not-because-of-bias/#e1aeb9d728e8https://newsstand.google.com/articles/CAIiEC3NNVEYk_j9uDC_J1soSDwqGQgEKhAIAC oHCAowgd31CjC749wCMMSKsQM.

[678] Retrieved from: https://www.theguardian.com/us-news/2017/may/17/donald-trump-presidency-media-coverage-russia-scandal.

[679] See: https://www.washingtonpost.com/people/jennifer-rubin/?utm_term=.e2 04197ea0c5.

However, his undisguised fury with investigators only gives weight to the accusation that he tried his best to stop—obstruct, that is—an investigation into his team's web of connections to Russia ... Trump's presidency is sinking into the quicksand of the Russia investigation. The more he decries his tormentors, the more support he provides for their investigation. Who can doubt that he was determined to stop the Russia investigation? In lashing out at prosecutors, he commits new acts of intimidation, vainly hoping to curtail their inquiry."[680]

She also thoughtfully reflected:

Trump's frustration over [Attorney General Jeff] Sessions' refusal to violate ethical standards stands out as further evidence that for Trump, loyalty is everything. Ethical and legal boundaries do not register with him; indeed, his loyal underlings are *expected* to disregard such niceties to protect him. Nothing better underscores his unfitness for office. He did, after all, take an oath to faithfully execute the laws, not to use government lawyers to shield him from inquiry. That concept is foreign to Trump, who sees the FBI and Justice Department as his supplicants.[681]

And in a similar tone, Benjamin Wittes,[682] a Senior Fellow (Governance Studies) at the Bookings Institution, elaborated in *Lawfare* on 20 July:

In an environment in which the President of the United States, in a single interview, expresses no confidence in the attorney general, the deputy attorney general, the special counsel, the acting FBI director, and the special counsel's staff, and in which he makes clear that the FBI should be his personal force and that all of law enforce-

---

680   Retrieved from: https://www.dailymaverick.co..za/article/2017-07-21-when-the-leadership-skills-are-missing-in-action-exhibit-trump/#.WXYAFyN95cw

681   Retrieved from: https://www.dailymaverick.co.za/article/2017-07-21-when-the-leadership-skills-are-missing-in-action-exhibit-trump/#.WXYAFyN95cw

682   See: https://www.brookings.edu/experts/benjamin-wittes/.

ment should be about serving him, the [principal] protection is having people with backbone who are willing to do their jobs and stand up for one another in the elevation of their oaths of office over political survival.[683]

The final White House word came on June 1 when Sean Spicer announced, as the White House Press Secretary: "We are focused on the president's agenda and going forward all questions on these matters [the on-going investigations into Donald Trump's alleged links to Russia] will be referred to outside counsel Marc Kasowitz."[684] Interestingly, the following day Putin cast a diverting red herring:

> Russian President Vladimir Putin, in an exclusive interview with NBC News' Megyn Kelly, insisted that hackers who interfered in the US presidential election could have come from "anywhere" [including "American hackers—and perhaps the CIA—could have framed Russia"[685]] and then they could have made it look like Russia was responsible.[686]

TRUMP'S DENOUEMENT: THE CHARLOTTESVILLE INCIDENT

This incident in mid-August—and Trump's breath-taking subsequent responses—brought to a head Trump's relationship with his far-right support base—including the White Nationalists,[687] the White Suprem-

---

683   Retrieved from: http://foreignpolicy.com/2017/07/20/trump-attacks-federal-law-enforcement-with-a-blunt-force-instrument-sessions-rosenstein-fbi-russia/.

684   Retrieved from:https://www.theguardian.com/us-news/2017/may/31/donald-trump-russia-investigation-sean-spicer-no-quess; http://time.com/4800 211/sean-spicer-james-comey-russia-marc-kasowitz-donald-trump/; but see: https://twitter.com/RaminTalaie/status/870311369580584960.

685   Retrieved from: https://newsstand.google.com/articles/CAIiEPhBDpNoyDcv 1OaI8TVjZAoqFQgEKg0IACoGCAowxYgCMIBNMOGXAg.

686   Retrieved from: http://www.nbcbayarea.com/news/politics/Vladimir-Putin-M egyn-Kelly-Hackers-Could-Have-Framed-Russia-426016984.html.

687   See: https://www.splcenter.org/fighting-hate/extremist-files/ideology/white-nationalist.

acists,[688] the Ku Kluz Klan (KKK),[689] and the neo-Nazis[690]—and the representation of the alt-right cabal in the White House.[691] The White Supremacists conducted a police-approved "Unite the Right" rally in Charlottesville, Virginia, on Sunday August 13 to protest the removal of a statue of a Confederate civil war[692] hero—General Robert E. Lee[693], an heroic symbol of white supremacy and a celebration of racial purity.[694] This rally, also attended by neo-Nazis and the KKK, turned into a Friday-to-Sunday event, one that attracted anti-racist protestors. Street violence on each day was the inevitable result.[695] This culminated in a White Supremacist—James Alex Fields—"being charged with second-degree murder after the authorities said he drove a car into a crowd [on Sunday August 13], leaving a 32-year-old woman dead and injuring at least 19 other people." [696] In some eyes—most notably Trump's National Security Advisor, Lieutenant General H.R. McMaster[697]—an act of terrorism had been committed. Trump's first reaction on the Saturday (12 August) was to the blame the street violence on the "many sides"[698] attending the rally:

> "We condemn in the strongest possible terms this egregious display of hatred, bigotry, and violence," he had

---

[688] See: https://www.adl.org/education/resources/reports/state-of-white-supremacy; http://www.rollingstone.com/politics/features/the-history-of-white-supremacy-in-america-w498334.

[689] See: https://www.splcenter.org/fighting-hate/extremist-files/ideology/ku-klux-klan.

[690] See: tps://www.splcenter.org/fighting-hate/extremist-files/ideology/neo-nazi.

[691] See: www.theatlantic.com/politics/archive/2017/01/far-right-taxonomy/509282/.

[692] See: http://www.telegraph.co.uk/news/0/robert-e-lee-confederate-hero-heart-charlottesville-unrest-statues/.

[693] See: https://www.civilwar.org/learn/biographies/robert-e-lee; but see also: https://www.nytimes.com/2017/08/18/us/robert-e-lee-slaves.html?mcubz=3; see also: http://www.bbc.co.uk/news/av/world-us-canada-40904081/trump-what-about-alt-left-violence-in-charlottesville.

[694] See: https://www.nytimes.com/2017/08/13/us/charlottesville-protests-unite-the-right.html.

[695] See: https://www.nytimes.com/2017/08/25/us/charlottesville-protest-police.html?mcubz=3; http://edition.cnn.com/2017/08/13/opinions/charlottesville-act-of-domestic-terrorism-bergen/index.html.

[696] See: https://www.nytimes.com/2017/08/13us/james-alex-fields-charlottesville-driver-.html?mcubz=3.

[697] See: http://www.slate.com/blogs/the_slatest/2017/08/13/national_security_adviser_h_r_mcmaster_on_charlottesville_of_course_it_was.html.

[698] Retrieved from: https://www.facebook.com/cnn/posts/10157177653201509.

said—before adding, apparently as an ad-lib[699]: "On many sides, on many sides."[700]

He, thereby, decline to condemn explicitly the violent behavior of racists groups in attendance, choosing instead to argue the moral equivalence of the all the protesters involved—whether racists (fascists) or anti-racist (anti-fascists),[701] although the First Lady, Melania Trump, and his daughter Ivanka, both did.[702]

A backlash quickly followed.[703] Then, "[a]fter reportedly facing pressure from his own staff, Trump on Monday [14 August] read a more politically correct presidential statement.[704] He began by talking about the economy,[705] and then he went on to talk about the incident, saying that members of KKK,[706] neo-Nazis, and White Supremacists who engendered violence were "criminals and thugs."[707] The response was seen as too little and too late.[708]

Then came Trump's spectacular retractions. The first was by twitter on

---

[699] See: https://www.theatlantic.com/entertainment/archive/2017/08/trump-press-conference-notes-image/537078/;http://www.bbc.co.uk/news/world-us-canada-40948812.

[700] Retrieved from: http://www.businessinsider.com/trump-gets-slammed-for-not-condemning-white-nationalists-in-charlottesville-2017-8.

[701] See: https://www.theguardian.com/commentisfree/2017/aug/15/mr-trump-were-not-same-neo-nazis-charlottesville.

[702] See: http://www.businessinsider.com/ivanka-trump-charlottesville-nazis-white-nationalists-alt-right-2017-8?_ga=2.150482677.296456635.1502692147-1316434574.1502692146;https://twitter.com/IvankaTrump/status/896705195228381187.

[703] See: http://www.businessinsider.com/trump-gets-slammed-for-not-condemning-white-nationalists-in-charlottesville-2017-8; http://edition.cnn.com/2017/08/13/opinions/charlottesville-trump-race-moral-leadership-joseph-opinion/index.html; https://www.theguardian.com/us-news/2017/aug/13/civil-rights-inquiry-for-charlottesville-rally-death.

[704] See: https://qz.com/1053270/full-text-donald-trumps-statement-on-charlottesville/.

[705] See: http://edition.cnn.com/2017/08/14/politics/trump-speech-monday-charlottesville/index.html.

[706] See: https://www.splcenter.org/fighting-hate/extremist-files/ideology/ku-klux-klan.

[707] See: http://www.businessinsider.com/trump-retweets-pizzagate-conspiracy-theory-jack-posobiec-charlottesville-2017-8; http://www.businessinsider.com/trump-second-statement-kkk-neo-nazis-charlottesville-2017-8.

[708] See: https://thinkprogress.org/asked-why-it-took-him-so-long-to-denounce-racists-trump-attacks-the-media-838504b8abf1/.

the same day:

> Made additional remarks on Charlottesville and realize
> once again that the #Fake News Media will never be sat-
> isfied ... truly bad people! (Tweet, 3.29 pm 14 August).[709]

Then, in a remarkable press conference held the following day (August 15) at Trump Tower in New York,[710] he more aggressively and colorfully repeated his initial allocation of blame for the street violence on the "many sides"[711] attending the rally. He went further—much further. In so doing he give more evidence of his lack of self-control, even when his words could be self-destructive—by tarnishing of the Trump brand in both politics and business[712]. He asserted that the "alt-left"[713]—incorrectly implying[714] that there is in America an organized radical left (anti-fascists)—had orchestrated the anti-racist protests[715]—were as much, if not more, to blame, because they seriously threatening White Supremacists engaged in a legal protest.[716] Indeed, he emphasized that—unlike the White Supremacist——the anti-racist

---

[709] Retrieved from: https://twitter.com/realDonaldTrump.

[710] See: https://www.vox.com/2017/8/15/16154028/trump-press-conference-transcript-charlottesville.

[711] See: https://www.nytimes.com/2017/08/15/us/politics/trump-press-conference-charlottesville.html?mcubz=3.

[712] See: https://newsstand.google.com/articles/CAIiELzvZ5vV74gWX2G0qtAdD ukqGQgEKhAIACoHCAowocv1CjCSptoCMPrWrwU; http://money.cnn.com /2017/08/18/news/companies/trump-mar-a-lago-fundraisers/index.html; https://www.washingtonpost.com/business/economy/cleveland-clinic-cancels -plans-for-gala-at-president-trumps-mar-a-lago/2017/08/17/a412f596-8369- 11e7-b359-15a3617c767b_story.html?utm_term=.129cbf140825; http://www. mypalmbeachpost.com/business/palm-beach-chamber-head-charities-have- conscience-mar-lago/Pp7jHFkUixKlK7eQaAArmM/; http://edition.cnn.com/ 2017/08/14/politics/charlottesville-nazi-trump-statement-trnd/index.htm- l?sr=.

[713] See: https://www.cbsnews.com/news/what-is-the-alt-left-trump-was-talking- about/; http://www.independent.co.uk/voices/donald-trump-charlottesville- altright-altleft-neonazis-moral-compass-facts-sad-a7898791.html.

[714] See: https://www.nytimes.com/2017/08/15/us/politics/alt-left-alt-right- glossary.html; see also http://heavy.com/news/2017/08/alt-left-trump-hannity- antifa-charlottesville-meaning/

[715] See: http://www.bbc.co.uk/news/av/world-us-canada-40904081/trump-what- about-alt-left-violence-in-charlottesville.

[716] See: http://www.bbc.co.uk/news/av/world-us-canada-40904081/trump-what- about-alt-left-violence-in-charlottesville; http://www.politifact.com/truth-o- meter/statements/2017/aug/17/donald-trump/donald-trump-wrong- charlottesville-counter-protest/.

protestors were conducting an illegal demonstration. He went so far as to state that there were some "fine people" amongst the White Supremacist,[717] who were defending "our history and heritage".[718] Exactly a month later, Trump told reporter on *Air Force One*: "You have some pretty bad dudes on the other side [anti-fascists] also and that is essentially what I said [a month ago]."[719]

The backlash—and what a backlash—against Trump quickly followed.[720] Some argued that:

- he has revealed his true racist feelings and far-right political leanings;[721]
- he has disgraced the Office of the President;[722]
- he has lost presidential credibility.[723]
- he has a flawed moral compass;[724]
- he has lost moral authority as president;[725]

---

[717] Retrieved from: https://www.vox.com/2017/8/15/16154028/trump-press-conference-transcript-charlottesville.

[718] Retrieved from: http://www.mailtribune.com/opinion/20170829/michael-gerson-trump-deepens-moral-damage-to-gop.

[719] Retrieved from: https://www.thetimes.co.uk/article/ivanka-trump-dad-isn-t-always-right-and-needs-to-be-told-n3vj5nrnm.

[720] See: http://edition.cnn.com/2017/08/17/politics/donald-trump-statement-fallout/index.html.

[721] See: https://www.cbsnews.com/news/afl-cio-president-says-trump-manufacturing-council-totally-ineffective/.

[722] See: http://www.huffingtonpost.com/entry/charles-krauthammer-trump-a-moral-disgrace-fox-news_us_5993c9f1e4b04b19336176fe; https://www.theguardian.com/us-news/2017/aug/15/donald-trump-press-conference-far-right-defends-charlottesville; https://www.usatoday.com/story/opinion/2017/08/13/trump-charlottesville-disgrace-white-nationalists-not-another-side-cheri-jacobus-column/562740001/.

[723] See: https://www.theatlantic.com/politics/archive/2017/08/trump-charlottesville-nazis-confederate-monument/537195/; https://www.usnews.com/opinion/articles/2017-08-16/is-president-trump-brave-enough-to-visit-charlottesville.

[724] See: https://www.algemeiner.com/2017/08/14trumps-charlottesville-response-shows-lack-of-moral-compass/; http://www.salon.com/2017/08/19/one-more-lesson-from-charlottesville-our-comedians-are-more-ethical-than-our-president/.

[725] See: http://edition.cnn.com/2017/08/17/politics/tim-scott-donald-trump-charlottesville/index.html; https://www.forbes.com/sites/victorlipman/2017/08/17/can-a-leader-without-moral-authority-lead/.

- he lacks the capacity to give moral leadership, as, is at best, an "amoral president"[726];[727] and
- he has made hate fashionable.[728]

His credibility and morality gaps certainly seem to have widened immensely,[729] perhaps even fatally fracturing his presidency.[730] He was condemned by both Republicans[731] and Democrats.[732]

The business community and others quickly disassociated itself from any hint of racism in the Trump administration.[733] Trump was forced to discontinue two presidential business advisory bodies—the Strategy and Policy Forum[734] and the Manufacturing Council[735]—in order to

---

[726]   Retrieved from: http://www.bbc.co.uk/news/av/world-us-canada-40944075/trump-and-charlottesville-amoral-president-stuns-world.

[727]   See: http://uk.businessinsider.com/tim-scott-trumps-charlottesville-response-compromised-moral-authority-lead-2017-8;https://www.washingtonpost.com/opinions/after-charlottesville-end-the-denial-about-trump/2017/08/13/05adbc6e-804a-11e7-b359-15a3617c767b_story.html?utm_term=.06a15cae38fc; https://www.forbes.com/sites/victorlipman/2017/08/17/can-a-leader-without-moral-authority-lead/.

[728]   See: https://www.theguardian.com/sport/2017/aug/15/lebron-james-charlottesville-violence-donald-trump-protest; see also: http://www.bbc.co.uk/news/av/world-us-canada-40944836/how-has-trump-responded-to-other-hate-crimes'.

[729]   See: https://www.usatoday.com/story/opinion/2017/01/25/trump-administrations-credibility-gap/96976224/; https://www.washingtonpost.com/news/comic-riffs/wp/2017/08/15/how-trumps-moral-leadership-went-awol-in-charlottesville-according-to-cartoons/?utm_term=.283bf375e637.

[730]   See: https://www.dailymaverick.co.za/article/2017-08-16-the-road-not-taken-donald-trumps-fatal-misstep/.

[731]   See: http://www.bbc.co.uk/news/world-us-canada-40946386; http://www.bbc.co.uk/news/world-us-canada-40919181; https://www.nytimes.com/2017/08/16/us/politics/trump-republicans-race.html; http://wtop.com/virginia/2017/08/lawmakers-weigh-in-on-trumps-comments-on-charlottesville/.

[732]   See: http://wtop.com/virginia/2017/08/lawmakers-weigh-in-on-trumps-comments-on-charlottesville/.

[733]   See: https://www.forbes.com/forbes/welcome/?toURL=https://www.forbes.com/sites/jeffkauflin/2017/08/15/a-closer-look-at-the-manufacturing-council-resignations-reveals-fascinating-moments-in-leadership/&refURL=https://www.google.co.uk/&referrer=https://www.google.co.uk/; http://uk.businessinsider.com/trump-manufacturing-council-whos-still-in-2017-8.

[734]   See: https://greatagain.gov/president-elect-trump-announces-additional-members-of-presidents-strategic-and-policy-forum-8aa8822eced9.

[735]   See: https://www.cnbc.com/2017/08/16trump-abruptly-ends-manufacturing-council-after-ceos-disband-strategy-and-policy-forum.html.

stem the flow of CEO resignations.[736] Although no member of the Strategy and Policy Forum actually resigned over the Charlottesville incident,[737] they threatened to do so unless the Forum was disbanded, as they were so "outraged" over his claimed there were "some 'very fine people' alongside the neo-Nazi protesters"[738].[739] The obvious, but remarkable, conclusion is:

Corporate America [has] decided that it could not be seen standing alongside a US president—and a Republican president at that.[740] Indeed:

> Following Trump's ban on refugees, his planned withdrawal from the Paris Climate Accord, a decision to ban transgender people from the military and (the final straw), him all but defending white supremacists, America's top business leaders started abandoning ship like there was no tomorrow. So, what does the President do? What he always does. He doubles down and disbands the councils to try to get ahead of a negative story. Sometimes, it seems like the only person who doesn't know the ship is sinking is the captain himself.[741]

Members of the National Infrastructure Advisory Council[742] and of the Committee on the Arts and Humanities[743] also resigned in protest of his

---

[736] See: https://www.cnbc.com/2017/08/16trump-abruptly-ends-manufacturing-council-after-ceos-disband-strategy-and-policy-forum.html; http://www.marketwatch.com/story/trump-today-president-blames-amazon-for-great-damage-to-retailers-2017-08-16; http://www.bbc.co.uk/news/business-40952820.

[737] See: https://ftalphaville.ft.com/2017/08/16/2192402/unlike-manufacturing-council-no-member-of-trumps-strategic-and-policy-forum-has-resigned-over-charlottesville/.

[738] Retrieved from: s://www.ft.com/content/adc17d2e-83f5-11e7-94e2-c5b903247afd.

[739] See: http://uk.businessinsider.com/trump-business-council-strategic-policy-forum-why-ceos-left-2017-8.

[740] Retrieved from: s://www.ft.com/content/adc17d2e-83f5-11e7-94e2-c5b903247afd; But definitely see: http://money.cnn.com/2017/08/19/news/trump-business-councils-ceos-charities/index.html.

[741] Retrieved from: https://www.forbes.com/sites/cartoonoftheday/2017/08/21/ceos-dumping-the-first-ceo-president-like-theres-no-tomorrow-advisory-council-rebellion/#79a48dc2423b.

[742] See: https://www.dhs.gov/national-infrastructure-advisory-council.

[743] See: https://www.pcah.gov/.

presumption of moral equivalence.[744] And, one member of his Evangelical Advisory Board resigned, when it "became obvious that there was a deepening conflict in values between myself and the [Trump] administration."[745] Even the military publicly distanced itself from any hints of racism.[746] TV comedians were ferocious and malicious in the way they expressed their outrage.[747] Trump's presidential performance rating tumbled further[748] as some of his supporters admitted to being disillusioned.[749]

Of course, the leaders of the alt-right and its allies came out in his support.[750]

The Charlottesville incident brought to a head the future of the alt-right cabal in the White House. From the reaction of Republic leaders in Congress, Trump had to decide, once and for all, whether he wish-

---

[744] Retrieved from: http://www.salon.com/2017/08/18/presidents-committee-on-the-arts-and-the-humanities-resigntion/; see also: http://www.abc.net.au/news/2017-08-19/trumps-arts-council-quits-with-hidden-message-in-letter/8823262; https://www.google.co.uk/search?q=Trump%27s+cybersecurity+advisors+resign+en+masse&oq=Trump%27s+cybersecurity+advisors+resign+en+masse&aqs=chrome..69i57j69i60j69i61.2460j0j1&sourceid=chrome&ie=UTF-8.

[745] Retrieved from: http://edition.cnn.com/2017/08/19/politics/pastor-bernard-trump-evangelical-advisory-board-don-lemon-cnntv/index.html. See: https://www.theguardian.com/us-news/2017/aug/18/donald-trump-evangelicals-charlottesville; but see also: http://www.npr.org/2017/08/26/546407356/faith-council-members-take-a-step-back-from-advising-trump; https://www.theatlantic.com/politics/archive/2017/08/evangelical-advisers-trump/537513/.

[746] See: http://edition.cnn.com/2017/08/16/politics/joint-chiefs-charlottesville-racism/index.html.

[747] See: http://edition.cnn.com/2017/08/15/entertainment/jimmy-fallon-charlottesville-monologue/index.html; http://www.indiewire.com/2017/08/lemon-brett-gelman-interview-racism-charlottesville-1201867538/; https://www.vanityfair.com/hollywood/2017/08/donald-trump-charlottesville-seth-meyers-colbert-late-night; http://www.chicagotribune.com/lifestyles/stevens/ct-life-stevens-tuesday-comedians-being-serious-0815-story.html.

[748] See: http://www.politico.com/story/2017/08/23/trump-charlottesville-polls-241917.

[749] See, for example, New York Times, Sunday Review opinion piece at https://www.nytimes.com/2017/08/17/opinion/sunday/i-voted-for-trump-and-i-sorely-regret-it.html?mtrref=undefined&gwh=8E69123B749CD685BBE81AE-C76D4A450&gwt=pay&assetType=opinion,

[750] See: http://www.huffingtonpost.co.uk/entry/alt-right-leaders-praising-donald-trump-response-charlottesville_uk_5993fe93e4b0e789a947f8a6; https://twitter.com/DrDavidDuke/status/897559892164304896.

es to run the country as a credible president for all Americans—or at least for all Republicans—or as a president who has been so publicly captured by alt-right and its allies. The White House Chief of Staff, General John Kelly's body language at Trump's recanting press conference,[751] clear suggests that Trump would have to confront that issue very quickly.[752] Anthony Scaramucci,[753] the short-lived former White House Director of Communication, summed up the situation quite well in mid-August:

> I think there are elements inside of Washington, also inclusive of the White House, that are not necessarily abetting the president's interests or his agenda. I absolutely believe that, yes ...
>
> I think the president is getting his arms around the fact that if he wants to prosecute his agenda he's got to bring in loyalists to him ... He's got to bring in a different strategy to the one he's been deploying ...
>
> At the end of the day, I think the president has a very good idea of who the leakers are inside the White House. The president has a very good idea of the people that are undermining his agenda that are serving their own interests[754] ...

751 See: http://uk.businessinsider.com/photo-of-john-kelly-during-trumps-wild-press-conference-says-it-all-2017-8; http://edition.cnn.com/2017/08/15/politics/john-kelly-news-conference/index.html; but see also: http://nypost.com/2017/08/16/trumps-aides-were-stunned-after-rogue-press-conference/; http://edition.cnn.com/2017/08/15/politics/trump-news-conference-twitter/index.html.

752 See: https://www.reuters.com/article/us-usa-trump-bannon-analysis-idUSKCN1AV2MZ; http://www.bbc.co.uk/news/av/world-us-canada-40944836/how-has-trump-responded-to-other-hate-crimes.

753 See: http://www.telegraph.co.uk/news/2017/07/21/anthony-scaramucci-new-white-house-communications-director-edged/; https://www.theguardian.com/us-news/2017/jul/31/trump-administration-firings-resignations-anthony-scaramucci.

Interestingly, he believes that the Earth is only 5,500 years old. See: https://www.forbes.com/forbes/welcome/?toURL=https://www.forbes.com/sites/trevornace/2017/07/27/trumps-new-white-house-communications-director-believes-earth-5500-years-old/&refURL=https://www.google.co.uk/&referrer=https://www.google.co.uk/.

754 See: https://www.theguardian.com/us-news/2017/jul/18/devils-bargain-

I think the president knows what he's going to do with Steve Bannon.[755]

Indeed, Trump did know his mind; he needed Bannon to consolidate his alt-right support base, perhaps by creating a new al-right party to contest the next round of elections of Congress (in 2018) and the presidency (in 2020), by, once again, being the driving force behind the right-wing *Breitbart News* website. So, he accepted Bannon's resignation "amid a public backlash to Mr Trump's response to a white supremacist rally in Charlottesville, Virginia"[756].[757] The *Washington Post* observed:

> While Bannon's ouster was the latest move by new Chief of Staff John F. Kelly to bring a greater sense of normalcy to the White House, even some of Trump's allies question how likely that is to take hold, particularly under a president who relishes changing the national conversation with a provocative tweet—a practice Kelly has not been able to curb.

TRUMP'S ALBATROSS: HIS LEADERSHIP STYLE

A central leadership paradox of any US president is that although he has a great deal of formal power, his real authority comes only if he has the power of persuasion. As President Harry Truman once reportedly said "I sit here all day long in the White House, trying to convince some damned fool to do what he should have had the sense to do in the first place."[758] Of course, Truman had paid his dues before becoming president,[759] so he knew, or at least had a good idea of, what the "damned

---

joshua-green-steve-bannon-trump-election-win; see also: https://www.theguardian.com/global/2017/jul/26/breitbart-news-donald-trump-jeff-sessions-white-nationalism.

[755] Retrieved from: https://www.theguardian.com/us-news/2017/aug/14/anthony-scaramucci-warns-trump-to-beware-enemy-within.

[756] Retrieved from: http://www.bbc.co.uk/news/world-us-canada-39826934.

[757] See: http://edition.cnn.com/2017/08/18/politics/steve-bannon-white-house/index.html; https://www.vox.com/vox-sentences/2017/8/18/16171890/vox-sentences-bannon-fired

[758] Retrieved from: https://www.dailymaverick.co.za/article/2017-07-21-when-the-leadership-skills-are-missing-in-action-exhibit-trump/#.WXYAFyN95cw.

[759] See: https://www.whitehouse.gov/1600/presidents/harrytruman.

fools" needed to do.

Good leadership is a critical determinant of any president's effectiveness. Stogdill's (1950, 3) timeless and classical definition of leadership—an influencing process aimed at setting and achieving goals—goes a long way in explaining why this is so:

> A leader must be able to influence the course of action in order to be able to develop a vision, stimulate buy-in, rally for execution and maintain the course. One can think of these things but doing them requires the participation of others.

> Influence takes the form of persuasion in order to bring people together for common cause. While leaders can command direct reports they cannot command respect nor can they command followership of those outside their span of control. That requires heaping amounts of influence. This is especially true when you are seeking to bring new followers into your camp. Influence dies when what a leader can do does not match what he should do.[760]

What makes a true political leader—the ideal ruler—has been speculated upon extensively over the millennia (Dixon 2003, 2016):

- *Confucius* ([fifth century BC] 1992)—emphasizing the importance of Right Conduct—considered that the ideal ruler should gave ethical primacy the hierarchy of relationships and adhered to the values of the benevolence (*ren*)—the affectionate concern for the wellbeing of close others; righteousness (*yi*)—the sense of rightness exercised in coping with changing life circumstances; and propriety (*li*)—the proper social patterns of conduct and relations in particular circumstances (Dixon and Wong 2015).

- *Aristotle* ([350 BCE] 2004)—emphasizing the importance of Right Thinking—considered that the ideal ruler should be a virtuous person who is naturally predisposed to acting in a virtuous

---

[760] Retrieved from: https://www.forbes.com/sites/johnbaldoni/2017/07/05/president-trump-yes-you-can-but-should-you/#7177558a204b

way, for virtuous reasons, and so feel pleasure in doing so, because it makes him a flourishing person. This requires the right intellectual and moral virtues, so that they are able to reflect on what they know and to reason properly about how to act:

> If we declare that the function of man is a certain form of life, and define that form of life as the exercise of the soul's faculties and activities in association with rational principle, and say that the function of a good man is to perform these activities well and rightly, and if a function is well performed when it is performed in accordance with its own proper excellence—from these premises it follows that the Good of man is the active exercise of his soul's faculties in conformity with excellence or virtue, or if there be several human excellences or virtues, in conformity with the best and most perfect among them (Sect. I, 7)

• *Plato* ([c360 BC] 1955, [c380s] 1952)—emphasizing the importance of a Wise Orderly Self—considered that the ideal ruler should have a self-controlled and well-ordered self, with wisdom (superior insight) and virtue, and a willingness and ability to get advice from elders who would draw upon their own experience.

• *Machiavelli* ([1513] 2011)—emphasizing the importance of Deceit and Intrigue—considered that the ideal ruler should be able to instill in his people both admiration and fear, but, unfortunately, in the end instilling fear is more important if he wants accomplishments: the "fear preserves you [the prince] by a dread of punishment which never fails" (p. 76).

• *Hobbes* ([1651] 1991—the emphasizing the importance of Peace and Unity—considered that the ideal ruler should be strong enough to sustain civil peace and social unity, thereby avoiding the collapse of society into a nasty and brutish world.

• *Smith* ([1776] 1819)—emphasizing the importance of Personal Liberty—considered that the ideal ruler should be willing to permit private ends to be peacefully pursued by limiting that state's role to ensuring society's safety and security, and to establishing and sustaining the rule of the law of property, tort and contract:

> The statesman who should attempt to direct private people in what manner they ought to employ their capitals, would not only load himself with a most unnecessary attention, but assume an authority ... [that] would nowhere be so dangerous as in the hands of a man who had folly and presumption enough to fancy himself fit to exercise it (p. 243).

- *Burke* ([1756] 1987)—emphasizing the importance of Customs and Traditions—considered the ideal ruler should be strong enough to produce a well-ordered state, one that is grounded in shared traditions, beliefs and habits: "custom reconciles us to everything". (p. 148).

- *Weber* (1946)—emphasizing Authority and Legitimacy—considers the ideal ruler should have legitimate authority—by being rightfully elevated to positions of authority. He gave particular prominence to a charismatic authority:

> Charismatic authority is often the most lasting of regimes because the leader is seen as infallible and any action against him will be seen as a crime against the state. Charismatic leaders eventually develop a cult of personality often not by their own doing ... power legitimised on the basis of a leader's exceptional personal qualities or the demonstration of extraordinary insight and accomplishment ... inspire[s] loyalty and obedience from followers (pp. 245-247).

Trump's leadership style draws upon Machiavelli and Weber—a combination of fear and charisma—seeking to be a Hobbesian strong leader. He is, however, bereft of the moral requisites for rulership demanded by Confucius, Aristotle and Plato, and of the cognitive capacities demanded by Burke and Smith.

Trump lacks the capacity to lead a large, complex and accountable system of public organizations. The *New York Times*, drawing upon opinions of a small a sample of business executives, concluded in February: "Thus far, the Trump administration is a textbook case of how not to run a complex organization like the executive branch. His management style was further scrutinized by experienced business executives in June; and was trashed. CNBC [Consumer News and Business Channel[761]] asked the members of its CNBC Global CFO Council[762]: "If you had to describe President Donald Trump's management style in one word, what would it be? That's the open-ended question in our quarterly survey."[763] Of the 35 respondents, only four remotely characterized his management style positively—as Business-style, Directive, Fluid and Unconventional. The remaining 31 respondents trashed it. They choose to characterize it as Antagonistic, Arrogant, Authoritarian, Autocratic, Chaotic, Chaos, Clueless, Confusing, Dictatorial, Disjointed, Disruptive, Divisive, Erratic, Reckless, Hubristic, Incompetent, Narcissistic, Obnoxious, Reckless, Self-absorbed, Terrible Unpredictable, and Volatile.[764]

As a political leader Trump is without a set of values, without an appreciation of presidential history and tradition, without the interest or ability to inspire people to rally behind a cause that goes beyond self-interest, and without the political nous to appreciate that he needs to build bridges beyond his core base. So, unchanged he is destined to leave to posterity only a legacy of bullshit rhetoric—innumerable tweets—disillusioned supporters, and even a Republican Party struggling to keep control of Congress.

Closer to home—the White House—John Baldoni, the author of *Lead Your Boss: The Subtle Art of Managing Up*,[765] observed in late July:

> Now comes arguably his ['Trump's] toughest challenge: transforming the White House into a smooth operating organization. While some Presidents would welcome

761 See: https://www.cnbc.com.

762 See: https://www.cnbc.com/2016/04/08/cnbc-global-cfo-council.html.

763 See: https://www.cnbc.com/2017/06/23/cfos-react-to-trumps-management-style-and-its-not-pretty-survey.html.

764 See: https://www.cnbc.com/2017/06/23/cfos-react-to-trumps-management-style-and-its-not-pretty-survey.html; http://time.com/money/4830055/president-donald-trump-leadership-management-style/?xid=homepage.

765 See: https://www.cnbc.com/2017/06/23/cfos-react-to-trumps-management-style-and-its-not-pretty-survey.html; http://time.com/money/4830055/president-donald-trump-leadership-management-style/?xid=homepage.

such discipline, Trump is not so inclined. He has had only one boss in his life: his father. He resents being told what to do much in the way of a rebellious teen. He does the opposite.[766]

In early October, Baldoni commented with insight:

Pride robs a boss of self-knowledge. And when you lack insight into yourself you cannot lead others because you are incapable of leading yourself. Self-glorification prevents empathy as well as compassion. The needs of others become subservient to the need for self-aggrandizement.

And that's not good for anyone![767]

Trump's actions so far during his presidency give rise only to pessimism about his presidential leadership capacity. His ego demands that he must have the best of everything, including advisors. But their mere presence, and any hint that they might be disloyal by highlighting, intentionally or otherwise, his inadequacies and incompetence, is likely to induce a knee-jerk reaction to cut them down to size—to show the world that he is still the boss. This is evidenced by the way he treats his senior officials.

Jeff Sessions, his Attorney General and loyal campaign supporter,[768] has been the subject of protracted and on-going humiliation by Trump because he offended, angered,[769] and, in his eyes, made him look "foolish and powerless."[770] This is all because he had recused himself from the

---

[766] Retrieved from: https://www.forbes.com/sites/johnbaldoni/2017/07/29/john-kelly-leada-your-boss/#7ad881e8499b.

[767] Retrieved from: https://www.forbes.com/sites/johnbaldoni/2017/10/08/pride-pettiness-and-the-presidency/#5fecf3534756.

[768] See:http://www.npr.org/2016/07/14/486011917/sen-jeff-sessions-loyal-to-trump-defined-by-race-and-immigration;https://www.theguardian.com/us-news/2017/jul/25/jeff-sessions-donald-trump-feud-russia;https://www.vox.com/policy-and-politics/2017/7/25/16025150/jeff-sessions-donald-trump-resigns.

[769] See: https://www.wbez.org/shows/npr/reports-ag-sessions-offered-to-resign-amid-trump-anger-at-recusal/fc8d7450-9a9f-4168-aa09-abef339fcdcc.

[770] Retrieved from: https://www.theguardian.com/us-news/2017/jul/25/jeff-

Justice Department's investigation into Russian meddling in the 2016 presidential election,[771] even though to do otherwise would have violated the Justice Department code of ethics.[772] Trump, who demands absolute loyalty, unconcerned with ethical propriety, stated publicly:

> Sessions should have never recused himself, and if he was going to recuse himself, he should have told me before he took the job, and I would have picked somebody else.[773]

Perhaps he was harboring the hope of inducing Sessions' resignation, although it was reported that he did offer it to him,[774] as firing him would not be easy, given his congressional connection as a former senator.[775]

Rex Tillerson, his Secretary of State, has had his foreign policy positions persistently undermined by Trump, perhaps to bring him down a peg or two because of his past disloyalty by not supporting his decisions and actions more forcefully.[776] Tillerson has been on the verge of resigning for some months.[777] The tenuousness of their relationship became publicly evident as a result of a very public presidential spat that occurred in early October. It was over whether Trump was a moron[778]—a fool

sessions-donald-trump-feud-russia?CMP=Share_AndroidApp_Gmail.

[771] See: http://www.washingtonexaminer.com/trump-on-his-relationship-with-jeff-sessions-it-is-what-it-is/article/2631207.

[772] See: http://www.businessinsider.com/jeff-sessions-recuse-trump-russia-investigation-james-comey-.2017-6.

[773] Retrieved from: http://www.bbc.co.uk/news/world-us-canada-40665891.

[774] See: http://www.npr.org/sections/thetwo-way/2017/06/06/531840626/reports-ag-sessions-offered-to-resign-amid-trump-anger-at-recusal.

[775] See: http://www.rollingstone.com/politics/features/republicans-are-not-thrilled-trump-might-fire-jeff-sessions-w494568; http://www.chicagotribune.com/sns-bc-us--trump-sessions-20170726-story.html.

[776] See: http://www.firstpost.com/world/donald-trumps-iq-jibe-deepens-feud-with-rex-tillerson-is-end-near-for-long-rocky-relationship-4131485.html.

[777] See: https://www.newyorker.com/magazine/2017/10/16/rex-tillerson-at-the-breaking-point; https://www.nbcnews.com/politics/white-house/tillerson-s-fury-trump-required-intervention-pence-n806451.

[778] "Moron was originally a scientific term, coined by psychologist Henry Goddard from a Greek word meaning 'foolish' and used to describe a person with a genetically determined mental age between 8 and 12 on the Binet scale. It was also once applied to people with an IQ of 51–70 and was a step up from 'imbecile' (IQ of 26–50) and two steps up from 'idiot' (IQ of 0–25)." Retrieved from: http://www.urbandictionary.com/define.php?term=moron.

or "an adult with a mental age of about 8–12."[779] It began when Trump became aware that, at the end of a Pentagon meeting on July 20, a frustrated Tillerson allegedly called Trump a "moron"[780]—or was it a "fucking moron"[781]—an allegation that Tillerson never denied.[782] The public reaction of a furious Trump[783] was to challenge Tillerson to an IQ test face-off.[784] The White House dismissed this as a presidential joke.[785] Their shaky relationship is destined to continue for a while yet, only because Trump is, according to an advisor, "loath to get rid of anyone" at the moment.[786] But, "[a]ccording to some White House officials, their relationship has deteriorated to the point of no return and that it is only a matter of time before Tillerson departs."[787] Indeed, the feud between them reached another peaked in early December, when it was reported:

President Donald Trump has failed to unequivocally back Secretary of State Rex Tillerson, after reports saying the White House is looking to remove the official from his post.

Asked by reporters if he still wanted Mr Tillerson in the job, the President merely said: "He's here. Rex is here."

---

[779] Retrieved from: https://en.oxforddictionaries.com/definition/moron.

[780] Retrieved from: https://www.wired.com/story/internet-week-140/; see also: https://www.newyorker.com/magazine/2017/10/16/rex-tillerson-at-the-breaking-point.

[781] See: https://www.newyorker.com/magazine/2017/10/16/rex-tillerson-at-the-breaking-point.

[782] See: https://www.theguardian.com/us-news/2017/oct/04/rex-tillerson-trump-moron.

[783] See: https://www.thedailybeast.com/stung-over-being-called-a-moron-donald-trump-now-insists-nbc-is-run-by-morons; http://foreignpolicy.com/2017/10/10/trump-stung-by-moron-moniker-challenges-tillerson-to-compare-iqs-intelligence-state-department-diplomacy/.

[784] See: https://www.theguardian.com/us-news/2017/oct/10/donald-trump-forbes-rex-tillerson-moron;https://www.washingtonpost.com/news/post-politics/wp/2017/10/10/trump-proposes-iq-tests-face-off-with-tillerson-after-secretary-of-state-calls-him-a-moron/?utm_term=.46b671066587. But see also particularly: http://www.mercurynews.com/2017/10/07/cartoons-rex-tillerson-and-the-moron/.

[785] See: http://www.politico.com/story/2017/10/10/trump-rex-tillerson-moron-iq-test-243624

[786] Retrieved from: http://www.firstpost.com/world/donald-trumps-iq-jibe-deepens-feud-with-rex-tillerson-is-end-near-for-long-rocky-relationship-4131485.html.

[787] Retrieved from: http://www.firstpost.com/world/donald-trumps-iq-jibe-deepens-feud-with-rex-tillerson-is-end-near-for-long-rocky-relationship-4131485.html.

Multiple reports suggest that Mr Trump had probably tasked Chief of Staff, John Kelly, with handling a transition that would see Mr Tillerson replaced with CIA Director Mike Pompeo within weeks.[788]

Trump has managed to fire four senior officials, including one of his longest-serving political aides, despite his alleged dislike of firing people:

> "I think Donald Trump doesn't like to fire people, period," the former House Speaker Newt Gingrich, a Trump adviser and friend, said Tuesday [July 25] on *Fox News*. During his presidential campaign and into his presidency, Trump has kept dismissals at arm's length, fuming in public at the state of his affairs, but rarely acting as the person who brings the hammer down on the person behind his ire.[789]

Those who have been fired are:

- *Sally Yates*, his Acting Attorney General, originally an Obama appointee, who he fired in late January, after she questioned the legality of Mr Trump's [first Executive Order] travel ban on seven Muslim-majority countries. Ms Yates ... believed it discriminated unconstitutionally against Muslims, and ordered justice department lawyers not to enforce the president's executive order.[790] A Federal Court subsequently vindicated her legal opinion.[791]

- *James Comey*,[792] the long-term FBI Director, who he fired in early May[793]—"He was crazy, a real nut job" according to Trump[794]—

---

788   Retrieved from: http://www.independent.co.uk/news/world/americas/us-politics/rex-tillerson-fired-secretary-state-department-mike-pompeo-replace-white-house-donald-trump-a8084966.html.

789   Retrieved from: http://edition.cnn.com/2017/07/26/politics/trump-firing-people-jeff-sessions-contrast/index.html.

790   Retrieved from: http://www.bbc.co.uk/news/world-us-canada-39826934

791   See: http://www.independent.co.uk/news/world/americas/seattle-federal-judge-restraining-order-donald-trump-immigration-ban-a7562406.html.

792   See: https://www.theguardian.com/us-news/2017/jul/31/trump-administration-firings-resignations-anthony-scaramucci.

793   See: http://edition.cnn.com/2017/06/10/politics/trump-comey-testimony-timeline-what-we-know/index.html.

794   See: https://www.theguardian.com/us-news/2017/may/19/officials-identify-white-house-person-of-interest-trump-russia.Butsee:https://www.washingtonpost.

because, according to Comey, he declined to exculpate Trump
publicly, to give him a pledge of his personal loyalty, and to discontinue the FBI's Flynn inquiry:

> The Trump administration first claimed Mr Comey's han-
> dling of the Clinton email investigation [in 2016] rendered
> him no longer able to credibly lead the bureau and that Mr
> Trump had acted on the deputy attorney general's recom-
> mendation.

> However, Mr. Trump soon contradicted this, calling him a
> "showboat" in a TV interview and saying he was thinking of
> the "Russia thing" when he made the decision to sack him.

> Later it emerged that he allegedly told Russian officials that
> the dismissal had taken "great pressure" off him.[795]

- *Anthony Scaramucci*, a brash, long-standing business associate who had repeatedly publicly defended Trump during his
presidential campaign, was his short-lived Director of White
House Communications, being fired 10 days—or was it 11
days as Scaramucci claims[796]—after his appointment decision
was made, but 15 days before was due to take up his appointment[797]. His crass and undignified public addresses generated
news headlines—taking the spotlight off Trump—and went
well beyond the pale in one epic media rant[798]:

> He appeared to accuse Chief of Staff Reince Priebus of being
> responsible for White House leaks[799] in a tweet (later delet-

com/news/the-fix/wp/2017/05/20/from-nut-job-to-wacko-trump-has-a-history-
of-insulting-others-mental-health/?utm_term=.2c87c3c21de9.

795 Retrieved from: http://www.bbc.co.uk/news/world-us-canada-39826934.

796 See: https://www.theguardian.com/us-news/2017/oct/03/anthony-scaramu
cci-post-media-company.

797 See: http://www.bbc.co.uk/news/world-us-canada-39826934; http://www.bbc.
co.uk/news/world-us-canada-40782299.

798 See: https://www.thesun.co.uk/news/4117622/donald-trumps-new-pr-chief-
anthony-the-mooch-scaramucci-launches-into-epic-rant-saying-he-wants-to-
kill-paranoid-schizophrenic-white-hous/; http://www.bbc.co.uk/news/av/
world-us-canada-40780842/anthony-scaramucci-sacked-10-memorable-
quotes-from-10-days.

799 See also: http://edition.cnn.com/2017/07/28/politics/trump-reince-priebus-
anthony-scaramucci-health-care/index.html.

ed) that also appeared to threaten him.

Mr Scaramucci then attacked Mr Priebus and President Trump's senior adviser Steve Bannon in an expletive-filled rant on the phone with a reporter from the New Yorker magazine.

Although he had boasted of reporting directly to the president, Mr Scaramucci's ill-discipline may have cost him any post alongside President Trump's new chief of staff—retired, four-star General John Kelly.[800]

- *George Gigicos*, one of Trump's four longest-serving political aides, was his White House Director of Presidential Advance,[801] whose job included organizing the campaign-style rallies as a contractor to the Republican National Committee. Trump fired him in late August for not filling his event venue for a campaign-style rally at Phoenix, Arizona:

  A Phoenix official estimated the crowd to be 10,000 strong, a rather midsize rally by Trump standards—the president was fuming. Afterward, he dispatched his longtime bodyguard, Keith Schiller—the same man he sent to fire James Comey—to tell Gigicos that he would never manage a Trump rally again. ... Gigicos's failure to create a comforting environment for the president's public therapy session, then, was the ultimate betrayal. Trump takes no joy from venting in a half-empty room.[802]

Trump has also facilitated, deliberately or otherwise, the resignations of:

---

[800] Retrieved from: http://www.bbc.co.uk/news/world-us-canada-39826934. See also: http://www.bbc.co.uk/news/world-us canada-40684697.

[801] See:https://www.whitehouse.gov/participate/internships/departments #Advance.

[802] Retrieved from: https://www.vanityfair.com/news/2017/08/donald-trump-fires-rally-organizer (emphasis in original). See also: https://www.bloomberg.com/news/articles/2017-08-28/trump-is-said-to-punish-longtime-aide-after-angry-phoenix-speech; https://www.washingtonpost.com/news/post-politics/wp/2016/10/29/yes-donald-trumps-crowds-are-big-but-not-quite-as-yuge-as-he-often-claims/?utm_term=.857e2776eeef.

- *Michael Flynn*,[803] his initial National Security Advisor and loyal campaign advisor,[804] who Trump asked to resign after 23 days in mid-February,[805] because he misled, among others, the Vice President, Mike Pense,[806] on his contacts with the Russian ambassador Sergei Kislyak.[807]

- *Katie Walsh*, his initial Deputy Chief of Staff, a former senior Republican National Committee official and ally of then White House Chief of Staff, Reince Priebus, who resigned at the end of March[808]: "... some [White House] staffers, especially those who worked on Trump's campaign, did not trust her and fed negative stories questioning her loyalties to conservative outlets like Brietbart."[809]

- *Walter Shaub*, the Director of the Office of Government Ethics, who resigned in early July, after he "sharply criticized President Donald Trump's conflicts of interest earlier this year ... choosing to become an ethics watchdog outside government rather than in it."[810]

- *Sean Spicer*, Trump's initial Press Secretary, who was required, repeatedly, to defend the indefensible, which made him look bad. He was:

---

803 See: https://www.theguardian.com/us-news/2017/jul/31/trump-administration-firings-resignations-anthony-scaramucci. See also: https://newsstand.google.com/articles/CAIiEK05bEKqOtkcHZtmud-rzc8qFggEKg0I ACoGCAowxYgCMIBNMJeP1AM.

804 See: http://www.businessinsider.com/trump-defending-mike-flynn-2017-5.

805 See: http://www.bbc.co.uk/news/world-us-canada-39826934.

806 See: https://newsstand.google.com/articles/CAIiEL0MS5mnD_VUUZgms IrkCRoqGQgEKhAIACoHCAowocv1CjCSptoCMPrTpgU.

807 See: http://abcnews.go.com/Politics/timeline-michael-flynns-interactions-russia-cost-job/story?id=45456031; https://www.washingtonpost.com/news/post-politics/wp/2017/02/14/trump-was-told-weeks-ago-that-flynn-misled-vice-president-about-russia-contacts-white-house-says/?utm_term=.360e723053c3; http://edition.cnn.com/2017/05/18/politics/mike-pence-michael-flynn-trump-russia/index.html; https://www.usnews.com/opinion/articles/2017-05-19/how-much-did-vice-president-mike-pence-know-about-michael-flynn.

808 See: http://time.com/4718902/white-house-staff-katie-walsh-departure/.

809 Retrieved from: http://time.com/4718902/white-house-staff-katie-walsh-departure/.

810 Retrieved from: https://www.vox.com/policy-and-politics/2017/7/6/1592 9742/walter-shaub-office-government-ethics-resigned.

[s]truggling with the task of defending Trump's every deed and tweet to the media. [Spicer's] pugnacious style has been lampooned mercilessly by Melissa McCarthy[811] on [NBC's] Saturday Night Live, complete with weaponized lectern.[812]

And he was

the subject of ridicule for feisty exchanges with reporters (inspiring Melissa McCarthy's caricature of Spicer on NBC's *Saturday Night Live*) and awkward comments by Spicer, like suggesting that Adolph Hitler never used chemical weapons.[813]

His resignation seemed inevitable. He stepped down in late July, just after Mr Scaramucci was appointed to a role he had partially filled [as Director of Communications], which he believed was "a major mistake."[814]

- *Reince Priebus,* Trump's initial Chief of Staff—a former Republican National Committee chairman and a Washington insider. He was set up by Trump to be unable to assert his authority over the contending White House factions,[815] and so he was unable to stop the flow of leaks emanating from the White House:

President Trump lost confidence in him and clearly wanted a shake-up in the White House, opting for a general to replace the Republican Party operative, who was seen as weak.[816]

---

811 See: http://www.imdb.com/name/nm0565250/.

812 Retrieved from: https://www.theguardian.com/tv-and-radio/video/2017/feb/12/melissa-mccarthy-revives-impersonation-sean-spicer-snl-video; see also: https://www.theguardian.com/us-news/2017/mar/10/donald-trump-first-50-days-white-house-administration.

813 See: https://www.forbes.com/sites/markjoyella/2017/07/21/sean-spicer-quits-because-donald-trumps-hit-show-made-him-look-bad/#5cfab0984905.

814 Retrieved from: http://www.telegraph.co.uk/news/2017/07/21/sean-spicer-resigns-white-house-press-secretary-anthony-scaramucci/. See also: http://www.bbc.co.uk/news/world-us-canada-40687521.

815 Retrieved from: http://edition.cnn.com/2017/07/31/opinions/white-house-shakeup-opinion-louis/index.html.

816 Retrieved from: http://www.bbc.com/news/world-us-canada-39826934.

- *Steve Bannon,* Trump's Chief Strategist and enthusiastic campaign supporter[817]—a "Cardinal Richelieu in cargo pants."[818] Trump initially designated him, along with Reince Priebus, as co-equal chief advisors. In April it was reported that Bannon is "enduring a 'bad time' partly due to low polling numbers for Trump and the growing influence of President Donald Trump's daughter Ivanka and son-in law Jared Kushner[819]."[820] He survived until August, when Trump accepted his resignation soon after the Charlottesville incident[821].[822]

Trump, by his actions, does seem to evidence the merit of the Master of Deceit and Intrigue's observation: "Princes, especially new ones, have found more fidelity and assistance in those men who in the beginning of their rule were distrusted than among those who in the beginning were trusted" (Machiavelli [1513] 2011, 94–95).

CONCLUSION

If Trump believes his own assessment of his presidential leadership, he still has a lot to learn about being president and leading the White House:

I think my team has been, well, I have different teams.

---

[817] See: http://www.bbc.com/news/world-us-canada-38996534; https://www.project-syndicate.org/commentary/trump-bannon-radical-ideology-by-mark-leonard-2017-03; http://google.com/newsstand/s/CBIwrYecwDQ; http://www.huffingtonpost.com/entry/jared-kushner-steve-bannon-national-security-council_us_58e5a8d1e4b0fe4ce0882c8c; http://edition.cnn.com/2017/04/12/politics/trump-bannon-backing/index.html; but see: http://edition.cnn.com/2017/04/13/opinions/bannon-departure-would-rip-fJung-off-blue-collar-trump-opinion-zelizer/index.html?iid=ob_lockedrail_topeditorial.

[818] Retrieved from: http://www.independent.co.uk/news/world/americas/us-politics/donald-trump-white-house-infighting-tweet-us-news-media-fake-news-michael-flynn-reince-priebus-steve-a7616486.html#gallery.

[819] See: https://www.vanityfair.com/news/2017/04/jared-kushner-steve-bannon-white-house-civil-war.

[820] Retrieved from: https://www.cnbc.com/2017/04/07/bannon-reportedly-told-to-lay-low-as-white-house-denies-reports-of-trump-shake-up.html?view=story&%24DEVICE%24=native-android-mobile.

[821] Retrieved from: http://www.bbc.co.uk/news/world-us-canada-39826934.

[822] See: http://edition.cnn.com/2017/08/18/politics/steve-bannon-white-house/index.html; https://www.vox.com/vox-sentences/2017/8/18/16171890/vox-sentences-bannon-fired.

I think my military team has been treated with great respect. As they should be. I think my other team hasn't been treated with the respect that they should get. We have some very talented people, and very diverse people.[823]

I think Reince (Priebus) [his then Chief of Staff] has been doing an excellent job. I think that, you know, this is a very tough environment not caused necessarily by me.[824]

Indeed, as has been observed:

So coming into the White House he [Trump] brings along his family-business style, no-holds barred executive style ... The irony of tough-guy leadership style is that it simply does not work long-term. You can bluster and bully in the short run, but pretty soon that act gets old. Good people say enough is enough and leave. The organization is left with hangers-on who seem loyal merely because they cannot get a job anywhere else ... This is no way to run a business let alone a country.[825]

---

[823] Retrieved from: https://apnews.com/c810d7de280a47e88848b0ac74690c83.

[824] Retrieved from: https://apnews.com/c810d7de280a47e88848b0ac74690c83.

[825] Retrieved from: https://www.forbes.com/forbes/welcome/?toURL=https://www.forbes.com/sites/johnbaldoni/2017/05/12/president-trump-knows-no-composure/&refURL=https://www.google.com.tr/&referrer=https://www.google.com.tr/.

5

DONALD J. TRUMP: ON PUBLIC POLICY AND HIS DOMESTIC AND INTERNATIONAL POLICIES

INTRODUCTION

Trump is disinterested and unwilling to master the art and science of making, enacting, and implementing policy. Dye's (2010, 1) classic definition of public policy captures its essence of what this means:

> Public policy is whatever governments choose to do or not to do. Governments do many things. They regulate conflict within society; they organize society to carry on conflict with other societies; they distribute a great variety of symbolic rewards and material services to members of the society; and they extract money from society, most often in the form of taxes. Thus public policies may regulate behavior, organize bureaucracies, distribute benefits, or extract taxes—or all these things at once.

Essentially, public policy comes down to answering five questions:

- What are the causes and consequences of an issue that has been identified as needing government intervention (issue analysis)?
- What should government do, or not do, in the public interest, about that issue (public interest analysis)?
- What can government do about that issue? (policy analysis)?
- How can a government do whatever needs to be done about it? (implementation analysis)?
- Who should pay for what the government decides needs to be done? (financing analysis)?

Behind these simple-looking questions is a labyrinth of tanged issues, most notably, those related to causation, consequences, political winners and losers, and constitutionality. Indeed, making good public policy is difficult, very difficult.

Politicians rarely know exactly what the consequences of a policy decision will be. Because policy decisions, inevitably, create winners and losers, making policy decisions is about making hard ethical judgments about how to trade-off the interests of one segment of society against those of another segment. Such trade-offs are also likely to difficult to justify. It is easier for politicians to foster the pretence that everyone is a winner, then, there is no need to acknowledge, accommodate, or compensate any losers. The inevitable outcome, of course, is the creation of an angry—even revengeful—group of losers. For Trump, untangling these issues on any given public policy domain is a near-impossible challenge, as he seems resolutely committed to the idea that there are simple and easy solutions to complex public policy issues.

TRUMP AND PUBLIC POLICY

Making and enacting public policy is a challenge for the most seasoned Washington politician, even those who, by inclination, are natural satisficers, and so are "pleased to settle for a good enough option, not necessarily the very best outcome in all respects."[826] They accept that policies are the product of multi-institutional activities conducted in a way that facilitates satisficing decision-making (Simon [1947] 1960). Pugh and Hickson (1996, 134) describe the satisficing decision-making process as envisaged by Simon:

> In this process decision-maker are content with gross simplifications, taking into account only those comparatively few relevant factors which their minds can manage to encompass. "Most human decision making whether individual or organizational, is concerned with the discovery and selection of satisfactory alternatives; only in exceptional cases is it concerned with the discovery and selection of optimal alternatives".

For Trump, however, satisficing policy decision-making—win–win policymaking—requires compromise, but, as he has remarked: "oftentimes

---

[826] Retrieved from: https://www.psychologytoday.com/blog/science-choice/201 506/satisficing-vs-maximizing.

compromise is the equivalent of defeat, and I don't like being defeated" (*Life*, January 1989, cited in Piehler 2016, 69). And for him, multi-institutional policymaking requires engaging, far more than he would prefer, with one or more of his scorned institutional nemeses—his policy thwarters—in the Washington swamp and well beyond:

- The federal executive—some of which is beyond his direct and immediate control—the intelligence agencies—and all which is actively defending their sources of autonomy (their statutory powers and obligations) and exercising their political power (through their influential stakeholders).

- Congress, particularly the disloyal factions within the Congressional Republican Part,[827] and, of course, the Democrats.

- Federal courts, which seeks to constrain his presidential power in a way that is contrary to the "will of the people."

- State governments, whether under Republican or Democrat control, which are forever seeking to get the edge on Washington.

- Foreign governments and influential international agencies, all of which are beyond his direct control.

- The news media, ever and always intent on closely unpicking, dissecting, and judging his every word—teasing out the contradictions and incongruities in the nooks and crannies of his mind—which, to his chagrin, remains beyond his direct control.[828]

For Trump, dealing with the minutiae of presidential policymaking has its challenges, for he lacks the necessary deliberative, implementation, or agent mindsets. He likes to deal only with the big picture—one that he can easily gain from a very succinct policy brief. He prefers to "forget about the little shit" policy details[829]—which challenge his short attention span and his strong preference for reading only "in small doses and when his own name appears prominently."[830] This means, of course, that

---

[827] See: http://www.vox.com/obamacare/2017/3/24/15055232/donald-trump-ahca-statement.

[828] See: ww.factcheck.org/person/donald-trump/.

[829] This is how Trump reportedly described healthcare policy minutae to the Freedom Caucus of the congressional Republican Party in March. See: http://talkingpointsmemo.com/livewire/trump-freedom-caucus-little-stuff-concern

[830] Retrieved from: http://www.independent.co.uk/voices/donald-trump-dimmest-

he does enjoy reading his very special large folder:

> Twice a day since the beginning of the Trump's admin-
> istration, a special folder is prepared for the president.
> The first document is prepared around 9:30 a.m., and
> the follow-up around 4:30 p.m. Former Chief of Staff
> Reince Priebus and former Press Secretary Sean Spicer
> both wanted the privilege of delivering the 20-to-25-
> page packet to President Trump personally, White
> House sources say.

> These sensitive papers [ruefully referred to by some
> White House insiders as "the propaganda docu-
> ment"].... are filled with screenshots of positive cable
> news chyrons (those lower-third headlines and crawls),
> admiring tweets, transcripts of fawning TV interviews,
> praise-filled news stories, and sometimes just pictures
> of Trump on TV looking powerful.

> One White House official said the only feedback [from
> Trump] the White House communications shop, which
> prepares the folder, has ever gotten in all these months
> is: "It needs to be more fucking positive."[831]

Trump is a naïve and impulsive president who prefers gathering the information he thinks he needs from the media. He is a news junkie. According to White House sources:

> Trump may not be a fan of briefing books, but he does
> devour the news. Most mornings, current and former
> aides say, Trump reads through a handful of newspa-
> pers in print, including The New York Times, New York
> Post, The Washington Post, and The Wall Street Jour-
> nal—all while watching cable news shows in the back-
> ground.

us-president-ever-personal-mobile-phone-number-security-concerns-a7766271.
html.

[831] Retrieved from: https://news.vice.com/story/trump-folder-positive-news-white
-house.

He uses the Internet minimally, other than tweeting and tracking his mentions, so what other news stories he sees can be more haphazard. Trump does receive a daily binder of news clippings put together by his communications team, but White House officials disagreed about how much he reads those. White House and former campaign aides have tried to make sure it includes regular doses of praise and positive stories to keep his mood up—a tactic honed by staff during the campaign to keep him from tweeting angrily[832].[833]

This novel information gathering approach provides an interesting insight into the way Trump thinks about policymaking. Reportedly, "he wants policy papers heavy on maps and graphics and not dense with boring words."[834] He is reported to have said he likes his briefings short: "I like bullets or I like as little as possible. I don't need, you know, 200-page reports on something that can be handled on a page. That I can tell you."[835] Still, according to White House sources:

> The best way to focus the president's attention on any story is to tell him about it personally, even if it is in one of the papers he has already thumbed through. But officials say it's a high-risk, high-reward proposition because Trump's frustrations at bad stories can easily boomerang against those delivering him the news.
>
> Still, Trump advisers are unwilling to give up the chance to directly bend the president's ear and hand him supporting documents because they have seen how he can be swayed.[836]

---

[832] See also: http://www.politico.com/story/2017/02/trump-twitterstaffer-235263.

[833] Retrieved from: http://www.politico.com/story/2017/05/15/donald-trump-fake-news-238379

[834] Retrieved from: https://www.nytimes.com/2017/02/18/opinion/sunday/trapped-in-trumps-brain.html?mcubz=3.

[835] Retrieved from: http://www.msnbc.com/rachel-maddow-show/intelligence-briefings-trump-prefers-little-possible; http://www.businessinsider.com/trump-daily-intelligence-briefings-short-and-full-of-killer-graphics-2017-5.

[836] Retrieved from: http://www.politico.com/story/2017/05/15/donald-trump-

Indeed, the task of giving Trump a policy briefing must be challenging, particularly if he perceives the advice being tendered to be critical or offensive, whether directly stated or implied, according to the web of fantasies he has built up to support his fragile ego. This is a recipe for policy delusion and, ultimately, an unimplemented presidential policy agenda.

Change, however looms, if the new Chief of Staff, General John Kelly, gets his way. He has imposed a rigorous new system to control over what Trump reads and whom he sees[837]: "The creation of policy will involve the drafting of 'decision memos' to collate recommendations from different agencies and outline options".[838] It may work, but only if Trump can discipline himself to read more boring words and to control his impulses and his twitter urges, and if Kelly can instil in him the judgment, wisdom, and emotional intelligence required for real presidential leadership; a tall order, even for a General.

TRUMP'S CAMPAIGN PROMISES AS EXPRESSIONS OF THE PUBLIC INTEREST

Trump holds the populist standpoint that, because he is now president in control of the Executive Branch, the people are now in control of the government.[839] Thus, he takes for granted that his campaign promises[840]—literally hundreds of promises, pledges, and threats—are expressions of the public interest. This has classically defined by Lasswell (1930, 264) as "the displacement of private affects upon public objects.

---

fake-news-238379

[837] See: https://www.nytimes.com/2017/08/24/us/politics/trump-white-house-kelly-memos.html?mcubz=3.

[838] Retrieved from: https://www.thetimes.co.uk/article/general-john-kelly-imposes-military-rule-on-west-wing-chaos-pg8pr7ltv.

[839] See: https://www.theguardian.com/world/2017/jan/20/donald-trump-inauguration-speech-full-text; but see: https://www.theguardian.com/world/2017/jan/20/donald-trump-inauguration-speech-analysis; but see also: https://www.theguardian.com/commentisfree/2017/jan/24/donald-trumps-warning-sign-populism-authoritarianism-inauguration. But see: http://www.huffingtonpost.co.uk/mark-malcomson/donald-trump_b_14200514.html.

[840] For a definitive list of Trump's campaign promises see: https://www.washingtonpost.com/news/post-politics/wp/2016/01/22/here-are-76-of-donald-trumps-many-campaign-promises/.

The affects which are organized in the family are redistributed upon various social objects such as the state." His presumption that his campaign promises require no further justifications is grounded in the proposition that political campaigns constitute the only process that gives rise to definitive "will of the people." This makes his campaign promises unchallengeable by others. But, of course, he can—and does—change or abandon them at a whim. He sees himself as the embodiment of the "will of the people," which means that he is free to act on their behalf as their proxy, regardless of what they think or or want—thereby he feels free to substitute what he wants for the what his supporters want.

In so sanctifying his campaign promises, he is conveniently ignoring that he is without a *bona fide* mandate from the American people. There are four reasons or this. The first is that he won the presidency because of an archaic and outmoded electoral method—the Electoral College[841]—one that has been gerrymandered[842]—the boundaries of an electoral constituency are changed so as to advantage a particular party[843]—to favor the Republican Party (McGann et al. 2016).[844] His 304 Electoral College votes—34 more than required (13%)—gave Trump a clear legal victory.[845] The second reason is that he became president with only a minority of the votes caste (46%, 62.9 million people[846]), which is 2.9 million less than his opponent[847] Hilary Clinton[848]and 10.9 million

---

[841] See: https://www.scholastic.com/teachers/articles/teaching-content/electoral-college/.

[842] See also: http://blogs.lse.ac.uk/usappblog/2017/02/08/gerrymandering-the-presidency-why-trump-could-lose-the-popular-vote-in-2020-by-6-percent-and-still-win-a-second-term/.

[843]   See: https://www.washingtonpost.com/news/wonk/wp/2015/03/01/this-is-the-best-explanation-of-gerrymandering-you-will-ever-see/?utm_term=.076f53e8bad0.

[844] See: https://www.brennancenter.org/blog/tying-presidential-electors-gerrymandered-congressional-districts-will-sabotage-elections; http://www.pewresearch.org/fact-tank/2016/12/20/why-electoral-college-landslides-are-easier-to-win-than-popular-vote-ones/; http://www.joycefdn.org/news/redistricting-reform-works?gclid=CjwKCAjw2N vLBRAjEiwAF98GMZBhfJim1ii6SOCZLf8kMfaNn95HP1NHAoK4wqf15MRewaTP_ lOSTxoCmokQAvD_BwE. See also: https://www.theguardian.com/us-news/2016/ nov/21/wisconsin-gerrymandering-district-court-2016-election-decision.

[845] See: https://www.nytimes.com/interactive/2016/12/18/us/elections/donald-trump-electoral-colmlege-popular-vote.html.

[846] See: https://transition.fec.gov/pubrec/fe2016/2016presgeresults.pdf.

[847] Ibid

[848] Ibid

less that all his opponents combine[849]—notwithstanding his outrageous claim, made—without any supporting evidence—of very extensive voter fraud involving "millions" of votes.[850] The third reason is that 41.1% of the 232 million eligible voters chose not to caste a vote (95.3 million people).[851] Thus, Trump attained the presidency with the support of only 27% of the eligible voter population. This means that 169 million people choose not to vote for Trump. The fourth reason is "the people" have also expressed their will when they elected 535 Senators and Representatives, who can also claim that their campaign promises represent at least a legitimate perspective on what constitutes the public interest, one, indeed, that cannot be arbitrarily dismissed. This gives rise to the complexities of the politics that has long prevailed in Washington, a legacy of the Founding Fathers of Federation.

Yet, Trump considers that he has no obligation to justify how implementing his campaign promises will advance the common or collective good of all the people—some 325 million men, women, and children.[852] This is of particular importance when his campaign promises are likely to create losers and well as winners, as with the repeal Obamacare, where the losers are well represented among his own core supporters,[853] who he seems willing to abandon in order to attain a much needed political "win"[854]. He is indifferent as to whether implementing his campaign promises will be in the interest of all Americans, or will be for the good of American society as a whole, rather than just in the interests of his core supporters. Indeed, the on-going public criticism about his presidency, and his poor approval ratings—under 40%—by the standards defined by his predecessors over some 40 years,[855] would strongly sug-

---

[849]   Ibid

[850]   See Trump's tweet on 27 November 2016, retrieved from: http://edition.cnn.com/2016/12/21/politics/donald-trump-hillary-clinton-popular-vote-final-count/index.html.

[851]   See: http://www.businessinsider.com/trump-voter-turnout-records-history-obama-clinton-2016-11.

[852]   Retrieved from: http://www.worldometers.info/world-population/us-population/.

[853]   See: http://www.vox.com/obamacare/2017/3/24/15055232/donald-trump-ahca-statement

[854]   See: https://newsstand.google.com/articles/CAIiEJ02VEFmviHj8DxbRemYx8YqFQgEKg0IACoGCAowrqkBMKBFMLKAAg

[855]   See: http://www.gallup.com/poll/201617/gallup-daily-trump-job-approval.aspx

gest that his campaign promises are not popularly perceived to be in the public interest.

TRUMP'S POLICY AGENDA

Ninety-four million Americans are out of the labor force. Over 43 million people are now living in poverty, and over 43 million Americans are on food stamps. More than one in five people in their prime working years are not working. We have the worst financial recovery in 65 years. In the last eight years, the past administration has put on more new debt than nearly all of the other Presidents combined.

We've lost more than one-fourth of our manufacturing jobs since NAFTA was approved, and we've lost 60,000 factories since China joined the World Trade Organization in 2001. Our trade deficit in goods with the world last year was nearly $800 billion dollars. And overseas we have inherited a series of tragic foreign policy disasters (Donald J. Trump, Address to Congress, February, 2017). [856]

Trump's vision of the good society is one in which there would be jobs for all, and everyone would be safe from foreigners—be they hostile foreign states, foreign terrorists, or just outsiders. Following are the major campaign promises that have become Trump's key policies:[857]

- Immigration policy:
  - Muslims: Impose a temporary ban on Muslims entering the US, block Syrian refugees, and create a Muslim registry.
  - Latinos: Build an American–Mexico border wall, for which

---

[856] Retrieved from: https://www.whitehouse.gov/the-press-office/2017/02/28/remarks-president-trump-joint-address-congress.

[857] See: https://www.washingtonpost.com/news/post-politics/wp/2016/01/22/here-are-76-of-donald-trumps-many-campaign-promises/; http://edition.cnn.com/interactive/2017/politics/tracking-trumps-promises/;http://www.bbc.com/news/world-us-canada-37982000; http://www.politifact.com/truth-o-meter/promises/trumpometer/; https://www.aol.com/news/trump-campaign-promises/.

Mexico will pay, and deport millions of undocumented immigrants.

- Domestic economic policy:
  - Rebuild America's infrastructure.
  - Lower taxes for individuals and corporations.
- Healthcare policy:
  - Repeal Obamacare.
  - Provide universal market-based health insurance.
- International trade policy:
  - Bring jobs back from overseas.
  - Impose tariffs on goods made in China and Mexico
  - Re-negotiate or withdraw from the North American Free Trade Agreement and the Trans-Pacific Partnership.
- Foreign policy:
  - Improve Russian relations.
  - Renegotiate the Iran deal.
  - Defeat ISIS.
- Defense policy:
  - Rebuild American military capacity.
  - Withdraw from the North Atlantic Treaty Organization.
- Climate change and environmental policy:
  - Withdraw from Paris climate agreement.
  - Cancel payments to all United Nations (UN) climate change programs.
  - Reverse all related environmental restrictions.

ON DOMESTIC POLICY

Trump, the reluctant collectivist, is a Keynesian market interventionist.[858] Thus, he accepts that the state should modestly seek to guide the

---

858   See: https://www.bloomberg.com/view/articles/2016-11-18/even-trump-is-a-

marketplace to achieve a desirable state of economic affairs. This differentiated him from the free-market perspectives held by the conservative mainstream of the Republican Party. It remains to be seen, however, whether he understands the logic of economics.

Trump's key domestic policies are premised on the public interest being advanced by:

- The creation of jobs, particularly in the manufacturing sector.[859]

- The implementation of "a pro-growth tax reform to help American workers and businesses keep more of their hard-earned dollars."[860]

- The repeal and replacement of Obamacare.[861]

Trump's Domestic Policies

Trump has indicated that his most important domestic policy aspiration is "to create 25 million new American jobs in the next decade and return to 4% annual economic growth."[862]

Rebuilding America's Infrastructure

During his presidential campaign, Trump lamented that America's airports were of third-world standard, that the country's roads were crumbling, and that there were wobbly bridges in need of repair.[863] He promised to spend $1 trillion on infrastructure rebuilding,[864] although the American Society of Civil Engineers' estimates that an investment of more than $4.5 trillion by 2025 may well be needed to restore America's

---

keynesian; https://mises.org/blog/keynes-would-have-loved-trumps-economic-plan; http://www.salon.com/2017/03/27/hes-a-kynesian-now-donald-trump-tells-nyt-he-wants-to-prime-the-pump/.

[859]   See: https://www.whitehouse.gov/bringing-back-jobs-and-growth.

[860]   Retrieved from: https://www.whitehouse.gov/bringing-back-jobs-and-growth.

[861]   See: https://www.whitehouse.gov/repeal-and-replace-obamacare.

[862]   Retrieved from: https://www.whitehouse.gov/bringing-back-jobs-and-growth.

[863]   Retrieved from: https://www.nytimes.com/2017/03/17/us/politics/trump-budget-in frastructure.html.

[864]   https://www.cnbc.com/2017/02/27/trump-pledges-to-spend-big-on-infrastructure. html

failing infrastructure.[865] When speaking to a group of governors in late February he indicated that he would be making a "big statement" about fixing roads and bridges in his Address to Congress (on February 28):

> We spend $6 trillion in the Middle East and we have potholes all over our highways and our roads ... so we're going to take care of that. Infrastructure—we're going to start spending on infrastructure big. Not like we have a choice. It's not like, oh gee, let's hold it off.[866]

His "big statement" to Congress was:

> Another Republican President, Dwight D. Eisenhower, initiated the last truly great national infrastructure program—the building of the Interstate Highway System. The time has come for a new program of national rebuilding. (Applause.) ... To launch our national rebuilding, I will be asking Congress to approve legislation that produces a $1 trillion investment in infrastructure of the United States—financed through both public and private capital—creating millions of new jobs. (Applause.) This effort will be guided by two core principles: buy American and hire American. (Applause.)[867]

In June, the White House announced the presidential infrastructure rebuilding plan. It involves:

- reducing dramatically the permitted time for the completion of these infrastructure projects from 10 years to 2 years and to get a "yes" or "no" quickly by slashing regulations;

- unleashing private sector capital and expertise to rebuild our cities and states;

- dedicating $200 billion in his 2018 budget for infrastructure

---

[865] Retrieved from: http://uk.businessinsider.com/us-invest-over-4-trillion-by-2025-to-fix-infrastructure-2017-3?r=US&IR=T.

[866] Retrieved from: https://www.cnbc.com/2017/02/27/trump-pledges-to-spend-big-on-infrastructure.html.

[867] Retrieved from: https://www.whitehouse.gov/the-press-office/2017/02/28/remarks-president-trump-joint-address-congress.

that can be leveraged for a $1 trillion infrastructure investment in crumbling systems;

- investing in rural infrastructure;

- investing in bold new transformative projects that will change America's approach to infrastructure; and

- making America ready for the future with a work-force training initiative focused on skill-based apprenticeship education.[868]

The Republican-controlled Congress does not see Trump's infrastructure debt-financed spending pledge as a priority.[869] And neither will business, as the wrecking ball of his neo-Nazi comments after the Charlottesville incident left his joint public–private infrastructure plan at least in a state of uncertainty.[870]

Trump's domestic economic policy is to increase public capital expenditure significantly—so far he has made a commitment of $18 trillion or more. This is nothing less than a long out-of-fashion Keynesian-pump-priming fiscal policy strategy designed, in part, to create jobs. Trump's hope is that this would reduce both unemployment (the number of people seeking employment) and economic inactivity (the number of people of working age who are not seeking employment, but should be). However, this would only happen if those without jobs want the jobs created—because they have the necessary skill profiles to do those jobs, and the jobs are offering a competitive wage and are in their preferred locations. The increased public expenditure would inevitably increase the budget deficit, even if only in the short term, as the only alternatives would be to impose higher taxes (at a time when reducing taxes is also a key element of his fiscal policy[871]) or to reduce further

---

868   See: https://www.whitehouse.gov/blog/2017/06/08/president-trumps-plan-re-build-americas-infrastructure.

869   See: https://www.cnbc.com/2017/02/27/trump-pledges-to-spend-big-on-infrastructure.html; https://www.vice.com/en_us/article/mbb7b3/trumps-infrastructure-plan-is-a-trainwreck; http://thehill.com/policy/transportation/334334-five-road-blocks-for-trumps-1t-infrastructure-planhttp://www.chicagotribune.com/news/nationworld/politics/ct-trump-infrastructure-plan-congress-20170606-story.html

870   See: https://www.theguardian.com/us-news/2017/aug/19/trump-infrastructure-charlottesville-neo-nazis-comments.

871   See: http://www.reuters.com/article/us-imf-g20-usa-treasury-idUSKBN17O0OJ?feedType=RSS&feedName=politicsNews; http://edition.cnn.com/2017/04/26/opinions/

other public expenditures (but not reducing social security (age pension) entitlements that Trump made sacrosanct by a campaign promise[872]). Only by increasing public debt can this deficit be financed in the short term. This requires the approval of Congress to lift the public debt ceiling—and hence his initiation of a dalliance with the congressional Democrats, which has its problems[873]. In the capital market, such increased public borrowing could crowd out of private investment, so diminishing the rate of private capital formation and thus the prospects for sustained economic growth. This increased debt-financed government expenditure would increase aggregate demand, which would also add to inflationary pressures, the monetary policy response to which would be to increase interest rates. In turn, inflation may well reduce any competitive advantage held by exporters, thereby increasing the prospect of increased unemployment in export industries. Making the economic situation worse would be the imposition of any new import duties and border taxes, which would increase the cost of imports, with the intention of making import-competing industries relatively more competitive, so raises the prospect more jobs being created in those industries. This combination of economic pressures could well configure in a way that may not reduce aggregate unemployment, but could increase inflation, could diminish economic growth, could initiate an economic restructuring away from once internationally competitive exports industries, toward relatively uncompetitive import-replacement industries, and could worsen the balance of trade. The economic outcome could well be the worst of all economic worlds.

Taxation Reform

Trump's campaign tax reform plan—"Tax Reform That Will Make America Great Again,"[874]—was issued on September 2016:

---

trump-is-giving-the-republicans-what-they-really-want-opinion-zelizer/index.html.

[872] See: https://www.washingtonpost.com/politics/trump-touts-spending-plan-but-promise-to-leave-entitlements-alone-puts-gop-in-a-quandary/2017/02/27/35f17d70-fd14-11e6-8ebe-6e0dbe4f2bca_story.html?utm_term=.c3dd426f0ac2.

[873] See: https://www.nbcnews.com/politics/congress/democrats-sour-trump-infrastructure-proposals-n768446.

[874] Retrieved from: https://www.donldjtrump.com/positions/tax-reform. See also: https://taxfoundation.org/details-analysis-donald-trump-tax-plan-2016/#_ftn1; http://www.investopedia.com/terms/t/trumponomics.asp.

My tax proposal has been graded as the most pro-growth of all the tax plans offered by any other [Republican presidential] candidate. The purpose of my tax reforms is to put more money in the pockets of middle class Americans. My proposal goes to four brackets, eliminates the death tax, eliminates carve outs for special interests and allows Americans to have more economic security. The most significant feature of my tax reform plan is in the corporate tax area. The plan reduces corporate taxes to 15% for ALL businesses, allows repatriation of off-shore funds at a 10% rate and reduces carve outs for special interests. This influx of capital will spur growth and encourage foreign direct investment. The jobs created will clear our 9 million job backlog and put us on a trajectory to unbridled economic growth.[875]

His plan specified in some detail his desired tax reform outcomes. For income tax, the main changes promised were:

- To reduce the current seven taxable income brackets to three and apply these to federal income and capital gains taxes.
- To raise the taxable income threshold for joint married tax filers from $12,600 to $30,000 with itemized deductions capped at $200,000 for them.
- To eliminate the personal exemption and introduce other child-care-related tax provisions.
- To repeal the gift and estate (inheritance) taxes (death taxes).

For business tax, the main changes promised were:

- To reduce the corporate income tax rate from 35% to 15%.
- To eliminate the corporate alternative minimum tax.
- To allow firms engaged in manufacturing in America to choose between the deductibility of the full cost of capital investment, and the deductibility of interest paid on those investments.

---

[875] Retrieved from: https://www.teapartypatriotscitizensfund.com/official-tppcf-primary-registration/donald-trump/?roi=echo7-22089092107-45865753-4d6e12f3e1e31f39739 a7595888b38e1&mid=9180712 (emphasis in original).

- To eliminate the domestic production activities deduction and all other business credits, except for the research and development credit.

- To establish a tax holiday (at a tax rate of 10%) for corporations to repatriate profits held overseas.

- To increase the cap for the tax credit for employer-provided day care from $150,000 to $500,000 and reduces its recapture period from 10 to 5 years.

The devil, of course, in any tax reform policy statement is the detail—or lack of it—given the complexities of a tax code that runs, allegedly, to some 70,000 pages.[876]

The brevity of Trump's one-page presidential tax policy statement, issued in April 26,[877] and formally announced in Indianapolis on September 27,[878] is intriguing. One plausible explanation for the emergence of this rather curt tax policy statement is, if true, very suggestive as to how Trump goes about policymaking. Four economists, Steve Forbes, Larry Kudlow, Arthur Laffer and Stephen Moore wrote in an op-ed piece for New York Times on April, 19 suggesting that "now is the time to move [tax reform] forward with urgency."[879] The White House drew this to Trump's attention in mid-May.

Trump summoned staff to talk about it. His message: Make this the tax plan, according to one White House official present. By Friday [19 May], Trump was telling The Associated Press, "I shouldn't tell you this, but we're going to be announcing, probably on Wednesday [24 May], tax reform," startling his aides, who had not yet prepared such a plan.[880]

---

[876] Retrieved from: http://www.investopedia.com/terms/t/trumponomics.asp, but see: https://twitter.com/ZekeJMiller/status/857287861019824131/photo/1; http://www.investopedia.com/terms/t/trumponomics.asp; https://taxfoundation.org/trump-administration-tax-proposal/; http://www.investopedia.com/news/trumps-tax-reform-what-can-be-done/.

[877] See: https://www.whitehouse.gov/blog/2017/04/26/president-trump-proposed-massive-tax-cut-heres-what-you-need-know.

[878] See: https://www.washingtonpost.com/news/fact-checker/wp/2017/09/28/fact-checking-president-trumps-tax-speech-in-indianapolis/?utm_term=.4f5cc6c96479.

[879] See: https://www.nytimes.com/2017/04/19/opinion/why-are-republicans-making-tax-reform-so-hard.html.

[880] See also: http://www.politico.com/story/2017/04/29/trump-100-day-deadline-237781.

Sure enough, the next Wednesday, Trump's economic team was rolling out a tax plan that echoed the op-ed. [Stephen] Moore was at the White House that day. "Several of the White House folks came up to us and said, 'It's your op-ed that got Trump moving on this,'" Moore said. "I've probably written 1,000 op-eds in my life, but that might have been the most impactful."[881]

The complete April statement follows.[882]

Goals for Tax Reform
- Grow the economy and create millions of jobs
- Simplify our burdensome tax code
- Provide tax relief to American families—especially middle-income families
- Lower the business tax rate from one of the highest in the world to one of the lowest

Individual Reform
- Tax relief for American families, especially middle-income families:
- Reducing the seven tax brackets to three tax brackets of 10%, 25%, and 35%
- Doubling the standard deduction [taxable income threshold]
- Providing tax relief for families with child and dependent care expenses
- Simplification:
  - Eliminate targeted tax breaks that mainly benefit the wealthiest taxpayers
  - Protect the home ownership and charitable gift tax deductions
  - Repeal the Alternative Minimum Tax
  - Repeal the death tax
  - Repeal the 3.8% Obamacare tax that hits small businesses and investment income

[881] Retrieved from: http://www.politico.com/story/2017/05/15/donald-trump-fake-news-238379.

[882] Retrieved from: http://edition.cnn.com/2017/04/26/politics/white-house-donald-trump-tax-proposal/index.html.

Business Reform
- 15% Business tax rate
- Territorial tax system to level the playing field for American companies
- One-time tax on trillions of dollars held overseas
- Eliminate tax breaks for special interests

Process
- Throughout the month of May, the Trump administration will hold listening sessions with stakeholders to receive their input and will continue working with the House and Senate to develop the details of a plan that provides massive tax relief, creates jobs, and makes America more competitive—and can pass both chambers.

With the hyperbole that has come to be expected of Trump, he tweeted on the following Sunday [May 28]: "The massive TAX CUTS/REFORM that I have submitted is moving along in the process very well, actually ahead of schedule. Big benefits to all!"[883] Submitted to whom it might be asked? Certainly to Treasury Secretary, Steven Mnuchin, who described it as a massive tax cut reform, and to the White House Office of Management and Budget[884] Director, Mick Mulvaney, who described it as a tax reform that would eliminate tax breaks and deductions to offset lower tax rates.[885] Obviously, the Trump administration has yet to decide on a final tax reform message.

The Urban-Brookings Tax Policy Center[886] has calculated that:

> the Trump tax reform policy would give those earning more than $3.4 million an average tax cut of $937,700, while the average family earning less than $25,000 would receive a cut of ... $40. Put another way, the plan would be 23,500 times better for the ultra-rich than the poor.[887]

[883] Retrieved from: http://www.marketwatch.com/story/trump-makes-puzzling-statements-in-pair-of-policy-tweets-2017-05-28.

[884] See: https://www.whitehouse.gov/omb.

[885] See: http://www.marketwatch.com/story/trump-makes-puzzling-statements-in-pair-of-policy-tweets-2017-05-28.

[886] See: http://www.taxpolicycenter.org/about.

[887] See: https://www.vanityfair.com/news/2017/07/trump-claims-he-has-a-secret-plan-

Trump's rationale for providing tax relief to high-income earners—a tax bracket, he claims, he would really have like to tax more, but could not because of the obstructionist Democrats[888]—is grounded in the principle of "trickle-down" economics.[889]

The "trickle-down" economics advances the proposition that benefits for the wealthy—usually in the form of tax cuts for businesses, high-income earners, and on capital gains and dividends—will trickle down to everyone else. With such tax reductions, the wealthy will be incentivized to use the tax savings to expand businesses—rather than to increase their conspicuous consumption—and so raise output and create more and better jobs. This presumes that the real drivers of economic growth are those who save, invest, and own companies. Such tax policies, however, are redistributive, transferring wealth—and so advantages—toward an already wealthy few. Its other crucial—and doubtful—assumption is that any increased economic growth benefits generated will benefit all members of society.

Reducing taxes is also seen as a strategy for increasing tax revenue—according to the logic of the Laffer Curve[890]—on the premise that as the economy expands and people will become more prosperous, so the tax bases will be enlarged. But, as Laffer cautions,[891] this effect works best when taxes are in what he called the prohibitive range (100% marginal tax rate down to some hypothetical mid-point rate) below which, further cuts would not stimulate economic growth, only lower government revenue:

---

to-tax-the-rich-but-democrats-wont-let-him. See also: http://www.taxpolicycenter.org/taxvox/trumps-campaign-rhetoric-may-have-been-populist-his-tax-plan-isnt.

[888] See: https://www.vanityfair.com/news/2017/07/trump-claims-he-has-a-secret-plan-to-tax-the-rich-but-democrats-wont-let-him

[889] See: https://www.ft.com/content/736ca456-a50f-11e7-b797-b61809486fe2; https://www.salon.com/2016/05/12/donald_trumps_supply_side_hacks_his_nonsensical_tax_plan_is_getting_the_trickle_down_treatment/.

[890] "The Laffer Curve is one of the main theoretical constructs of supply-side economics, and is often used as a shorthand to sum up the entire pro-growth world view of supply-side economics. However, the Laffer Curve itself simply illustrates the tradeoff between tax rates and the total tax revenues actually collected by the government."
Retrieved from: http://www.laffercenter.com/the-laffer-center-2/the-laffer-curve/.

[891] Retrieved from: http://www.laffercenter.com/the-laffer-center-2/the-laffer-curve/.

Importantly, the Laffer Curve does not say whether a tax cut will raise or lower revenues, nor does it predict that any and all tax rate reductions would necessarily bring in more total revenues. Instead it says that tax rate reductions will always result in a smaller loss in revenues than one would have expected when relying only on the static estimates of the previous tax base.[892]

The Urban-Brookings Tax Policy Center has, however, calculated that the under the Trump tax reform policy, if adopted, "Federal revenues would fall by $6.2 trillion over the first decade before accounting for added interest costs. Including interest costs, the federal debt would rise by $7.2 trillion over the first decade and by $20.9 trillion by 2036."[893]

Tax reform is never easy, anywhere and at any time. The London-based *Financial Times* on July 31 concluded:

> The Trump administration's hopes of achieving tax reform this year are already being questioned by current and former congressional aides as Washington faces a fiscal quagmire over the next three months and intense wrangling over the details of changes.[894]

The prospects of tax reform legislation being negotiated by the Trump administration are contingent upon the various factions of the Republican Party being willing to compromise of the specifics of tax reform. However, with the Congressional elections coming up in 2018, compromise became an imperative. By early December, both the House of Representatives and the Senate had passed separate and different tax reform bills. This means that both chambers will have to constitute "a conference committee to agree on differences... [among which] are the bills' treatment of individual tax rates, the alternative minimum tax and the Obamacare individual mandate."[895] It seems likely, however, that Trump

---

[892] Ibid

[893] Retrieved from: http://www.taxpolicycenter.org/publications/analysis-donald-trumps-revised-tax-plan.

[894] Retrieved from: https://www.ft.com/content/1641ad70-760d-11e7-90c0-90a9d1bc9691.

[895] Retrieved from: https://www.cnbc.com/2017/12/04/republican-house-and-senate-tax-plan-differences.html.

will achieve his much desired enactment of, essentially, his corporate tax reform policy.

Obamacare Repeal and Replacement

Trump promised, at a late night presidential campaign rally in Grand Rapids, Michigan, on October 31, that he would immediately upon becoming President "repeal and replace the disaster known as Obamacare"[896]—the Patient Protection and Affordable Care Act, 2010.[897]

Obamacare's sought to extend health insurance coverage to some of the estimated 15% of Americans who lack it, because:

- they were not covered by their employers;

- they could not afford the health insurance premiums;

- they choose to self-insure (directly pay their own health costs); or

- they were not protected by federal health programmes—Medicare[898] and Medicaid[899]—that target the poor and elderly.

To achieve this coverage extension, all adult Americans were legally obliged to take out health insurance coverage, so as to reduce the cost of insurance by bringing younger, healthier people into the health insurance risk pool. Those who chose not to do so were obliged to pay a penalty tax. To make coverage more affordable federal subsidies were provided to health insurance providers. People with pre-existing health conditions were protected from being denied coverage by health insurance providers. Businesses with more than 50 full-time employees were required to offer health insurance. Obamacare created a network of health insurance marketplaces in various US states, where individuals are able to compare online health insurance premiums for govern-

---

[896] Retrieved from: http://www.politifact.com/truth-o-meter/promises/trumpometer/pro mise/1388/repeal-obamacare/; see LSO: http://www.freep.com/story/news/local/ michigan/2016/11/08/donald-trump-holds-late-night-rally-grand-rapids/93447114/.

[897] See: https://www.hhs.gov/sites/default/files/ppacacon.pdf; see also: https://www.whit ehouse.gov/repeal-and-replace-obamacare.

[898] See: https://www.medicare.gov/sign-up-change-plans/decide-how-to-get-medicare/ whats-medicare/what-is-medicare.html.

[899] See: https://www.medicaid.gov/apply-for-coverage/index.html.

ment-approved insurance products. Some states chose not to participate in Obamacare, so their residents have been able to shop online for
health insurance on a site run by the federal government.[900]

Trump has been consistent throughout his campaign, and during his
presidency, about his intention to abolish Obamacare.[901] In his first Address to Congress in February, he declared:[902]

> Tonight, I am also calling on this Congress to repeal
> and replace Obamacare—(applause)—with reforms
> that expand choice, increase access, lower costs, and, at
> the same time, provide better healthcare. (Applause.)
>
> Mandating every American to buy government-ap-
> proved health insurance was never the right solution for
> our country. (Applause.) The way to make health insur-
> ance available to everyone is to lower the cost of health
> insurance, and that is what we are going do. (Applause.)
>
> Obamacare premiums nationwide have increased by
> double and triple digits. As an example, Arizona went up
> 116% last year alone. Governor Matt Bevin of Kentucky
> just said Obamacare is failing in his state—the state of
> Kentucky—and it's unsustainable and collapsing.
>
> One-third of counties have only one insurer, and they
> are losing them fast. They are losing them so fast. They
> are leaving, and many Americans have no choice at all.
> There's no choice left. Remember when you were told
> that you could keep your doctor and keep your plan?
> We now know that all of those promises have been to-
> tally broken. Obamacare is collapsing, and we must act
> decisively to protect all Americans. (Applause.)

---

[900] See: https://www.hhs.gov/healthcare/; http://www.bbc.com/news/world-us-canada-24370967; https://obamacarefacts.com/whatis-obamacare/; http://www.his-inc.com/what-is-obamacare-exactly/.

[901] Retrieved from: https://www.whitehouse.gov/repeal-and-replace-obamacare.

[902] Retrieved from: https://www.whitehouse.gov/the-press-office/2017/02/28/remarks-president-trump-joint-address-congress

Action is not a choice, it is a necessity. So I am calling on all Democrats and Republicans in Congress to work with us to save Americans from this imploding Obamacare disaster. (Applause.)

He has, however, long been ambivalent about with what precisely should replace Obamacare: universal health insurance[903] (as in Australia[904]); single-payer healthcare—Medicare for all[905] (as in Canada[906]), even publicly funded—fully socialized—healthcare (as in Scotland[907]). He has, however, opted for a free-market strategy that will provide universal coverage,[908] by creating a national network of health insurance providers in a deregulated, interstate (national) health insurance market, with tax-deductible premiums and a Medicaid safety net.[909]

In his inaugural address to Congress in February, Trump identified his proposed universal healthcare system design principles:[910]

Here are the principles that should guide the Congress as we move to create a better healthcare system for all Americans:

First, we should ensure that Americans with preexisting conditions have access to coverage, and that we

---

903 See: https://www.youtube.com/watch?v=TPJfKdp3bDs; https://www.vox.com/policy-and-politics/2017/5/5/15556008/trump-australia-universal-health-care-better.

904 See: http://www.aihw.gov.au/australias-health/2016/health-system/. See also: https://www.vox.com/policy-and-politics/2017/5/5/15556008/trump-australia-universal-health-care-better

905 See: https://www.washingtonpost.com/news/the-fix/wp/2017/05/05/trumps-forbidden-love-singe-payer-health-care/?utm_term=.64898974a779.

906 See: https://www.canada.ca/en/health-canada/services/health-care-system/reports-publications/health-care-system/canada.html.

907 See: https://nhsnss.org/.

908 See: http://www.reuters.com/article/us-usa-trump-obamacare-idUSKBN15005C; http://www.reuters.com/article/us-usa-trump-obamacare-idUSKBN15005C.

909 See: http://www.genfkd.org/donald-trump-healthcare-plan-free-market-coverage-everyone.

910 Retrieved from: https://www.whitehouse.gov/the-press-office/2017/02/28/remarks-president-trump-joint-address-congress.

have a stable transition for Americans currently enrolled in the healthcare exchanges. (Applause.)

Secondly, we should help Americans purchase their own coverage through the use of tax credits and expanded Health Savings Accounts—but it must be the plan they want, not the plan forced on them by our government. (Applause.)

Thirdly, we should give our great state governors the resources and flexibility they need with Medicaid to make sure no one is left out. (Applause.)

Fourth, we should implement legal reforms that protect patients and doctors from unnecessary costs that drive up the price of insurance, and work to bring down the artificially high price of drugs, and bring them down immediately. (Applause.)

And finally, the time has come to give Americans the freedom to purchase health insurance across state lines—(applause)—which will create a truly competitive national marketplace that will bring costs way down and provide far better care. So important.

Trump's universal healthcare policy—oxymoronically dubbed Trumpcare[911]—has a seven-point platform:[912]

1. Completely repeal Obamacare. Our elected representatives must eliminate the individual mandate. No person should be required to buy insurance unless he or she wants to.

2. Modify existing law that inhibits the sale of health insurance across state lines. As long as the plan purchased complies with state requirements, any vendor ought to be able to offer insurance in any state. By allowing full competition in this market, insurance costs will go down and consumer satisfaction will go up.

---

[911] See: http://edition.cnn.com/videos/cnnmoney/2017/07/19/late-night-health-care-bill-defeated-orig-vstan-jnd.cnn.

[912] See: https://trumpcare.org/?SRC=tc_google.

3. Allow individuals to fully deduct health insurance premium payments from their tax returns under the current tax system. Businesses are allowed to take these deductions so why wouldn't Congress allow individuals the same exemptions? As we allow the free market to provide insurance coverage opportunities to companies and individuals, we must also make sure that no one slips through the cracks simply because they cannot afford insurance. We must review basic options for Medicaid and work with states to ensure that those who want healthcare coverage can have it.

4. Allow individuals to use health savings accounts (HSAs). Contributions into HSAs should be tax-free and should be allowed to accumulate. These accounts would become part of the estate of the individual and could be passed on to heirs without fear of any death penalty. These plans should be particularly attractive to young people who are healthy and can afford high-deductible insurance plans. These funds can be used by any member of a family without penalty. The flexibility and security provided by HSAs will be of great benefit to all who participate.

5. Require price transparency from all healthcare providers, especially doctors and healthcare organizations like clinics and hospitals. Individuals should be able to shop to find the best prices for procedures, exams or any other medical-related procedure.

6. Block-grant Medicaid to the states. Nearly every state already offers benefits beyond what is required in the current Medicaid structure. The state governments know their people best and can manage the administration of Medicaid far better without federal overhead. States will have the incentives to seek out and eliminate fraud, waste, and abuse to preserve our precious resources.

7. Remove barriers to entry into free markets for drug providers that offer safe, reliable, and cheaper products. Congress will need the courage to step away from the special interests and do what is right for America. Though the pharmaceutical industry is in the private sector, drug companies provide a public service.

Allowing consumers access to imported, safe and dependable drugs from overseas will bring more options to consumers.

To facilitate the implementation of Trumpcare in 2018, Trump tweeted on May 28: "I suggest that we add more dollars to Healthcare and make it the best anywhere. ObamaCare is dead—the Republicans will do much better!"[913] Surprisingly, or not, his "hard-power" budget plan[914] submitted to Congress[915] in mid-May only included healthcare expenditure cuts.[916]

The implementation of Trumpcare requires the cooperation of Congress, state governors, and the health insurance industry. His first challenge is for Congress to completely repeal Obamacare, which after three failed attempts to do so, represents a challenge still to be met.[917] It is now apparent that the Republican Party's 7 years of anti-Obamacare rhetoric has placed it in an impossible repeal and replace position:

> The party had promised not only to repeal the [Patient Protection and] Affordable Care Act, but to replace it with something that would offer better coverage at a lower price—while also spending less public money and cutting the taxes that financed the whole thing. This was clearly impossible. Yet nobody dared say what everybody knew.[918]

Complicating the politics of repeal and replacement, the Obamacare discourse within the Republican Party began to shift subtly.

---

913   Retrieved from: http://www.marketwatch.com/story/trump-makes-puzzling-statements-in-pair-of-policy-tweets-2017-05-28.

914   Retrieved from: https://www.cnbc.com/2017/03/15/trump-budget-out-now-congressional-battle-begins.html.

915   See: https://www.usatoday.com/story/news/politics/2017/05/22/dont-expect-congress-pass-trump-controversial-budget-plan/102009962/.

916   See: http://www.marketwatch.com/story/trump-makes-puzzling-statements-in-pair-of-policy-tweets-2017-05-28.

917   See: https://www.theatlantic.com/politics/archive/2017/08/the-real-reason-trumps-obamacare-repeal-push-failed/535500/; https://www.nytimes.com/2017/07/18/us/politics/republicans-obamacare-repeal-now-replace-later.html.

918   See: https://www.theatlantic.com/politics/archive/2017/08/the-real-reason-trumps-obamacare-repeal-push-failed/535500/.

During the Obama presidency, the Republican Party had the luxury of advancing a hard-line rhetoric of absolute hostility to Obamacare, advocating to all and sundry that it must be repealed at any cost. When Trump gained the presidency this rhetorical luxury disappeared, for it was now expected that the Republican Party would deliver its promise to provide a better replacement. At this point, the Obamacare discourse rhetoric began to shift to one of concern for the human consequences of repealing Obamacare without a replacement to deal with the up to 30 million or so people who could lose their health insurance coverage.[919] Blame for any repeal consequences would definitely be attributed to the Republican Party.[920] Trump stepped back from the faction feuding within the congressional Republican Party. He did nothing to mobilize public opinion in support of any of the failed repeal and replace bills. He did little to build consensus in Congress, whether within the Republican Party or between the Republicans and Democrats. He preferred to limit his interventions to occasional empty threats against opposing Republican senators. Effectively he did too little too late to bring about the repeal and replacement of Obamacare.[921] This, at least, ensured the deflection any future blamed for his failure to repeal Obamacare to the Republican Party and its leadership.

Trump has made it clear that his fall-back—but risky—strategy is just to let Obamacare fail[922] and then blame the Democrats[923]:

---

[919]   See: https://www.cbo.gov/publication/52486; https://www.cbo.gov/publication/52939; http://money.cnn.com/2017/07/19/news/economy/senate-repeal-bill-cbo/index.html.

[920]   See: https://www.theguardian.com/us-news/2017/jul/18/dopes-replacement-healthcare-bill-trump-senate; https://www.theguardian.com/us-news/2017/jul/22/republicans-face-two-unpalatable-options-on-replacement-healthcare-bill; http://www.politico.com/story/2017/07/17/obamacare-senators-turn-on-mcconnell-240646.

[921]   See: http://www.slate.com/articles/news_and_politics/politics/2017/07/obamacare_repeal_failed_because_of_trump_s_inaction.html.

[922]   See: https://www.nytimes.com/2017/07/18/us/politics/republicans-obamacare-repeal-now-replace-later.html; https://www.theguardian.com/us-news/video/2017/jul/18/donald-trump-lays-out-healthcare-plan-let-obamacare-fail-video; http://www.bbc.com/news/world-us-canada-40646625; but see also; http://www.lifezette.com/polizette/trumps-risky-let-obamacare-explode-approach/.

[923]   See: https://www.vox.com/policy-and-politics/2017/7/18/15988402/trump-blame-democrats-health-care-confused.

"I think we're probably in that position where we'll let Obamacare fail," Trump said at the White House [on 18 July]. "We're not going to own it. I'm not going to own it. I can tell you, the Republicans are not going to own it."

Once Obamacare collapses, Trump said Democrats would join Republicans so Congress would be able to "come up with new plan [his Trumpcare plan?], really good for people."[924]

This takes the future of Obamacare out of the hands of the Republicans in Congress, and puts in his hands, where he, no doubt, wants it to be. He is already facilitating its eventual demise by weakening the bureaucratic enforcement of the individual mandate, by imposing work requirements for Medicaid recipients, and by failing to advertise or do any outreach to potential Obamacare applicants.[925] More aggressively, he could seek to make tax credits for premiums less generous, and stop funding subsidies.[926]

In any event, all Trump can do at this stage is to wait for the worst—a failed Obamacare, which may well take a while[927] and for which he may well be blamed—and then await its eventual repeal. Of more concern to him is the implication of his failure to repeal Obamacare for his tax reform policy aspirations, where, again, the devil is in the detail. He can now be in no doubt that the factional feuding within the Republican Party has gone a long way to establish that governing with a Republican-controlled Congress is a real challenge.

---

[924] Retrieved from: http://www.nbcnews.com/politics/donald-trump/trump-lays-blame-health-care-bill-failure-n784006; see also; http://www.politico.com/story/2017/07/18/trump-tweet-obamacare-repeal-failure-240664.

[925] See: https://www.nytimes.com/2017/07/18/us/politics/republicans-obamacare-repeal-now-replace-later.html; https://www.theguardian.com/us-news/video/2017/jul/18/donald-trump-lays-out-healthcare-plan-let-obamacare-fail-video; http://www.bbc.com/news/world-us-canada-40646625; but see also; http://www.lifezette.com/poli zette/trumps-risky-let-obamacare-explode-approach/.

[926] See: https://www.nytimes.com/interactive/2017/07/19/us/what-trump-can-do-to-let-obamacare-fail.html.

[927] See: http://money.cnn.com/2017/07/18/news/economy/obamacare-trump-fail/index.html?iid=EL.

ON INTERNATIONAL POLICY

Trump holds a very distinctive set of views of the world at large and the role of the United States in it.

Trump's Moral Compass

It is clear that Trump has a black and white moral compass in relation to international affairs, one permitting no hint of moral ambiguity. Being a man of his time, his moral compass was no doubt informed by Hollywood's 1950s Western film genre,[928] which was so dominant in American popular culture at that time. In that celluloid world there were "the good guys"—traditionally those wearing white hats—and "the bad guys"—traditionally those wearing black hats or feathers. The "good guys"—the righteous—were:

- the white male town Sheriffs and roving US Marshalls, the upholders of law and order and protectors of property rights, however acquired;[929]
- the white male ranch owners and their white male cowboys, ever willing to take the law into their own hands as vigilantes posses; and
- the law abiding and salt-of-the-earth shopkeepers, always and ever serving their community through thick and thin.

The "bad guys"—the wicked—were:

- the gunslinging white male drifters, always from other parts and always with trouble-making in mind;
- the native American Indians, of ever intent, in raiding parties, on terrorizing stage coaches and small communities by killing, looting, and kidnapping;
- the Mexicans crossing into America in marauding bands, ever intent on pillage and rape to terrorize communities and property owners and their families;[930] and, of course,

---

928 See: http://www.123helpme.com/characteristics-of-a-typical-western-view.asp?id=170209.

929 Indifferent to any unjustness created in the process of the land acquisition (Locke [1688] 1960; Nozick1974).

930 See: https://qz.com/934680/donald-trump-wall-with-mexico-america-helped-create-

- the Chinese, with their pig-tails, opium dens, and very foreign ways of dressing, behaving, and eating.

All of whom, of course, disturbed the God-fearing Christian communities, but, of course, in the Hollywood movies the "good guys" always won.

Trump's "good-guy" countries—albeit metaphorically wearing off-white rather that white hats—would definitely include:

- The United Kingdom (UK), despite his belief that British intelligence tapped his telephone at Obama's request.[931]

- Europe, despite his evident misgiving about the EU's political integration agenda[932]; Angela Merkel's gender and intelligence, a person with whom Trump has a "fairly unbelievable" relationship"[933]; and his frustrations with NATO not pulling its weight financially and in the war against terrorism.[934]

- Japan, despite his evident frustrations with its unfair trade practices[935] and its inadequate contribution toward the cost of its defense, although he loves the Japanese practice of bowing: "In Japan, they bow. I love it. Only thing I love about Japan" (*Washington Post* Interview, September 2004, cited in Piehler 2016, 76).[936]

- South Korea, despite his evident frustration that it is not contributing enough toward the cost of its defense,[937] and that it is

---

the-racist-myth-of-the-violent-mexican-that-trump-is-exploiting-today/.

[931] See: http://google.com/newsstand/s/CBIw6cLfzDQ; but see http://google.com/newsstand/s/CBIwkv7ezTQ. But see: http://www.bbc.com/news/38777762.

[932] See: http://www.bbc.com/news/world-us-canada-38846565; http://www.bbc.com/news/world-europe-38808504; http://google.com/newsstand/s/CBIwp-rC1DQ; http://www.newsweek.com/donald-trump-europe-nato-g7-eu-577321.

[933] This is the judgment of Sean Spicer, the White House Press Secretary. Retrieved from: http://www.independent.co.uk/news/world/americas/us-politics/trump-merkel-sean-spicer-fairly-unbelievable-press-conference-us-germany-relationship-a7764201.html.

[934] See: http://www.bbc.com/news/world-europe-38972695.

[935] See: http://business.financialpost.com/news/economy/donald-trump-to-about-to-order-probe-of-16-countries-to-ferret-out-trade-abuse-and-canada-is-on-the-list.

[936] See: http://edition.cnn.com/2017/04/14/politics/vice-president-pence-trip-asia-pacific/index.html.

[937] Ibid

engaging in unfair trade competition.[938]

- Israel,[939] despite his evident frustrations with Prime Minister Benjamin "Bibi" Netanyahu's planned expansion Palestinian settlements.[940]

- Egypt, despite some concerns about its human rights record.[941]

- Saudi Arabia,[942] despite his evident frustration over its inadequate contribution toward the cost of its defense,[943] its very public feud with Qatar,[944] and its military excursions into Yemen,[945] but because its leadership significantly stroked his ego[946]—by Saudi King Salman greating him the Order of Abdulaziz medallion.[947]

- Canada, despite being bested by the battle of the handshakes by Prime Minister Justin Trudeau,[948] and his evident misgiving about its unfair trade practices.[949]

---

[938] See: https://www.washingtonpost.com/news/wonk/wp/2017/09/02/trump-plans-withdrawal-from-south-korea-trade-deal/?utm_term=.c1d346bb4e36.

[939] See: http://google.com/newsstand/s/CBIw-LHF7zQ; http://google.com/newsstand/s/CBIw36H2zzk.

[940] See: http://edition.cnn.com/2017/03/25/politics/netanyahu-trump-settlements-aipac/index.html?iid=ob_article_footer_expansio; http://google.com/newsstand/s/CBIw1oyN9DQ.

[941] See: http://www.reuters.com/article/us-usa-trump-egypt-idUSKBN17227M.

[942] See: https://www.theguardian.com/commentisfree/2017/jun/07/saudi-arabia-donald-trump-qatar-conflict; http://www.independent.co.uk/voices/saudi-arabia-qatar-donald-trump-sanctions-middle-east-jared-kushner-uae-rex-tillerson-a7824701.html; https://www.theguardian.com/commentisfree/2017/jun/07/saudi-arabia-donald-trump-qatar-conflict.

[943] See: http://google.com/newsstand/s/CBIw_6K1wDk

[944] Retrieved from: http://www.reuters.com/article/us-gulf-qatar-usa-idUSKBN18R1AA.

[945] See: http://www.defensenews.com/articles/us-military-aid-in-limbo-as-trump-welcomes-egyptian-president.

[946] See: https://www.theguardian.com/us-news/2017/may/20/trump-visit-hailed-by-saudi-leaders-as-reset-of-regional-order; https://www.theguardian.com/commentisfree/2017/may/23/trump-administrations-iran-policy-dangerous-flawed.

[947] See: http://www.salon.com/2017/05/22/president-cuck-trump-supporters-are-freaking-out-over-the-presidents-tone-change-on-islam/.

[948] See: http://www.telegraph.co.uk/news/2017/07/14/marathon-handshake-ends-trump-bastille-day-trip-paris-macron/.

[949] See: http://www.bbc.com/news/world-us-canada-38971859.

- Australia, despite his robust telephone exchanges with Prime Minister Malcolm Turnbull[950] and his evident misgivings about its "dumb deal" with the Obama administration on refugees.[951].

- France, despite its new President, Emmanuel Macron,[952] coining of the expression "Make the Planet Great Again"[953] and besting Trump in the battle of the handshakes,[954] but because Marcon very publicly stroked his ego in Paris[955].[956]

Trump during his presidential campaign would certainly have included Russia in this category. His very apparent fixation on Russian President Vladimir Putin[957] has continued after he became president:

> President Trump said on Thursday [August 10] that he was "very thankful" that Russian President Vladimir Putin had ordered the expulsion of hundreds of US diplomats from the country in response to sanctions— because the administration needs to cut the State Department's budget anyway.
>
> "I want to thank him because we're trying to cut down

---

950   See: http://www.bbc.com/news/world-us-canada-38849257

951   Retrieved from: https://www.reuters.tv/v/4mF/2017/02/02/dumb-deal-drags-australia-u-s-ties-to-new-low?utm_source=taboola_int&utm_medium=referral&utm_term=eslmedia-theindependent.

952   See: https://www.theguardian.com/world/2017/jul/14/macron-pulls-out-all-stops-bastille-day-parade-trump-france; http://www.bbc.co.uk/news/av/world-us-canada-40602788/trump-in-paris-compliments-and-a-hint-of-compromise; http://www.bbc.co.uk/news/world-us-canada-40613719.

953   Retrieved from: https://www.theguardian.com/world/2017/jun/03/make-our-planet-great-again-macron-praised-for-response-to-trump#img-1.

954   See: https://www.theguardian.com/us-news/video/2017/may/25/macron-trump-handshake-battle-video.

955   See: http://edition.cnn.com/2017/07/01/opinions/trump-france-bastille-opinion-andelman/index.html; https://www.ft.com/content/c4ee8aca-6887-11e7-9a66-93fb352ba1fe; http://news.sky.com/story/trump-hails-french-ties-as-he-joins-bastille-day-celebrations-in-paris-10948183.

956   See: http://edition.cnn.com/2017/07/01/opinions/trump-france-bastille-opinion-andelman/index.html; https://www.ft.com/content/c4ee8aca-6887-11e7-9a66-93fb352ba1fe; http://news.sky.com/story/trump-hails-french-ties-as-he-joins-bastille-day-celebrations-in-paris-10948183.

957   See: http://www.bbc.co.uk/news/world-europe-40683083

our payroll, and as far as I'm concerned, I'm very thankful that he let go of a large number of people [sic] because now we have a smaller payroll," Trump told reporters at his Bedminster, N.J., golf club.

As president, such a Russian rapprochement scenario has increasingly became politically untenable, given the disclosures from the FBI and Congressional on-going investigation of the alleged Russian meddling in the 2016 presidential election,[958] and the rumors that the Russian government has compromising information on Trump,[959] and given Putin's intransigent support of the al-Assad regime in Syrian[960] and his continued, albeit recently more constrained, support of the Kim Jong-un regime in North Korea.[961]

Trump's "bad-guy" countries—metaphorically wearing the darkest of black hats—are:

- North Korea, because of its nuclear bombs and its intercontinental missile aspirations.[962]

- Syria, because of its heinous head of state[963]—Bashar al-Assad[964,]—and his despicable use of poisonous gas on his citizens, particularly women amd children.[965]

---

[958] See: http://www.zerohedge.com/news/2017-03-20/preview-james-comeys-testimony-russian-hacking-us-elections-trumps-allegedwiretap?utm_source=feedburner&utm_medium=feed&utm campaign=Feed%3A+zerohedge%2Ffccd+I%28zero+hedge+-+on+a+long+enough+timeline%2C+the+survival+rate+for+everyone+drops+to+zero%29; https://thinkprogress.org/this-congressmans-short-speech-crisply-lays-out-the-evidence-of-collusion-between-trump-and-russia-d166801a11fa#.jeep2zcbo.

[959] See: http://www.independent.co.uk/news/world/europe/russia-donald-trump-kompromat-nikita-isaev-new-russia-movement-state-tv-us-president-a7929966.html.

[960] See: https://www.theguardian.com/world/2017/apr/06/postmortems-confirm-syria-chemical-attack-turkey-says.

[961] See: http://edition.cnn.com/2017/04/19/asia/russia-un-veto-north-korea/index.html.

[962] See: http://edition.cnn.com/2017/02/28/politics/north-korea-obama-trump-threat/; http://www.aljazeera.com/news/2017/03/trump-kim-jong-acting-badly-170320043115740.html; http://google.com/newsstand/s/CBIw7YC1zTQ.

[963] See: http://google.com/newsstand/s/CBIw4Yau8zQ; https://www.youtube.com/watch?v=WZ5sZm0pBco&list=UU52X5wxOL_s5yw0dQk7NtgA&index=26.

[964] See: http://edition.cnn.com/2012/12/06/world/meast/bashar-al-assad--fast-facts/index.html.

[965] See: http://www.independent.co.uk/news/world/middle-east/syria-latest-bashar-al-

- Iran, because of its continued sponsoring of global terrorism and its ballistic missile aspirations.[966]

- Venezuela, because of the anti-democratic actions of its socialist dictator, President Nicolás Maduro[967].[968]

Trump, when a presidential candidate, rather unfairly, would certainly have included both Mexico and China in this category. He accused Mexico of "sending rapist, criminal gangs, and drugs to the US".[969] He accused China of raping America[970] by using unfair trade practices.[971] These countries now regularly vacillate between black and white poles of his presidential moral compass.

Trump's International Policies

Trump's ascension to the Oval Office followed a campaign during which, as a populist, he resorted to controversial rhetoric that was disdainful of both international diplomacy and international opinion—particularly his vilification of China[972] and Mexico[973]—not to mention personal sensitivities. At the forefront of his campaign rhetoric[974]—

---

assad-chemical-attack-donald-trump-white-house-claim-a7809641.html.

[966] See: http://www.bbc.com/news/world-us-canada-38868039; http://blink.htcsense.com /web/articleweb.aspx?regionid=3&articleid=84872360; https://www.theguardian.com/ commentisfree/2017/may/23/trump-administrations-iran-policy-dangerous-flawed.

[967] See: https://www.britannica.com/biography/Nicolas-Maduro.

[968] See: http://thehill.com/homenews/administration/344905-trump-denounces-venezuelan-dictatorship-calls-for-release-of; http://www.bbc.com/news/world-latin-america-40798128; but see: http://www.reuters.com/article/us-venezuela-usa-idUSKCN18F2HB.

[969] Retrieved from: https://qz.com/934680/donald-trump-wall-with-mexico-america-help ed-create-the-racist-myth-of-the-violent-mexican-that-trump-is-exploiting-today/.

[970] See: http://www.bbc.com/news/election-us-2016-36185012; http://www.politico. com/blogs/2016-gop-primary-live-updates-and-results/2016/05/trump-china-rape-america-222689.

[971] See: http://www.reuters.com/article/us-usa-china-idUSKBN1792KA; http://google. com/newsstand/s/CBIwjJnPyjQ.

[972] See: http://www.cnbc.com/2016/11/10/trumps-foreign-policy-heres-a-recap-of-what-the-president-elect-said-about-asia-during-the-campaign.html.

[973] See: https://www.youtube.com/watch?v=WSWF71EKp6g.

[974] See: https://www.nytimes.com/2016/10/15/us/politics/trump-speech-highlights.html?_ r=1&mtrref=undefined&gwh=9B4413B7D25B0F22E600D02AD6D74BBF&gwt=pay; http://www.newyorker.com/culture/cultural-comment/plot-america-donald-trumps-

under the rubric "Make America Great Again"[975] was his "America First" political slogan[976]—no more foreign nation-building and no more regime changing adventures.[977] In so doing, he was dismissing the long-standing foreign policy principle of American exceptionalism.[978] This is the proposition that by virtue of America's origins and ideals—the democratic principles of liberty, equality, individualism, and *laissez faire* attitude life and business—its values and political institutions are unique and worthy of universal replication (see Lipset 1996). Trump foreshadowed his position on CNN's *Piers Morgan Tonight* in September 2013 when he praised Putin for his criticism of that principle:

> "You think of the term as being fine, but all of a sudden you say, what if you're in Germany or Japan or any one of 100 different countries? You're not going to like that term," Trump told CNN. "It's very insulting and Putin really put it to him [Obama] about that."[979]

And again in August 2017:

> I share the American people's frustration. I also share their frustration over a foreign policy that has spent too much time, energy, money, and most importantly lives, trying to rebuild countries in our own image, instead of pursuing our security interests above all other considerations.[980]

---

rhetoric.

975   See: http://www.businessinsider.com/donald-trump-great-again-website-2016-11.

976   See: http://time.com/4309786/read-donald-trumps-america-first-foreign-policy-speech/.

977   See: http://www.businessinsider.com/trump-first-100-days-promises-2017-4?utm_source=googleplaynewsstand&utm_medium=referral.

978   See: http://www.bbc.com/news/world-us-canada-39133677; but see also: https://www.theatlantic.com/politics/archive/2017/02/how-trump-wants-to-make-america-exceptional-again/515406/.

979   Retrieved from: http://edition.cnn.com/interactive/2017/03/politics/trump-putin-russia-timeline/; see also: https://www.buzzfeed.com/andrewkaczynski/donald-trump-praised-putin-for-bashing-the-term-american-exc?utm_term=.ubWoZO3A1#.enLP2aQ7r.

980   Retrieved from: https://www.whitehouse.gov/the-press-office/2017/08/21/remarks-president-trump-strategy-afghanistan-and-south-asia.

Trump's rhetoric calls for an isolationist and zenophobic America[981]: "If our presidents would have just gone to the beach and enjoyed the ocean and the sun, we would've been much better off in the Middle East" (*New York Times*, March 2016, cited in Piehler 2016, 85). Isolationism is a long-standing and, from time-to-time, influential[982] American tradition dating back to President John Quincy Adams[983] (1825–1829): "[America] goes not abroad, in search of monsters to destroy. She is the well-wisher to the freedom and independence of all. She is the champion and vindicator only of her own."[984]

Certainly, it looks as if Trump is determined to do no less than to reconsider fully Washington's international strategy. He wants to substitute the bluffing poker card game[985] for the mind-challenging grand geopolitical chess game.[986] Yet:

> There's an argument to be made that Trump is at his most successful in foreign affairs when he is at his most unpredictable for the simple reason that is when he is most feared.
>
> The Assad regime will surely hesitate before ordering another chemical strike.
>
> Nato's Secretary General Jens Stoltenberg said he is already seeing the effect of Trump's focus on financial burden-sharing within the military alliance ...

---

[981]   See: https://news.vice.com/story/trumps-birthday-present-to-america-is-a-xenophobic-travel-ban; https://medium.com/everyvote/xenophobic-america-found-its-leader-in-trump-41e593b606b.

[982]   See: http://www.newyorker.com/news/john-cassidy/donald-trump-cant-turn-back-history.

[983]   He was the sixth US president, who had also been a sometime diplomat, US Senator, and member of the US House of Representatives. See: https://www.whitehouse.gov/1600/presidents/johnquincyadams.

[984]   Retrieved from:.http://teachingamericanhistory.org/library/document/speech-on-inde pendence-day/.

[985]   "There is plenty of luck in Poker, but the game requires incredibly great skill as well, and each player is the master of his own fate." Retrieved from: http://www.bicyclecards.com/how-to-play/basics-of-poker/.

[986]   "The purpose of the game is to checkmate the opponent's king." See: https://www.chess.com/learn-how-to-play-chess.

At the United Nations, there is a new focus on reform, especially of peacekeeping operations. This is partly because there is a new reformist Secretary General, Antonio Guterres, but mainly because of the fear that the US, by far the organization's biggest donor, could pull funding. Trump has brought a fear factor to the American presidency often absent during the Obama years.[987]

Trump seems to be proposing that America—he—should be the world's policeman, albeit one with an eye on current and future wrong-doings against America. This is evidenced by his military interventions in Syria,[988] and his imposing of sanctions on Iran[989] and Venezuela,[990] and his threatening military action on the latter.[991] His preferred policing strategy is in line with his proclivity for brinkmanship—the long out-of-fashion madman theory of diplomacy[992] associated with Richard Nixon (Matusow 1999).[993] This is premised on the belief that the cultivation

---

[987] Retrieved from: http://www.bbc.co.uk/news/world-us-canada-39724045.

[988] See: http://foreignpolicy.com/2017/04/09/trumps-humanitarian-intervention-in-syria-is-just-getting-started/; but see also; http://www.nationalreview.com/article/446546/us-airstrikes-syria-intervention-not-our-vital-interest; https://www.theatlantic.com/politics/archive/2017/04/president-trumps-syria-strike-was-unconstitutional-and-unwise/522228/.

[989] See: https://www.theguardian.com/us-news/2017/feb/03/trump-administration-iran-sanctions; see also: http://www.jpost.com/Arab-Israeli-Conflict/Analysis-Will-Trump-waive-sanctions-against-Iran-490738.

[990] See: https://www.nytimes.com/2017/07/26/world/americas/venezuela-sanctions-treasury.html; http://www.latimes.com/politics/washington/la-na-essential-washington-updates-trump-hits-venezuela-with-more-1501087930-htmlstory.html.

[991] See: http://www.cetusnews.com/news/Trump-makes-military-threat-against-Venezuela-.BylORJ72DW.html. But see: https://www.reuters.com/article/us-usa-venezuela-military-idUSKBN1AR2GR; http://www.telesurtv.net/english/news/The-World-Reacts-to-Trumps-Military-Threat-Against-Venezuela-20170812-0007.html.

[992] See: http://www.vox.com/the-big-idea/2017/1/4/14165670/madman-theory-nuclear-weapons-trump-nixon; https://www.washingtonpost.com/blogs/post-partisan/wp/2016/12/15/how-might-nixons-madman-theory-apply-to-trump/?utm_term=.30ec6377bfb3; https://www.wired.com/story/donald-trump-madman-strategy-north-korea-nuclear-weapons/; http://www.trinidadexpress.com/20170825/features/trump-administration-imposes-sweeping-sanctions-on-venezuela.

[993] See: http://www.politico.com/magazine/story/2017/08/11/donald-trump-nuclear-weapons-richard-nixon-215478; http://foreignpolicy.com/2017/04/18/trumps-madman-theory-isnt-strategic-unpredictability-its-just-crazy/https://www.theatlantic.com/international/archive/2017/10/madman-theory-trump-north-korea/542055/.

of uncertainty breeds the fear needed to get the "bad guys" to change their objectionable behavior. This requires the use of increasingly aggressive rhetoric—including frequent and aggressive Trump tweets—with the clear and strong message that if the desired behavior change is not forthcoming, then American military force will be used without warning (including the use of big, bunker-busting non-nuclear bombs or even nuclear missiles). The success of such policing tactic depends on whether Trump can bully the "bad guys," without them, responding in kind and even calling his bluff.

Trump's "America First" international policy orientation means all bilateral and multilateral trade and defense agreements, alliances, and coalitions are expected to produce a net benefit to America. This became his signature presidential slogans: "Make America Great Again" and "Buy American, Hire American".[994] These became the focus of a Presidential Executive Order in April.[995] In Trump's mind, what was required was to abandon or radically renegotiate various international trade agreements—the Trans-Pacific Partnership (TPP)[996] and the North American Free Trade Agreement (NAFTA)[997]—and to end what he saw as one-sided defense alliances, whether bilateral, particularly with Japan,[998] South Korea,[999] and Saudi Arabia,[1000] or multilateral, particularly, the North Atlantic Treaty Organization (NATO). To Trump, "Make America Great Again" also means "Make America Safe Again."[1001] This meant expanding American military capability, after all, as Trump declared in an interview with Bill O'Reilly at *Fox News*

---

[994] See: http://money.cnn.com/2017/01/20/news/economy/donald-trump-jobs-wages/.

[995] See: https://www.whitehouse.gov/the-press-ofice/2017/04/18/presidential-executive-order-buy-american-and-hire-american.

[996] See: http://www.nbcnews.com/business/economy/why-trump-killed-tpp-why-it-matters-you-n710781.

[997] See: http://money.cnn.com/2016/11/15/news/economy/trump-what-is-nafta/.

[998] See: http://www.cnbc.com/2016/11/10/trumps-foreign-policy-heres-a-recap-of-what-the-president-elect-said-about-asia-during-the-campaign.html.

[999] Ibid

[1000] See: https://www.bloomberg.com/politics/articles/2015-08-16/donald-trump-adds-saudi-arabia-to-list-of-countries-ripping-off-the-u-s-.

[1001] See: https://www.whitehouse.gov/the-press-office/2017/02/04/promise-make-america-safe-again.

in January 2015: "There's nobody bigger or better at the military than I am,"[1002] despite his lack of any military knowledge and experience. Interestingly, Trump has delegated war-making authority to the Pentagon:

> What he has done is cede war-making authority to Secretary of Defense James Mattis,[1003] who now reportedly has plenary power to set objectives, allocate resources, and move troops to fight in both countries [Iraq and Afghanistan] ... it's clear from Trump's own statements and reporting on the White House[1004] that the president has delegated his war powers down to Mattis—along with whatever political risk[1005] may come from bad outcomes.

> Such a delegation of war power may be attractive to Trump ... Nonetheless ... he cannot escape responsibility for the strategic decisions about objectives, nor evade his duty to marshal public support and resources from Congress to pursue those ends.[1006]

More cynically: "He is using the troops as props, hiding behind their bright medals, and using their credibility for political gain."[1007] Trump's engagement with the American military is designed to give him what he needs to shore-up his core support base—a war—albeit not the isolationist alt-right.

[1002] Retrieved from: https://www.forbes.com/sites/lorenthompson/2017/02/28/trump-historic-defense-increase-is-barely-above-what-obama-planned-and-faces-similar-obstacles/#4c8bf76165cd.

[1003] See: https://www.nytimes.com/2017/06/13/world/asia/mattis-afghanistan-military.html?_r=0&mtrref=www.slate.com&gwh=72F848744C0135DFE57B98D85F34D-B8&gwt=pay.

[1004] See also: https://www.washingtonpost.com/news/checkpoint/wp/2017/06/14/whats-your-end-game-trump-delegating-afghan-war-decisions-to-the-pentagon-faces-scrutiny/?utm_term=.9166729bd9af.

[1005] See: http://www.slate.com/articles/news_and_politics/politics/2017/05/trump_s_afghanistan_strategy_could_get_us_sucked_back_into_the_forever_war.html.

[1006] Retrieved from: http://www.slate.com/articles/news_and_politics/politics/2017/07/donald_trump_is_abdicating_his_role_as_commander_in_chief.html.

[1007] Ibid

It has been suggested, as an alternative explanation, that Trump has fallen into the clutches of the military—even subjected to a behind the scenes military coup:

> He is now so enfeebled that the Generals and Admirals are not just emboldened to ignore his orders with contempt (not a blind bit of notice was taken of his ban[1008] on transgender people in the military[1009]). They are dictating foreign policy even when it directly undermines the support of Trump's base.[1010]

Trump's "Make America Safe Again" also meant deporting "illegal immigrants"[1011] coming from or through Mexico, and deporting Syrian refugee re-settlers,[1012] and taking steps to deter Iran's and North Korea's ballistic missile program.[1013]

It was expected that Trump, on becoming president, would put in place a set of policy to fulfill his major campaign promises on international affairs.[1014]

[1008] See: http://www.independent.co.uk/news/world/americas/us-politics/trump-transgender-ban-trans-troops-medical-treatment-latest-a7913686.html.

[1009] The Secretary of Defense, James Mattis, is "convening a panel of experts to examine the implications of prohibiting transgender Americans from serving in the armed forces, seeking to determine 'what is best for the military's combat effectiveness leading to victory on the battlefield....' In the interim, current policy with respect to currently serving members will remain in place. Mr. Mattis said." Retrieved from: http://www.independent.co.uk/news/world/americas/us-politics/trump-transgender-ban-general-mattis-frozen-defence-secretary-a7919331.html. See also: http://www.independent.co.uk/news/transgender-us-military-donald-trump-ban-james-mattis-a7914746.html; http://www.independent.co.uk/news/transgender-us-military-donald-trump-ban-james-mattis-a7914746.html.

[1010] Retrieved from: http://www.independent.co.uk/voices/donald-trump-afghanistan-speech-military-troops-taliban-isis-president-military-coup-a7906741.html.

[1011] See: http://www.foxnews.com/politics/2017/04/18/trump-illegal-immigrant-criminals-are-getting-hell-out.html; https://www.lifezette.com/polizette/trumps-forfeits-valuable-immigration-bargaining-chip/.

[1012] See: https://www.theguardian.com/us-news/2016/sep/02/donald-trump-syria-refugees-us-immigration-security-terrorism.

[1013] See: http://www.cbsnews.com/pictures/wild-donald-trump-quotes/.

[1014] See: https://www.washingtonpost.com/opinions/global-opinions/what-president-trumps-foreign-policy-will-look-like/2016/11/09/3ab88670-a632-11e6-ba59-a7d93165c6d4_story.html?utm_term=.ba61cd170421.

Muslim Travel and Immigration Ban

Trump's campaign rhetoric emphasized the threat of Islamic terrorism:

> We can't let them [Islamist terrorists] come over here.
> I have to say, there is an end. And it has to be humilia-
> tion. There is an end. Otherwise it's really tough. But
> there is an end. We are really eradicating some very bad
> people. When you take a look at what's going on with
> the cutting off of the heads. We haven't seen that since
> medieval times. Right.

> He holds this position because he believes that every
> living Muslim is a potential terrorist[1015] (political Is-
> lam[1016]) on the premise that the hatred of the West that
> is an intrinsic Islamic belief.[1017]

Perhaps Trump's most contentious campaign promise was the "total and complete shutdown of Muslims entering the US until our country's representatives can figure out what is going on."[1018] Very soon after his inauguration, Trump issued an Executive Order—*Protection of The Nation From Foreign Terrorist Entry Into The United States.*[1019] This imposed

---

[1015] See: http://www.nbcnews.com/politics/2016-election/his-words-donald-trump-muslim-ban-deportations-n599901. Retrieved from: https://www.theguardian.com/us-news/2017/jan/27/donald-trump-executive-order-imm.

[1016] See: https://www.whitehouse.gov/the-press-office/2017/01/27/executive-order-protecting-nation-foreign-terrorist-entry-united-states. See: https://www.politicalislam.com/product-category/pdf-downloads/; but see https://www.cmi.no/publications/file/1548-political-islam-in-the-middle-east.pdf.

[1017] See: https://www.buzzfeed.com/andrewkaczynski/donald-trump-praised-putin-for-bashing-the-term-american-exc?utm_term=.ubWoZO3A1#.enLP2aQ7r; https://www.buzzfeed.com/andrewkaczynski/donald-trump-praised-putin-for-bashing-the-term-american-exc?utm_term=.ubWoZO3A1-.enLP2aQ7r; https://www.buzzfeed.com/andrewkaczynski/donald-trump-praised-putin-for-bashing-the-term-american-exc?utm_term=.ubWoZO3A1#.enLP2aQ7r; http://www.bbc.com/news/world-us-canada-38886496; http://vestnikkavkaza.net/analysis/Bannon%E2%80%99s-war-in-the-Middle-East.html.

[1018] See: http://www.nbcnews.com/politics/2016-election/his-words-donald-trump-muslim-ban-deportations-n599901.

[1019] Retrieved from: https://www.theguardian.com/us-news/2017/jan/27/donald-trump-executive-order-immigration-full-text

a temporary a travel ban[1020] on visitors, refugees, and immigrants from selected countries with a Muslim majority—Iran, Iraq, Libya, Somalia, Sudan, Syria, and Yemen. These, Trump considered, were "some of the most dangerous countries in the world, including those "that have a history of exporting terrorism,"[1021] and so they pose a threat to America.[1022] Yet, "[r]efugees from those countries ... have killed zero Americans in terrorist attacks in America since 1975."[1023]

The ban was for 120 days, the time needed to install a system of "extreme" immigration vetting".[1024] This is expected to involve requiring visitors to provide their 'phone contacts and social media passwords, and would certainly involve "ideological" vetting.[1025] The travel ban was, however, blocked by a federal court.[1026] A subsequent attempt to initiate such a ban[1027] was similarly blocked.[1028] Ultimately, however:

> The Supreme Court gave a short-term win to the Trump administration Tuesday [3 September], bolstering part of a travel ban that will allow the administration to block new refugees arriving from six majority-Muslim nations. In a brief order and with no dissents, the justices reversed rulings by a federal judge in Hawaii and the 9th Circuit Court of Appeals in San Francisco ... The Supreme Court in late June said the travel ban may not be enforced against foreigners who have a "close"

[1020] See: https://www.whitehouse.gov/the-press-office/2017/01/27/executive-order-protec ting-nation-foreign-terrorist-entry-united-states.

[1021] See: http://www.nbcnews.com/politics/2016-election/his-words-donald-trump-musli m-ban-deportations-n599901.

[1022] Ibid

[1023] Retrieved from: https://www.indy100.com/article/white-supremacists-killed-more-peo ple-week-refugee-terrorists-trump-travel-ban-countries-40-years-7761101

[1024] See: http://www.businessinsider.com/trump-first-100-days-promises-2017-4?utm_ source=googleplaynewsstand&utm_medium=referral.

[1025] See: http://www.cbsnews.com/news/where-donald-trump-stands-on-terrorism/.

[1026] See: http://www.independent.co.uk/nws/world/americas/seattle-federal-judge-restraining-order-donald-trump-immigration-ban-a7562406.html.

[1027] This time, Iraq was omitted. See: https://www.whitehouse.gov/the-press-office/2017/03/06/executive-order-protecting-nation-foreign-terrorist-entry-united-states.

[1028] See: https://www.theguardian.com/us-news/2017/mar/16/trump-new-travel-ban-bloc ked-explainer-what-next.

family tie with someone in this country, and the 9th Circuit said that may include grandparents, in-laws and cousins.[1029]

This may well be one of the rare occasions when that American immigration policy is to be used as a foreign policy instrument.[1030]

Resident Syrian Refugees

Trump's campaign promise was to deport all resident Syrian refugees.[1031] His solution to the Syrian refugee crisis is to create a safe zone in Syria: "He suggested to 'take a big swatch of land' for 'the right price' and build 'a big beautiful safe zone' that will make Syrian refugees 'happier.'"[1032] This he expected to be financed by the Persian Gulf states.[1033] Since becoming president, Trump has said he will "absolutely do safe zones in Syria."[1034] No actions toward meeting this campaign promise has been taken, as the idea of such a safe zone has been taken up by Iran, Russia, and Turkey,[1035] thereby excluding American participation.

Mexico

Perhaps Trump's signature campaign themes were the unpatriotic emigration of US manufacturing capacity to Mexico and the illegal immigrants coming to, and living in, the US. He colorfully combined these themes in a speech he made in Iowa in October 2015: "They're going to

---

[1029] Retrieved from: http://www.latimes.com/politics/washington/la-na-essential-washington-updates-supreme-court-blocks-new-refugees-under-1505255496-htmlstory.html.

[1030] See: http://www.salon.com/2017/03/16/iran-trump-and-bannons-war-in-the-middle-east_partner/.

[1031] See: http://www.cbsnews.com/news/donald-trump-proposes-ideological-test-immigration-u-s/; http://www.nbcnews.com/politics/2016-election/his-words-donald-trump-muslim-ban-deportations-n599901

[1032] Retrieved from: http://www.aljazeera.com/indepth/opinion/2017/01/trump-real-estate-approach-safe-zones-syria-170130135423734.html.

[1033] See: http://www.businessinsider.com/trump-first-100-days-promises-2017-4?utm_source=googleplaynewsstand&utm_medium=referral.

[1034] Retrieved from: http://www.huffingtonpost.com/david-l-phillips/safe-zones-in-syria_b_14439356.html.

[1035] See: http://www.huffingtonpost.com/david-l-phillips/safe-zones-in-syria_b_14439356.html; https://www.theguardian.com/world/2017/may/04/syrian-opposition-rejects-deal-to-create-safe-zones.

build a plant [in Mexico] and illegals are going to drive those cars right over the border. And they'll probably end up stealing the cars" (cited in Piehler 2016, 63).

Trump's campaign promise on illegal migrants came in three parts. He promised to deport all undocumented Latino immigrants (up to 11 million people); of which an estimated 2 million are "criminal aliens" (including gang members).[1036] He promised to terminate the granting of citizenship to US-born children of undocumented immigrants (birth right citizenship[1037]). He promised to build a great new "impenetrable physical wall" along the length of the American-Mexico border[1038]— some 1,600 km: "I will build a great wall—and nobody builds walls better than me—and I'll build them very inexpensively. I will build a great, great wall on our southern border; and I will make Mexico pay for that wall. Mark my words" (Trump Tower, June 2015, cited in Piehler 2016, 67).[1039] To which he added a little later: "They [the Mexicans] will put my name on it, I want a gorgeous wall, ah the Trump wall" (Dallas, Texas, September 2015, cited in Piehler 2016, 68). This incredibly difficult wall to build[1040] has been made necessary because Mexico is "sending" illegal immigrants—"drugs and rapists"[1041]—across the border. It would be paid for by Mexico. A cheeky response has come from a Mexican lawyer-businessman, Antonio Battaglia. He was so offended by Trump's comments that he decided to produce and sell "'Trump' brand toilet paper, marketed under the slogans 'Softness without borders' and 'This is the wall that, yes, we will pay for.'"[1042]

[1036] See: http://www.bbc.com/news/world-us-canada-34789502.

[1037] See: https://www.washingtonpost.com/news/wonk/wp/2015/08/17/understanding-trumps-plan-to-end-citizenship-for-undocumented-immigrants-kids/?utm_term=.f0a0df123fc7.

[1038] Retrieved from:http://www.businessinsider.com/trump-first-100-days-promises-2017-4?utm_source=googleplaynewsstand&utm_medium=referral.

[1039] But see also: http://www.express.co.uk/news/politics/730583/Donald-Trump-will--President-build-wall-border-Mexico-America-Mexican-illegal-immigrants.

[1040] See: http://www.bbc.co.uk/news/resources/idt-d60acebe-2076-4bab-90b4-0e9a5f62ab12.

[1041] Retrieved from: http://www.bbc.com/news/av/world-us-canada-37230916/what-trump-has-said-about-mexicans.

[1042] Retrieved from: https://www.theguardian.com/world/2017/may/31/donald-trump-mexico-toilet-paper-antonio-battaglia.

Under Operation Wetback, illegal immigrants are being identified and detained prior to deportation,[1043] which extends to previously tolerated non-violent undocumented immigrants.[1044] This prompted a critical response from one Federal Judge Stephen Reinhardt in relation to the Andres Magana Ortiz case:[1045]

> Judge Reinhardt wrote [in his judgment] that the government had forced the panel [of federal judges considering this case] to participate in ripping apart a family, and observed that this result was contrary to President Trump's claim that his immigration policies would target "bad hombres" and his promise of an immigration system with "a lot of heart." Judge Reinhardt found no such compassion in the government's choice to deport [Andres] Magana Ortiz, writing that judges, forced to participate in such inhumane acts, suffer a loss of dignity and humanity.[1046]

Deportation even extends to illegal immigrants who are military veterans[1047] and young children covered by Obama's executive amnesties.[1048] It seems, however, that Trump has had a change of heart about deporting undocumented children: "Does anybody really want to throw out good, educated and accomplished young people who have jobs, some serving in the military? Really!" (Trump tweet, 11.28 am, 14 September).[1049]

[1043] See: https://newrepublic.com/article/132988/operation-wetback-revisited.

[1044] See: https://www.usatoday.com/story/news/world/2017/03/22/faces-of-deportations-under-president-trump/99455428/.

[1045] "Andres Magaña Ortiz is a 43-year old Mexican [illegal] immigrant who, in his 30 years of living in the United States, worked his way up from a fruit picker to owner of a 20-acre coffee farm and manager of about 150 acres of land for other farmers who can't manage on their own. He is married to an American citizen and his three children were born in the United States." Retrieved from: https://www.thenation.com/article/andres-magana-ortizs-deportation-is-indefensible-help-reverse-it/.

[1046] Retrieved from: http://cdn.ca9.uscourts.gov/datastore/opinions/2017/05/30/17-1601 4.pdf, pp. 2-3.

[1047] See: http://www.snopes.com/united-states-deporting-veterans.

[1048] See: https://townhall.com/tipsheet/conncarroll/2014/11/21/everything-you-need-to-know-about-obamas-executive-amnesty-n1922199; http://www.dailymail.co.uk/news/article-2843174/We-not-going-deport-Obama-announces-amnesty-millions-anchor-baby-parents-illegal-immigrant-children-long-ve-five-years.html.

[1049] Retrieved from: https://twitter.com/realDonaldTrump/status/908276308265795585.

Some illegals have been deported to Mexico,[1050] much to Mexico's chagrin,[1051] under threat that if it did not take back deported criminals then American visas would be cancelled.[1052]

The reduced scope of birth right citizenship—*jus soli* (literally "right of the soil"—has been incorporated into proposed legislation introduced in Congress on January 3, 2017.[1053] This specified that citizenship would be granted only to individuals born in America who have at least one parent who is a citizen, a lawful permanent resident, or an immigrant who is in active military service. It has yet to become law, and is not likely to do so.

As to the financing of the border wall, Mexico has already firmly refused to pay for it,[1054] despite Trump's threatened penalties (such as withholding billions of dollars in remittance payments to Mexico, increasing fees and possibly cancelling visas issued to Mexicans, and increasing fees at ports of entry into the US from Mexico). So, the wall's future is contingent on Congress agreeing to its funding (estimated to be $10–12bn,[1055] but it could be as much as $21.6bn[1056]).[1057] This may well give him a zero-sum policy choice:

> That means the president is going to have to decide, very soon, how he wants the fall policy debate to play out. Does he want Congress to spend the next few months battling over the budget and funding a border wall? Or does he want lawmakers to try to pass a tax cut? If he does not develop and sell a coherent policy

1050 See: http://edition.cnn.com/2017/04/17/americas/mexico-airport-deportees/.

1051 See: http://www.reuters.com/article/us-usa-mexico-idUSKBN16127O.

1052 See: http://www.businessinsider.com/trump-first-100-days-promises-2017-4?utm_source=googleplaynewsstand&utm_medium=referral.

1053 See: http://www.sandiegouniontribune.com/news/immigration/sd-me-birthright-citizenship-20170503-story.h.

1054 See: http://www.express.co.uk/news/politics/730583/Donald-Trump-will--President-build-wall-border-Mexico-America-Mexican-illegal-immigrants.

1055 See: http://www.bbc.com/news/world-us-canada-37243269.

1056 See: http://www.reuters.com/article/us-usa-trump-immigration-wall-exclusive-idUSK.BN15O2ZN.

1057 See: https://www.forbes.com/sites/nathanielparishflannery/2017/04/28/media-round up-trumpty-dumptys-wall-falls-down/#abe8785affe7.

choice to Congress ... it is likely that the congressional GOP leadership will choose for him.[1058]

And the wall would almost certainly the looser. Indeed, it is already off the immediate agenda—at least temporarily deferred—in Trump's discussions with the Democrats about raising the public debt ceiling.[1059]

Iran

Trump's campaign rhetoric positioned Iran as most dangerous "bad guy" in the Middle East;[1060] as the major state sponsor of terrorism globally[1061] (supporting, among others, rebels in Yemen and militias in Iraq and Lebanon) and as a key ally of the al-Assad regime in Syria. Trump's main campaign promise was to renegotiate or withdraw from the Iran nuclear agreement[1062]—the Joint Comprehensive Plan of Action signed by Iran and the five permanent UN Security Council members plus Germany and the EU (the Paris Agreement[1063])—neither has happened, as Trump has come to accept, perhaps very reluctantly,[1064] that Iran is in formal compliance with requirements of the Paris Agreement,[1065] but, as

---

[1058] See, for example: http://thehill.com/policy/finance/347680-ryan-shutdown-over-border-wall-not-necessary; http://edition.cnn.com/2017/08/23/politics/paul-ryan-border-security-funding/index.html; http://talkingpointsmemo.com/livewire/paul-ryan-government-shutdown-not-necessary-trump-threat.

[1059] Retrieved from: https://www.thetimes.co.uk/article/trump-backers-in-despair-at-democrat-talks-ck283xk7f.

[1060] See: http://www.salon.com/2017/03/16/iran-trump-and-bannons-war-in-the-middle-east_partner/; http://edition.cnn.com/videos/politics/2017/03/29/trump-iraq-troops-starr-lead-dnt.cnn/video/playlists/president-donald-trump/Europeam Union; http://www.aljazeera.com/indepth/features/2017/02/trump-leading-warpath-iran-170203105946707.html; http://blink.htcsense.com/web/articleweb.aspx?regionid=3&articleid=84872360.

[1061] See: http://www.bbc.com/news/world-us-canada-38868039.

[1062] See: http://foreignpolicy.com/2016/11/16/president-trump-and-the-iran-nuclear-deal/.

[1063] See: http://www.ipcs.org/article/nuclear/the-paris-agreement-and-iranian-nuclear-case-1606.html.

[1064] http://www.aljazeera.com/news/2017/10/trump-threats-iran-nuclear-deal-matter-171009071238924.html.

[1065] See: http://www.reuters.com/article/us-iran-nuclear-usa-tillerson-idUSKBN17L08I?feedType=RSS&feedName=topNews; but see also: https://www.nytimes.com/2017/10/03/world/middleeast/mattis-iran-deal-trump.html.

this Agreement has to be re-certified every 90 days, he may well change his mind and de-certify it.[1066]

Trump also promised to negotiate the release of all American prisoners held in Iran; none have yet been released. Iran's ballistic missile program is considered by Trump to be bigger threat to America.[1067] This has solicited more targeted sanctions.[1068] Trump, seeking to build a coalition of support for his anti-Iran position, "denounced Shi'ite Iran's "destabilizing interventions" in Arab lands in an address to a summit of Muslim leaders in Saudi Arabia in May, at which he told them that they need to stand united against Iran."[1069] This solicited—10 days later—an unexpected outcome; a very public feud between Saudi Arabia and the United Arab Emirates with Qatar over "Qatar's conciliatory line on Iran, their regional arch-rival, and its support for Islamist groups, in particular the Muslim Brotherhood, which they regard as a dangerous political enemy."[1070] Trump has had his first lesson on the complexities of Middle East politics.[1071]

Russia

Trump's most startling campaign rhetoric and promise was that he would build a strong relationship with Russia and the Russian President, Vladimir Putin. He has described Putin as "a man so highly respected within his own country and beyond"[1072] and, more recently, as "a tough cook-

---

[1066] See: https://www.cnbc.com/2017/08/25/strong-indications-trump-wont-recertify-iran-nuclear-deal.html.

[1067] See: http://edition.cnn.com/2017/04/19/politics/tillerson-iran-nuclear-deal-review/index.html.

[1068] See: http://www.bbc.com/news/world-us-canada-38860352; see also https://www.whitehouse.gov/legislation/hr-3364-countering-americas-adversaries-through-sanctions-act.

[1069] Retrieved from: http://www.reuters.com/article/us-gulf-qatar-usa-idUSKBN18R1AA.

[1070] Ibid

[1071] See: http://www.ooyuz.com/geturl?aid=15855891; http://www.ooyuz.com/geturl?aid=15865086; http://www.ooyuz.com/geturl?aid=15885436; https://worldview.stratfor.com/article/us-charges-head-gulf-crisis; http://www.aljazeera.com/news/2017/07/trump-good-relations-qatar-170714230137824.html.

[1072] Retrieved from: http://www.politico.com/story/2015/12/trump-vladimir-putin-praise-216892; see also: http://edition.cnn.com/2016/07/28/politics/donald-trump-vladimir-putin-quotes/index.html.

ie".[1073] Trumps has said: "I also believe we can find common ground with Russia in the fight against ISIS. Wouldn't that be a good thing? Wouldn't that be a good thing?"[1074]

Improving relations with Russia has, however, proven to be more difficult than Trump ever imagined.[1075] In the face of veritable flood of rumors, disclosures, and allegations of collusion by the Trump Campaign with respect to the alleged Russian meddling in the 2016 presidential election, Trump has had little choice but to distance himself publicly from Putin,[1076] by publicly renouncing, perhaps reluctantly,[1077] his desire to proceed with his Putin overtures. However, somewhat clandestinely, he has initiated such overtures.[1078] He has spoken with Putin by telephone[1079] and they met for formally in early July in Germany at the G20 Summit,[1080] and, again, informally, after the Summit dinner.[1081,1082]

[1073] See: http://www.bbc.com/news/world-us-canada-37920224

[1074] See: http://www.bbc.com/news/world-us-canada-37920224; http://www.bbc.com/news/world-us-canada-37920224; http://www.cbsnews.com/news/where-donald-trump-stands-on-terrorism/; http://transcripts.cnn.com/TRANSCRIPTS/1608/16/acd.01.html.

[1075] See: http://www.bbc.com/news/world-us-canada-39157527.

[1076] See: http://edition.cnn.com/2017/04/14/politics/trump-china-russia/index.html?iid=ob_lockedrail_topeditorial.

[1077] See: https://www.bloomberg.com/news/articles/2017-03-16/behind-trump-s-russia-romance-there-s-a-tower-full of oligarchs; and http://www.bbc.com/news/world-europe-38969166.

[1078] See: http://google.com/newsstand/s/CBIw1NzY8TQ.

[1079] See: https://www.rferl.org/a/us-russia-trump-putin-meeting-july-7-g20-hamburg/28595565.html.

[1080] See: https://www.rferl.org/a/us-russia-trump-putin-meeting-july-7-g20-hamburg/28595565.html; http://www.bbc.co.uk/news/av/world-40534300/g20-trump-and-putin-shake-hands.

[1081] See: http://matzav.com/trump-putin-met-for-nearly-an-hour-in-second-g20-meeting/; http://www.bbc.co.uk/news/world us canada-40658999; but see http://www.telegraph.co.uk/news/2017/07/18/white-house-admits-donald-trump-had-second-meeting-vladimir/; http://edition.cnn.com/2017/07/18/politics/trump-putin-g20/index.html. But see also: http://www.telegraph.co.uk/news/2017/07/18/white-house-admits-donald-trump-had-second-meeting-vladimir/.

[1082] See: https://www.vox.com/world/2017/6/30/15904366/trump-putin-agenda-2016-election-interference-g20-comey; https://www.vox.com/world/2017/6/30/15904366/trump-putin-agenda-2016-election-interference-g20-comey; http://www.bbc.co.uk/news/world-europe-40527359.

Another stumbling block to any rapprochement is Putin's commitment to the regimes of al-Assad in Syrian[1083] and Kim Jong-un in North Korea.[1084] The overall outcome is that American–Russian relations reached a 25-year low, with any future rapprochement contingent upon the outcome of the various Russian collusion investigations. Putin began testing Trump's resolve to challenge Russia's future actions by having Russian bombers fly near Alaska[1085]—perhaps with a view to Russia moving back into Ukraine.[1086]

The Islamic State in Iraq and Syria

Trump's campaign rhetoric emphasized and responded to the barbarity of ISIS: "In the Middle East, we have people chopping the heads off Christians, we have people chopping heads off many other people. ...I would bring back waterboarding and I'd bring back a hell of a lot worse than waterboarding (Address to St Anselm College (Manchester, New Hampshire), February 2016, cited in Piehler 2016, 54). Trump even proposed killing terrorists' families: "When they say they don't care about their lives, you have to take out their families (*Fox News* interview, December 2015, cited in Piehler 2016, 63). Over two years before becoming president, Trump publicly declared that he considered himself to be "the worst thing that's ever happened to ISIS" (Barbara Walters Interview, December 2015 cited in Piehler 2016, 61).

Trump's campaign promise was that America would to join with Russia and Syrian in a joint military effort to defeat ISIS. The keeping this promise has had to be been abandoned following the souring of American relations with both Russia and Syria, after the alleged Syrian chemical weapons attack on its citizens and the Russian response.[1087] Instead,

---

[1083] See: https://www.theguardian.com/world/2017/apr/06/postmortems-confirm-syria-chemical-attack-turkey-says.

[1084] See: http://edition.cnn.com/2017/04/19/asia/russia-un-veto-north-korea/index.html.

[1085] See: http://www.newsweek.com/russian-aircraft-nuclear-bombers-near-alaska-jets-587743.

[1086] See: https://www.salon.com/2017/04/20/putin-on-the-move-russia-is-moving-back-into-ukraine-as-the-trump-administration-does-nothing/ but see http://blink.htcsense.com/web/articleweb.aspx?regionid=3&articleid=86247002 and see also http://www.bbc.com/news/world-37930957.

[1087] See: http://www.nydailynews.com/news/national/assad-u-s-missile-strike-fuel-syria-civil-war-article-1.3029925.

he decided to reinforce with his supporters that his primary foreign policy priority is still to defeat ISIS, he authorized the dropping of a massive (9,800 kg) conventional bomb (a GBU-43/B Massive Ordnance Air Blast Bomb)—the "mother-of-all-bombs—on an ISIS camp with underground tunnels in Afghanistan.[1088] This tactic is not very different to Obama's strategy,[1089] which he once strongly condemned.[1090]

Trump, having abandoned his Russia–Syrian–American joint military effort to defeat ISIS, has moved on to defeating terrorism in Afghanistan:

> During a July 19 meeting in the White House Situation Room, Trump demanded that his top national security aides provide more information on what one official called "the end-state" in a country where the United States has spent 16 years fighting against the Taliban with no end in sight.
>
> The meeting grew stormy when Trump said Defense Secretary James Mattis and Joint Chiefs of Staff Chairman Joseph Dunford, a Marine general, should consider firing Army General John Nicholson, commander of American forces in Afghanistan, for not winning the war.[1091]

A month later, Trump announced that he would deliver victory over ISIS, al Qaeda, and the Taliban in Afghanistan: "From now on, victory will have a clear definition. Attacking our enemies, obliterating ISIS, crushing al Qaeda, preventing the Taliban from taking over Afghanistan and stopping mass terror attacks against America before they emerge."[1092]

[1088] See: http://www.abc.net.au/news/2017-04-22/afghan-moab-evidence-increasingly-interventionist-donald-trump/8463184.

[1089] See: http://www.nbcnews.com/news/us-news/trump-s-secret-plan-beat-isis-looks-lot-obama-s-n735171; http://edition.cnn.com/2017/04/07/politics/obama-syria-airstrikes-trump/; http://www.thedailybeast.com/revealed-trumps-still-secret-plan-to-crush-isis.

[1090] See: http://edition.cnn.com/2017/04/13/politics/moab-trump-afghanistan/.

[1091] Retrieved from: https://www.reuters.com/article/us-usa-trump-afghanistan-idUSKBN1AI2Z3.

[1092] Retrieved from: https://www.nytimes.com/2017/08/21/world/asia/trump-speech-afghanistan.html?smid=tw-nytimes&smtyp=cur&_r=0. But see: http://www.politifact.com/truth-o-meter/article/2017/aug/21/donald-trumps-afghanistan-address-fact-checked/.

What Trump insisted was "new" about his approach to Afghanistan—"the integration of all instruments of American power—diplomatic, economic, and military—toward a successful outcome"; the refusal to "be silent about Pakistan's safe havens for terrorist organizations, the Taliban and other groups that pose a threat"; and so on—could be ripped from the pages of Obama-era strategy documents.[1093] Indeed, not only does the blatant conceptual continuity belie any claim to novelty, but the unanswered question of *how* again undercuts Trump's claim to be able to deliver on these elements of his approach.[1094]

The outcome is that more American troupes will go to Afghanistan, which means that its 16-year-old war against the terrorists will continue for some years to come. This is a major reversal of his long-standing opposition to America's military engagement there:

> "When will we stop wasting our money on rebuilding Afghanistan?" [2011] ...

> "We have wasted an enormous amount of blood and treasure in Afghanistan. Their government has zero appreciation. Let's get out!" [2013].[1095]

North Korea

Trump's campaign rhetoric emphasized, and the promise was made, that the US would make a pre-emptive strike on North Korea[1096] if it

---

[1093] See: http://www.tampabay.com/news/perspective/politifact-tracking-trumps-afghanistan-policy-against-previous/2335045.

[1094] Retrieved from: https://www.theatlantic.com/international/archive/2017/08/trump-afghanistan-speech-old-ideas/537588/.

[1095] Retrieved from: http://www.washingtontimes.com/news/2017/aug/24/afghanistan-policy-has-trump-deploying-more-troops/. See also: http://www.tampabay.com/news/perspective/politifact-tracking-trumps-afghanistan-policy-against-previous/2335045.

[1096] For Trump on North Korea, see https://www.theatlantic.com/international/archive/2016/11/trump-nuclear-north-korea/506750/; https://www.nytimes.com/2017/05/09/world/asia/south-korea-election-north-korea-trump-moon-jae-in.

continued to pursue nuclear weapons technology and the development of an intercontinental ballistic missile that could reach the American mainland. The foreign policy context is that North Korea, which has been taunting the US for years,[1097] has already conducted six successful nuclear tests over the last 11 years,[1098] and may well be nearly able to launch a nuclear-tipped intercontinental ballistic missile that could reach the American mainland.[1099] North Korea could also seek, perhaps alone or with the support of a terrorist organization, to place a bomb in America, perhaps to deter America from protecting South Korea in the event of an invasion from the north.[1100]

Early in his Presidency, Trump declared that the North Korean threat would not happen.[1101] Then, in late February, he judges that this was the greatest threat to the US.[1102] In early March, he acknowledged that the threat had entered a more serious "new phase."[1103] By late April, the alarm bells began ringing across Washington,[1104] after Trump declared that Kim Jong-un, who he hopes is rational,[1105] is "acting very, very badly."[1106] He considered that the threat has escalated,[1107] so justifying his

---

html?mtrref=undefined&gwh=731FC688F1EA46B1E872258825762E70&gwt=pay.

[1097] See: http://edition.cnn.com/2017/04/25/politics/trump-north-korea-taunts/index.html.

[1098] See: http://edition.cnn.com/2013/10/29/world/asia/north-korea-nuclear-timeline---fast-facts/index.html.

[1099] See:https://www.nytimes.com/2016/09/10/science/north-korea-nuclear-weapons.html?_r=0&mtrref=www.theatlantic.com &gwh=884E2CB1FB0629F811FD1F7F849AB100&gwt=pay.

[1100] See: https://www.theatlantic.com/international/archive/2016/11/trump-nuclear-north-korea/506750/.

[1101] See: http://edition.cnn.com/2017/01/02/politics/north-korea-icbm-threat-trump/index.html.

[1102] See: https://www.theguardian.com/world/2017/mar/07/donald-trump-threat-north-korea-new-phase.

[1103] Retrieved from: https://www.theguardian.com/world/2017/mar/07/donald-trump-threat-north-korea-new-phase.

[1104] See: http://www.sacbee.com/article147000464.html.

[1105] See: https://www.theguardian.com/us-news/2017/apr/28/i-thought-being-president-would-be-easier-trumps-reuters-interview-highlights; http://google.com/newsstand/s/CBIwqvu48TQ

[1106] Retrieved from: http://www.aljazeera.com/news/2017/03/north-korea-afraid-military-strike-170320210348513.html.

[1107] See: http://www.reuters.com/article/us-northkorea-usa-idUSKBN17T0AW?feedType=RSS&feedName=topNews.

more aggressive posturing (including imposing tighter sanctions to be imposed by the US and the UN[1108]), more American military action,[1109] more diplomatic pressure on America's Asian Allies. Trump clearly hopes, like his last three predecessors (Presidents Clinton, Bush Jr, and Obama), that China will intervene to deter North Korea from continuing on its nuclear missile program.[1110] His optimism is grounded in his belief that his new "friend" President Xi Jin-ping,[1111] "doesn't want to see turmoil and death [on the Korean peninsula]. ...I know he would like to be able to do something. Perhaps it's possible that he can't."[1112] He has also sought to the support of other Asian allies, starting with the Philippine.[1113]

Trump has escalated the tension with his hostile rhetoric since early August, when he warned of "fire and fury like the world has never seen"[1114]

[1108] See: https://www.reuters.com/article/us-northkorea-missiles-un-idUSKBN18T2X3; https://www.theguardian.com/world/2017/sep/12/north-korea-sanctions-un-security-council-unanimously-agrees-new-measures; http://edition.cnn.com/2017/09/11/politics/north-korea-un-security-council-vote/index.html.

[1109] See: http://www.telegraph.co.uk/news/2017/03/03/trump-administration-considering-military-force-among-measures/; https://newsstand.google.com/articles/CAIiEAj1xnkp5HyQzwPA-lKPcSYqFggEKg4IACoGCAowzdp7ML-3CTCtyxU;http://edition.cnn.com/2017/04/24/politics/uss-michigan-nuclear-sub-south-korea/index.html; https://mail.google.com/mail/u/0/#inbox/15bb3015bf3f1682; http://www.bbc.com/news/av/world-us-canada-39749828/us-committed-to-defending-asia-allies; http://www.bbc.com/news/av/world-us-canada-39749828/us-committed-to-defending-asia-allies.

[1110] See: http://www.foxnews.com/politics/2017/04/24/trump-discusses-north-korea-tensions-with-asian-leaders.html; https://newsstand.google.com/articles/CAIiEJ02VEFmviHj8DxbRemYx8YqFQgEKg0IACoGCAowrqkBMKBFMLKAAg.

[1111] Retrieved from: http://news.sky.com/video/trump-says-chinas-xi-is-friend-of-mine-10855345; see also: https://qz.com/966591/donald-trump-great-chemistry-with-chinese-president-xi-jinping-is-actually-not-that-great/.

[1112] Retrieved from: https://www.theguardian.com/us-news/2017/apr/28/i-thought-being-president-would-be-easier-trumps-reuters-interview-highlights.

[1113] See: http://www.telegraph.co.uk/news/2017/04/30/trump-invites-philippines-duterte-washington-white-house-says/and; http://edition.cnn.com/2017/04/30/politics/reince-priebus-philippines-president/index.html. But see: http://www.bbc.com/news/world-asia-39762742.

[1114] Retrieved from: http://www.bbc.co.uk/news/world-us-canada-40871754; but see: https://newsstand.google.com/articles/CAIiEGEKE0R0PsQsBaKF55pRzDEqGQgEKhAIACoHCAowocv1CjCSptoCMPrTpgU; but see: https://newsstand.google.com/articles/CAIiEPY4Vig0tmnwTSJjbK5dVxoqGQgEKhAIACoHCAowocv1CjCSptoCMKrUpgU;

if North Korea continues to threaten America. North Korea response was to announce that it was considering a missile strike on Guam,[1115] a US island territory in Micronesia in the western Pacific Ocean.[1116] The US then imposed sanctions.[1117] A US-sponsored UN resolution was then passed condemning North Korea and imposing sanctions.[1118] North Korea then put its proposed missile strike on Guam on hold.[1119] In retaliation to the next round of UN sanctions—its eighth—imposed in early September, North Korea has, matching Trump's earlier "fire and fury" rhetoric, threatened the US with "the greatest pain it has ever experienced".[1120] In return, Trump threatened, in his speech to the UN on September 20, to "totally destroy" North Korea if necessary, mocking its leader as "rocket man."[1121] In response North Korea threaten to test a nuclear bomb over the Pacific Ocean.[1122] Both Kim and Trump have now called each other mad.[1123] Indeed, North Korea considers that the

---

https://www.theguardian.com/politics/2017/aug/13/jeremy-corbyn-tells-trump-kim-stop-war-rhetoric-north-korea.

[1115] See: http://guam-online.com/.

[1116] See: http://www.bbc.co.uk/news/world-asia-40871416; see also http://www.telegraph.co.uk/news/2017/08/09/guam-paradise-island-hosts-nuclear-bombers-north-koreas-cross/; http://thediplomat.com/2016/08/guam-where-the-us-military-is-revered-and-reviled/.

[1117] See: https://www.treasury.gov/resource-center/sanctions/Programs/pages/nkorea.aspx. But see: https://www.washingtonpost.com/world/china-bristles-at-us-imposed-sanctions-on-north-korea-trade/2017/08/23/32bfba3c-87ba-11e7-9ce7-9e175d8953fa_story.html?utm_term=.0579988d8d5f.

[1118] See: http://edition.cnn.com/2017/04/21/politics/unsc-north-korea-resolution/index.html; http://www.independent.co.uk/news/world-0/us-politics/trump-north-korea-un-sanctions-vote-nuclear-threat-security-council-a7878911. But see: https://www.nytimes.com/2017/08/07/world/asia/north-korea-responds-sanctions-united-states.html?mcubz=3; http://comment-news.com/source/www.nytimes.com/2017/08/07/world/asia/north-korea-responds-sanctions-united-states.html/.

[1119] See: http://news.sky.com/story/north-korea-carefully-examining-plan-to-strike-guam-with-missiles-10980468; http://www.abc.net.au/news/2017-08-15/north-korea-kim-holds-off-on-guam-missile-plan/8810174.

[1120] Retrieved from: https://www.thetimes.co.uk/article/alarm-as-north-korea-fires-missile-over-japan-bzzc7p07q.

[1121] See: https://www.nbcnews.com/news/us-news/trump-un-north-korean-leader-suicide-mission-n802596; http://www.bbc.com/news/world-us-canada-41327130; http://www.bbc.com/news/world-asia-41357315

[1122] Retrieved from: https://www.nytimes.com/2017/09/22/world/asia/kim-trump-north-korea.html?mcubz=3.

[1123] See: http://www.bbc.com/news/world-asia-41356836.

US has declared war on it.[1124]

Yet, despite all this escalating rhetoric, secret talks are taking place,[1125] which Trump considers to be a "waste of time."[1126] Only time will tell whether Trump, with or without China's support, can bully—"out-cra-zy"[1127]—Kim Jong-Un, who he has said is a "smart cookie"[1128] who he would be 'honored"[1129] to meet—into abandoning his nuclear missile program, without Kim calling his bluff. Trump's threats and counter threats have, themselves, become a threat to Trump's threadbare believ-ability: should he keep his campaign promise and authorize pre-emp-tive military strike on North Korea? Trump's next moves are crucial:

> he discussed with his cabinet at the weekend [Septem-ber 9–10] options to confront Kim Jong-un. They in-clude cyberwarfare[1130] and possibly positioning nuclear weapons in South Korea for the first time in 26 years, White House officials told NBC News.

> Keeping the nuclear option open could be a useful tac-tic as the US pressures China ... to rein in Pyongyang ... a key part of the diplomatic strategy is to raise the pros-pect of a nuclearize South Korea and Japan—which

---

[1124] See: http://www.bbc.com/news/world-asia-41391978. But See: http://www.bbc.com/news/world-asia-41395970

[1125] See: http://www.telegraph.co.uk/news/2017/09/30/us-confirms-direct-talks-north-korea-nuclear-programme/

[1126] Retrieved from: https://www.ft.com/content/cd2087a0-a5f1-11e7-ab55-27219df83c97; see also: http://edition.cnn.com/2017/10/07/politics/donald-trump-mike-huckabee-interview-tnb/index.html; http://www.hurriyetdailynews.com/trump-says-n-korea-diplomacy-has-failed-only-one-thing-will-work-120518. But see also: https://www.theatlantic.com/international/archive/2017/10/trump-tillerson-self-respect-north-korea-puerto-rico-diplomacy/541695/.

[1127] Retrieved from: http://edition.cnn.com/2017/04/24/opinions/north-korea-threat-opinion-kirby/index.html.

[1128] Retrieved from: http://www.bbc.com/news/world-asia-39764834.

[1129] Retrieved from: https://www.washingtonpost.com/news/post-politics/wp/2017/05/01/trump-says-hed-be-honored-to-meet-with-north-korean-dictator/?utm_term=.83d4ae756d27.

[1130] See: https://www.nytimes.com/2017/03/04/world/asia/north-korea-missile-program-sabotage.html?mcubz=3. But see particularly: http://www.wired.co.uk/article/us-cyber-war-against-north-korea.

Beijing opposes—if the North [Koreans] continues down the path of weapons development.[1131]

So, the avoidance of military conflict remains in the hands of the Chinese.[1132] They alone still have the trust of both parties, which would enable them to initiate a process that could give rise not only to an acceptable negotiated solution but also to an opportunity to extract significant trade and other concessions from the Trump administration. But time is running out.[1133] Only time will tell at what price Trump might have to pay for outbreak of peace—or war—on the Korean peninsula.

Cuba

Trump's campaign rhetoric emphasized that he would reverse the decision made by Obama to reopen diplomatic relations and improve trade with, and travel to, Cuba.[1134] Soon after his inauguration, Trump ordered a review of the current Cuba policy, suggesting that he might be considering the reinstate the restrictions on Cuban trade and travel. If he deactivates Obama's détente, it would probably be detrimental for American business—especially the tourist industry[1135] and agriculture[1136]. Trump told an audience in Miami in mid-June, however, that he was "cancelling the Obama administration's one-sided deal"[1137] In reality, however, he has only placed restrictions on:

[1131] Retrieved from: https://www.thetimes.co.uk/article/us-plans-cyberwar-as-kim-jongun-celebrates-missile-tests-mk9trzqdq.

[1132] See: https://www.vox.com/world/2017/8/10/16125076/china-north-korea-donald-trump-xi-jinping-kim-jong-un; but see: https://www.forbes.com/forbes/welcome/?toURL=https://www.forbes.com/sites/sarahsu/2017/08/13/china-has-nothing-to-gain-from-sanctioning-north-korea/&refURL=https://www.google.co.uk/&referrer=https://www.google.co.uk/; http://nypost.com/2017/07/05/asking-china-to-fix-north-korea-is-a-waste-of-time/;https://www.cfr.org/backgrounder/china-north-korea-relationship.

[1133] See: http://nypost.com/2017/07/05/asking-china-to-fix-north-korea-is-a-waste-of-time/; http://www.scmp.com/week-asia/opinion/article/2079968/real-reason-china-wont-exert-economic-pressure-north-korea.

[1134] See: http://www.bbc.co.uk/news/world-us-canada-3798200.

[1135] See: https://www.nytimes.com/2017/06/01/travel/how-a-shift-in-us-policy-could-affect-travel-to-cuba.html?mtrref=undefined&gwh=687FE26901756F4B743AEBB2C578463D&gwt=pay.

[1136] See: http://foreignpolicy.com/2017/05/30/cuba-rollback-could-cost-trump-on-jobs-front/.

[1137] Retrieved from: http://www.telegraph.co.uk/news/2017/06/16/american-travel-cuba-restricted-donald-trump-announces-partial/.

- Travel to Cuba: "The US government will ensure travellers are pursuing a 'full-time schedule of educational exchange activities.'"[1138] This means "[US] citizens travelling in licensed groups with an American tour leader, and counterpart Cuban guide, on state-owned coaches, staying in state-run hotels, and following an itinerary approved by the Cuban government."[1139]

- Business with Cuba: specifically curtailed is doing business with GAESA[1140]—the Cuban conglomerate run by the Castro family jointly with the military—and any of its "affiliates, subsidiaries or successors."[1141]

Diplomatic relations remain in place, as do US commercial flights and cruise ships visits.

Defence Expenditure

Trump's campaign rhetoric emphasized that "[o]ur military is a disaster."[1142] His campaign promise was for an "historic increase in defense spending",[1143] so as to increase the size and readiness of the armed forces, including a cutting edge ballistic missile defense system, and up grading particular classes of Navy warships. Trump's first budget outline to Congress requested a $54 billion increase in defense expenditure (10%), taking it to $603 billion in 2018.[1144] This request came with no

---

[1138] Retrieved from: http://www.aljazeera.com/news/2017/06/cuba-rejects-donald-trump-hostile-rhetoric-170617040048115.html.

[1139] Retrieved from: http://www.telegraph.co.uk/travel/destinations/caribbean/cuba/articles/what-now-for-cuba-is-trump-going-to-spoil-the-party/. See also: http://www.telegraph.co.uk/travel/destinations/caribbean/cuba/articles/what-now-for-cuba-is-trump-going-to-spoil-the-party/.

[1140] Grupo de Administración Empresarial SA, "which operates state-owned companies that account for at least half the business revenue produced in Cuba." Retrieved from: http://www.huffingtonpost.com/daniel-williams2/castro-inc-cuba-as-family_b_960938.

[1141] Retrieved from: http://www.telegraph.co.uk/travel/destinations/caribbean/cuba/articles/what-now-for-cuba-is-trump-going-to-spoil-the-party/.

[1142] Retrieved from: http://www.pbs.org/newshour/rundown/fact-checking-gop-candidate-statements-on-obamas-military-spending/.

[1143] Retrieved from: https://www.forbes.com/sites/lorenthompson/2017/02/28/trump-historic-defense-increase-is-barely-above-what-obama-planned-and-faces-similar-obstacles/#4c8bf76165cd.

[1144] See: http://marketrealist.com/2017/03/big-defense-spending-trumps-first-budget-plan/.ist.

suggestions as to how it should be funded. If achieved, it would only be the ninth largest defense expenditure increase in the past 40 years, with both the Ronald Reagan and George W. Bush presidencies achieving higher defense expenditure increases.[1145]

Defence Expenditure Recoupment from Allies

Trump's campaign rhetoric made it clear that he would the end what he sees as one-sided defense alliances, highlighting in particular the US's bilateral alliances with Japan,[1146] South Korea,[1147] and Saudi Arabia[1148]. His promise was to require those countries to pay more for their own defense—including payments to the US—otherwise the US will withdraw its military support. He even went as far as to suggest that each country should develop its own nuclear weapons. Early in his presidency, Trump found this aspiration quite problematic in the face of events in Yemen (with Saudi military engagement)[1149] and North Korea (given the strategic importance of Japan[1150] and South Korea[1151]). He seemed to have quietly abandoned the meeting of this promise, but it was resurrected briefly in late April, when he was questioning who is paying the $1 billion cost of the THAAD—Terminal High Altitude Area Defense—system being installed in South Korea: "Why are we paying? Why are we paying a billion dollars? We're protecting. Why are we paying a billion dollars?"[1152] Nevertheless, the US is paying for it.[1153]

[1145] See: http://foxtrotalpha.jalopnik.com/trumps 668-billion-defense-budget-still-doesnt-match-h-1795485916.

[1146] See: http://www.cnbc.com/2016/11/10/trumps-foreign-policy-heres-a-recap-of-what-the-president-elect-said-about-asia-during-the-campaign.html.

[1147] See: http://www.cnbc.com/2016/11/10/trumps-foreign-policy-heres-a-recap-of-what-the-president-elect-said-about-asia-during-the-campaign.html.

[1148] See: https://www.bloomberg.com/politics/articles/2015-08-16/donald-trump-adds-saudi-arabia-to-list-of-countries-ripping-off-the-u-s-.

[1149] See: https://www.washingtonpost.com/news/josh-rogin/wp/2017/03/16/trump-resets-u-s-saudi-relations-in-saudi-arabias-favor/?utm_term=.cf9c0764baf9.

[1150] See: http://blink.htcsense.com/web/articleweb.aspx?regionid=3&articleid=85779082.

[1151] See: https://www.nytimes.com/2017/01/30/world/asia/trump-north-korea-south.html.

[1152] Retrieved from:https://www.theguardian.com/us-news/2017/apr/28/i-thought-being-president-would-be-easier-trumps-reuters-interview-highlights; But see: https://www.forbes.com/sites/johnbrinkley/2017/04/28/trump-Is-belligerence-toward-n-korea-with-belligerence-toward-s-korea/#47d7d24672cb.

[1153] See: https://www.nytimes.com/2017/04/30/world/asia/donald-trump-south-korea-

North Atlantic Treaty Organization

Trump's campaign rhetoric made it clear that he would change America's engagement with NATO, which he saw as a one-sided multilateral defense alliance. His campaign promise was to require the other NATO members[1154] to "pull their weight in the military alliance."[1155] Indeed, NATO became one of Trump's a major early foreign policy focuses as president. He warned NATO allies that they must spend more on their own defense—no less than the agreed target of 2% of GDP, which Germany, at least, considered "unrealistic"[1156]—or the US will give it less support.[1157]

He also saw NATO as being obsolete and in need of reform. It was far too focused on containing Russia and rather than on addressing the terrorist threat: "It's become very bureaucratic, extremely expensive and maybe is not flexible enough to go after terror. Terror is very much different than what NATO was set up for."[1158] His ultimate threat was to withdraw the US from this alliance, which raised anxieties in Europe about America's intentions and the future of America–Europe relations.[1159] It may well be that by issuing that threat Trump solicited the response he sought from other NATO members.[1160] The final outcome after a robust 3-month discourse is that Trump declared that NATO is

---

missile-system-thaad.html.

[1154] Comprising: Albania, Belgium, Bulgaria, Canada, Croatia, Czech Republic, Lithuania, Denmark, France, Germany, Hungary, Iceland, Italy, Latvia, Luxembourg, Netherlands, Norway, Poland, Portugal, Romania, Slovakia, Slovenia, Spain, Turkey, the United Kingdom, and the United States.

[1155] Retrieved from: http://www.express.co.uk/news/politics/733103/Donald-Trump--President-elect-snub-EU-UK-Russia-key-global-allies.

[1156] Retrieved from: http://www.telegraph.co.uk/news/2017/03/31/germany-says-nato-defence-spending-targets-unrealistic-rex-tillerson.

[1157] See: http://www.euronews.com/2017/02/15/mad-dog-mattis-warns-nato-members-to-spend-more-or-us-spends-less/; https://www.theatlantic.com/magazine/archive/2017/05/the-plan-to-end-europe/521445/?utm_source=feed.

[1158] See: https://www.theatlantic.com/magazine/archive/2017/05/the-plan-to-end-europe/521445/?utm_source=feed.

[1159] See: https://mail.google.com/mail/u/0/#inbox/15a55417b842325b; http://www.bbc.com/news/world-europe-39017879.

[1160] See: http://www.bbc.com/news/world-us-canada-39413655 [integrated in Melania Trump item].

no longer obsolete[1161] and that, in principle, the US is fully committed to it,[1162] although he remains a NATO sceptic. It was, indeed, a testy, oafish, and boorish Trump who attended his first NATO/G7 meeting in late May,

> [One who] might have recognized the sacrifices of nations much smaller than his fighting the Taliban in Afghanistan instead of delivering a scolding to virtually every other member nation allegedly for stiffing the American taxpayer in their contributions to the Alliance. He might also have refrained from calling the Germans "very bad" for being very good at selling their cars in America.[1163] This left European leaders "strangely shaken"[1164] but clearly not stirred.

Foreign Trade Agreements

Trump's campaign rhetoric recognized that in recent decades, millions of manufacturing jobs have disappeared, for which he blamed unfair trade practices made possible by flawed bilateral and multilateral trade agreements. His position can be colorfully summarized as:

> We're gonna bring businesses back. We're gonna have businesses that used to be in New Hampshire, that are now in Mexico, come back to New Hampshire, and you can tell them to go fuck themselves. Because they let you down, and they left (Speech in New Hampshire, February 2016, cited in Piehler 2016, 69).

His campaign promise was to "to bring back our jobs. We will bring back

---

[1161] See: http://www.bbc.com/news/world-us-canada-39585029.

[1162] See: https://www.wsj.com/articles/president-trump-says-u-s-and-germany-share-much-in-common-on-security-and-prosperity-1489776222; but see: http://www.dw.com/en/as-trump-re-evaluates-nato-nato-must-rethink-russia/a-37514599?maca=en-gk-volltext-newsstand-topstories-en-10709-xml-media.

[1163] Retrieved from: https://www.nytimes.com/2017/06/09/world/europe/trump-nato-defense-article-5.html; http://www.independent.co.uk/voices/donald-trump-nato-g7-paris-treaty-russia-dwindling-base-a7758401.html.

[1164] Retrieved from: https://www.theguardian.com/us-news/2017/may/27/donald-trumps-europe-tour-leaves-leaders-shaken.

our borders. We will bring back our wealth, and we will bring back our dreams."[1165] He is intent on stopping the use of unfair trade practices (if necessary, by renegotiating or abandoning all 14 bilateral and regional free-trade agreements).[1166] He particularly promised to reverse the loss of manufacturing jobs to Mexico, China, and elsewhere by bringing that production capacity back to America.[1167]

Trump was clearly committing himself to fair and reciprocal foreign trade[1168] as the means by which the manufacturing sector can be resurrected. This, he thought, would stem the loss of American jobs,[1169] because of unfair trade practices. He believed that cheap imports were not just because of cheap labor; foreign governments were also providing hidden support[1170] by, he believed, deliberately undervalued their exchange rates.[1171] Such unfair trade practices, he asserted, have been adopted by China and Mexico, as well as Japan and Germany,[1172] and contribute to America's balance of trade deficit, of which 77% of comes from trade with China,[1173] the European Union,[1174] and Japan.[1175]

[1165] Retrieved from:http://money.cnn.com/2017/01/20/news/economy/donald-trump-jobs-wages/.

[1166] See: http://fortune.com/2017/03/24/trump-executive-order-trade-deal/; https://www.nytimes.com/2017/01/23/us/politics/tpp-trump-trade-nafta.html.

[1167] See: http://www.ontheissues.org/2016/Donald_Trump_Jobs.htm.

[1168] See: https://www.economist.com/news/briefing/21721935-idea-reciprocity-animates-white-houses-view-trade-what-donald-trump-means-fair; https://www.cnbc.com/video/2016/03/10/donald-trump-free-trade-has-to-be-fair-trade.html; https://www.usatoday.com/story/money/2017/03/06/trump-advisor-free-fair-and-reciprocal-trade-deals-priority/98801640/.

[1169] See: http://www.nydailynews.com/news/politics/trump-executive-orders-fall-short-u-s-manufacturing-jobs-vow-article-1.3016023.

[1170] See: http://www.bbc.com/news/world-us-canada-38971859.

[1171] See: http://www.bbc.com/news/election-us-2016-36185012; http://www.politico.com/blogs/2016-gop-primary-live-updates-and-results/2016/05/trump-china-rape-america-222689.

[1172] See: https://www.axios.com/trumps-tweets-for-the-past-6-years-tell-a-different-story-2357875234.html.

[1173] See: https://www.forbes.com/sites/douglasbulloch/2017/04/24/why-the-u-s-trade-deficit-with-china-does-matter-after-all/#6b2528da7956.

[1174] See: http://www.strategic-culture.org/news/2017/04/28/trump-revive-us-eu-trade-deal.html; http://www.zerohedge.com/news/2017-01-31/euro-surges-after-trump-trade-advisor-accuses-germany-using-grossly-undervalued-curr; https://www.thelocal.it/20170331/vespa-wars-italy-fears-sting-of-trump-trade-barriers.

[1175] See: http//www.economist.com/news/finance-and-economics/21719499-it-will-find-

For Trump to go down the protectionist path would require the adoption of import replacement strategies. This would begin with the imposition of import duties or quotas on all or selected imports from all or selected countries, and border taxes on all or selected imported products manufactured offshore by American corporations (such as Apple and Nabisco,[1176] for example, in China, Mexico, and Ireland). Such strategies would increase the cost of imports, thereby allowing more expensive domestic suppliers to enter the market. Trump clearly envisaged that these domestic suppliers would be labor-intensive, rather than the more likely capital intensive production processes involving automation,[1177] thereby creating skilled and semi-killed jobs that would pay competitive wages, and would be located in regions that previously had a concentration of manufacturing industries. His hope is that this would reduce both unemployment and economic inactivity overall, but particularly in the Mid-West. The extent to which this occurs would depend on the capital intensity of the manufacturing production processes adopted, which would also determine the skill profile of the required workforce. This means that only those without jobs who want—and have the required skill profile for—the jobs created would be employed. The higher cost of imports or their domestic substitutes would increase inflation (aggravated by any debt-financed increase in public expenditure) and so would diminish the competitive advantage of exports, thereby worsening unemployment in the export sector, and, of course, the balance of trade. This combination of economic pressures could configure in a way that may not reduce unemployment, either in aggregate or in any particular region, but may increase inflation, could initiate an economic restructuring away from internationally competitive exports industries, toward relatively uncompetitive import-replacement industries, and so diminish economic growth and. In this eventuality, the balance of trade could well worsen. The economic outcome could well be the worst of all economic worlds.

---

they-are-not-blame-americas-trade-deficit-trump.

[1176] See: http://www.businessinsider.com/trump-first-100-days-promises-20174?utm_source=googleplaynewsstand&utm_medium=referral.

[1177] See: https://www.forbes.com/sites/markhendrickson/2017/02/03/trump-on-trade-the-good-the-bad-and-the-ugly/2/#432a63725bbb.

Trans-Pacific Partnership

Trump's campaign promise was to withdraw from the TPP.[1178] This he did very early in his presidency.[1179] His rationale was that American workers would be protected against competition from low-wage countries like Vietnam and Malaysia.[1180]

North American Free Trade Agreement

Trump's campaign promise was to withdraw from, or renegotiate the terms of, the multilateral NAFTA[1181].[1182] He considered this to be "the worst trade deal" America had ever signed.[1183] As President, Trump decided not to withdraw, preferring to renegotiate that agreement, although he was, in his own words, "psyched to terminate NAFTA,"[1184] leaving the option of withdrawal on the table.[1185] Tim Fernholz, in *Quartz* on May 30, colorfully explains Trump's NAFTA reform dilemma:

The White House has started the clock. The re-negotiation of the North American Free Trade Agreement (NAFTA), which underpins $1.1. trillion in trade between the US, Canada, and Mexico, will start no later than August 16. But will it be a spruce-up or a gut renovation?

When US Trade Representative Robert Lighthizer calls these trade talks an effort at "modernization,"[1186] one pictures a contractor talking about fixing a small leak in the bathroom. But when the walls come down and the pipes are exposed, little problems can multiply. That leak turns out

---

[1178] Comprising Australia, Brunei, Canada, Chile, Japan, Malaysia, Mexico, New Zealand, Peru, Singapore, United States and Vietnam.

[1179] See: http://www.nytimes.com/2017/01/23/us/politics/tpp-trump-trade-nafta.html.

[1180] See: https://www.nytimes.com/2017/01/23/us/politics/tpp-trump-trade-nafta.html.

[1181] Comprising Canada, Mexico and the US.

[1182] See: http://www.businessinsider.com/trump-first-100-days-promises-2017-4?utm_source=googleplaynewsstand&utm_medium=referral.

[1183] Retrieved from: https://www.nytimes.com/2017/03/30/business/nafta-trade-deal-trump.html.

[1184] Retrieved from:http://www.reuters.com/article/us-usa-trade-nafta-idUSKBN17S2DG.

[1185] See: https://www.nytimes.com/2017/03/30/business/nafta-trade-deal-trump.html; but see https://mail.google.com/mail/u/0/#inbox/15bade1db6465f29.

[1186] Retrieved from: https://ustr.gov/sites/default/files/files/Press/Releases/NAFTA%20Notification.pdf

to be over-pressure in the water heater, which must be replaced. Now your septic tank is overflowing into the neighbor's yard. And soon, you are enmeshed in a total, and expensive, plumbing overhaul.[1187]

The Key Mexican Unfair Trade Issue. Trump's campaign promise was to impose 20% border adjustment tax[1188] to be imposed on companies that moved their manufacturing operations to Mexico and then exported their products back into America. However, Trump abandoned this initiative in late April, as part of his tax reform negotiations with Congress.[1189]

The Key Canadian Unfair Trade Issue. Trump argued during his campaign that Canada was engaging in unfair trade practices.[1190] Trump's first NAFTA trade dispute was over Canada's exporting to the US of lumber (timber)[1191] and dairy products (the milk war)[1192] that were receiving hidden government support. Indeed, The US imposed a 19.88% duty on Canadian lumber exports in April 2017, with a further 6.87% added in June,[1193] and has sought the lowering or elimination of Canadian tariffs on above quota US exports of dairy, chicken, and egg industries.[1194]

China: Unfair Trade Practice

One of Trump's more startling campaign statement related to China "raping" the US, evidenced by the bilateral balance of trade deficit,[1195]

[1187] Retrieved from: https://qz.com/992847/donald-trumps-plan-for-a-swift-update-to-nafta-is-about-to-hit-reality-like-a-brick-wall/.

[1188] See: https://taxfoundation.org/faqs-border-adjustment/.

[1189] See: https://www.nytimes.com/2017/04/25/us/politics/orrin-hatch-trump-tax-cuts-deficit-economy.html; http://www.marketwatch.com/story/trump-drops-support-for-border-adjustment-tax-report-2017-04-25.

[1190] See: http://www.bbc.com/news/world-us-canada-38971859.

[1191] See: http://www.sciencedirect.com/science/article/pii/S1389934102001041.

[1192] See:http://www.randomlengths.com/in-depth/us-canada-lumber-trade-dispute/.

[1193] See: http://business.financialpost.com/news/economy/u-s-slaps-more-duties-on-canadian-lumber-shipments/wcm/390653ed-2379-4a98-b072-b2d4407b41fa.

[1194] See also: https://www.thestar.com/news/world/2017/04/18/canadian-dairy-farmers-being-very-unfair-to-us-counterparts-trump-says.html.

[1195] See: http://www.bbc.com/news/election-us-2016-36185012; http://www.politico.com/blogs/2016-gop-primary-live-updates-and-results/2016/05/trump-china-rape-america-222689.

an assertion he first made in 2011.[1196] He judged that China was engaging in unfair trade practices that harmed the US—most notably some of its businesses and workers, but certainly not its consumers. This he has described as "the greatest theft in the history of the world,"[1197] for which he blames not China but previous US administrations: "What China has done—and I like China—I've made a lot of money with China ... I mean, China's great. No problem. I'm not angry with China."[1198] This trade deficit, Trump believed, was the result of China manipulating its currency so as to make its exports more competitive. His promise was to immediately designate China a currency manipulator, as a precursor to imposing trade penalties, include a 45% tariff on Chinese imports.[1199] This, the Hyundai Research Institute in South Korea, estimates would reduce Chinese exports to the US by 39.1%.[1200] The imposition of such tariffs would, however, "strongly hurt the American consumer."[1201]

Trump reversed his position on China's currency manipulation after the US Treasury declined to name China as a currency manipulator.[1202] He has not imposed any tariff on Chinese imports, but he has initiated negotiations on a new trade agreement with China:

> China will open its market to US credit rating agencies
> and credit card companies as well as resume imports of
> US beef, part of a package hailed by the Trump admin-
> istration as the first step in redefining the trade relation-
> ship between the world's two largest economies.[1203]

[1196] See: http://www.bbc.com/news/election-us-2016-36185012.

[1197] Retrieved from: http://www.politico.com/blogs/2016-gop-primary-live-updates-and-results/2016/05/trump-china-rape-america-222689.

[1198] Retrieved from: http://www.politico.com/blogs/2016-gop-primary-live-updates-and-results/2016/05/trump-china-rape-america-222689.

[1199] See: https://www.nytimes.com/politics/first-draft/2016/01/07/donald-trump-says-he-favors-big-tariffs-on-chinese-exports/?mtrref=www.businessinsider.com&gwh=7241970FCB6BC0FF55D865D5A0DB21B6&gwt=pay.

[1200] See: https://sputniknews.com/us/201701311050199982-us-china-tariffs/.

[1201] Retrieved from: https://www.brookings.edu/blog/up-front/2017/01/06/trumps-trade-policy-protecting-american-workers-at-the-expense-of-american-consumers/.

[1202] See: http://www.cnbc.com/2017/04/14/trump-administration-says-no-us-trading-partners-manipulate-currency.html.

[1203] Retrieved from: https://www.ft.com/content/9a5ee6b8-36c0-11e7-bce4-9023f8c0fd2e.

As could be expected, Trump has linked progress on the trade negotiations with China's support in bringing North Korea to heal:

> 'Trade between China and North Korea grew almost 40 percent in the first quarter. So much for China working with us—but we had to give it a try!' Trump said on Twitter.[1204]

In relation to the trade negotiation process:

> "It is US-China commercial negotiations to be considered a success," said Jacob Parker, vice president of China operations at the US–China Business Council (USCBC) in Beijing.[1205]

However, the big American trade irritants with China remain unaddressed, leaving open the possibility of a trade war.[1206] American firms still do not have access to China's services and high-tech markets; and China still continues to dump its steel and aluminum on the global market—selling it for a price less than their fair market value—rather than reducing its excess domestic production capacity of those commodities. The Trump administration is considering the imposition of broad tariffs or quotas on steel:

> "Steel is a big problem," Trump said on board Air Force One. "I mean, they're dumping steel. Not only China, but others. We're like a dumping ground, OK? They're dumping steel and destroying our steel industry. They've been doing it for decades, and I'm stopping

---

[1204]   Retrieved from: http://www.reuters.com/article/us-usa-china-trade-idUSKBN1A109V.

[1205]   Ibid

[1206]   See: https://www.cnbc.com/2017/08/08/us-china-trade-war-brewing-trade-deficit-sticks at 25 billion dollars.html; https://www.forbes.com/sites/sarahsu/2017/09/12/rising-u-s-protectionism-may-hurt-chinas-economy-and-begin-a-trade-war/#8b61f151a326; http://fortune.com/2017/08/07/donald-trump-trade-war-china-301-investigation/; https://www.forbes.com/sites/timworstall/2017/08/19/here-comes-the-trade-war-us-to-investigate-ip-china-wont-sit-by/#38a6e4476b02; http://www.businessinsider.com/us-begins-section-301-investigation-2017-8. But see: https://www.uschina.org/reports/understanding-us-china-trade-relationship; https://www.forbes.com/sites/franklavin/2017/05/22/china-us-trade-issues-how-bad-is-it/#580d210e416f; https://thediplomat.com/2017/03/the-future-of-us-china-trade-relations/.

it. It'll stop."[1207]

Asked how he would do that, Trump replied: "There are two ways — quotas and tariffs. Maybe I'll do both."

So, "the stage is set for a global showdown over steel [dumping]."[1208] On this trade issue, Trump is, perhaps, conveniently ignorant:

> It would be very convenient for his narrative if China were flooding the United States with steel, but that's not the case. China did not make the Top 10 sources[1209] for US steel imports in 2016; it accounted for roughly 3 percent of US supply.[1210]

Paris Climate Accord

Trump's most astonishing campaign rhetoric was his assertion that the Paris Climate Accord was founded on a Chinese hoax: "the concept of global warming was created by and for the Chinese in order to make [US] manufacturing non-competitive."[1211] Trivializing the climate change issue, Trump twittered on December 7, 2012: "It's freezing and snowing in New York—we need global warming" (cited in Piehler 2016, 69). Could it be that he does not understand the science behind climate research?[1212]

His campaign promise was to withdraw the US from this Accord and cancel payments to all UN climate change programs and.[1213] It is evi-

---

[1207]   Retrieved from: https://www.forbes.com/forbes/welcome/?toURL=https://www.forbes.com/sites/phillevy/2017/07/16/president-trumps-steel-confusion/&refURL=https://www.google.co.uk/&referrer=https://www.google.co.uk/.

[1208]   Retrieved from: https://www.ft.com/content/d8413fe8-25e6-11e7-8691-d5f7e0cd0a16.

[1209]   See: http://www.ita.doc.gov/steel/countries/pdfs/imports-us.pdf.

[1210]   Retrieved from: https://www.for bes.com/sites/phillevy/2017/07/16/president-trump s-steel-confusion/

[1211]   Retrieved from: http://www.businessinsider.com/trump-did-call-climate-change-a-hoax-created-by-china-2016-9.

[1212]   See: https://www.reuters.com/article/us-usa-climatechange-trump-mit-idUSKBN 18S6L0; https://www.edf.org/blog/2017/06/01/what-you-need-know-about-trumps-retreat-paris-climate-agreement.

[1213]   See: https://www.nytimes.com/2017/04/19/podcasts/the-daily/trump-paris-climate-accord.html; vox.com/vox-sentences/2017/6/1/15724910/vox-sentences-trump-paris-

dent that early in his presidency Trump was under pressure to change his mind about this Accord,[1214] in the face of lobbying by the energy business sector—especially the oil, gas, and coal industries[1215]—and the negative responses of other sections of business[1216] and environmental activists.[1217] So, he had to decide whether it is better to try and renegotiate America's commitments under this Accord rather than to leave it.[1218] He ultimately decided to withdraw the US and then possibly re-negotiate re-entry.[1219] The UN was officially advised of this on August 4.[1220] But, as Bob Ward, Policy and Communications Director of the London School of Economics' Grantham Research Institute on Climate Change and the Environment[1221], remarked:

> ... the [Paris] agreement states that no country can withdraw within three years of it coming into force, and the

agreement.

[1214] See: https://www.theguardian.com/us-news/2016/nov/22/donald-trump-paris-clima te-deal-change-open-mind; http://www.salon.com/2017/06/01/top-ceos-make-last-ditch-appeal-to-trump-keep-u-s-in-the-paris-climate-agreement-to-save-the-economy/; https://www.yahoo.com/news/us-may-stay-paris-climate-accord-caveats-210305667. html; but see: http://edition.cnn.com/2017/03/16/politics/trump-latest-news/index. html?iid=ob_lockedrail_bottomlist;

[1215] See: http://www.dw.com/en/why-coal-companies-want-trump-to-stay-in-the-paris-climate-pact/a-38344216?maca=en-gk-volltext-newsstand-topstories-en-10709-xml-media; http://thehill.com/policy/energy-environment/330621-oil-tech-giants-tell-trump-to-stay-in-paris-deal; http://fuelfix.com/blog/2017/04/18/oil-and-gas-majors-press-trump-on-paris/. But see particularly: https://www.forbes.com/sites/davidblackmon/2017/10/09/luminant-announcement-proves-trump-repeal-of-cpp-wont-save-coal/#7d51d277391c; http://www.newsnow.co.uk/h/Industry+Sectors/Energy/Coal

[1216] See also: https://www.forbes.com/sites/mikescott/2017/04/27/trump-might-not-believe-in-the-risks-of-climate-change-but-investors-do-and-they-are-taking-action/#34142bb2aa13.

[1217] See: http://www.bbc.com/news/av/world-us-canada-39759960/protests-against-trump s-climate-plans.

[1218] See: https://www.yahoo.com/news/us-may-stay-paris-climate-accord-caveats-210305667.html; https://thinkprogress.org/3-reasons-trump-would-be-crazy-to-pull-out-of-the-paris-climate-agreement-d110b44c8f7.

[1219] See: https://www.mprnews.org/story/2017/06/01/npr-trumps-speech-on-paris-clima te-agreement-withdrawal-annotated.

[1220] See: http://www.euronews.com/2017/08/05/us-offically-tells-un-it-wants-out-of-paris-climate-deal.

[1221] See: http://www.lse.ac.uk/GranthamInstitute/about/about-the-institute/.

process of withdrawal takes a further year to complete. That means the United States cannot complete withdrawal from the Paris Agreement before November 5, 2020, the day after the next presidential election in the United States. So Mr Trump will not have withdrawn from the agreement within this presidential term.[1222]

Trump's withdrawal decision was criticized by US business[1223] (such as, Goldman Sax,[1224] SpaceX,[1225] Tesla,[1226] Walt Disney,[1227] Uber,[1228] Twitter,[1229] and Square[1230]), the popular media (such as "Jimmy Kimmel Live!" on American Broadcasting Corporation/YouTube),[1231] and other popular opinion-makers (including Al Gore,[1232] Arnold Schwarzenegger,[1233] and Michael Bloomberg, the Secretary-General's Special Envoy for Cities and Climate Change[1234]). The global reaction was for the sig-

---

[1222] Retrieved from: http://www.bbc.com/news/science-environment-40128046.

[1223] See: http://www.salon.com/2017/06/01/top-ceos-make-last-ditch-appeal-to-trump-keep-u-s-in-the-paris-climate-agreement-to-save-the-economy/; https://www.forbes.com/forbes/welcome/?toURL=; https://www.forbes.com/sites/kensilverstein/2017/06/01/will-pulling-out-of-the-paris-accord-end-up-costing-u-s-businesses-economic-opportunities/&refURL=https://www.google.com.tr/&referrer=https://www.google.com.tr/https://www.wired.com/2017/05/trump-paris-economics/.

[1224] See: http://www.telegraph.co.uk/news/2017/06/02/goldman-sachs-ceo-lloyd-blankfein-tweets-first-time-ever-slam/. For Trump's hostile response see: https://www.bloomberg.com/news/articles/2017-06-01/blankfein-tweets-iger-quits-trump-council-in-ceo-climate-fury.

[1225] See: https://qz.com/997738/all-the-ceos-who-are-staying-on-trumps-elite-advisory-board-after-the-paris-climate-decision/.

[1226] Ibid

[1227] Ibid

[1228] Ibid

[1229] See: https://www.forbes.com/sites/katevinton/2017/06/02/zuckerberg-benioff-and-other-billionaires-sound-off-on-trumps-decision-to-leave-paris-climate-accord/#531db8fa7090.

[1230] Ibid

[1231] See: https://finance.yahoo.com/news/jimmy-kimmel-skewers-trump-controversial-140020952.html.

[1232] See: http://edition.cnn.com/2017/06/04/politics/al-gore-paris-climate-accord/index.html.

[1233] See: https://www.un.org/sg/en/content/other-high-level-appointments.

[1234] See: https://www.un.org/sg/en/content/other-high-level-appointments; https://www.forbes.com/sites/noahkirsch/2017/06/01/billionaire-out-billionaire-in-bloomberg-

natory countries "to reiterate their commitment to the global pact."[1235] The Vatican compares Trump to "flat earthers" over climate change.[1236] When Pope Francis met Trump in late May, he gave him his land-mark 2015 *Encyclical Letter Laudato Si' of the Holy Father, Francis, Care For Our Common Home*,[1237] which called for strong action on climate change, because of its likely disproportionately impact on developing countries.[1238] The French President, Emmanuel Macron's response to Trump's decision was swift, smart, and typically self-assured[1239]: we should all seek to "make our planet great again."[1240]

And what of the prospect of a global consumer boycott of US goods?[1241]

Trump has isolated the United States[1242] as one of only three countries not committed to the Paris Climate Accord—Nicaragua and Syria both declined to ratify the agreement in 2015.[1243] Essentially, only, but certainly not all, Republicans agrees with Trump's decision.[1244] Tantalisingly, Trump has since hinted at the possibility of a US com-promise on the Paris Accord when he was meeting with President Macon in Paris in mid-July[1245] and again in September, the context

pledges-15m-to-climate-as-trump-ditches-paris-deal/#2bf59414bda3.

[1235] Retrieved from: https://www.theatlantic.com/news/archive/2017/06/the-global-reacti on-to-trumps-climate-change-decision/528777/. See also: https://www.reuters.com/ article/us-usa-trump-viewsroom-breakingviews-idUSKBN18S6A3.

[1236] See: http://gizmodo.com/vatican-compares-trump-to-flat-earthers-over-climate-ch-1795722005.

[1237] Available at: http://w2.vatican.va/content/francesco/en/encyclicals/documents/papa-francesco_20150524_enciclica-laudato-si.html.

[1238] See: http://time.com/3925520/pope-francis-climate-change-encyclical/.

[1239] See: https://www.forbes.com/sites/davidschrieberg1/2017/07/03/trump-macron-and-the-official-photos-that-actually-bare-their-souls/.

[1240] Retrieved from: https://www.theguardian.com/world/2017/jun/03/make-our-planet-great-again-macron-praised-for-response-to-trump.

[1241] See: https://www.forbes.com/sites/kotlikoff/2017/06/01/will-boycott-america-follow-trumps-paris-accord-withdrawal/#653a5a6a2dda.

[1242] See:https://www.nytimes.com/2017/07/14/opinion/mr-trump-the-climate-change-loner.html?mtrref=undefined&gwh=D67BE4F471B4C4A5373C471A-B4E52ECE&gwt=pay&assetType=opinion; https://www.edf.org/blog/2017/06/01/what-you-need-know-about-trumps-retreat-paris-climate-agreement.

[1243] See: https://www.theatlantic.com/news/archive/2017/06/the-global-reaction-to-trumps-climate-change-decision/528777/.

[1244] See: http://edition.cnn.com/2017/06/05/politics/climate-change-polling/index.html

[1245] See: http://www.bbc.co.uk/news/av/world-us-canada-40602788/trump-in-paris-

of his negotiations with the Democrats over raising the public debt ceiling.[1246]

CONCLUSION

To Trump, winning the presidential campaign transformed his campaign promises into unchallengeable expressions of the public interest—the "will of the people". Thereby ignoring that he was elected by only 27% of the eligible voter population. So, he considers that he has no obligation to justify how the implementation of his campaign promises will advance the common good rather than just the interests of his core supporters, be the members of the Trump Tribe, followers of the alt-right and allied movements, or fellow billionaires. Indeed, the on-going public criticism about his presidency would strongly suggest that his campaign promises are not popularly perceived to be in the public interest. When it comes to enacting and implementing his campaign promises he sees this as a matter of policy minutiae, and so is someone else's responsibility.

Trump is disinterested in trying to master the art and science of being a President who can make policy a reality. This would be a near-impossible challenge for him, because he lacks a policy mindset, he is not a natural win–win compromiser, and he dislikes reading or otherwise engaging in detailed policy discussions and situational briefings. This has become all too apparent.

Trump's populist presidential campaign revealed his disdainfulness of political correctness, international diplomacy, and public opinion, whether domestic or international. His campaign promises called for an isolationist America, one that would be led by an activist— Keynesian pump-priming—president intent on making America great again, by always putting America first, by always buying American and hiring Americans, and definitely by making America safe again from foreigners.

---

compliments-and-a-hint-of-compromise.

[1246] See: http://www.bbc.co.uk/news/world-us-canada-41300036; https://www.reuters. com/article/us-usa-climate/tillerson-says-u-s-could-stay-in-paris-climate-accord-idUSKCN1BS0LW.

Yet, once ensconced the White House the policy outcomes he has achieved are:

- to polarize American society;

- to drive a wedge between himself from the Republican dominated Congress;

- to isolate himself from his international peers; and

- to isolate America in the international community, in terms of both globalization-free trade and the climate change agendas, making it increasingly likely that it will find itself being caste as a pariah nation on the global stage.

One candidly damning judgment on Trump on the international stage came from Chris Uhlmann, the political editor of the *Australian Broadcasting Corporation*, in his reporting of the July G20 Summit.[1247] He described Trump as being "isolated and friendless" at that summit:

> He was an uneasy, lonely, awkward figure at this gathering and you got the strong sense that some of the leaders are trying to find the best way to work around him. ... [He had] no desire and no capacity to lead the world. ... We learned that Donald Trump has pressed fast-forward on the decline of the United States as a global leader. He managed to isolate his nation, to confuse and alienate his allies and to diminish America.

Understanding the mercurial Trump's approach to public policy begs quite a few key questions:

- Does he realize how foolish it is to promise simple solutions to complex policy problems?

- Does he realize the importance of conducting duty-of-care policy analysis before making any policy decision?

[1247] Retrieved from: https://www.theguardian.com/us-news/2017/jul/09/biggest-threat-to-the-west-australian-journalist-demolishes-trump-after-g20. But see: https://www.youtube.com/watch?v=y6_ckWZCHW4; see also: http://www.abc.net.au/news/2017-07-10/how-chris-uhlmanns-g20-takedown-of-donald-trump-went-viral/8695144; http://www.abc.net.au/news/about/backstory/digital/2017-07-14/why-uhlmanns-viral-critique-of-donald-trump-nearly-didnt-happen/8709664; http://deadline.com/2017/07/australian-chris-uhlmann-donald-trump-viral-g20-video-1202125801/.

- Does he realize and appreciate the intrinsic difficulties involved in dealing effectively with domestic or international politico-administrative reality?

- Does he realize that military intervention—anywhere and any-time—is a fraught project?

- Does he realize that remaining an isolationist president means that he is overseeing the decline of America as a global leader, despite its economic and military might?

The answers to these questions would, on the basis of his presidential words and actions, seem to be in the negative. This makes problematic understanding, let alone predicting, what Trump as president might do in the future on the domestic or world stages.

6
DONALD J. TRUMP:
UN BAILLEUR DE CANARD# PAR EXCELLENCE

INTRODUCTION

Donald J. Trump's governance and policy rhetoric and actions so far in his first year as the US President become more understandable by reference to his public persona, how he constructs his worldview, and his view of the world. Although he does not govern alone—much to his chagrin—he has considerable authority to make policy—particularly foreign policy. So, his personality traits and how he takes meaning from his encounters with reality matters, as does from whom he takes advice, particularly as he is a very inexperienced—and a not very knowledgeable—president.

TRUMP'S PUBLIC PERSONA

Trump is self-centered, with a strong sense of his own importance, albeit with a very fragile ego. This fragility is insistent. He demands constant positive psychological strokes—expressions of recognition, praise, and appreciation, and unquestioning compliance with his wishes. He also demands that criticism, censure, and disapproval must be, at all costs, deflected to others, as he is unable to handle any negative feedback, particularly when it is expressed as humor, irony, exaggeration, or ridicule.

He has many character foibles that stand him well apart. He is disdainfully flexible with the truth; ever willing divert attention away from unpalatable truths about, or related to, himself—what he says and does—by deliberately conveying false impressions.[1250] He sees life as a game

---

The *Dictionnaire de la Langue Française* (1863–1877) provides a 1612 citation for the expression *bailleur de canards* (literally, a deliverer of ducks) giving its meaning as "a teller of absurd stories." Retrieved from: https://www.grammarphobia.com/blog/2016/04/canard.html.

[1250] See, for example: http://money.cnn.com/2017/07/14/media/trump-russian-lawyer-veselnitskaya-theories-obama/index.html.

that he must win and, most importantly, his opponents must definitely lose, and be seen to have lost. This end justifies the use of any means necessary, which extends to making outlandish and unsubstantiated allegations and insinuations about his opponents, even their families. In essence, Trump's public persona suggests that:

- He has a grandiose sense of self.
- He becomes upset when his all too fragile ego is challenged.
- He is inclined to act quickly, without adequate deliberation.
- He considers himself to be superior to most people.
- He is reluctant to accept new ideas that threaten his worldview and his view of the world-at-large.

He evidences a bewildering array of defense mechanisms to deal with any contradictory or unpalatable anxiety-provoking understandings (product cognitions) with which he is confronted. These give him his denial and self-deception capacities. Thus, he is able

- to deny the validity of any contrary anxiety-provoking factual evidence that threatens any of his preferred understandings;
- to reconcile any contrary anxiety-provoking factual evidence with a preferred understanding by using plausible but erroneous arguments, perhaps with a hint of a supportive conspiracy theory that cannot be readily disproven;
- to assert the rightness of a preferred understanding in the face of contrary anxiety-provoking factual evidence, by asserting supportive "alternative facts"—bullshit, even lies; and
- to revert to an earlier stage of development—behaving like a child—to avoid facing the anxiety-provoking unsustainability of a preferred understanding when confronted with contrary factual evidence.

Indeed, his mental state has been the subject of speculation by psychiatrists, psychologists, and other mental health professionals, some of whom have associated his observed public persona personality traits with those of a narcissist, a sociopath, and even a psychopath.

TRUMP'S EXISTENTIAL INCLINATIONS

He is, intuitively, existential in his thoughts and actions. He lives only in the present, perhaps with the conviction that the future maps itself. He individually constructs the meaning and significance of reality on the basis of his existential subjectivity. This makes the trustworthiness of any information he is presented with contingent upon the vagaries of his thoughts and experiences. He presumes that he has the existential freedom to be who he wants to be—able to make the necessary leap in the dark in expectation of inevitable success—by exercising his will to power. He believes that he is able to engage with reality as he imagines it to be in any way he chooses. So, he has the drive for success and power over others that make any possibility his possibility. Yet, Trump's life experience seems to have taught him that to be successful he must be hyper-competitive, in order to take up and defeat life's endless cycle of trials and tribulations, for life can never be entirely under anyone's control—luck, fate, and unpredictable external forces are always lurking—with malintent.

Trump holds opinions on the basis of what is useful for him to say. He is willing to deliberately convey a false impression by confidently assert "alternative facts" as proposition deserving to be believed. So, he is inevitably caught between denial and delusion. This permits a pragmatic approach to decision-making, one that makes him impetuous, unpredictable, and even unprincipled. His policies are poorly considered—simplistic and held without apparent commitment—as he is so utterly dominated by his vulnerable ego—which means that any outcome is imaginable.

TRUMP'S ASCENSION TO THE OVAL OFFICE

Trump became president with the support of only 27% of the eligible voter population. During his presidential campaign, he presented himself as a billionaire populist—the heroic champion of the forsaken—ever and always willing, to take-on—take over—the Washington politico-administrative establishment and even the extant World Order—both of which he has long considered to be ineffective, corrupt, and badly in need of reform. He resorted to controversial policy rhetoric that was disdainful of political correctness, international—not mention personal—sensitivities, and Washington politico-administrative reality. His jingoistic aspiration is to have an America that is safe from foreigners, buys American, and hires Americans. This he considers would be in the best interest of his core support base—not too mention corporate America—and, so, in the best interest of those who are, or should be, in work. He fails, of course, to acknowledge its detrimental consequences for the American consumer.

Trump was expected, on becoming president, to put in place a set of policy to fulfill his campaign promises. Some of these, however, had been so hype-up, they were unrealistic, even misleading, thereby raising the expectations of his enthusiastic supporters beyond those that he could possibly deliver with any certainly. Examples would be his promise, effectively, to restore the American manufacturing Rust Belt to its former glory, and to have the Mexican's finance the building of his cherished Southern Border wall.

TRUMP IN THE OVAL OFFICE

He entered the White House with a very naïve view of governance, government, and the Office of the Presidency. He believed that he was the embodiment of the "will of the people"—not to mention the will of God—so he became at least "the voice of the people." This allowed him in his inaugural presidential address to assert, in the populist tradition, that the people now control the US government. He considered that as he held the highest political office in the land, he has the right to one-man rule. Little wonder Trump finds governing messy, complicated, and requiring very hard work.

Trump's election victory divided America and alarmed much of the world. He has brought to presidential politics and practice a very different set of perspectives on what a president does—or does not—do. These are grounded in very idiosyncratic set of cognitive assumptions about reality, himself, other people, and the world-at-large that he would probably be unwilling—if not unable—to change. He has, indeed, heralded in a new style of presidency.

- A president who constructs the meaning and significance of reality in his own head, in the process of which he blurs the boundary between the truth, firmly held beliefs, unproven propositions, and propositions that deliberately convey a false impression.

- A president who distrusts the national and international media, which he believes spreads fabricated—"fake"—news that is critical of him and his administration.

- A president who has social media savvy, which enables him to directly communicate in a way that simplifies the complex, gives a lie emotional resonance by hinting conspiracy that cannot be disproved, and avoids subtlety.

- A president who thinks like a reality TV performer.

- A president whose paranoia leads him to distrust everyone, with the possible exception of co-opted family members, thereby fostering an organizational culture of distrust in the White House, so making paranoia and chaos its natural state.

- A president who demands personal loyalty of all who work for, and with, him, and who is always seeking evidence of their disloyalty, any hint of which feeds his proclivity for presidential witch-hunts, which, in turn, feeds his paranoia in a way that demands retribution (public humiliation or employment termination).

- A president who thought that running the US would be easier and certainly less work than running his global family business, because he thought that once he became president he would be the Chief Executive Officer of America Inc., and so able to implement his campaign promises—as indisputable expressions of the public interest—by issuing instructions or making exhortations.

The idea that government should be run like a business is not an unpopular idea in the US, but being run by business magnates with no public sector experience is a novel experiment—a dream come true to some. However, a president running the US government as he would manage his family business is more than a little worrying. Little wonder Trump finds governing complicated, after all bullshitting is easier than governing. In his family business, where he is accountable only to himself, he was accustomed to telling people what to do and if they do not he fires them. But government does not work that way. He needs the bureaucracy to come up with concrete policies that will implement his policy aspirations. His power is limited not only by the size, but also by the controllability of his party's Congressional majorities, and by the legislative rules and the courts. Finally, he cannot presume nor expect support from the Democrats. Trump certainly faced a steep presidential learning curve after his presidential inauguration. Sadly, he does not seem to have learnt much.

Trump seems to be genuinely surprised about what it means to be, and what is expected of, a US president. His presidential conduct has been somewhat reminiscent of a dear or a rabbit in a car's headlights. He is surprised by:

- The scope of his duties and responsibilities.
- The importance of the human factor in public policy.
- The contending interests he must balance when making any decisions.
- The limited methods he has at his disposal, and under his control, to get things done.

This should not, of course, be surprising. Before becoming president he had no interest in understanding how the US government worked—and why it does not always work—or the nature of the public policy and legislative processes. He did little to prepare himself for the presidency, perhaps because he did not expect to become president. It is very evident that he still has a lot to learn about Washington politics and policy-making and about leading the Executive Branch.

Trump is disinterested, even unwilling, to master the art and science of being a President. He seems to have no idea about how to make his policy hopes and aspirations a reality. That would be a near-impossible challenge for him. He does not have the right mindset—he is a spectator not an agent-implementer. He is not a natural win–win compromiser—he hates losing. He is not a man of detail—he dislikes reading about, or listening to, policy minutiae. He likes to deal only with the big picture, preferably one that can be expressed in 140 characters.

TRUMP'S DOMESTIC POLICIES

His domestic campaign promises were premised on the need to "Make America Great Again." So his domestic strategies are intended to stimulate real economic growth, and, as a bi-product, to create jobs and to increase tax revenue. He has ambitious expectations that a Republican-controlled Congress will approve increasing public debt to finance his job-creating government spending plans (to rebuild the national infrastructure, to build the Mexican wall, and to build up military capacity); and his reducing of the financial burdens imposed by government on business and taxpayers (by lowering taxes and abolishing mandatory health insurance). It remains to be seen whether he understands the logic of Keynesian and "trickle down" supply-side economics.

TRUMP'S INTERNATIONAL POLICIES

His international campaign promises were premised on putting "America First"—no more trade rip-offs, no more expensive foreign nation-building initiatives, and no more regime changing adventures. So, his international strategies are intended to ensure all bilateral and multilateral trade and defense agreements, alliances, and coalitions must produce a net benefit to America. This meant "Making America Safe Again"—by expanding US military capability, deporting illegal immigrants, blocking all Muslims wishing to enter the United States, deporting Syrian refugee re-settlers, and taking steps to deter Iran's and North Korea's ballistic missile programs.

Yet, once ensconced in the White House he became more of an internationalist—the world's policeman with an eye on current and future wrongdoings against America. He pompously basks in the glory of being on the international stage as the President of the US of America. The international outcomes that he has so far achieved are, however, to isolate himself from his fellow heads of state, and to isolate America in the international community, disempowering it in terms of the globalization-free trade agenda and the climate change agenda.

Donald J. Trump: A Complex Multi-Faceted Man

Trump publicly portrays himself in diverse ways:

- the self-satisfied Trump;
- the billionaire populist Trump;
- the hero-of-the-forsaken Trump;
- the savior-of-business Trump;
- the bullying Trump;
- the blame-shifting Trump;
- the rhetorical Trump;
- the hyperbole-addicted Trump;
- the uninformed and ill-informed Trump;
- the alternative facts Trump;
- the politically naïve Trump;
- the economically naïve Trump;
- the anti-politics Trump;
- the authoritarian Trump;
- the public interventionist Trump;
- the isolationist Trump;
- the war hawk madman Trump;
- the global policeman Trump;
- the international peace negotiator Trump; and, above all,
- the flip-flop Trump.

In essence, he is a president who evidences deficiencies in dignity, discipline, knowledge, truthfulness, and ability to engage in logical thought. He appears to be constitutionally unable—unwilling—to be presidential.

Can the mercurial Trump change the way he conducts his presidency? This begs a profound question: Does he have the necessary capacity and will:

- To learn quickly what he needs to know, say, and do to be an effective president, by acquiring the necessary political judgment—which one former head of state believes takes 20 or so years of experience in politics[1251]—and aligning his rhetoric with realistic policies?[1252]

- To deliver his campaign promises—his presidential policy agenda—by giving effective leadership to a confounded White House, and to a Congress raven by ideological divisions?

The answers to all these questions would, on the basis of his presidential words and actions so far in his first year, would seem to be in the negative. It is difficult to imagine Trump having:

- the cognitive aptitude to grapple with the minutiae of presidential business;

- the motivations to soften his acerbic political rhetoric, so as to become more conciliatory and even, heaven forbid, more compromising; and

- the self-discipline to be less impulsive and more considered in his decision-making and actions.

CONCLUSION

To understand, even predict, what Trump might do in the remainder of his presidency—however long than may be—is to appreciate that to him being president is "all about me." Thus, his Achilles' heal is his mammoth, fragile, and very demanding ego. This makes him both predictable and vulnerable. So, ignore his rhetoric—his tweets and his off-the-cuff remarks—ever mindful that his words do not always reveal what he wants to achieve: "I aim very high, and then I just keep pushing and pushing and pushing to get what I'm after. Sometimes I settle for less than I sought, but in most cases I still end up with more than I want" (Trump and Schwartz 1987, 32). Instead, watch his actions very

---

1251 Retrieved from: ttps://www.theguardian.com/media/2017/sep/22/paul-keating-could-teach-malcolm-turnbull-a-thing-or-two-says-laurie-oakes.

1252 This requires, in the words of Paul Keating, a former Australian Prime Minister (1991–1996), "long straight lines of rhetoric that stay straight for years at a time." Retrieved from: https://www.theguardian.com/media/2017/sep/22/paul-keating-could-teach-malcolm-turnbull-a-thing-or-two-says-laurie-oakes. See also: http://www.keating.org.au/.

closely—Trump's personality gives good reasons to believe that actions do not always follow his words. And, above all, never underestimate the fragility of his ego, always be aware that it responds very well to stroking, even when it is done with a manipulative intent.

REFERENCES

Adler, A. [1933] 1973. "On the Origins of the Striving for Superiority and of Social Interest." In *Superiority and Social Interest: A Collection of Later Writings* (eds. H.L. Ansbacher and R.R. Ansbucher). New York: Viking.

Adorno, T.W., E. Frenkel-Bruns, D.J. Levinson, and R.N. Sanford. 1950. *The Authoritarian Personality*. New York: Harper.

Albrecht, K. 2017. "Why the Pundits Can't Figure Out Donald Trump." *Psychology Today* January 5. Available at: https://www.psychologytoday.com/blog/brainsnacks/201701/why-the-pundits-cant-figure-out-donald-trump.

Allison, L. 1996. "Power." In *The Concise Oxford Dictionary of Politics* (ed. I. McLean). Oxford: Oxford University Press.

Allport, G.W. 1937. *Personality: A Psychological Interpretation*. New York: Holt.

Allport, G.W. 1955. *Becoming: Basic Considerations for a Psychology of Personality*. New Haven, CT: Yale University Press.

Alston, W.P. 1989. *Epistemic Justification: Essays in the Theory of Knowledge*. Ithaca, NY: Cornell University Press.

Ankony, R.C. 1999. "The Impact of Perceived Alienation on Police Officers' Sense of Mastery and Subsequent Motivation for Proactive Enforcement." *Policing: An International Journal of Police Strategies and Management* 22 (2): 120–132.

Aquinas, T. [1259–64] 1905. *Summa Contra Gentiles [On the Truth of the Catholic Faith Against the Unbelievers]* (abridged) (tr. and ed. J. Rickaby). London: Burns and Oates. Available at: http://www2.nd.edu/Departments/Maritain/etext/gc.htm.

Archer, M.S. 2000. *Being Human: The Problem of Agency*. Cambridge: Cambridge University Press.

Aristotle. [350 BC] 2004. *Nicomachean Ethics* (tr. W.D. Ross). Available at: http://www.etext.library.adlaide.edu.au/mirror/classics.mit.edu/Aristotle/nicomachaen.html.

Ashford, N. 2016. "What is Classical Liberalism?" Available at: http://www.learnliberty.org/blog/what-is-classical-liberalism/.

Austin, J. [1832] 1995. *The Province of Jurisprudence Determined.* Cambridge: Cambridge University Press.

Bacon, F. ([1597–1625] 1972. "Essays or Counsels Civil and Moral." In *The Harvard Classics* (ed. C.W. Elliot). New York: Collier.

Bacon, F. [1623] 1997. *The Great Instauration: The Novum Organum.* Whitefish, MT: Kessinger.

Baggini, J. 2017. *A Short History of Truth: Consolations for a Post-Truth World.* London: Quercus.

Bambrough, R. 1979. *Moral Scepticism and Moral Knowledge.* London: Routledge and Kegan Paul.

Banfield, E.C. 1958. *The Moral Basis of a Backward Society.* New York: Free Press.

Barnard, C. 1938. *The Functions of the Executive.* Cambridge, MA: Harvard University Press.

Barrett, W. 1958. *Irrational Man: A Study in Existential Philosophy.* Westport, CT: Greenwood.

Baumeister, R. 1993. *Self-Esteem.* New York: Plenum Press.

Bentham, J. [1789] 1970. *An Introduction to the Principles of Morals and Legislation* (eds. J.H. Burns and H.L.A. Hart). London: Athlone.

Berger, P.L. and T. Luckmann. 1966. *The Social Construction of Reality: A Treatise in the Sociology of Knowledge.* Harmondworth, UK: Penguin.

Berlin, I. 1969. *Four Essays on Liberty.* London: Oxford University Press.

Bilton, T., K. Bonnett, P. Jones, T. Lawson, D. Skinner, M. Stanworth, and A. Webster. 1996. *Introductory Sociology* (3ʳᵈ ed.). London: Macmillan.

Black, M. 1983. *The Prevalence of Humbug, and Other Essays*. Ithaca, NY: Cornell University Press.

Blackburn, S. 2001. *Being Good*. Oxford: Oxford University Press.

Booth, W. C. 1961. *The Rhetoric of Fiction*. Chicago, IL: University of Chicago Press.

Boulder, K. 1990. *Three Faces of Power*. Newbury Park, CA: Sage.

Brandimonte, M.A., N. Bruno, and S. Collina. 2006. "Cognition." In *Psychological Concepts: An International Historical Perspective* (eds. P. Pawlik and G. d'Ydewalle). Hove, ES, UK: Psychology Press.

Brzezinski, Z. 1997. *The Grand Chessboard: American Primacy and Its Geostrategic Imperatives*. New York: Basic Books.

Buber, M. [1923] 1958. *I and Thou* (tr. R.G. Smith). New York: Charles Scribner's Sons.

Burke, E. [1756] 1987. *A Philosophical Enquiry into the Origin of our Ideas of the Sublime and Beautiful* (2ⁿᵈ ed.). Oxford: Blackwell.

Bushman, B. and R. Baumeister. 1998. "Threatened Egoism, Narcissism, Self-esteem, and Direct and Displaced Aggression: Does Self-love and Self-hate Lead to Violence." *Journal of Personality and Social Psychology* 75 (1): 219–129. Available at: http://www-personal.umich.edu/~bbushman/bb98.pdf.

Butterfield, J. 1998. "Determinism and Indeterminism." In *Routledge Encyclopedia of Philosophy* (ed. E. Craig). London: Routledge.

Camus, A. [1942] 2005. *The Myth of Sisyphus* (tr. J. O'Brien) Harmondworth, UK: Penguin.

Cattell, R.B. 1965. *The Scientific Analysis of Personality*. Baltimore, MD: Penguin.

Cattell, R.B. 1980. *Personality and Learning Theory*. New York: Springer.

Chesterton, G.K. [1908] 2007. *Orthodoxy*. New York: Filiquarian. Available at: http://books.google.co.uk/books?id=W6j4Qx2UF2AC&pg=PA97&lpg=PA97&dq=chesterton+%22the+real+trouble+with+this+world+of+ours+is%22&source=web&ots=yunxnJFil&sig=0zbAi2pTbtupcCvt9JjErodLw2Y&hl=en.

Cicero [44 BC] 1971. *De Fato* [*On Fate*] (tr. R.W. Sharples). Warminister, WT, UK: Aris & Phillips.

Cipolla, C.N. 1976. "The Basic Laws of Human Stupidity." Available at: http://harmful.cat-v.org/people/basic-laws-of-human-stupidity/.

Cliff, T. 1960. "Trotsky on Substitutionism." Available at: https://www.marxists.org/archive/cliff/works/1960/xx/trotsub.htm.

Cohen, M., J. March, and J. Olsen. 1972. "A Garbage Can Model of Organizational Choice." *Administrative Science Quarterly* 17 (1): 1–23.

Coleman, W.D. and G. Skogstad, eds. 1990. *Policy Communities and Public Policy in Canada*. Toronto, ON: Copp Clark Pitman.

Confucius [Kongfuzi] [5th century BC] 1992. *Lanyo* [*Analects*] (tr. D.C. Lau). Hong Kong: Chinese University Press.

Costa, P.T. and R.R. McCrae. 1992. "Four Ways Five Factors are Basic." *Personality and Individual Differences* 13 (6): 653–665.

Coulter, A. 2016. *In Trump We Trust: E Pluribus Awesome!* New York: Sentinel.

Cramer, P. 1991. *The Development of Defense Mechanisms: Theory, Research and Assessment*. New York: Springer-Verlag.

Cresswell, M.J. 1985. *Structured Meanings. The Semantics of Propositional Attitudes*. Cambridge, MA: MIT Press.

Crumbaugh, J.C. 1973. "The Validation of Logotheropy." In *Direct Psychotheropy* (ed. R. M. Jurjrvich). Coral Gables, FL: University of Miami Press.

Cutting, B. and A. Kouzmin. 1997. "Towards an Ontological Understanding of Good Governance Based on a Synthesis of Weber's Concept of 'Ideal Types' and the Enneagram Typology." *Indian Journal of Public Administration* 2 (2): 85–112.

D'Andrade, R.G. 1984. "Cultural Meaning Systems." In *Culture Theory: Essays on Mind, Self, and Emotion* (eds. R.A. Shweder and R.A. LeVine). New York: Cambridge University Press.

D'Antonio, M. 2015. *Never Enough: Donald Trump and the Pursuit of Success.* New York: St. Martin's Press.

D'Antonio, M. 2017. *The Truth about Donald Trump.* New York: St. Martin's Press.

Dahl, R.A. 1999. "The Anti-reflexive Revolution: On the Affirmation of the New Right." In *Spaces of Culture: City, Nation, World* (eds. M. Featherstone and S.E. Lash). London: Sage.

Davison, G.C. and J.M. Neale. [1976] 2001. *Abnormal Psychology* (8th ed.). New York: Wiley.

Dawson, T. 1977. "Literary Criticism and Analytical Psychology." In *The Cambridge Companion to Jung* (eds. P. Young-Eisendrath and T. Dawson). Cambridge: Cambridge University Press.

de Board, R. 1978. *The Psychoanalysis of Organizations: A Psychoanalytic Approach to Behavior in Groups and Organizations.* London: Tavistock.

de Haven-Smith, L. 1988. *Philosophical Critiques of Policy Analysis.* Gainesville, FL: University of Florida Press.

Deaux, K. 1996. "Social Identification." In *Social Psychology: Handbook of Basic Principles* (eds. E. Tory Higgins and A.W. Kruglansk). New York: Guilford.

DePaul, M. (ed.) 2000. *Resurrecting Old-Fashioned Foundationalism.* Blue Ridge Summit, PA: Rowman & Littlefield.

Descartes, R. [1641] 1975. "Discourse on Method and Meditations on

First Philosophy." In *The Philosophical Writings of Descartes* (vol. 2) (eds. J. Cottingham, R. Stoothoff, and M.D. Dugald Murdoch). Cambridge: Cambridge University Press.

Devitt, M. 1984. *Realism and Truth*. Princeton, NJ: Princeton University Press.

Dewey, J. [1895–98] 1972. *The Collected Works of John Dewey* (vol. 5: 1929–1930) (ed. A. Borydston, intro. P. Kurtz). Carbondale, IL: Southern Illinois University Press.

Digman, J.M. 1990. "Personality Structure: Emergence of the Five-factor Model." *Annual Review of Psychology* 41: 417–440.

Dixon, J. 2003. *Responses to Governance: The Governing of Corporations, Societies and the World*. Westport, CT: Praeger.

Dixon, J. 2015. *The Public Administrator: Contenders, Contentions, and Tensions*. Washington, DC: Westphalia Press.

Dixon, J. 2016. *Neoliberalism: The Emperor has Threadbare Contemporary Clothes*. Washington, DC: Westphalia Press.

Dixon, J. and P. P.-S. Wong. 2015. "Organization Traits under Conditions of Relational Dominance: The Archetypal Confucian Organization." *AFBE Journal* 8 (1): 41–55. Available at: http://www.afbe. biz/main/wp-content/uploads/AFBEJournal-Vol8No1.pdf.

Dixon, J., R. Dogan, and A. Sanderson. 2009. *Situational Logic of Social Actions*. New York: Nova Science.

Doherty, B. 2012. *The Rise of the President's Permanent Campaign*. Lawrence: University Press of Kansas.

Douglas, M. 1994. *Risk and Blame: Essays in Culture Theory*. London: Routledge.

Douglas, M. 1996. "Prospects for Asceticism." In *Thought Style: Critical Essays on Good Taste* (ed. M. Douglas). London: Sage.

Douglas, M. and S. Ney. 1998. *Missing Persons: A Critique of the Social*

Sciences. Berkeley: University of California Press.

Duncker, K. [1935] 1945. *On Problem Solving* (Psychological Monographs, 58, No. 270) (tr. L.S. Lees). Washington, DC: American Psychological Association.

Durkheim, E. [1897] 1952. *Suicide: A Study in Sociology*. London: Routledge and Kegan Paul.

Dworkin, G. 1988. *The Theory and Practice of Autonomy*. Cambridge: Cambridge University Press.

Dye, T. R. 2010. *Understanding Public Policy* (13th ed.). New York: Pearson.

Eagly, A. H., S. Chen, S. Chaiken. and K. Shaw-Barnes. 1999. "The Impact of Attitudes on Memory: An Affair to Remember." *Psychological Bulletin* 125: 64–89.

Eilon, S. 1974. "The Board: Functions and Structure." *Management Decisions* 12 (2): 167–190.

Ellis. A. 2005. *The Myth of Self-esteem: How Rational Emotive Behavior Therapy Can Change Your Life Forever*. Buffalo, NY: Prometheus.

Elster, J. 1985. *Sour Grapes: Studies in the Subversion of Rationality*. Cambridge: Cambridge University Press.

ErEel, H. and N. Meiran. (2011). "Mindset Changes Lead to Drastic Impairments in Rule Finding." *Cognition* 119 (2): 149–165.

Etzioni, A. 1961. *A Comparative Analysis of Complex Organizations*. New York: Free Press.

Etzioni, A. 1968. *The Active Society: A Theory of Societal and Political Processes*. New York: Free Press.

Eysenck, H.J. 1970. *The Structure of Human Personality* (3rd ed.). London: Methuen.

Farthing, G.W. 1992. *The Psychology of Consciousness*. Englewood Cliffs, NJ: Prentice Hall.

Festinger, L. 1957. *A Theory of Cognitive Dissonance*. Evanston, IL: Row, Peterson.

Flanagan, O. 1992. *Consciousness Reconsidered*. Cambridge, MA: MIT Press.

Foucault, M. 1978. *The History of Sexuality* (vol 1: *An Introduction*) (tr. R. Hurley). New York: Pantheon.

Foucault, M. 1991. "Governmentality." In *The Foucault Effect: Studies in Governmentality* (eds. G. Burchell, C. Gordon, and P. Miller). Hemel Hempstead, HD, UK: Harvester Wheatsheaf.

Frankfurt, H. [1971] 2002. "Freedom of the Will and the Concept of a Person." In *Free Will* (ed. R. Kane). Malden, MA: Blackwell.

Frankfurt , H. 2005. "On Bullshit." Available at: https://www.stoa.org. uk/topics/bullshit/pdf/on-bullshit.pdf.

Frankl, V. E. [1948/75] 2000. *Man's Search for Ultimate Meaning* (for. S. Hunt). New York: Perseus.

French, J.R.P. and B. Raven. 1959. "The Bases of Social Power." In *Studies in Social Power*m (ed. D. Cartwright.) Ann Arbor, MI: University of Michigan Press.

Freud, A. [1936] 1948. *The Ego and the Mechanisms of Defense*. London: Horgart and the Institute of Psychoanalysis.

Fujita, K., P.M. Gollwitzer, and G. Oettingen. 2007. "Mindsets and Pre-Conscious Open-Mindedness to Incidental Information." *Journal of Experimental Social Psychology* 43 (1): 48–61.

Galinsky, A.D. and L.J. Kray. 2004. "From Thinking About What Might Have Been to Sharing What We Know: The Effects of Counterfactual Mind-Sets on Information Sharing in Groups." *Journal of Experimental Social Psychology* 40 (5): 606–618.

Gambetta, D. 1988. "Can We Trust?" In *Trust: Making and Breaking* (ed. D. Gambetta). Oxford: Oxford University Press.

Garland, D. 1997. "'Governmentality' and the Problem of Crime: Foucault, Criminology. Sociology." *Theoretical Criminology* 1 (2): 173–214.

Geertz, C. 1983. "The Way We Think Now: Towards an Ethnography of Modern Thought." In *Local Knowledge* (ed. C. Geert). New York: Basic Books.

Gergen, K.J. and T.J. Thatchenkey. 1998. "Organizational Science in Postmodern Context." In *In the Realm of Organization: Essays for Robert Cooper* (ed. R.C.H. Chia). London: Routledge.

Gilbert, N. and B. Gilbert. 1989. *The Enabling State*. Oxford: Oxford University Press.

Gingrich, N. 2017. *Understanding Trump* (for. E. Trump). New York: Hachette Books.

Goethe, J.W. von [1749] 2011. *The Sorrows of Young Werther* (tr. R. D. Boylan). Istanbul: BS World Classics.

Goffman, E. 1974. *Frame Analysis*. Cambridge, MA: Harvard University Press.

Goldberg, L.R. 1993. "The Structure of Phenotypic Personality Traits." *American Psychologist* 48 (1): 26–34.

Gollwitzer, P.M. and U. Bayer. 1999. "Deliberative Versus Implemental Mindsets in the Control of Action." In *Dual-Process Theories in Social Psychology* (eds. S. Chaiken and Y. Trobe). New York: Guilford Press.

Gouinlock, J. 1972. *John Dewey's Philosophy of Value*. New York: Humanities Press.

Grave, S.A. 1960. *The Scottish Philosophy of Common Sense*. Oxford: Clarendon.

Green, J. 2017. *Devil's Bargain: Steve Bannon, Donald Trump and the Storming of the Presidency*. New York: Penguin Press.

Green, T.H. [1895] 2006. *Lectures on the Principles of Political Obliga-*

tion. New York: Antiquarian Booksellers' Association of America.

Hägerström, A. 1964. *Philosophy and Religion* (tr. R.T. Sandin). London: Allen and Unwin.

Hales, C. 2001. *Managing Through Organization: The Management Process, Forms of Organisation and the Work of Managers*. London: Business Press.

Haselbach, A. 1994. "On Ways and Patterns of Thinking 'Identity.'" In *The Multiple Identity: What is it and How does it Work* (ed. S. Novak-Lukanovic). Ljubljana, SL: Slovenian National Commission for UNESCO and Institute for Ethnic Studies (European project: Overlapping Cultures and Plural Identities/Cultures Partielles et Identités Multiple).

Hay, C. 1998. "The Tangled Web We Weave: The Discourse, Strategy and Practice of Networking." In *Comparing Policy Networks* (ed. D. Marsh). Buckingham: Open University Press.

Hayman, R. 1997. *Nietzsche: Nietzsche's Voices*. London: Pheonix.

Hegel, G.W.F. [1806] 1998. "Independence and Dependence of Self-consciousness Lordship and Bondage." In *Hegel Reader* (ed. Houlgate). Oxford: Blackwell.

Hegel, G.W.F. [1807] 1977. *Phenomenology of Spirit* (tr. A.V. Miller). Oxford: Oxford University Press.

Heidegger, M. [1927] 1967. *Being and Time* (tr. J. Macquarrie and E. Robinson). Oxford: Basil Blackwell.

Hendriks, F. and S. Zouridis. 1999. "Cultural Biases and New Media for the Public Domain: Cui Bono." In *Cultural Theory as Political Science* (eds. M. Thompson, G. Grendstat, and P. Selle). London: Routledge.

Hirschman, A.O. 1991. *The Rhetoric of Reaction: Perversity, Futility, Jeopardy*. Cambridge, MA: Harvard University Press.

Hobbes, T. [1651] 1991. *Leviathan* (ed. R. Tuck). Cambridge: Cambridge University Press.

Holling, C.S. 1986. "The Resilience and Vulnerability of Eco-systems." In *The Sustainable Development of the Biosphere* (eds. W.C. Clark and R.E. Munn). Cambridge: Cambridge University Press.

Hollis, M. 1994. *The Philosophy of Social Science*. Cambridge: Cambridge University Press.

Hood, C. 1998. *The Art of the State: Culture, Rhetoric, and Public Management*. Oxford: Clarendon.

Hoppe, R. 2000. "Grid-Group Culture Theory and the Politics of Problem Definition." A paper presented at the 8th Biennial Jerusalem Conference in Canadian Studies. Jerusalem, Israel.

Horney, K. 1937. *The Neurotic Personality of our Times*. New York: Norton.

Horney, K. 1945. *Our Inner Conflicts*. New York: Norton.

Hume, D. [1777] 1902. *An Enquiry Concerning the Human Understanding* [1748] *and Concerning the Principles of Morals* [1751] (ed. L.A. Selby-Biggs) (2nd ed.). Oxford: Clarendon.

Inglehart, R. and P. Norris. 2016. "Trump, Brexit, and the Rise of Populism: Economic Have-Nots and Cultural Backlash." HKS Working Paper No. RWP16-026. Available at: https://papers.ssrn.com/sol3/papers.cfm?abstract_id=2818659.

Jacobi, J. 1962. *The Psychology of C.G. Jung*. New Haven, CT: Yale University Press.

James, P. 2006. *Globalism, Nationalism, Tribalism*. London: Sage. Available at: https://www.researchgate.net/publication/2651415 55_Globalism_Nationalism_Tribalism.

James, W. [1897] 1979. *The Will to Believe and Other Essays in Popular Philosophy*. Cambridge, MA: Harvard University Press.

James, W. [1907] 1995. *Pragmatism [a New Name for Some Old Ways of Thinking]*. Toronto, ON: General Publishing.

James, W. 1896. *The Will to Believe: An Address to the Philosophical Clubs of Yale and Brown Universities*. Available at: http://falcon.jmu.

edu/~omearawm/ph101willto-believe.html.

Jung, C.G. [1934] 1981. *The Archetypes and the Collective Unconscious* (2nd ed.) (tr. R.F.C. Hull). Princeton, NJ: Bollingen.

Kane, R. 2002. "Introduction." In *Free Will* (ed. R. Kane). Malden, MA: Blackwell.

Kant, I. [1781–87] 1956. *Critique of Pure Reason* (tr. L.W. Beck). Indianapolis, IN: Bobbs-Merrill.

Katz, D. 1960. "The Functional Approach to the Study of Attitudes." *The Public Opinion Quarterly* 24 (2): 163–204.

Kelly, G.A. 1955. *The Psychology of Personal Constructs*. New York: Norton.

Keynes, J.M. [1936] 2007. *The General Theory of Employment, Interest and Money*. London: Macmillan.

Keynes, J.M. 1972. *The Collected Writings of John Maynard Keynes, Volume IX, Essays in Persuasion*. London: Macmillan.

Kierkegaard, S. [1846] 1941. *Concluding Unscientific Postscript* (trs. D.F. Swenson and W. Lowrie). Princeton, NJ: Princeton University Press.

Kierkegaard, S. [1847] 1962. *Works of Love* (trs. H. Hong and E. Hong, pref. R.G. Smith). New York: HarperCollins.

Kirkham, R.L. 1992. *Theories of Truth: A Critical Introduction*. Cambridge, MA: MIT Press.

Klapp, O.E. 1964. *Symbolic Leaders: Public Dramas and Public Men. Observations*. Chicago, IL: Aldine.

Koffka, K. 1935. *The Principles of Gestalt Psychology*. New York: Harcourt Brace and World.

Kooiman, J. 1999. "Social–Political Governance: Overview, Reflection and Design." *Public Management* 1 (1): 67–92.

Kooiman, J. ed. 1993. *Modern Governance: New Government-Society Inter-*

actions. Newbury Park, CA: Sage.

Laffer, A.B. 2004. "The Laffer Curve: Past, Resent, and Future." Backgrounder (The Heritage Foundation), 1765 (I June). Available at: http://sobelrs.people.cofc.edu/Readings/2A-7.%20Laffer%20-%20The%20Laffer%20Curve.pdf.

Lake, T. 2016. *Unprecedented: The Election That Changed Everything* (ed. J. Eda, for. J. Tapper, intro. D. Brinkley). Atlanta, GA: CNN Press.

Lasch, C. 1979. *The Culture of Narcissism: American Life in an Age of Diminishing Expectations.* New York: Norton.

Lasswell, H.D. 1930. *Psychopathology and Politics.* Chicago, IL: University of Chicago Press.

Levenson, H. 1981. "Differentiating among Internality, Powerful Others, and Chance." In *Research with the Locus of Control Construct, 1: Assessment Methods* (ed. H.M. Lefcourt). Orlando, FL: Academic Press.

Lewin, K. 1948. "Experimenting in Social Space." In *Resolving Social Conflicts* (ed. G. W. Lewin). New York: Harper and Row.

Lewin, K. 1952. "Defining the Field at a Given Time." In *Field Theory in Social Sciences: Selected Theoretical Papers* (ed. D. Cartwright). London: Tavistock.

Lewin, K. 1972. "Needs, Force and Violence in Psychological Fields." In *Classic Contributions to Social Psychology* (ed. E.P. Hollander and R.G. Hunt). London: Oxford University Press.

Lewis, C. 2014. *935 Lies: The Future of Truth and the Decline of America's Moral Integrity.* New York: PublicAffairs.

Lipset, S.M. 1996. *American Exceptionalism: A Double-Edged Sword.* New York: Norton.

Locke, J. [1688] 1960. "The First Treatise of Government." In *Two Treatises of Government* (ed. P. Laslett). Cambridge: Cambridge University Press.

Lucey, K. G. ed. 1996. *On Knowing and the Know: Introductory Readings on Epistemology*. Buffalo, NY: Prometheus.

Lycan, W. ed. 1990. *Mind and Cognition*. Oxford: Blackwell.

Machiavelli, N. [1513] 1961. *The Prince* (tr. G. Bull). Harmondsworth, UK: Penguin.

Machiavelli, N. [1513] 2011. *The Prince* (tr. by W.K. Marriott). Istanbul: World Classics: Political Science.

Madge, J. 1962. *The Origins of Scientific Sociology*. New York: Free Press of Glencoe.

Malebranche, N. [1774–75] 1980. *The Search after Truth* (trs. T. Lennon and P.J. Olscamp). Columbus: Ohio State University Press.

Marbe, K. 1901. *Experimentell-Psychologische*. Leipzig, DE: Untersuchung über das Urteil.

Marcel, G. 1952. *Men against Humanity* (tr. G.S. Fraser). London: Harvill.

March, J.G. 1999. *The Pursuit of Organizational Intelligence*. Malden, MA: Blackwell.

March, J.G. and J.P. Olsen. 1976. *Ambiguity and Change in Organizations*. Bergen, NO: Universitets Forlaget.

Marino, G.D. 2001. *Kierkagaard in the Present Age*. Milwaukee, WI: Marquette University Press.

Marx, K. [1844] 1963. "Estranged Labour." In *Early Writings* (tr. and ed. T.B. Bottomore). London: Watts.

Marx, K. [1844] 1967. "Economic and Philosophical Manuscripts." In *Writings of the Young Marx on Philosophy and Society* (eds. L.D. Easton and K.H. Guddat). New York: Doubleday.

Maslow, A.H. [1962] 1968. *Towards a Psychology of Being*. New York: Nostrand.

Matheson, P.E. 1916. *Epictetus: The Discourses and Manual, Together with Fragments of his Writings* (2 vols.). Oxford: Clarendon Press. Available at: http://www archive. org/details/epictetus01epicuoft; http://www.archive.org/details/epictetus02epicuoft.

Mathews, K.A. 1997. *Hostility*. Available at: http://www.macses.ucsf.edu/research-/Psychosocial/notebook/hostility.

Matusow, A.J. 1999. "Review: Nixon as Madman." *Reviews in American History* 27 (4): 623–629.

May, R. 1967. *Psychology and the Human Dilemma*. New York: Van Norstrand.

Mayntz, R. 1993. "Governing Failure and the Problem of Governability: Some Comments on a Theoretical Paradigm." In *Modern Governance: New Government-Society Interactions* (ed. J. Kooiman). London: Sage.

McGann, A.J., C.A. Smith, M. Latner, and A. Keena. 2016. *Gerrymandering in America: The House of Representatives, the Supreme Court, and the Future of Popular Sovereignty.* New York: Cambridge University Press.

McKinney, J. P. 1981. "The Construct of Engagement Style: Theory and Research." In *Research with the Locus of Control Construct, 1: Assessment Methods* (ed. H.M. Lefcourt). Orlando, FL: Academic Press.

Merrien, F-X. 1998. "Governance and Modern Welfare States." *International Social Science Journal* 50 (1): 57–67.

Messner, D. 1997. *The Network Society: Economic Development and International Competitiveness as Problems of Social Governance.* London: Frank Cass.

Mill, J.S. [1843] 1988. *A System of Logic* (ed. A. J. Ayer). London: Duckworth.

Mill, J.S. [1859] 1963. "On Liberty." In *The Collected Works of John Stuart Mill* (ed. J. M. Robson). Toronto, ON: University of Toronto Press.

Mill, J.S. [1861] 1968. "Utilitarianism." In *Utilitarianism, Liberty and Representative Government* (au. J. S. Mill). London: Denton.

Mises, L. von. 1944. *Bureaucracy*. New Haven, CT: Yale University Press.

Moore, G.E. 1959. *Philosophical Papers*. London: George Allen and Unwin.

Moran, D. 2000. *Introduction to Phenomenology*. London: Routledge.

Morgan, G. 1986. *Images of Organizations*. Newbury Park, CA: Sage.

Morris, P. 1987. *Power: a Philosophical Analysis*. Manchester, UK: Manchester University Press.

Moser, P.K. 1989. *Knowledge and Evidence*. Cambridge: Cambridge University Press.

Mounce, H.O. 1997. *The Two Pragmatisms: From Peirce to Rorty*. London: Routledge.

Murphy, J.P. 1990. *Pragmatism: From Peirce to Davidson*. Boulder, CO: Westview Press.

Nadler, S. ed. 1993. *Causation in Early Modern Philosophy: Occasionalism and Preestablished Harmony*. University Park, PA: Pennsylvania State University Press.

Nagel, T. [1976] 1993. "Moral Luck." In *Moral Luck* (ed. D. Statman). Albany, NY: SUNY Press.

Natanson, M. ed. 1963. *Philosophy of the Social Sciences*. New York: Random House.

Navia, L.E. 2007. *Socrates: A Life Examined*. Amherst, NY: Prometheus Books.

Nietzsche, F. [1871] 1993. *The Birth of Tragedy* (tr. R.J. Hollingdale). Harmondworth, UK: Penguin.

Nietzsche. F. [1878] 1994. *Human, All Too Human* (tr. M. Faber). Harmondworth, UK: Penguin.

Nietzsche, F. [1881] 1997. *Daybreak: Thoughts on the Prejudices of Morality* (eds. M. Clarke and M. Leiter, tr. R.J. Hollingdale). Cambridge:

Cambridge University Press.

Nietzsche, F. [1886] 1998. *Beyond Good and Evil* (tr. M. Faber, intro. R.C. Holub). Oxford: Oxford University Press.

Nietzsche, F. [1887] 2006. *On the Genealogy of Morals* (ed. K. Ansell-Earson, tr. C. Diethe). Cambridge: Cambridge University Press. Available at: http://www.mala.bc.ca~joh-nstoi/Nietzche/genealogytofc.htm.

Nietzsche, F. [1888] 1969. *Twilight of the Idols and the Anti-Christ* (tr. R.J. Hollingdale). Harmondworth, UK: Penguin.

Nietzsche, F. [1895] 1967. *The Will to Power: Attempt at a Revaluation of all Values* (tr. R.J. Kaufmann). New York: Random House.

Nietzsche. F. [1883] 1967. "Thus Spoke Zarathustra." In *The Portable Nietzsche* (tr. W. Kaufman). New York: Viking.

Nozick, R. 1974. *Anarchy, State and Utopia*. New York: Basic Books.

Oborne, P. and T. Roberts. 2017. *How Trump Thinks: His Tweets and the Birth of a New Political Language*. London: Head of Zeus Press.

Olli, E. 1995. *Cultural Theory Specified—The Coherent, Sequential and Synthetic Individual Approaches* (Paper 230). Bergen, NO: University of Bergen: Department of Comparative Politics.

Ortega y Gasset, J. [1929–1931] 2002. *What is Knowledge?* (tr. J. García-Gómez). Albany: State University of New York Press.

Ortega y Gasset, J. [1935] 2001. *Towards a Philosophy of History*. Chicago: University of Illinios Press.

Owen, D. 2007. *The Hubris Syndrome: Bush, Blaire and the Intoxication of Power*. London: Methuen.

Owen, D. and J. Davidson. 2009. "Hubris Syndrome: An Acquired Personality Disorder? A Study of US Presidents and UK Prime Ministers over the last 100 Years." *Brain* 132 (5): 1296–1406.

Parsons, W. 1995. *Public Policy: An Introduction to the Theory and Prac-*

tice of Policy. Cheltenham, GR, UK: Edward Elgar.

Partridge, G.E. 1930. "Current Conceptions of Psychopathic personality." *The American Journal of Psychiatry,* 1 (87): 53–99. Available at: https://ajp.psychiatryonline.org/doi/abs/10.1176/ajp.87.1.53?-journalCode=ajp.

Pascal, B. [1670] 1966. *Pensée.* Harmondsworth, UK: Penguin.

Peirce, C.S. 1877. "The Fixation of Belief." *Popular Science Monthly,* 12 (November): 1–15. Available at: http://www.peirce.org/writings/p107.html.

Peirce, C.S. 1932. *Collected Papers of Charles Sanders Peirce* (vol. 1: *Principles of Philosophy*) (eds. C. Hartshorne and P. Wiess). Cambridge, MA: Harvard University Press.

Pettit, P. 1997. *Republicanism: A Theory of Freedom and Government.* Oxford: Oxford University Press.

Phares, E.J. and W.F. Chaplin. 1997. *Introduction to Personality* (4th ed.). New York: Prentice Hall.

Phelan, J. 2005. *Living to Tell about It.* Ithaca, NY: Cornell University Press.

Piehler, M. ed. 2016. *"Weil ich einfach sehr gut aussehe": Erschreckend wahre Worte von Donald J. Trump.* Hamburg, DE: Rowohlt Taschenbuch Verlag.

PlanetPsych 1999–2006. "Defense Mechanisms." Available at: http://www.planetpsych.com.Psychology_101/defense_mechanisms.htm.

Plato. [c360 BC] 1955. *The Republic* (tr. and intro. H. P. D. Lee). Harmondworth, UK: Penguin.

Plato. [c380s] 1952. *Phaedras* (tr. R. Hackforth). Cambridge: Cambridge University Press.

Portes, A. 1972. "Rationality in the Slum: An Essay on Interpretive Sociology." *Comparative Studies in Sociology and History* 14 (3): 268–286.

Posner, R. 2004. "Basic Tasks of Cultural Semiotics." In *Macht der Zeichen, Zeichen der Macht: Festschrift für Jeff Bernard* [*Signs of Power— Power of Signs. Essays in Honor of Jeff Bernard*] (eds. G. Withalm and J. Wallmannsberger). Vienna, AT: INST, Available at: http://faculty.georgetown.edu/irvinem/theory/Posner-basictasksofcultur-alsemiotics.pdf.

Pross, P. 1986. *Group Politics and Public Policy*. Toronto, ON: Oxford University Press.

Pugh, D.S. and D.J. Hickson. 1996. *Writers on Organizations* (5th ed.). Harmondworth, UK: Penguin.

Ramnarayan, S. 2003. "Changing Mindsets of Middle Level Officers in Government Organizations." *Vikalpa: The Journal for Decision Makers* 28 (4): 63–76.

Rand, A. 1962. "Introducing Objectivism." *The Objectivist Newsletter*, August. Available at: http://aynrandlexicon.com/ayn-rand-ideas/introducing-objectivism.html.

Rand, A. 1967. *Capitalism: The Unknown Ideal*. New York: Signet.

Rein, M. and D.A. Schön. 1993. "Reframing Policy Discourse." In *The Argumentative Turn in Policy Analysis and Planning* (eds. F. Fischer and J. Forester). London: UCL Press.

Rescher, N. 1973. *The Coherence Theory of Truth*. Oxford: Oxford University Press.

Rey, G. 1997. *Contemporary Philosophy of Mind*. Oxford: Blackwell.

Riesman, D. 1950. *The Lonely Crowd*. New Haven, CT: Yale University Press.

Ring, P. and A. Van de Ven. 1994. "Developmental Processes of Cooperative Interorganizational Relationships." *Academy of Management Review* 19 (1): 90–118.

Roese, N. J. 1994. "The Functional Basis of Counterfactual Thinking." *Journal of Personality and Social Psychology* 66 (5): 805–818.

Rofe, A. 2001. "Revealed Wisdom: From the Bible to Qumran." A paper presented at the Sixth Orion International Symposium on "Sapiential Perspectives: Wisdom Literature in Light of the Dead Sea Scrolls," Hebrew University of Jerusalem. Available at: http://orion.mscc.huji.ac.il/symposiums/6th/rofeFullPaper.html.

Rogers, C.R. 1961. *On Becoming a Person*. Boston, MA: Houghton Mifflin.

Rosenberg, M. 1979. *Conceiving the Self*. New York: Basic Books.

Rosenkrantz, R. 1977. *Inference, Method, and Decision*. Boston, MA: Reidal.

Rothstein, B. 2005. *Social Traps and the Problem of Trust*. Cambridge: Cambridge University Press.

Rousseau, J.–L. [1762] 1973. "The Social Contract." In *The Social Contract and Discourses* (ed. and tr. G.D.H. Cole). London: Dent.

Rozenblit, B. 2008. *Us Against Them: How Tribalism Affects The Way We Think*. Kansas City, MO: Transcendent Publications.

Rumi, J. 1956. *Rumi, Poet and Mystic* (tr. and ed. R.A. Nicholson). London: George, Allen and Unwin.

Russell, B. 1946. *A History of Western Philosophy*. London: George Allen & Unwin.

Russell, B. 1948. *Human Knowledge: Its Scope and Its Limitations*. London: George Allan & Unwin.

Sagan, C. 1996. *The Demon-Haunted World*. London: Headline.

Sartre, J.-P. [1943] 1957. *Being and Nothingness: An Essay of Phenomenological Ontology* (tr. H.E. Barnes). London: Methuen.

Sartre, J.-P. [1946] 1973. *Existentialism and Humanism* (tr. P. Mairet). London, Methuen.

Sartre, J.-P. [1960] 2004. *Critique of Dialectical Reason* (vol. 1: *Theory of Practical Ensembles*) (tr. A. Sheridan-Smith, ed. J. Rée, for. F. Jameson). London: Verso. Available at: https://libcom.org/files/jean-paul-sartre-critique-of-dialectical-reason-volume-1.compressed.pdf.

Scheffler, S. 1974. *Four Pragmatists: A Critical Introduction to Peirce, James, Mead and Dewey*. London: Routledge & Kegan Paul.

Schlafly, P., E. Martin, and B.M. Decker. 2016. *The Conservative Case for Trump*. Washington, DC: Regnery.

Schofield, M. 2007. "The Noble Lie." In *The Cambridge Companion to Plato's Republic* (ed. G. Ferrari). Cambridge: Cambridge University Press.

Schopenhauer, A. [1813/1877] 2017. *Delhi Collected Works of Arthur Schopenhauer*. Hastings, ES: Delhi Classics.

Schopenhauer, A. [1818/1844] 1969. *The World as Will and Representation* (tr. E.F.J. Payne) (2 vols.). New York: Dover.

Schopenhauer, A. [1839] 1999. *Prize Essay on the Freedom of the Will* (tr. E.F.J. Payne (ed. G. Zöller). Available at: http://assets.cambridge.org/97805215/71418/sample/9780521571418web.pdf.

Schopenhauer, A. [1851] 1970. *Essays and Aphorisms* (tr. R.J. Hollingdale). Harmondworth, UK: Penguin.

Schwartz, B. 2004. *The Paradox of Choice: Why More is Less*. New York: HarperCollins.

Schwarz, M. and M. Thompson. 1990. *Divided We Stand: Redefining Politics, Technology and Social Choice*. Philadelphia, PA: University of Pennsylvania Press.

Shavitt, S. 1989. "Operationalizing Functional Theories of Attitude." In *Attitude Structure and Function* (eds. A.R. Pratkanis, S.J. Breckler, and A.G. Greenwald). Hillsdale, NJ: Laurance Erlbaum.

Shope, R.K. 1983. *The Analysis of Knowing: A Decade of Research*. Princeton, NJ: Princeton University Press.

Shweder, R.A. 1984. "Preview: A Colloquy of Culture Theorists." In

Culture Theory: Essays on Mind, Self, and Emotion (eds. R.A. Shweder and R.A. LeVine). New York: Cambridge University Press.

Siefkes, M. 2010. "Power in Society, Economy, and Mentality: Towards a Semiotic Theory of Power." *Journal of the International Association for Semiotic* 181-1/4: 225–261. Available at: http://siefkes.de/dokumente/Siefkes_Power.pdf.

Simon, H.A. [1947] 1960. *Administrative Behavior* (2nd ed.). New York: Macmillan.

Simon, H.A. 1956. "Rational Choice and the Structure of the Environment." *Psychological Review* 63 (2): 129–138. Available at: http://digitalcollections.library.cmu.edu/awweb/awarchive?type=-file&item=33544.

Smith, A. [1776] 1819. *Inquiry into the Nature and Causes of The Wealth of Nations* (vol. 2). London: W. Allason, J. Maynard, and W. Blair. Available at: https://books.google.co.uk/books?id=R5MuAAAAYAAJ&pg=PA243&lpg=PA243&dq=The+statesman+who+should+attempt+to+direct+private+people+in+what+manner+they+ought+to+employ+their+capitals&source=bl&ots=uw243ULPeG&sig=pxh8hbcL0C9snHC7cIoVgDSesuA&hl=en&sa=X&ved=0ahUKEwjwxLDh5ZXWAhUrBcAKHXSEA7UQ6AEIMjAC#v=onepage&q=The%20statesman%20who%20should%20attempt%20to%20direct%20private%20people%20in%20what%20manner%20they%20ought%20to%20employ%20their%20capitals&f=fals.

Smith, D. 1980. "The Impact of World Views on Professional Life-styling." *The Personnel and Guidance Journal* 58 (9): 584–587.

Smith, M.B., J.S. Bruner, and R.W. White. 1956. *Opinions and Personality*. New York: Wiley.

Spadaro, A. and M. Figueroa. 2017. "Evangelical Fundamentalism and Catholic Integralism: A Surprising Ecumenism." *La Civiltà Cattolica*. Available at: http://www.laciviltacattolica.it/articolo/evangelical-fundamentalism-and-catholic-integralism-in-the-usa-a-surprising-ecumenism/.

Stack, G.J. 1977. *Kierkegaard's Existential Ethics* (Studies in the Humanities, 16 Philosophy). Montgomery: Alabama University Press.

Stevens, A. 1990. *On Jung.* London: Routledge.

Stevenson, C.L. 1944. *Ethics and Language.* New Haven, CT: Yale University Press.

Stevenson, C.L. 1963. *Facts and Values: Studies in Ethical Analysis.* New Haven, CT: Yale University Press.

Stogdill, R.M. 1950. Leadership, Membership and Organization. *Psychological Bulletin* 47 (1): 1-14.

Strawson, G. 1986. *Freedom and Belief.* Oxford: Clarendon.

Streeck, W. 1991. "Interest, Heterogeneity and Organizing Capacity—Two Class Logics of Collective Action." In *Political Choice, Institutions, Rules and Limits of Rationality* (eds. R. Czada and B. Windhoff-Heritier). Frankfurt am Main: Campus Verlag.

Swain, C. M. [2002] 2004. *The New White Nationalism in America: Its Challenge to Integration.* New York: Cambridge University Press.

Sztompka, P. 1996. "Trust and Emerging Democracy: Lessons from Poland." *International Sociology* 11 (1): 37–62.

Teresa, Mother and Kolodieichuk, B. 2007. *Mother Theresa: Come Be My Light.* New York: Doubleday.

Thompson, J.D. 1967. *Organizations in Action.* New York: McGraw-Hill.

Thompson, M. and P. Taylor. 1986. *The Surprise Game: An Exploration of Constrained Relativism* (Warwick Papers in Management 1). Coventry: University of Warwick, Institute for Management Research and Development.

Thorngate, W. 2001. "The Social Psychology of Policy Analysis." *Journal of Comparative Policy Analysis* 3 (1): 85–112.

Thucydides [401 BC] 1972. *History of the Peloponnesian War* (rev. ed.) (tr. R. Warner) Harmondsworth, UK: Penguin.

Triandis, H.C. 1971. *Attitude and Attitude Change*. New York: Wiley.

Trump, D.J. with T. Schwartz. 1987. *The Art of the Deal*. New York: Random House.

Tupes, E.C. and R.E. Christal. [1961] 1962. "Recurrent Personality Factors Based on Trait Ratings." *Journal of Personality* 60 (2): 225–251.

Urmson, J.O. 1968. *The Emotive Theory of Ethics*. London: Hutchinson.

Uslaner, E. 2002. *The Moral Foundations of Trust*. Cambridge: Cambridge University Press.

Vallentyne, P. and B. van der Vossen. 2014. "Libertarianism." *The Stanford Encyclopedia of Philosophy* (Fall ed.) (ed. E. N. Zalta). Available at: https://plato.stanford.edu/archives/fall2014/entries/libertarianism.

Vickers, G. [1983] 1995. *The Art of Judgment: A Study of Policy Making* (*Rethinking Public Administration*) (2nd ed.). Thousand Oaks, CA: Sage.

Walsh, W. 1972. "Open and Closed Morality." In *The Morality of Politics* (eds. B. Parekh and R. Berki). London: George Allen & Unwin.

Warnock, M. 1970. *Existentialism*. Oxford: Oxford University Press.

Weber, M. 1946. *From Max Weber: Essays in Sociology* (eds. trs. and intro. H.H. Gerth and C.W. Mills). New York: Oxford University Press.

Weick, K.E. 1979. *The Social Psychology of Organizing*. Reading, MA: Addison Wesley.

Weick, K.E. 1995. *Sensemaking in Organizations*. Newbury Park, CA: Sage.

Wertheimer, M. 1945. *Productive Thinking*. New York: Harper and Row.

Wildavsky, A. 1984. *The Nursing Father: Moses as a Political Leader*. Montgomery: Alabama University Press.

Wilkins, A. L. and W. G. Ouchi. 1983. "Efficient Cultures: Exploring the Relationship Between Culture and Organizational Performance." *Administrative Science Quarterly* 28 (3): 468–481.

Williams, B. [1976] 1993. "Moral Luck." In *Moral Luck* (ed. D. Statman). Albany, NY: SUNY Press.

Williams, B. 1981. *Moral Luck.* Cambridge: Cambridge University Press.

Williams, L. C. 2017. *White Working Class: Overcoming Class Cluelessness in America.* Boston, MA: Harvard Business Review Press.

Wilson, C. [1956] 1957. *The Outsider* (2nd ed.). London: Pheonix.

Wilson, C. [1956/1967] 2001. *The Outsider* (Indigo ed.). London: Pheonix.

Wilson, E. 2007. *The Death of Socrates: Hero, Villain, Chatterbox. Saint.* London: Profile Books.

Yamigishi, T. and M. Yamigishi. 1994. "Trust and Commitment in the United States and Japan." *Motivation and Emotion* 18 (2): 129–166. Available at: https://www.researchgate.net/profile/Toshio_Yamagishi/publication/225182584_Trust_and_Commitment_in_the_United_States_and_Japan/links/0c96052705d9fdadd7000000/Trust-and-Commitment-in-the-United-States-and-Japan.pdf.

Young, O. R. 1994. *International Governance: Protecting the Environment in a Stateless Society.* Ithaca, NY: Cornell University Press.

INDEX

All index entries relate to Donald J. Trump

ABOUT THE AUTHOR

John Dixon B Econ., M Econ., Ph.D., FAcSS is Professor of Public Administration in Department of Politics and Public Administration at the Middle East Technical University, Ankara, Turkey. He was previously the Distinguished Professor Public Policy and Administration at KIMEP University (2009–21-5) in Almaty, Kazakhstan. He is Emeritus Professor of Public Policy and Management at the University of Plymouth in the UK. He is a fellow of the British *Academy of the Social Science* (nominated by the British Social Policy Association) and an honorary life member of the American *Phi Beta Delta Honor Society for International Scholars* (nominated by the Policy Studies Organization and the American Political Science Association). He has published very extensively—39 books, 13 journal symposia, 95 refereed articles and 52 book chapters—in the fields of international public and social policy and administration.

www.ingramcontent.com/pod-product-compliance
Lightning Source LLC
Chambersburg PA
CBHW062047270326
41931CB00013B/2977